Manet

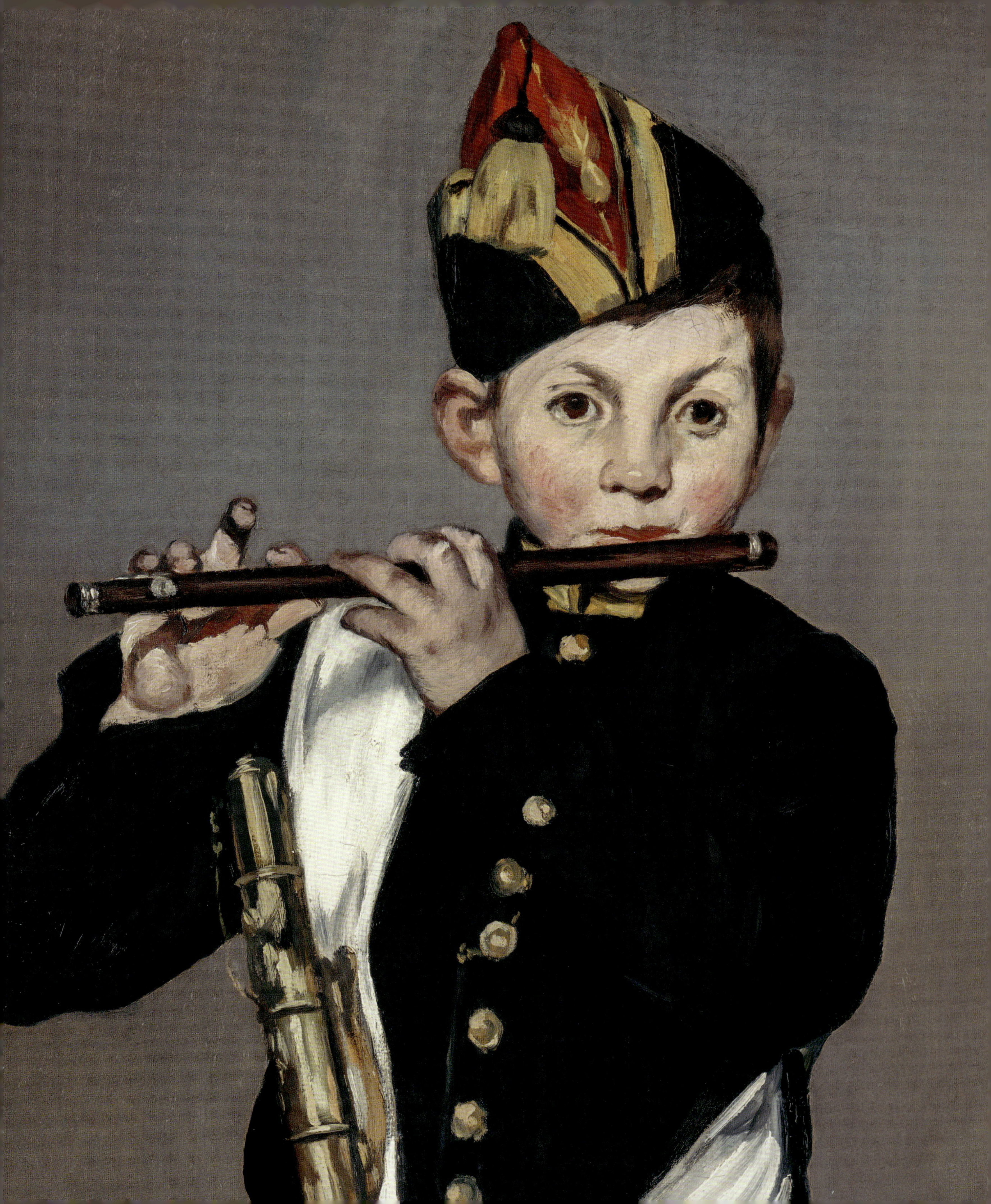

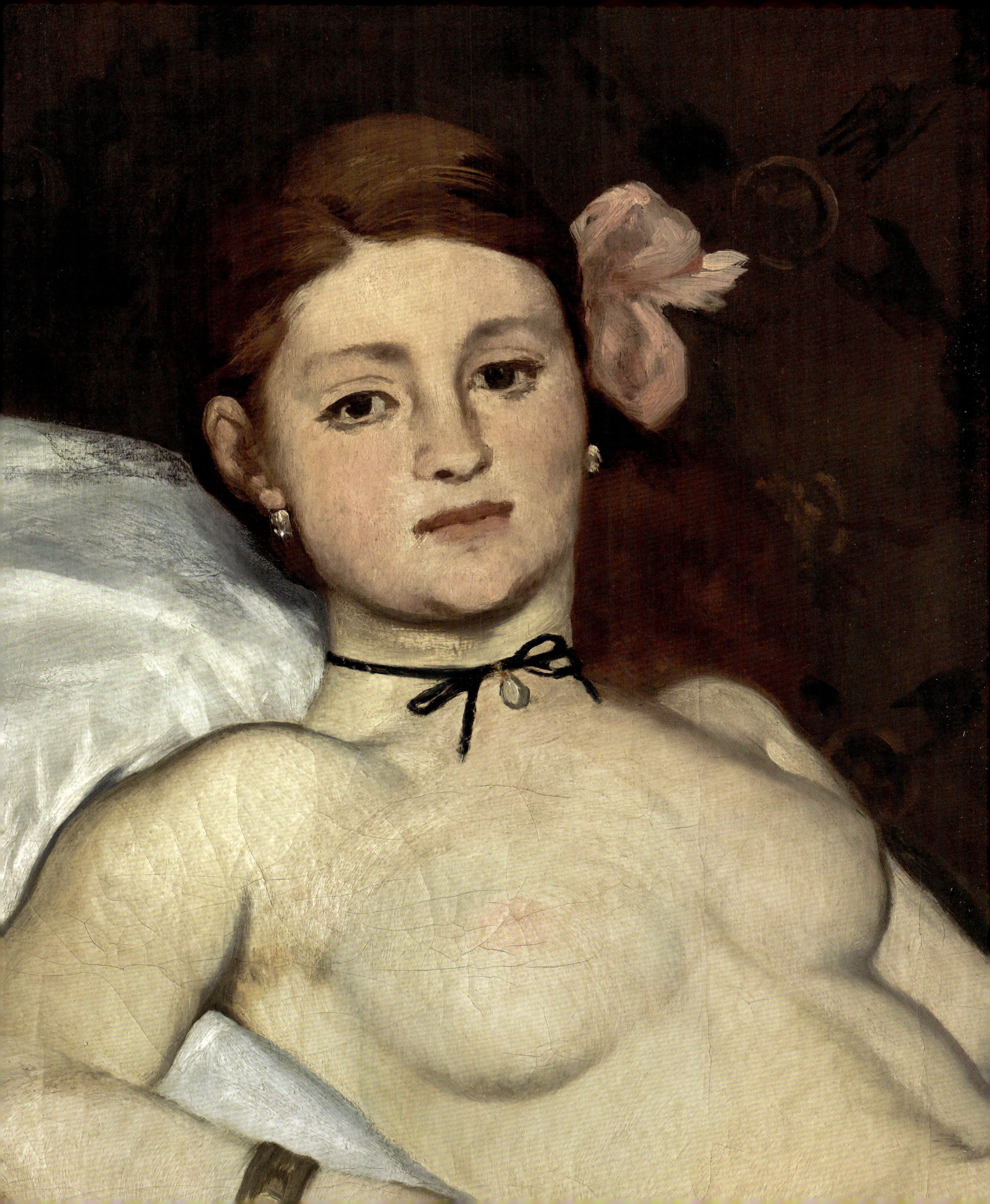

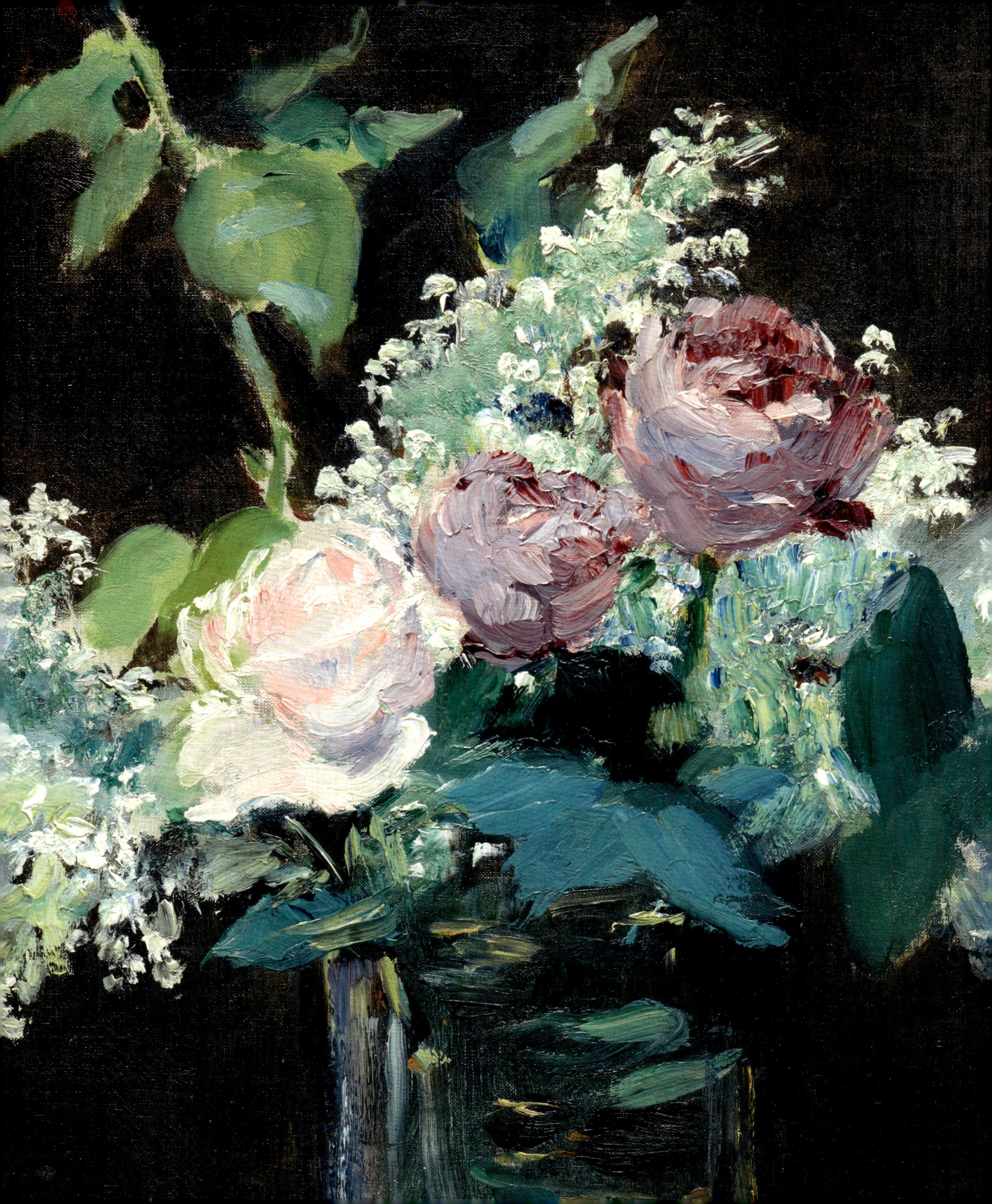

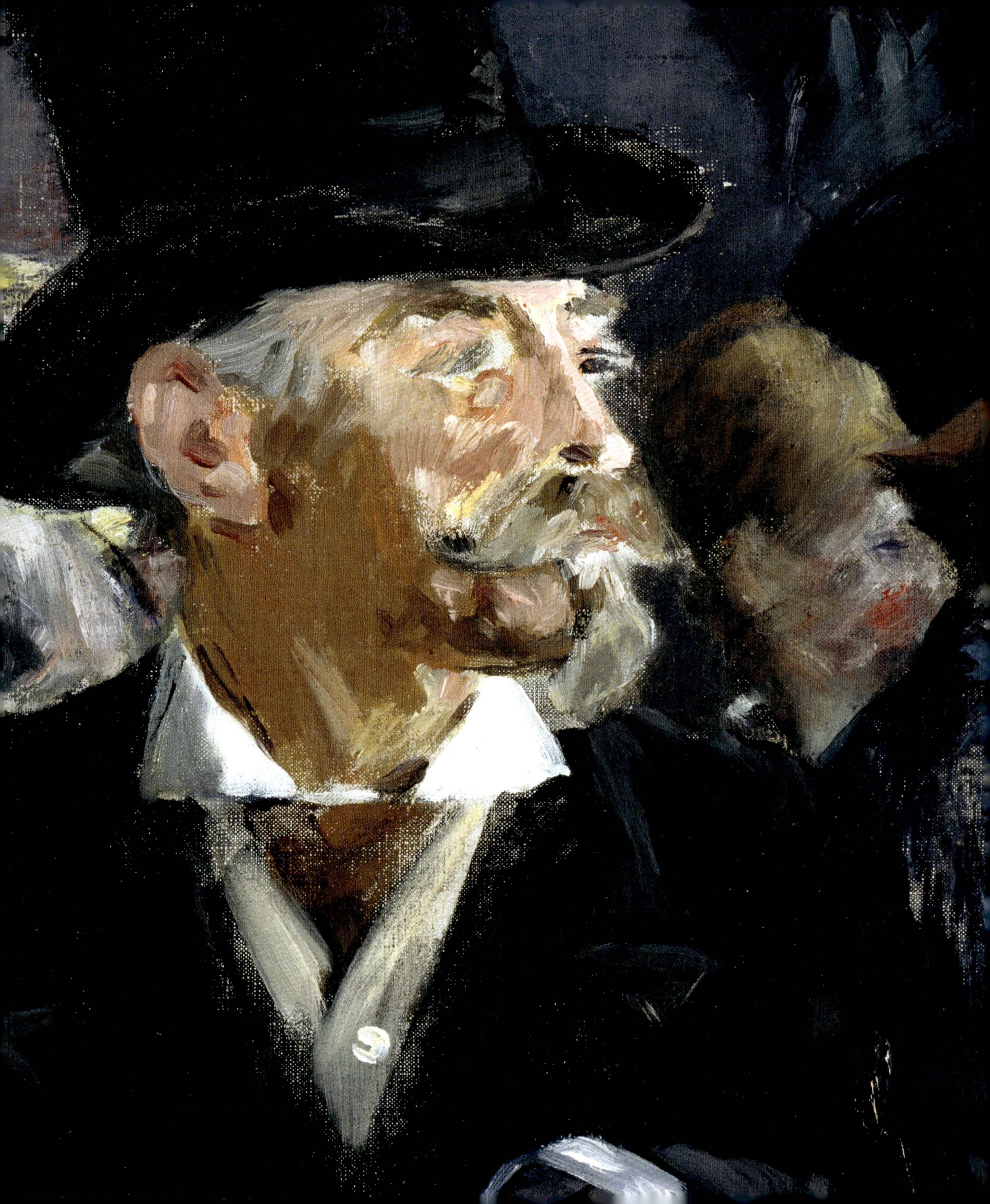

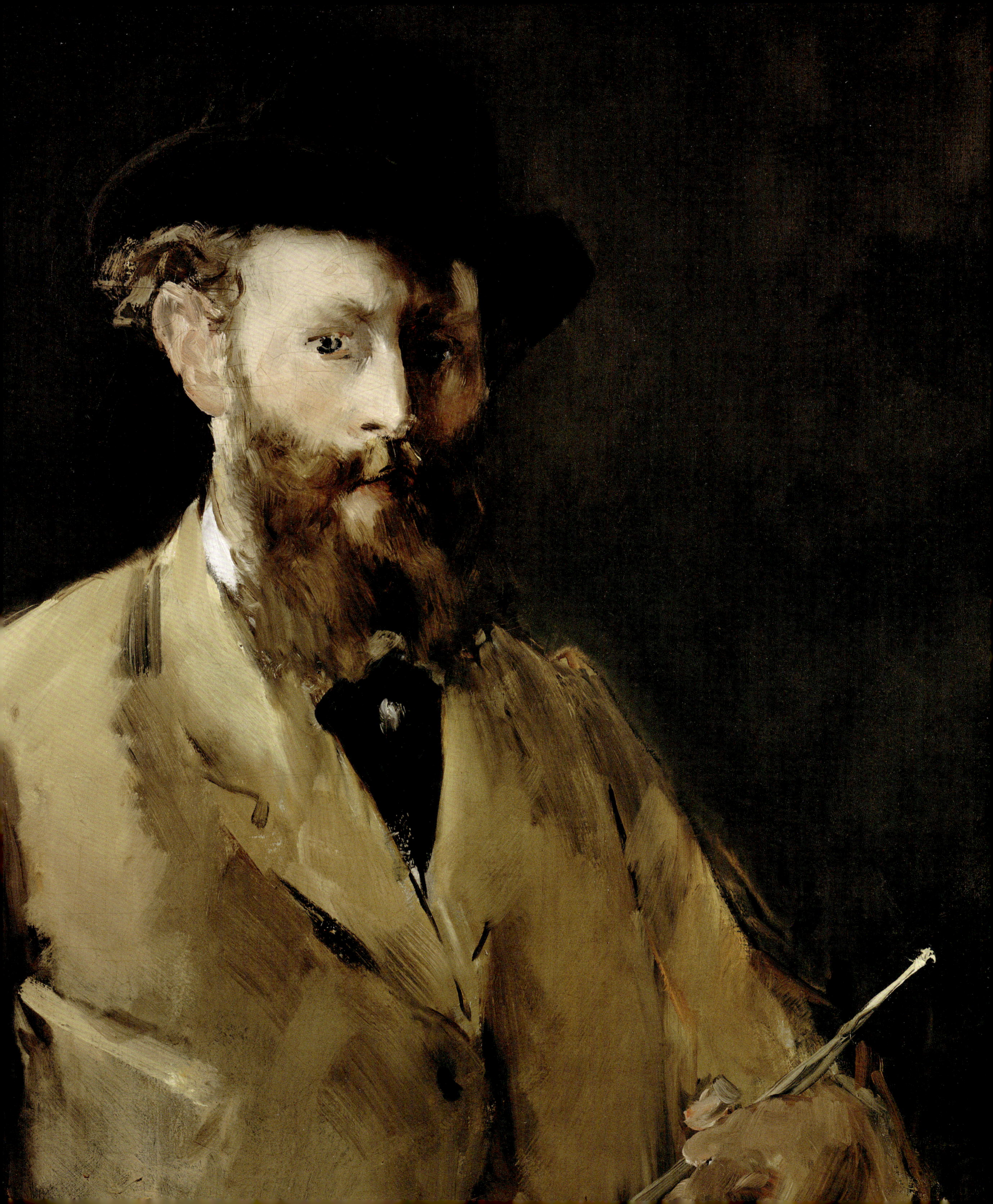

THE GREAT WORKS

Manet

Kathryn Calley Galitz

Rizzoli Electa

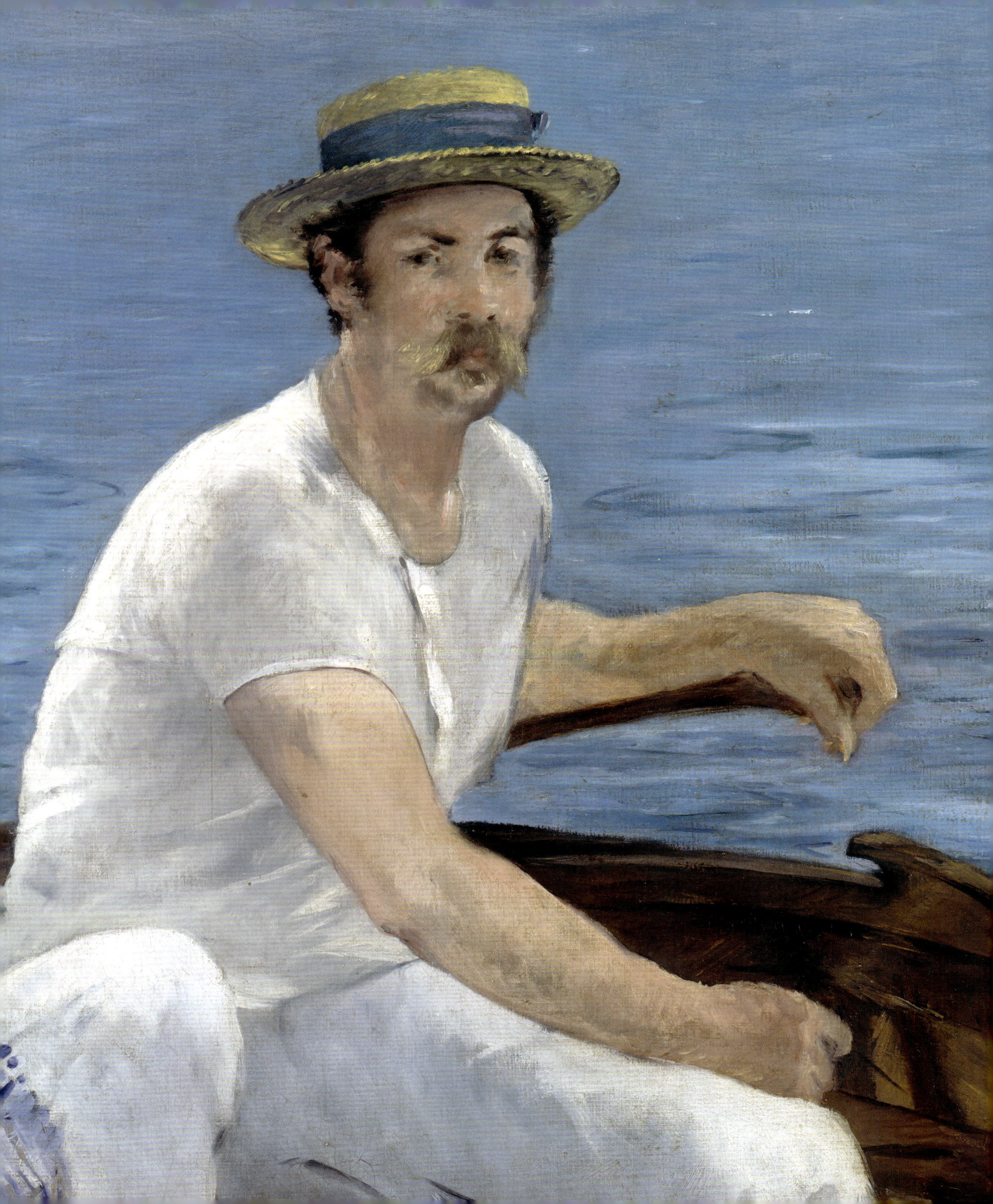

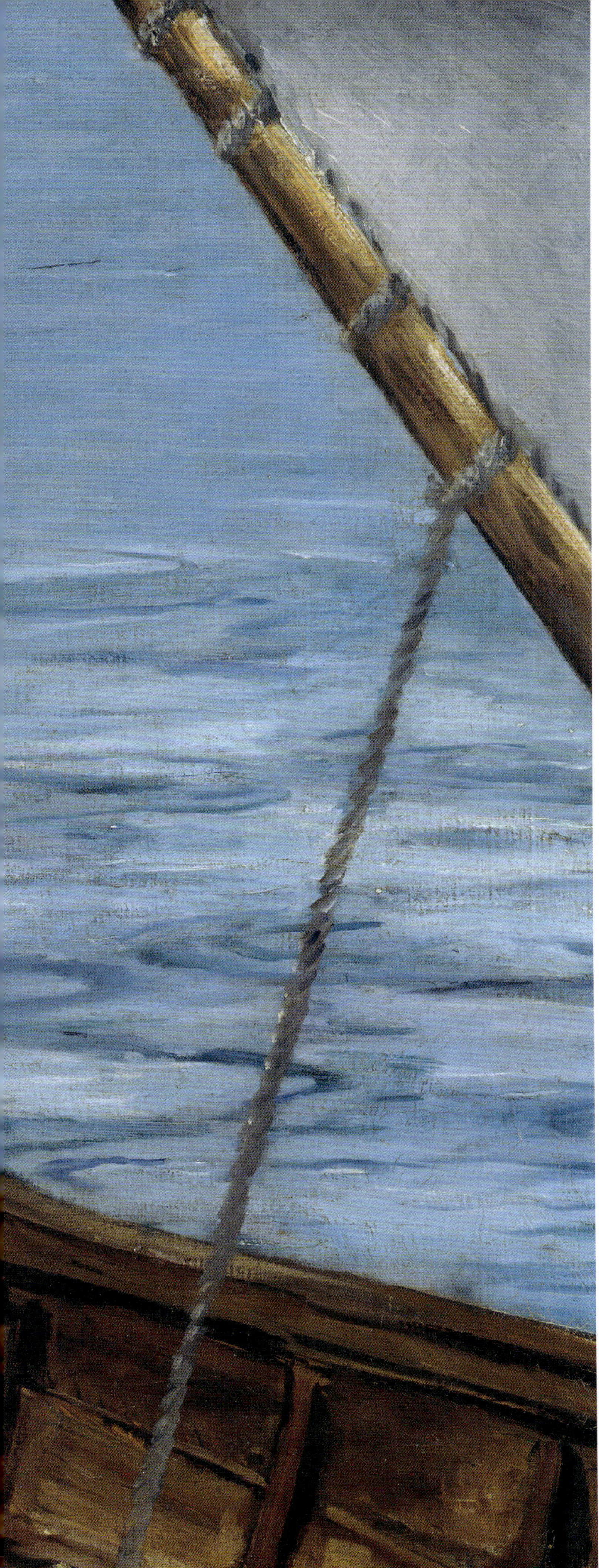

Contents

11 Introduction: Picturing Manet

17 Family Man

39 Past Made Present

75 The 1860s: Scandals and Notoriety

115 Painting Modern Life

151 Manet and Impressionism

181 Brush with History

207 Legacy

233 Timeline

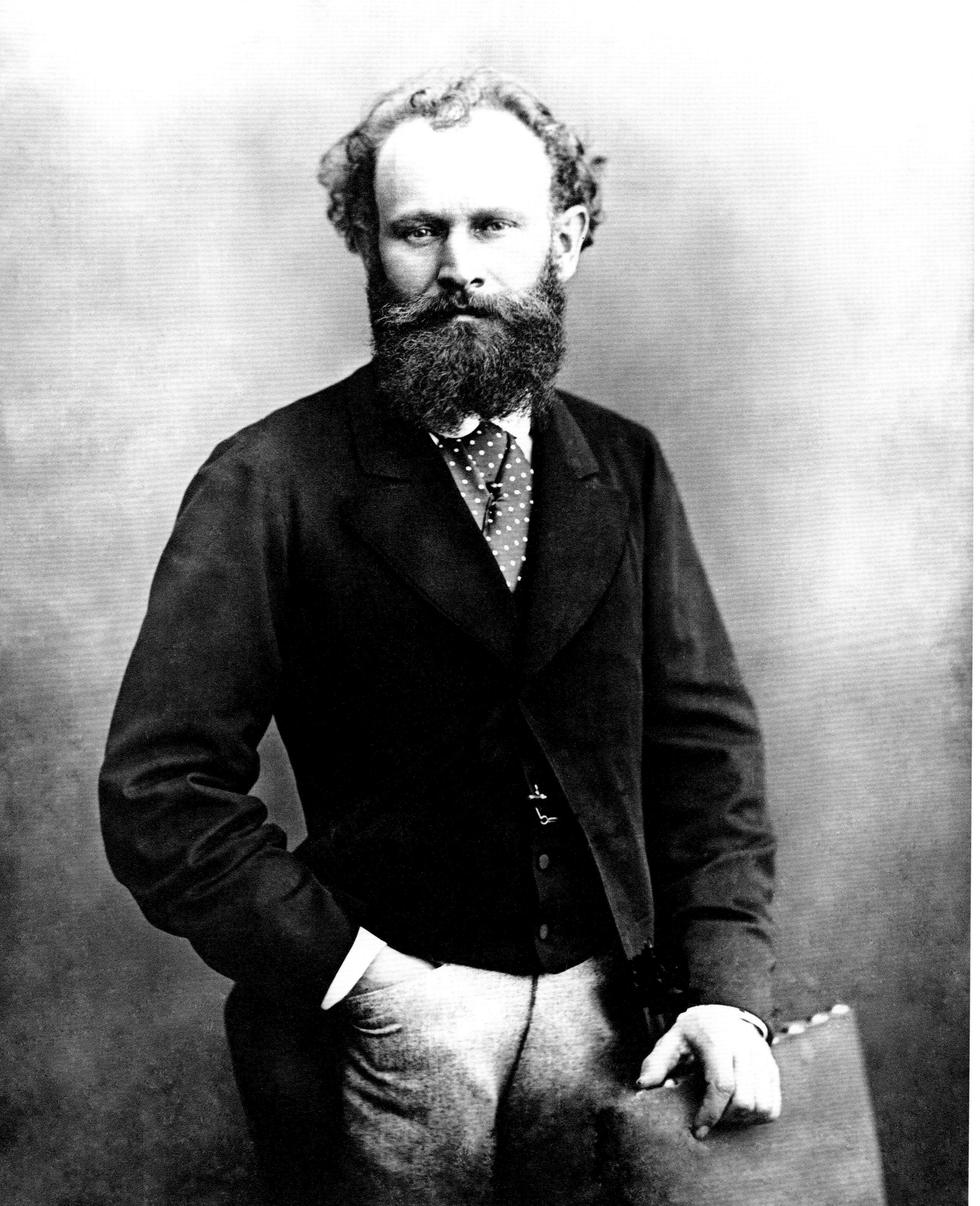

Introduction: Picturing Manet

In 1867, Édouard Manet posed for a portrait painted by his friend Henri Fantin-Latour. At the time, Manet was the most notorious living artist in France, dubbed "the painter of the black cat" in reference to *Olympia*, the painting that had scandalized Paris in 1865 at the state-sponsored exhibition known as the Salon (fig. 36). His portrait, though, emanates an air of haute-bourgeois elegance and cultivated nonchalance that belies the public perception of Manet as a radical bohemian based on the provocative nature of his modern-life subjects. As if in response to the artist's detractors, the portrait was exhibited at the Salon of 1867. That same year, the writer Émile Zola, then a young journalist, penned an ardent defense of Manet and his work; addressing his character, Zola observed, "we find in Édouard Manet a man of extreme amiability and exquisite politeness, with a distinguished manner and a sympathetic appearance."[1]

Manet's attire—the impeccably tailored frock coat, top hat, and walking stick—typifies that of the *flâneur*, the passionate observer of urban life, a quintessential modern type, as celebrated in the writings of his friend Charles Baudelaire. As Manet's lifelong friend, Antonin Proust, recalled, "Paris never knew a *flâneur* like him and a *flâneur* who strolled more usefully."[2] A few years earlier, Manet, similarly attired, made a cameo appearance in the form of a self-portrait on the margins of a crowd of his fellow *flâneurs* mingling in the newly fashionable Tuileries Gardens in Paris (fig. 19).

Portraits of Manet mark significant milestones in his life and career, which spanned less than a quarter-century. Manet, widely hailed as the first modern artist, redefined painting through his radical technique and his embrace of modern-life subjects at a time of profound social, technological, and cultural change. This book considers his now-iconic works in the context of his family, whose members frequently modeled for him, his ongoing dialogue with the art of the past as well as contemporary avant-garde art, and his engagement with modern Paris and contemporary history.

Édouard Manet standing beside a chair, ca. 1865. Photograph by Félix Nadar. Paris, Bibliothèque nationale de France

A portrait of Manet by his friend Edgar Degas, painted around the same time as Fantin-Latour's work, offers a rare glimpse of Manet's private life (see p. 21). Caught in an unguarded moment and seemingly unaware of being painted, Manet listens to his wife, Suzanne, playing the piano in the Manet family apartment on 49, rue de Saint-Pétersbourg in Paris. When the pair wed in 1863, Suzanne was the mother of an eleven-year-old boy. Their marriage apparently surprised even the artist's closest friends. The new family appears in a work known as *Fishing*, thought to have been painted by Manet to commemorate the event (fig. 7). Both Suzanne and her son frequently modeled for Manet in the early years of his career; after the artist's untimely death at the age of fifty-one, they oversaw his legacy.

In 1870, Manet again posed for Fantin-Latour, this time for a group portrait that celebrates his ascension as the leader of the avant-garde after a tumultuous decade, punctuated by a succession of scandals that played out in the public forum of the Salon (see p. 119). Throughout his career, Manet sought acceptance by the official art establishment but always on his own terms. Here, "the painter of the black cat" is shown at work on a portrait of his friend, the writer Zacharie Astruc, surrounded by his young acolytes in his studio in the Batignolles neighborhood of Paris. The mood is somber, respectful, attesting to the seriousness of their shared enterprise. Among the group are several artists on the cusp of fame as leaders of the nascent Impressionist movement, including Frédéric Bazille, who was then at work on a view of his own studio on the rue de la Condamine (see p. 118). Manet also figures among the artists in Bazille's informal group portrait, further attesting to his close ties with the young painters who shared his interest in painting modern life.

Over the course of the 1870s, Manet's art evolved in a lively dialogue with Impressionism. Near the end of the decade, Manet realized two independent self-portraits, the only such works of his career, which were not publicly exhibited in his lifetime.[3] His motive in painting them remains unknown. Their similar handling reflects his assimilation of the loose, visible brushwork characteristic of Impressionist art. At the same time, both recall Manet's own early works, which were painted under the influence of the seventeenth-century Spanish master, Diego Velázquez, whose art served as a touchstone for Manet. His pose in *Self-portrait with a Palette* (fig. 1) has been likened to Velázquez's appearance in *Las Meninas* of 1656, which Manet saw during his 1865 visit to the Prado Museum in Madrid. A full-length self-portrait, set against a freely brushed, neutral background, evokes his own early figure paintings, which, in turn, assimilated Velázquez's precedent (fig. 2). Manet's confident stance, arms akimbo, gives no hint of his declining health; by 1879, he was suffering from the effects of tertiary syphilis, which caused difficulties in walking and movement. He continued to paint until the final months of his life, succumbing to the disease on April 30, 1883, the day before the Salon opened.

The fusion of past and present in Manet's late self-portraits embodies the ongoing artistic dialogue that would define his modernity. Four years after his death, the critic Armand Silvestre recalled Manet's influence on the emerging Impressionist artists around 1870, adding that Manet

Henri Fantin-Latour, *Édouard Manet*, 1867, oil on canvas, 46 ¼ × 35 7⁄16 in. (117.5 × 90 cm). Chicago, The Art Institute of Chicago, Stickney Fund, 1905.207

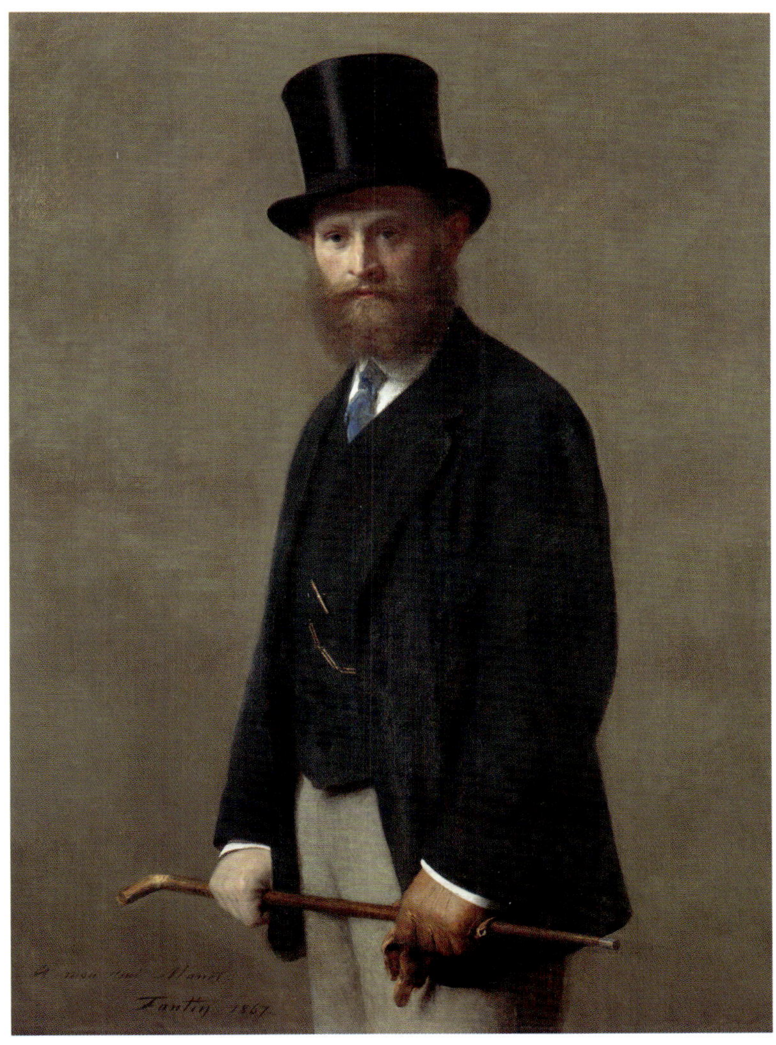

"asserted in painting . . . a sense of modernity which may have been widely aspired to but which had not yet seen the light of day."[4] His influence has continued to resonate. Just as Manet turned to the past to forge a new vision for the art of his time, successive generations of artists responding to his art, from Paul Cézanne in the 1870s to the contemporary artist Nicole Eisenman, ensure that his legacy endures.

1 Émile Zola, *Looking at Manet*, introduced by Robert Lethbridge (Los Angeles: The J. Paul Getty Museum, 2018), 33.

2 Antonin Proust, *Édouard Manet, Souvenirs* (Caen: L'Échoppe, 1988), 20.

3 On these works, see Mary Anne Stevens (ed.), *Manet: Portraying Life* [exhibition catalogue], Toledo, Museum of Art and London, Royal Academy, 2012–13, 176.

4 Cited in Charles S. Moffett, "Manet and Impressionism," in Françoise Cachin and Charles S. Moffett (eds.), *Manet, 1832–1883* [exhibition catalogue], Paris, Galeries Nationales du Grand Palais and New York, The Metropolitan Museum of Art, 1983, 31.

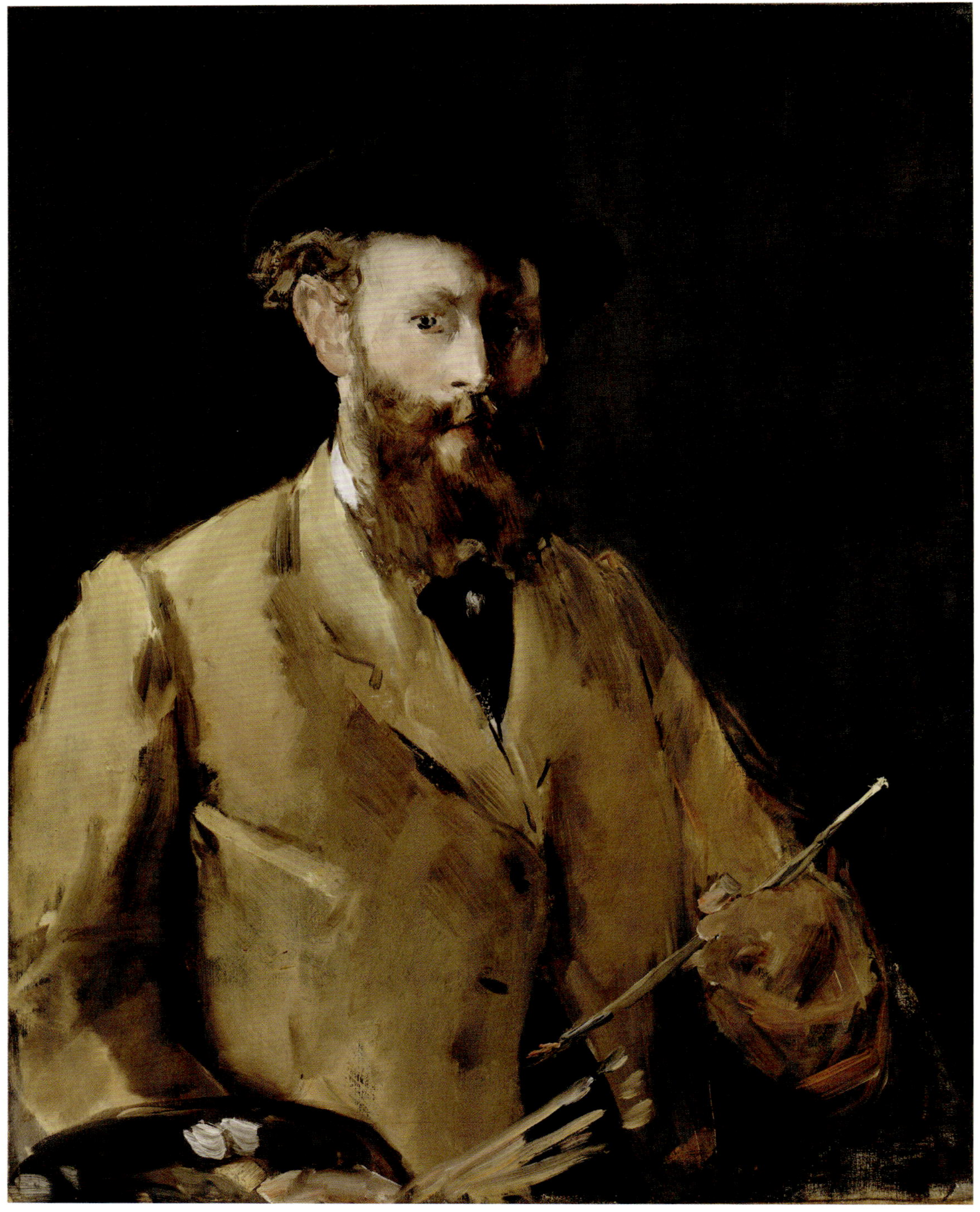

1

Self-portrait with a Palette

1879
Oil on canvas, 33 ⅝ × 28 in.
(85.5 × 71 cm)
Private collection

2

Self-portrait

1879
Oil on canvas, 37 ½ × 25 in.
(95.4 × 63.4 cm)
Tokyo, Artizon Museum

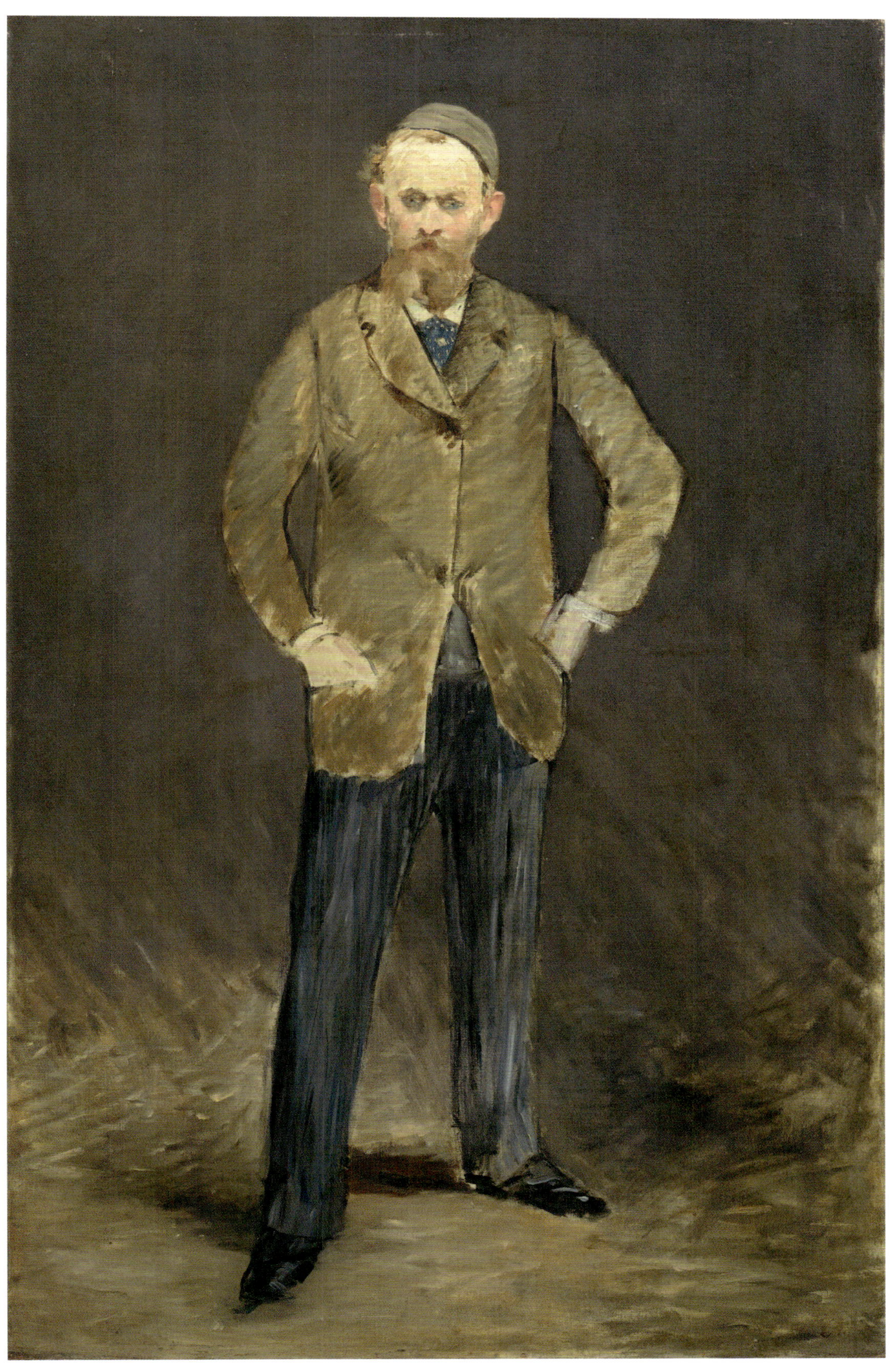

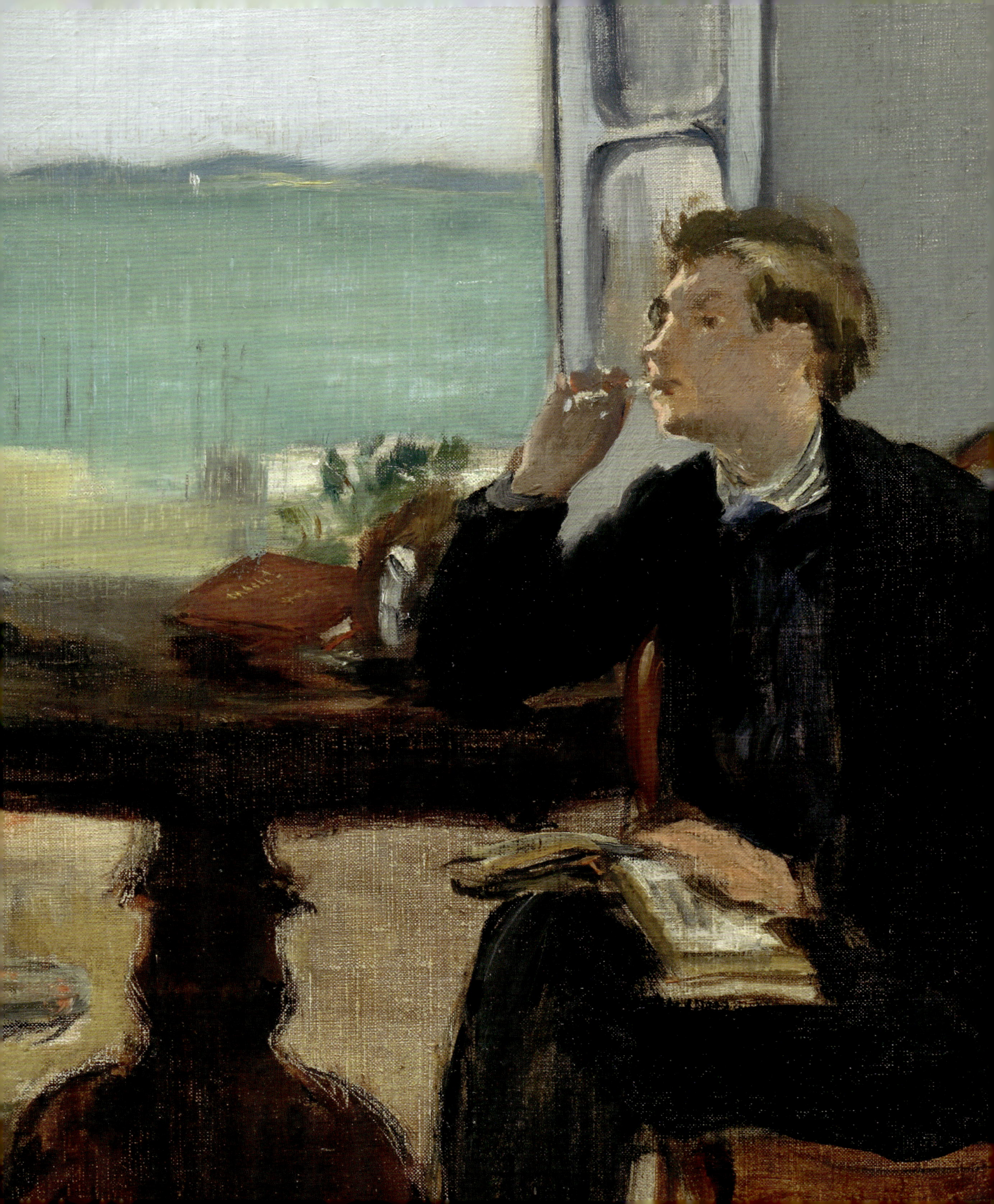

Family Man

A portrait by Édouard Manet of his wife, Suzanne Leenhoff, known today simply as *Woman with a Cat*, remains in its unfinished state (fig. 3). It was abandoned by the artist, who was then in the final years of life, suffering the effects of the disease that ultimately killed him. He portrayed his wife in a domestic interior, possibly that of the Manet family apartment on 49, rue de Saint-Pétersbourg in Paris.[1] The work is loosely painted, the application of paint evocative of Manet's handling of the pastel medium in which he had recently begun to work. Suzanne, her expression pensive, wears a simple peignoir, and the family cat, Zizi, is curled up on her lap in the place Manet reserved for her, its blue outlines visible. This intimate scene of quiet domesticity is possibly the last portrait that Manet painted of his wife, who had served as his model since the late 1850s and is the subject of at least eighteen works. Painted between 1880 and 1882, it is also one of his last portraits. As Manet often borrowed from his own imagery, it is tempting to see in it echoes of his earlier paintings, from the pink peignoir worn by Victorine Meurent in 1867 (fig. 38) to the infamous black cat of *Olympia* (fig. 36).

Manet's art is inextricably bound with his family. Members of the Manet family figure prominently in the artist's oeuvre as the subject of portraits as well as models in his innovative figure paintings and scenes from modern life, including *Luncheon on the Grass* (fig. 31) and *Young Man in the Costume of a Majo* (fig. 33).[2] Attesting to Manet's familial bonds, these works also offer tantalizing glimpses into the artist's private life, one that to this day remains shrouded in mystery and belies his conventional upbringing.

Born January 23, 1832, Manet was the eldest of three sons in an upper-middle class Parisian household. His maternal uncle, Edmond Fournier, encouraged the young Manet's budding interest in art with regular visits to the Louvre and sketching excursions. Manet's friend and early biographer, Théodore Duret, observed, "He grew up in an atmosphere of ancient tradition. The characteristics, social and moral, which he had inherited remained as firmly planted in him throughout his life as his innate artistic instinct."[3] Similarly, his lifelong friend Antonin Proust

Detail of fig. 10

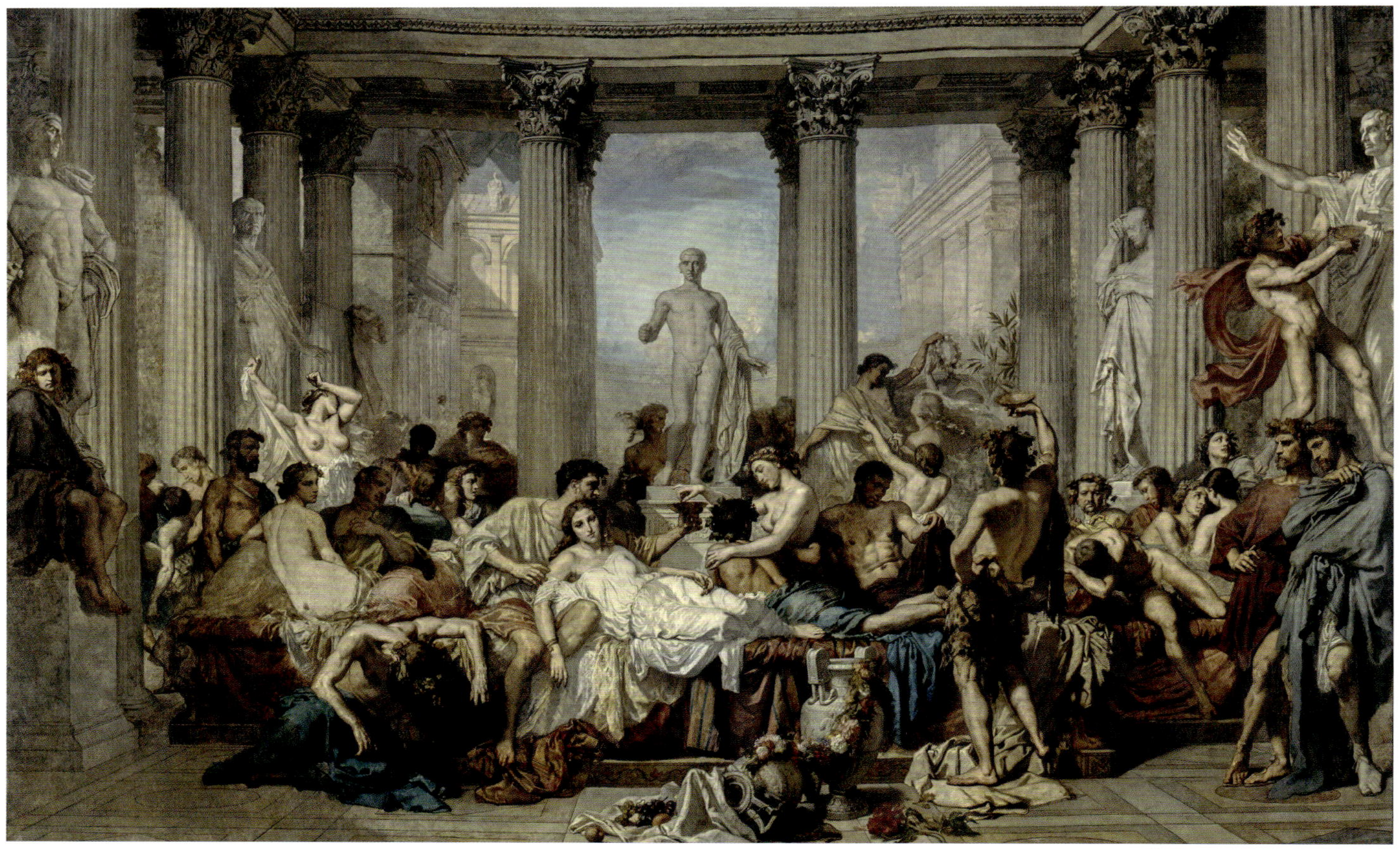

Thomas Couture,
The Romans of the Decadence, 1847,
oil on canvas,
189 × 304 in.
(472 × 772 cm).
Paris, Musée d'Orsay, 3451

described Manet as "the expression of this state of mind of his ancestors; French to the core . . ."[4] As such, Édouard was expected to pursue a legal career like his father and, before him, his grandfather, who had also served as the mayor of the rural town of Gennevilliers, where generations of Manet's family were landowners. He attended the prestigious Collège Rollin, its classical curriculum intended to prepare him for the study of law; however, as Proust recalled, the young Manet was an unmotivated student, more interested in his drawing class than academics.

When Manet was sixteen, it was decided that he would attend the Naval Academy, but he failed the entrance examination. As an alternative, he served as a naval cadet on *Le Havre et Guadeloupe*, a merchant ship that sailed to Rio de Janeiro from the French port of Le Havre on December 9, 1848. Following his six-month stint at sea, where he served as the ship's drawing master, he overcame his father's objections to his unconventional career choice and entered the studio of Thomas Couture in September 1850, where he spent the next six years. In 1847, Couture had made his name at the Salon, the state-sponsored, juried art exhibition in Paris, with a monumental history painting, *The Romans of the Decadence*. In his teaching, Couture emphasized the study of the art of the past as well as sketching from life, both of which would play a formative role in Manet's artistic development.

Portraits of his immediate family figure among Manet's earliest independent works of art. His parents, Auguste Manet (1797–1862) and Eugénie-Désirée Fournier (1811–85), appear in a double portrait of 1860, which Manet painted in their Parisian apartment (fig. 4). Clad in indoor dress, the couple projects an image of bourgeois respectability. His father, a civil court judge, wears his judicial hat and the red ribbon of the Legion of Honor, a national order of merit and the highest French civilian decoration, which stands out against the black lapel of his jacket; his mother, the daughter of a diplomat and goddaughter of the king of Sweden, hovers solicitously by his side, holding a basket of yarn, an emblem of female domesticity that also signals Manet's early interest in still-life subjects. Despite their physical closeness, they do not engage with each other, and their divergent gazes underscore the lack of connection. In 1857, Manet's father began suffering from the effects of tertiary syphilis, resulting in partial paralysis and, eventually, loss of speech; changes that Manet made to the figure of his father as the composition evolved suggest that he was responding to his father's declining health.[5] He originally painted Auguste gazing outward, his right hand relaxed on the arm of the chair. In the finished work, the family patriarch, visibly older, poses stiffly with downcast eyes and tightly clenched hand, while his wife's features register concern, suggesting the disruptive currents at play in the Manet household.[6]

In 1849, twenty-year-old Suzanne Leenhoff (1829–1906), a musician born in the Netherlands, entered the family orbit when she was hired to teach piano to Manet's younger brothers. On February 29, 1852, she gave birth to a son, Léon Édouard Koëlla, better known as Léon Leenhoff (1852–1927), whose paternity remains unknown, having been variously assigned to Manet himself, his father, and, more recently, a traveling Swiss musician surnamed Koëlla.[7] Suzanne became an early and frequent model for Manet, appearing in some dozen paintings as well as works on paper spanning more than thirty years; her central role as a model in Manet's nascent efforts to rival the Old Masters has only recently been fully recognized.[8]

Suzanne posed nude in *The Surprised Nymph*, a seminal canvas of 1861 (fig. 5). Her seated pose recalls images of the goddess Diana, surprised while bathing, and the biblical heroine Susanna, watched by the elders as she bathes. As such, *The Surprised Nymph* is an early example of Manet's artistic dialogue with the art of the past. The canvas was cut from a larger, multi-figured composition, *Moses Saved from the Waters*; x-radiographs reveal that Manet also painted over a second figure, that of an attendant attired in historicizing dress. He subsequently returned to the painting, adding the head of a satyr in the foliage at upper right, thereby grounding the nude in a mythological realm (the satyr's head was painted over at an unknown date).[9] Manet's thinly veiled mythological nude, her discarded clothing and jewelry at her feet, prefigures the unequivocally secular image of a nude Victorine Meurent in *Luncheon on the Grass*, painted just two years later.

Suzanne's son, Léon, also grew up modeling regularly for Manet, whom he called his godfather in the privacy of family. Publicly, Léon referred to Manet as his brother-in-law and Suzanne as his sister. As he later recalled, "We lived happily, the three of us; above all I lived happily with no concerns. Therefore, I had no need to question my birth."[10] Léon appears in at least fourteen paintings made between 1859 and 1873, which range from costumed studio paintings to variations on Old Master prototypes and scenes from modern life.[11] An early work, *Boy with a Sword* (fig. 6), painted in 1861, reflects Manet's burgeoning interest in Spanish art, especially the work of the seventeenth-century painter, Diego Velázquez, whose work served as a touchstone for Manet. Clad in historicizing dress and wielding a borrowed sword, a seven-year-old Léon, silhouetted against a neutral background, conjures the Spanish artist's portraits. However, Manet's work is a posed scene painted in his studio for which the child served as his model. It was not intended to be seen as a portrait of Léon.

Life in the Manet family was irrevocably altered with the death of the artist's father, Auguste, in 1862 at the age of sixty-five. Manet married Suzanne in her native Netherlands the following year, making public a relationship that had been a closely guarded secret. Their marriage surprised even the artist's closest friends, as evidenced by the reaction of Charles Baudelaire, who wrote in a letter of October 1863: "Manet has just announced . . . the most unexpected news. He is leaving this evening for Holland, when he will bring back *his wife*."[12] *Fishing*, a landscape with figures painted around 1862–63, has been interpreted as a commemoration of Manet's marriage to Suzanne (fig. 7) It is the only known painting by Manet in which he and Suzanne are shown together.[13] The couple appear in the lower right; dressed in seventeenth-century costume, they are modeled after a self-portrait of Peter Paul Rubens and his wife in a landscape, which Manet would have known from a recently published engraving of the Flemish master's work. Suzanne's son, Léon, sits alone on the opposite riverbank, fishing rod in hand. The child's physical isolation in the composition seemingly underscores his ambiguous status in the Manet family.

In 1866, Manet, Suzanne, and Léon moved in with his widowed mother, who lived in the family apartment at 49, rue de Saint-Pétersbourg. Around the same time, Manet painted a portrait of the family matriarch (fig. 8). Rendered life-size, Eugénie Manet commands attention with the directness of her gaze. Her imposing portrait later prompted Léon Leenhoff to characterize Manet's relationship with his mother as "not an ordinary filial affection, but a genuine worship."[14] Dressed in mourning attire, Eugénie evokes the black-clad burghers' wives portrayed by the seventeenth-century Dutch artist Frans Hals, whose art Manet admired and would have seen in the Netherlands in 1863.[15] She presided over the Thursday

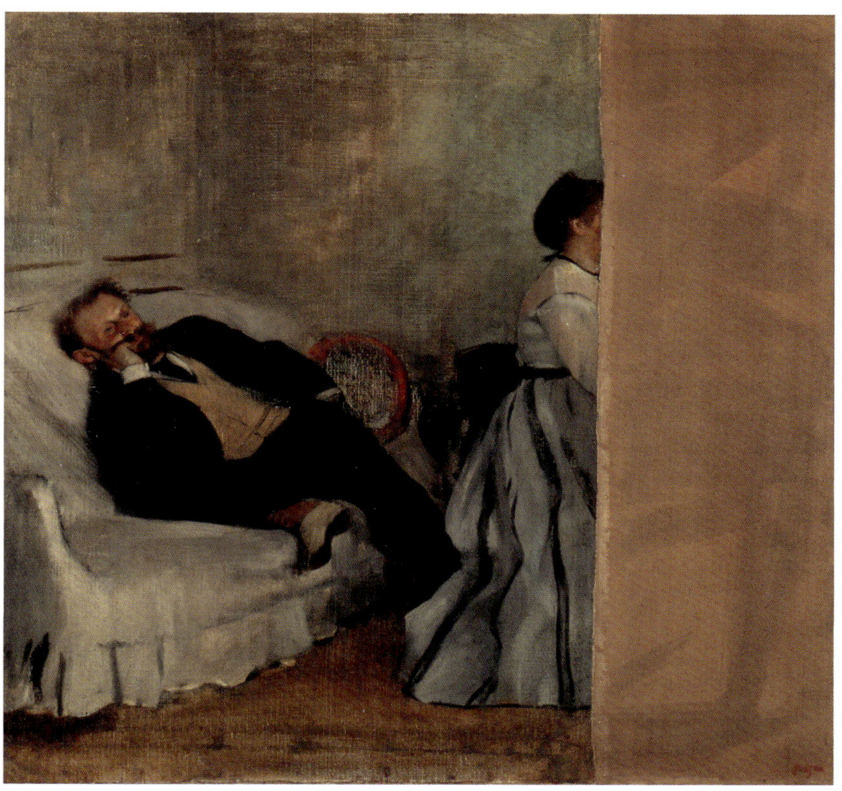

Edgar Degas, *Monsieur and Madame Édouard Manet*, 1868–69, oil on canvas, 25 9/16 × 27 15/16 in. (65 × 71 cm). Kitakyushu, Kitakyushu Municipal Museum of Art, O-119

salons attended by her son's friends, including artists such as Edgar Degas and Berthe Morisot and the writer Émile Zola.

Manet's wife, Suzanne, often played the piano during these evenings, and she also performed privately for her husband. In 1868, Degas captured in paint one such intimate performance; however, all that remains of this double portrait is the truncated, faceless figure of Suzanne seated at the piano and Manet, casually lounging on the sofa behind her in an unguarded moment. For reasons that remain unknown, Manet himself slashed the canvas, a gift from Degas, which the artist then took back.[16] That same year, Manet completed his own portrait of Suzanne, shown in profile while playing the piano in the drawing room of the Manet fa mily apartment, where Degas had also portrayed her (fig. 9). A contemporary account of Suzanne performing at other social gatherings evokes Manet's portrait: "Madame Manet, the painter's wife, a tall and heavy Dutchwoman, would play classical pieces, her exceptionally beautiful hands running over the keyboard with a lightness and a feeling so little suggested by her appearance that it was enchanting."[17] Much later, when Manet was ill and convalescing in the Parisian suburb of Bellevue in 1880, Suzanne would entertain him by playing "sonatas that delighted him," as Proust recalled.[18]

Suzanne posed for other portraits set in domestic interiors, including a work known as *Reading* (fig. 11). Manet began the painting in the mid-1860s as an intimate portrait of

Suzanne at home in the Manet family apartment, informally attired in a white muslin dress and backlit by the curtained living room window. Around 1873, Manet added the partially cropped figure of Léon Leenhoff, absorbed in a book. Despite other modifications Manet made to the work, he did not alter Suzanne's original, youthful features although her son was by this date a young man of about twenty.[19] This domestic scene embodies the blurred boundaries separating portraiture and scenes from modern life, which are characteristic of Manet's modern pictorial approach.[20] The composition also marks one of the first in which "Manet is entirely freed from the art of the past," as art historian Françoise Cachin observed.[21]

Although both Suzanne and Léon frequently modeled for Manet, they rarely appear together. Their portrayal in *Reading* recalls an earlier domestic scene, which Manet painted after spending five months apart from his family during the Franco-Prussian war of 1870–71 (fig. 10). He remained in Paris to serve in the National Guard but sent his mother, Suzanne, and Léon to southwestern France for their safety. While Paris was under siege, Manet wrote almost daily letters to his wife, which were often sent by balloon. In a letter of November 23, he asked after Léon and added, "Remind him that I sent him with you to replace me and to protect you. I hope he is worthy of my faith in him." On New Year's Day in 1871, Manet wrote to his wife, "I think of you all the time. I think it's the first time since I've known you that I can't kiss you on New Year's Day. Still no word from you. It is very cruel, and we may have another month of this."[22] In March, a newly reunited Manet family sojourned in the coastal town of Arcachon, where Manet depicted mother and son in the salon of their rented vacation villa, lost in their own reflections and seemingly unaware of being painted. Suzanne pauses from writing, a moment that recalls the letters written during the family's recent separation. Manet never exhibited this family portrait, whose sketch-like handling underscores its private aspect.

In the summer of 1873, the Manet family spent three weeks in Berck-sur-Mer, where the artist realized a painting of Suzanne and his younger brother Eugène (1833–1892) on the beach of this seaside town in northern France (fig. 12). Grains of sand embedded in the paint surface indicate that it was probably painted on site, a choice likely influenced by the practice of Manet's younger contemporary and future Impressionist, Claude Monet (1840–1926).[23] Despite their proximity to each other, Suzanne and Eugène do not interact in this outdoor scene, recalling Manet's portrayals of his wife and son in *Reading* and *Interior at Arcachon*. Eugène's reclining pose might intentionally echo his earlier appearance in *Luncheon on the Grass*, for which he posed in his brother's studio.

Throughout his career Manet portrayed members of his family, both as portrait subjects and as models in his groundbreaking scenes from modern life. In the 1860s, Manet's repertoire broadened to include other models, notably Victorine Meurent, as well as his widening circle of friends, including the artist Berthe Morisot, who married Manet's brother, Eugène, in 1874. However, his family played an essential role in the creation of paintings that came to define Manet's modernity as an artist. These works served as the foundation for the scandals and successes that followed.

1 See the discussion of the work in Emily A. Beeny, "Suzanne: The Private Portraits," in Diana Seave Greenwald (ed.), *Manet: A Model Family* [exhibition catalogue], Boston, Isabella Stewart Gardner Museum, 2024, 54, and Scott Allan et al. (eds.), *Manet and Modern Beauty, the Artist's Last Years* [exhibition catalogue], Chicago, The Art Institute of Chicago and Los Angeles, The J. Paul Getty Museum, 2019, 295.
2 On this subject see Boston 2024.
3 Théodore Duret, trans. J. E. Crawford Finch, *Manet* (New York, Crown Publishers, 1937), 8.
4 Proust 1988, 12.
5 Nancy Locke, *Manet and the Family Romance* (Princeton, Princeton University Press, 2001), 51.
6 These changes are detailed in Paris and New York 1983, 48, 50.
7 Diana Seave Greenwald, "Édouard Manet: A Family Story," in Boston 2024, 24, 27.
8 Juliet Wilson-Bareau, "Suzanne Leenhoff: Manet's Early Inspiration," in Boston 2024, 41–49.
9 For an analysis of the work's different stages, see Juliet Wilson-Bareau, "The Hidden Face of Manet: An Investigation of the Artist's Working Processes," *Burlington Magazine* 128, 997 (1986): pp. 35–36.
10 Boston 2024, 27.
11 Ibid., 116, for a list of works.
12 Ibid., 14.
13 Paris and New York 1983, 72.
14 Locke 2001, 54, 190, n. 62.
15 Boston 2024, 136.
16 On Degas's work and Manet's response, see Isolde Pludermacher, "Cut Paintings, Illegitimate Children, and Two Exceptional Artists: Edgar Degas and the Manet Family," in Boston 2024, 75–80.
17 Boston 2024, 105.
18 Ibid., 105.
19 Gary Tinterow and Henri Loyrette (eds.), *Origins of Impressionism* [exhibition catalogue], Paris, Galeries Nationales du Grand Palais and New York, The Metropolitan Museum of Art, 1994, 407.
20 On this subject in relation to the work of Manet and the Impressionists, see Henri Loyrette, "Portraits and Figures," in Paris and New York 1994, 183–231.
21 Paris and New York 1983, 259.
22 Mina Curtiss, "Letters of Édouard Manet to His Wife During the Siege of Paris: 1870–71," *Apollo* 113 (June 1981): 384, 386.
23 Paris and New York 1983, 344–45.

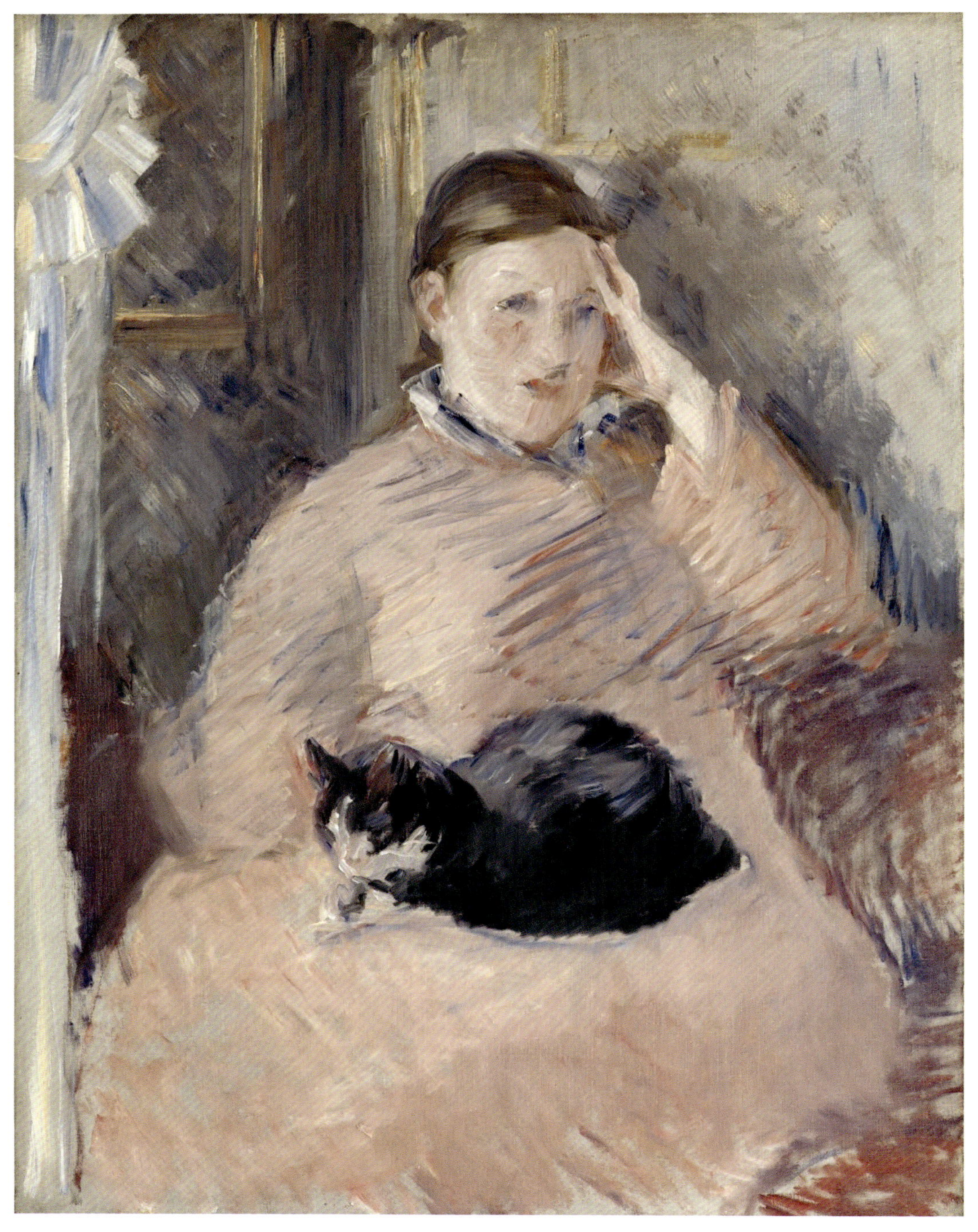

3

Woman with a Cat

1880–82
Oil on canvas,
36 ⅓ × 29 in. (92.1 × 73 cm)
London, The Tate Gallery,
N03295

4

Portrait of Monsieur and Madame Auguste Manet

1860
Oil on canvas,
43 ⅓ × 35 ½ in. (110 × 90 cm)
Paris, Musée d'Orsay,
RF 1977 12

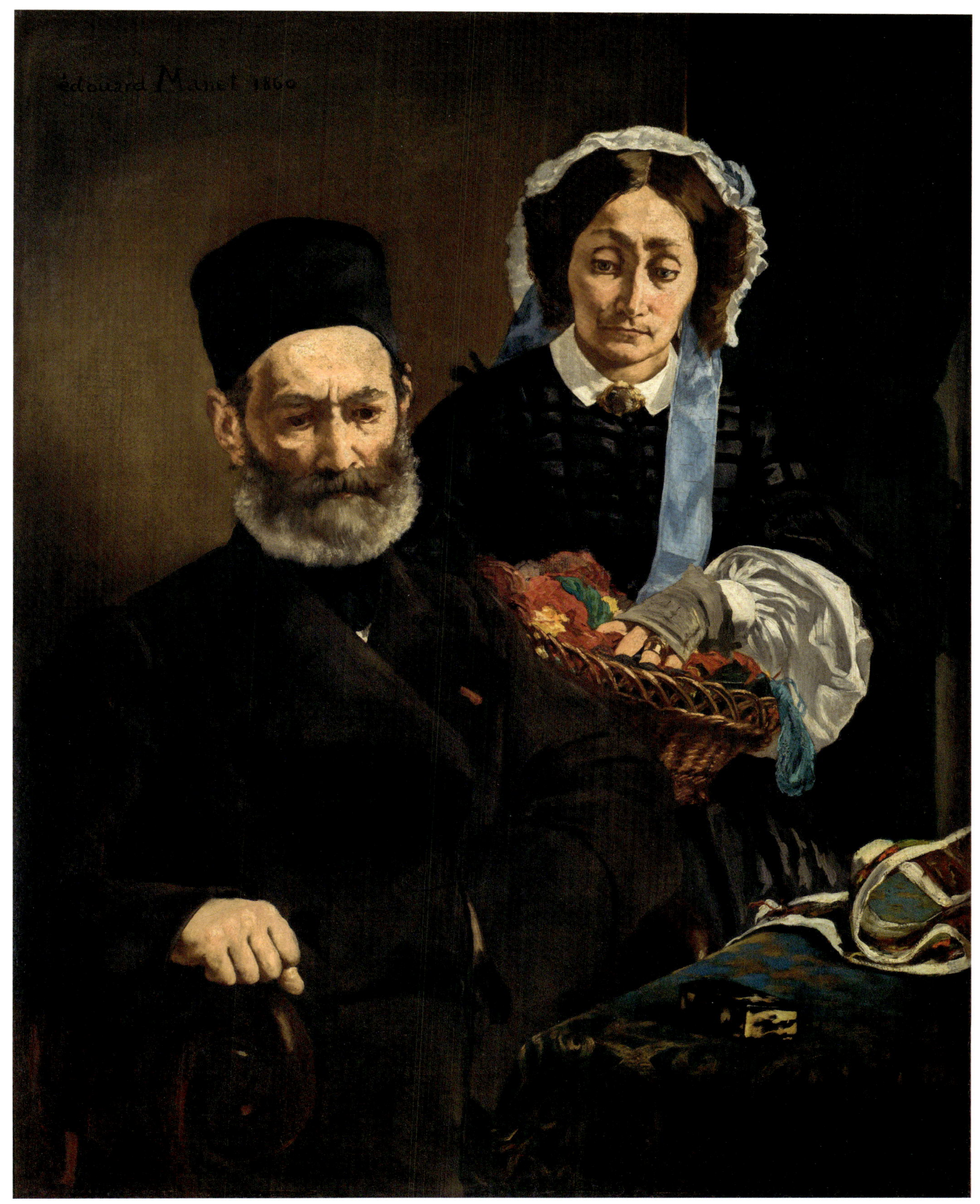
édouard Manet 1860

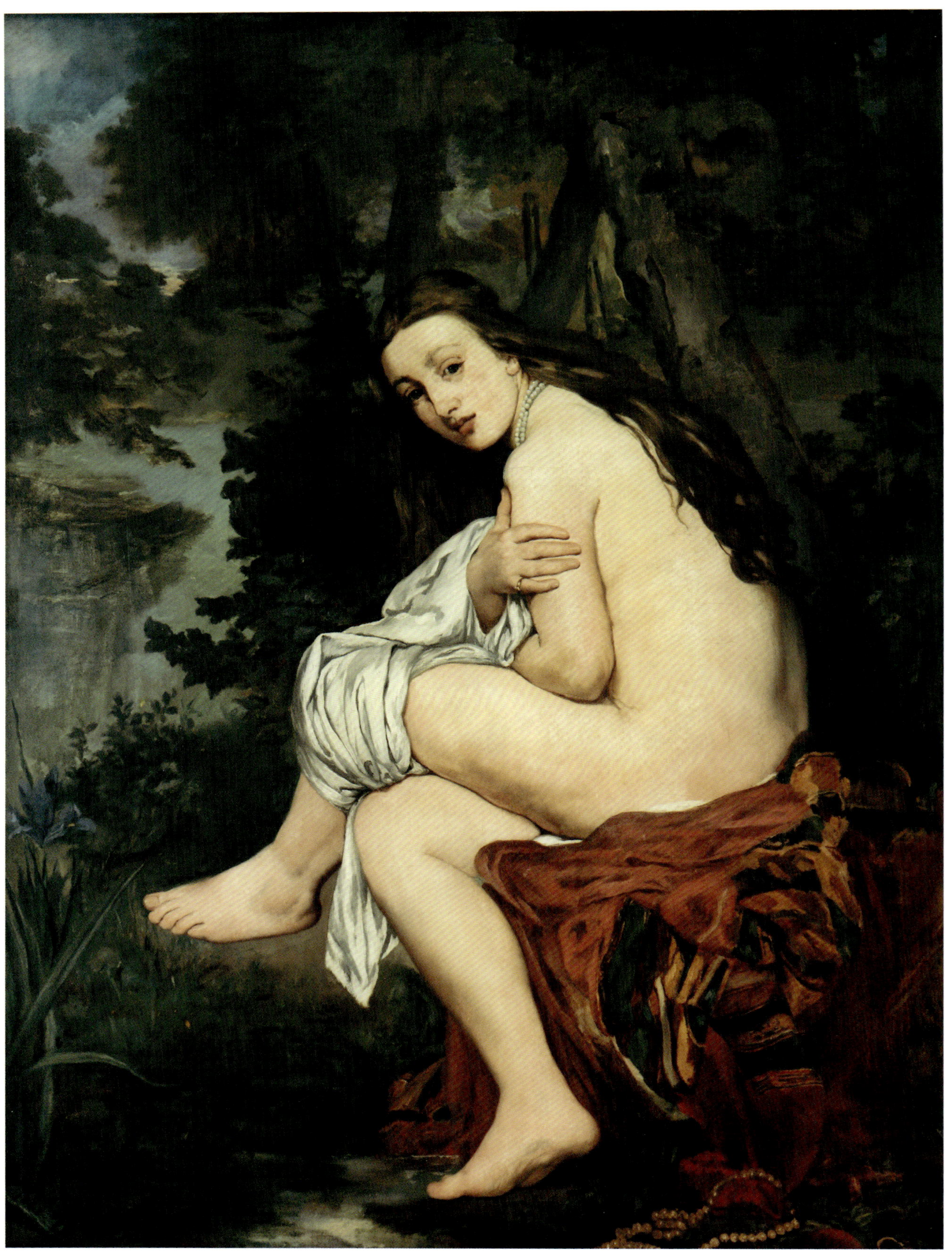

5

The Surprised Nymph

1861
Oil on canvas,
57 × 44 ⅓ in.
(144.5 × 112.5 cm)
Buenos Aires, Museo Nacional de Bellas Artes, 2712

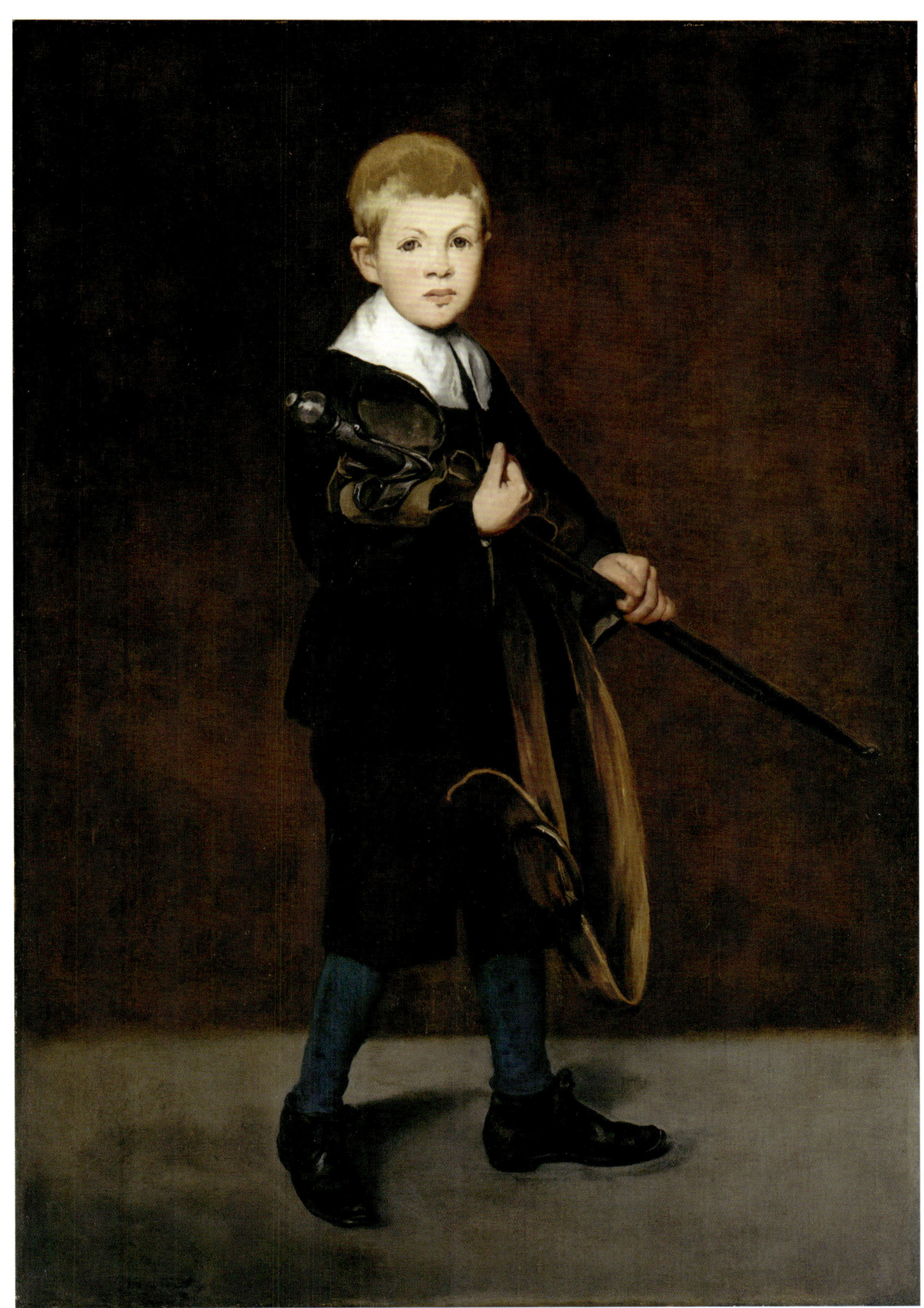

6

Boy with a Sword

1861
Oil on canvas, 51 ⅝ × 36 ¾ in.
(131.1 × 93.4 cm)
New York, The Metropolitan Museum of Art, Gift of Erwin Davis, 1889, 89.21.2

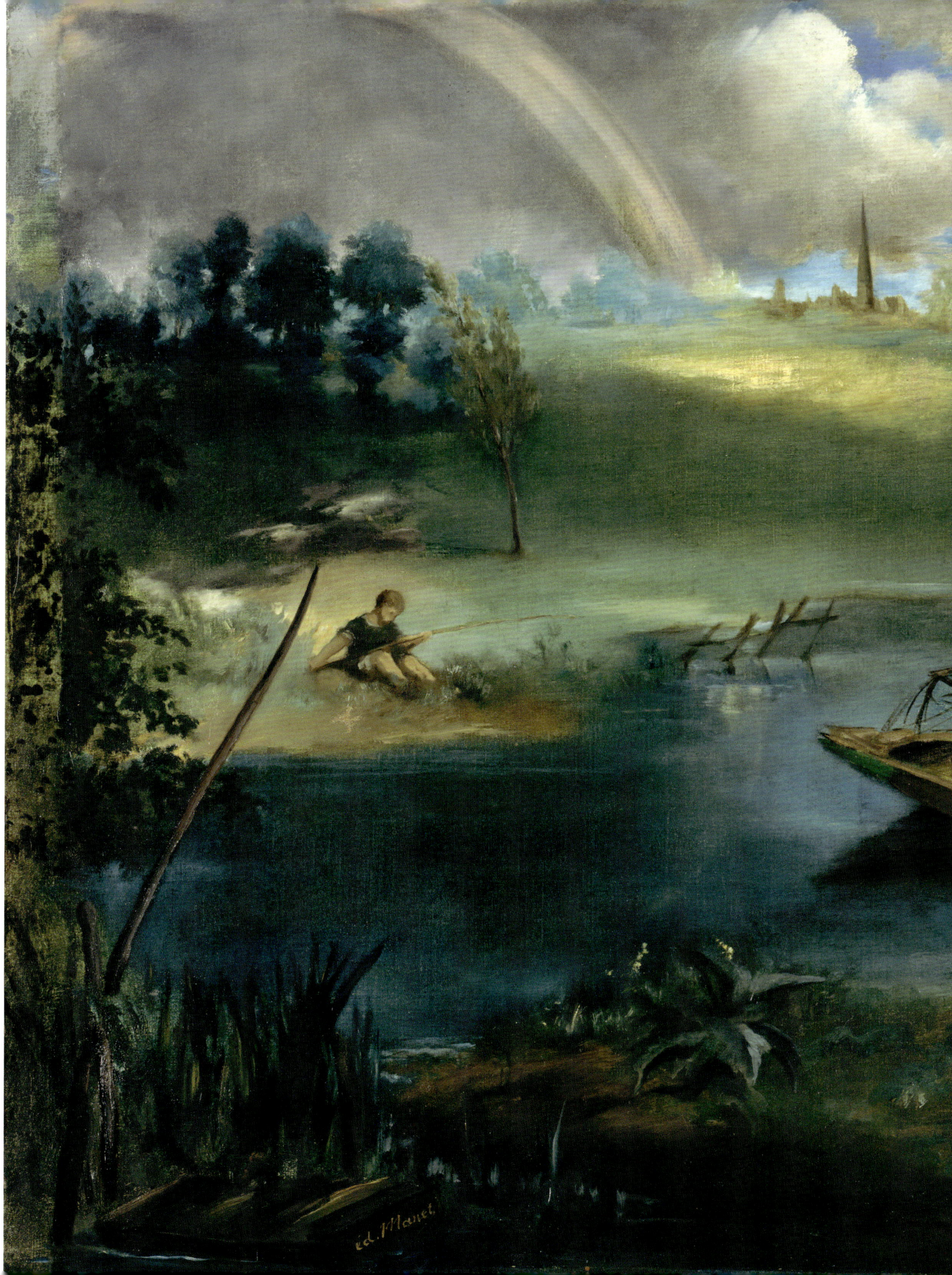

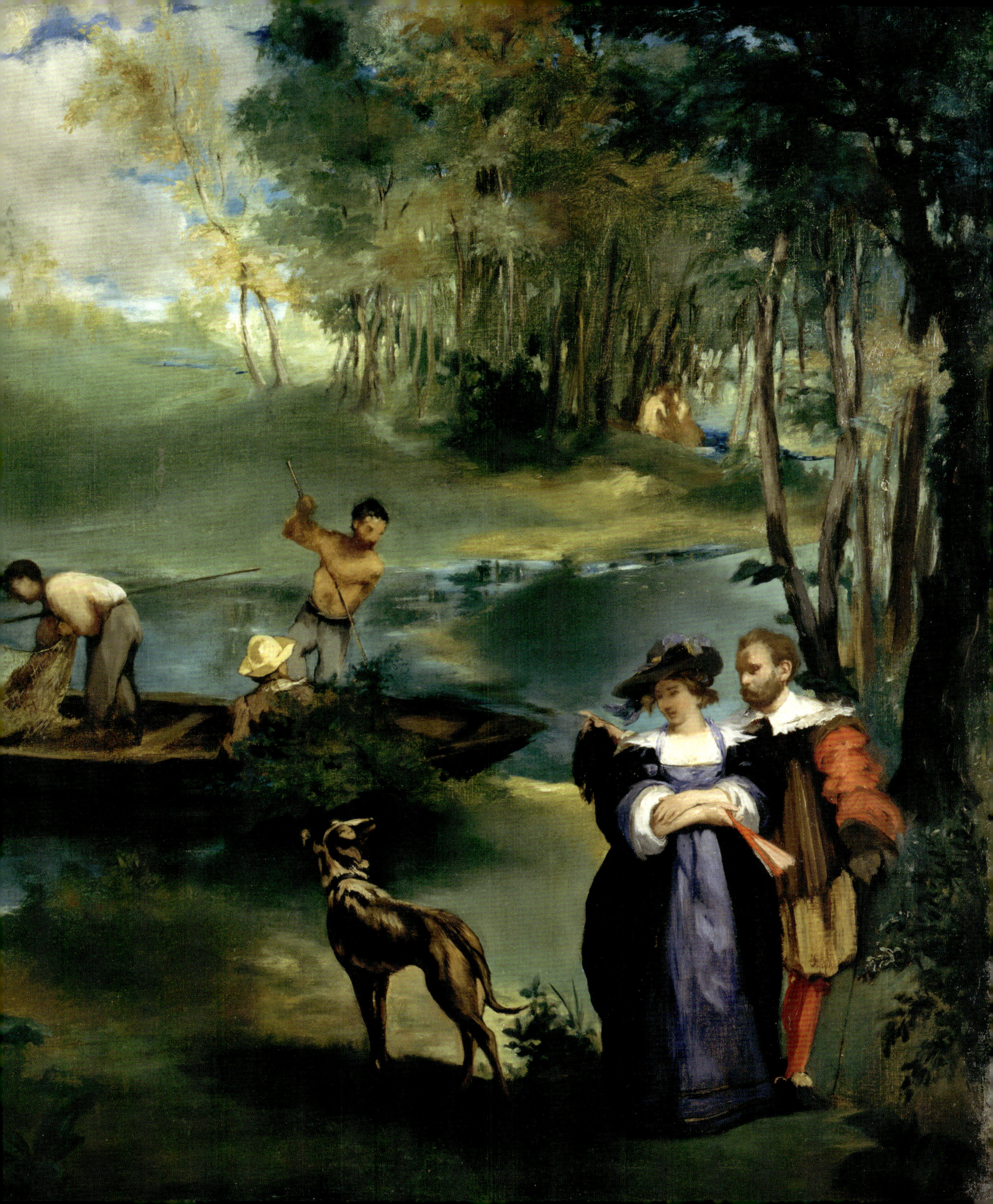

PREVIOUS PAGES

7

Fishing

1862–63
Oil on canvas, 30 ¼ × 48 ½ in.
(76.8 × 123.2 cm)
New York, The Metropolitan Museum of Art, Purchase, Mr. and Mrs. Richard J. Bernhard Gift, 1957, 57.10

8

Madame Auguste Manet

ca. 1866
Oil on canvas, 38 9/16 × 31 ½ in.
(98 × 80 cm)
Boston, Isabella Stewart Gardner Museum, P3s4

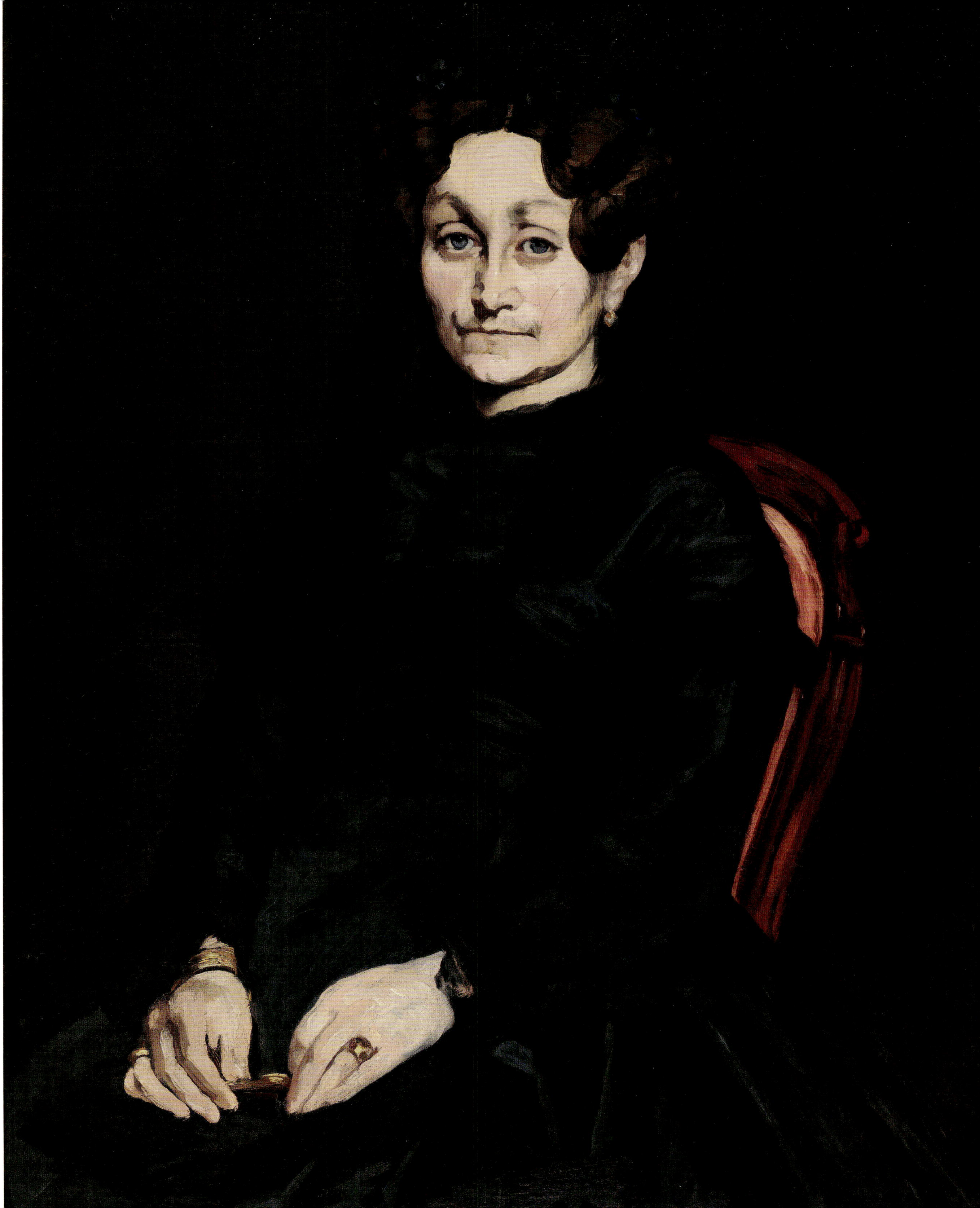

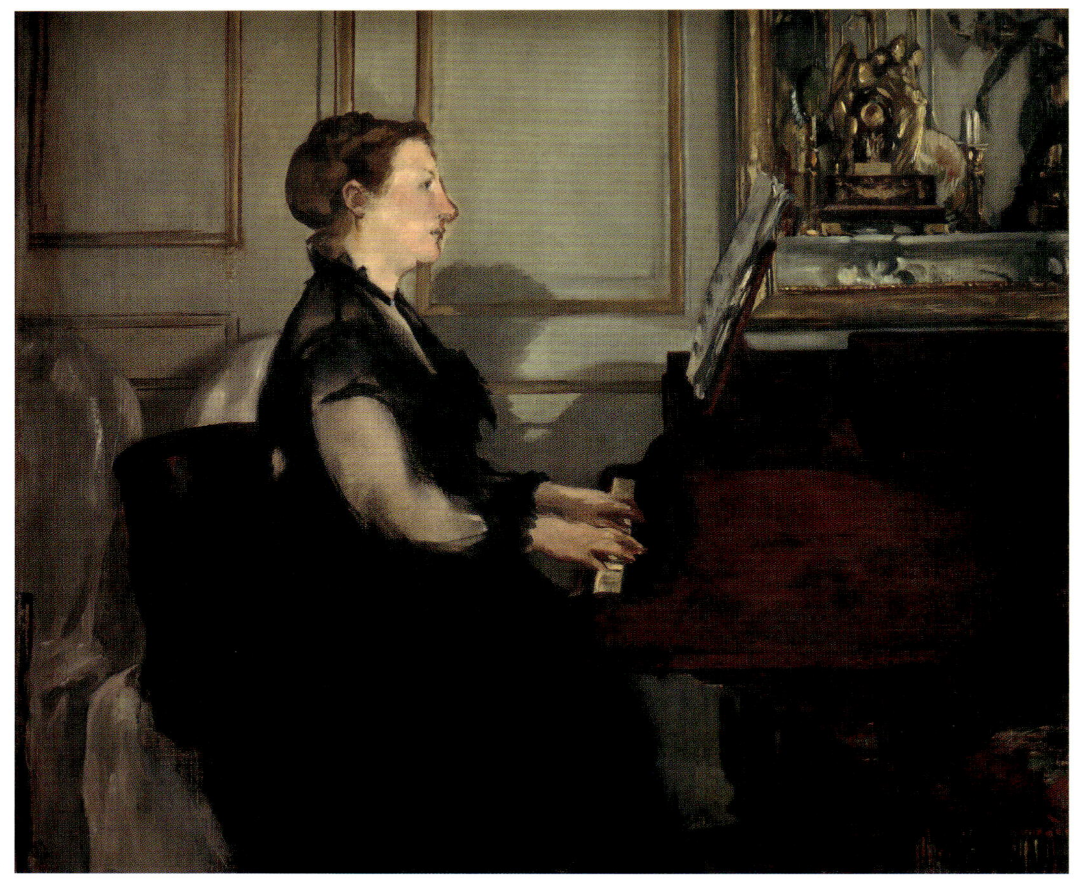

9

Madame Manet at the Piano

1868
Oil on canvas,
15 × 18 ⅓ in.
(38.5 × 46.6 cm)
Paris, Musée d'Orsay,
RF 1994

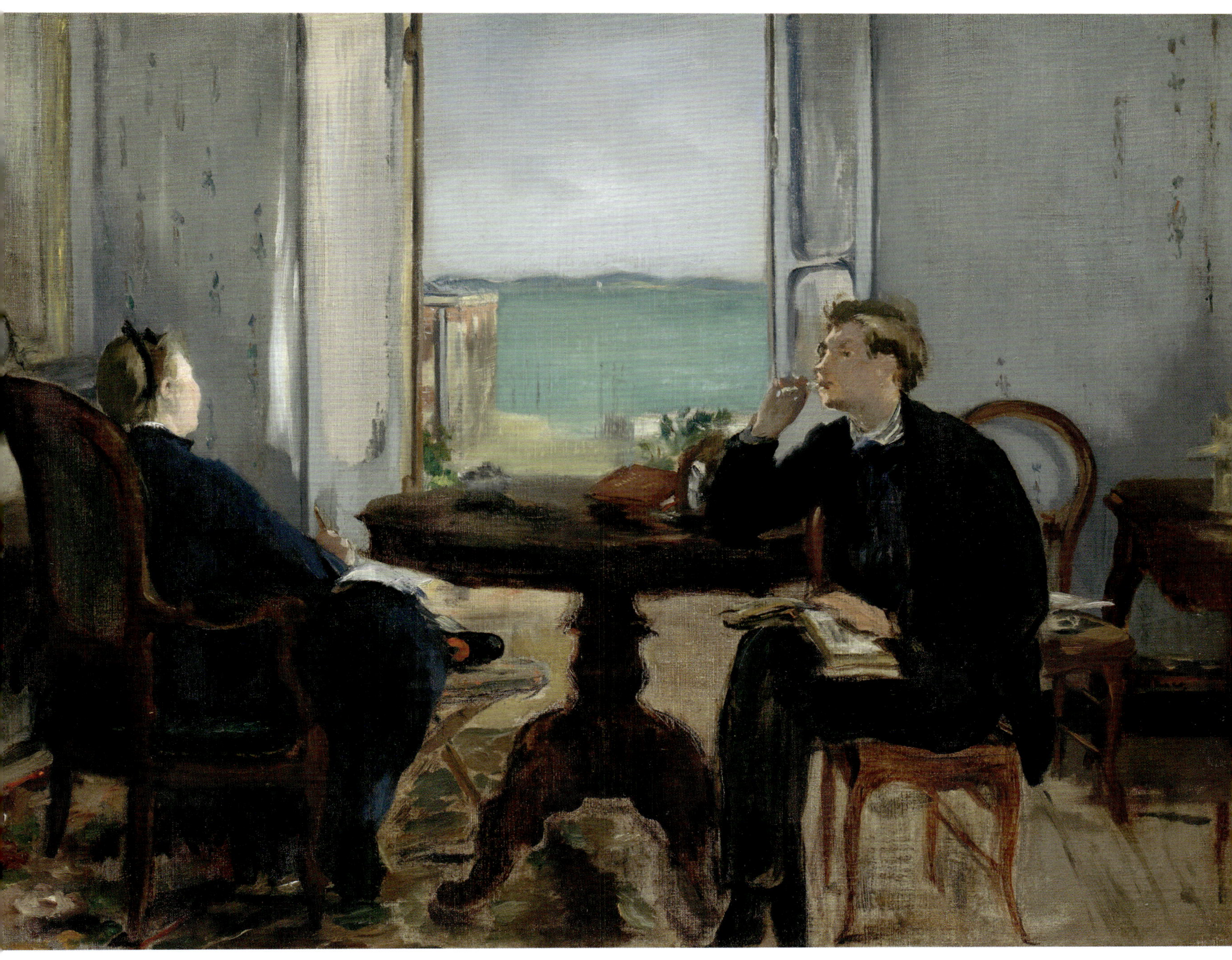

10

Interior at Arcachon

1871
Oil on canvas, 15 7/16 × 21 1/4 in.
(39.2 × 54 cm)
Williamstown, Clark Art
Institute, 1955.552

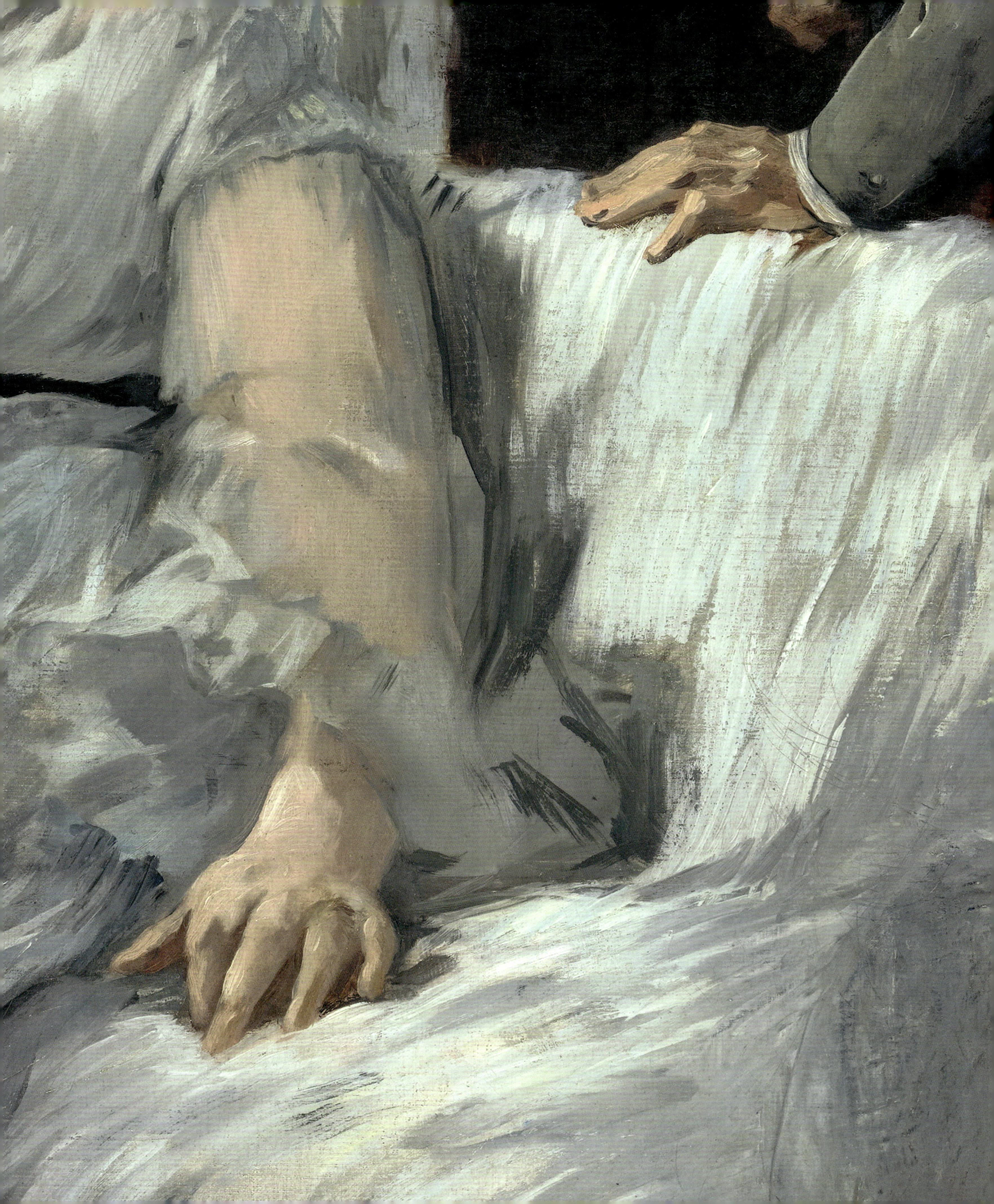

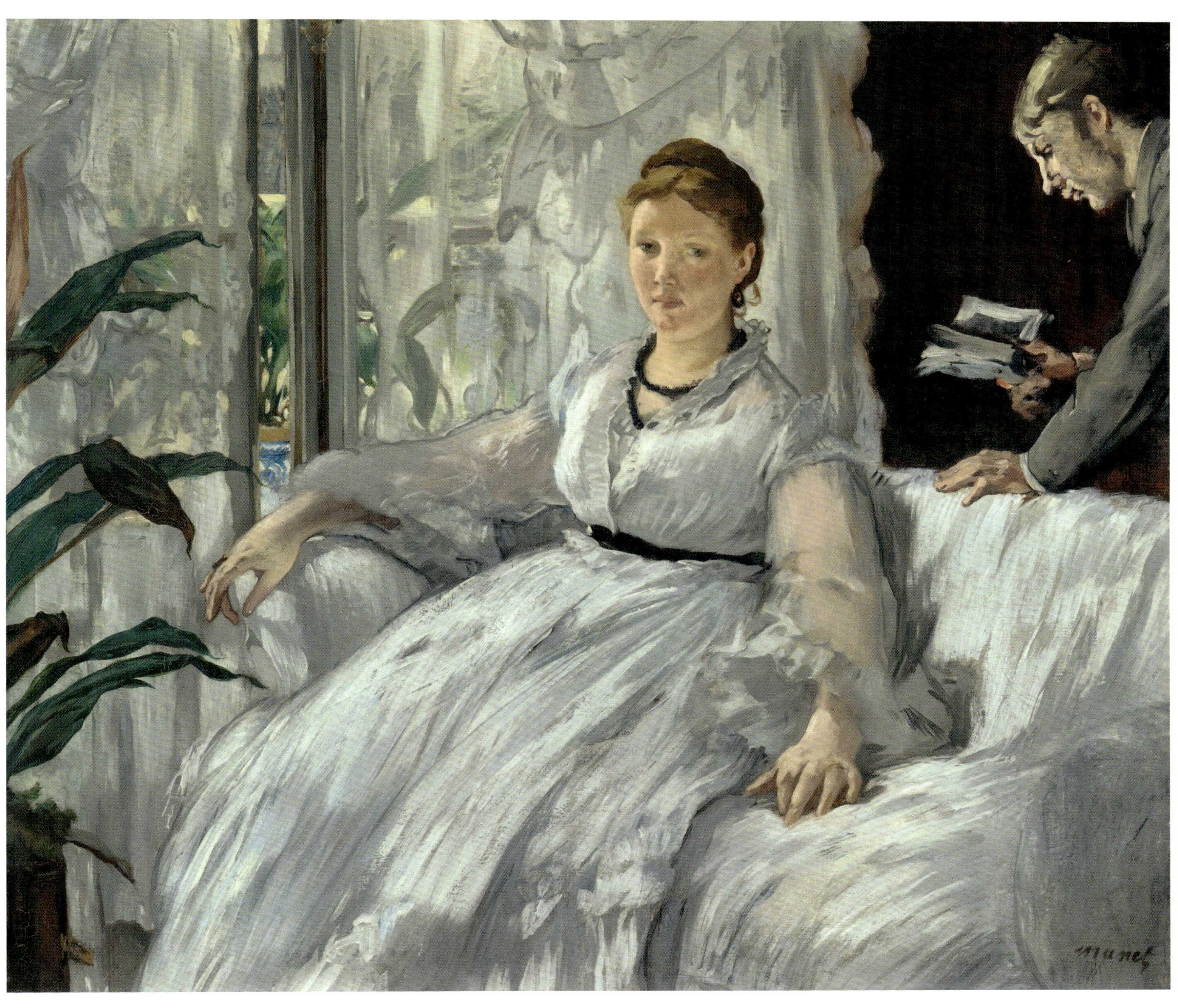

11

Reading

ca. 1866, probably resumed ca. 1873
Oil on canvas, 24 × 28 13⁄16 in. (61 × 73.2 cm)
Paris, Musée d'Orsay, RF 1944 17

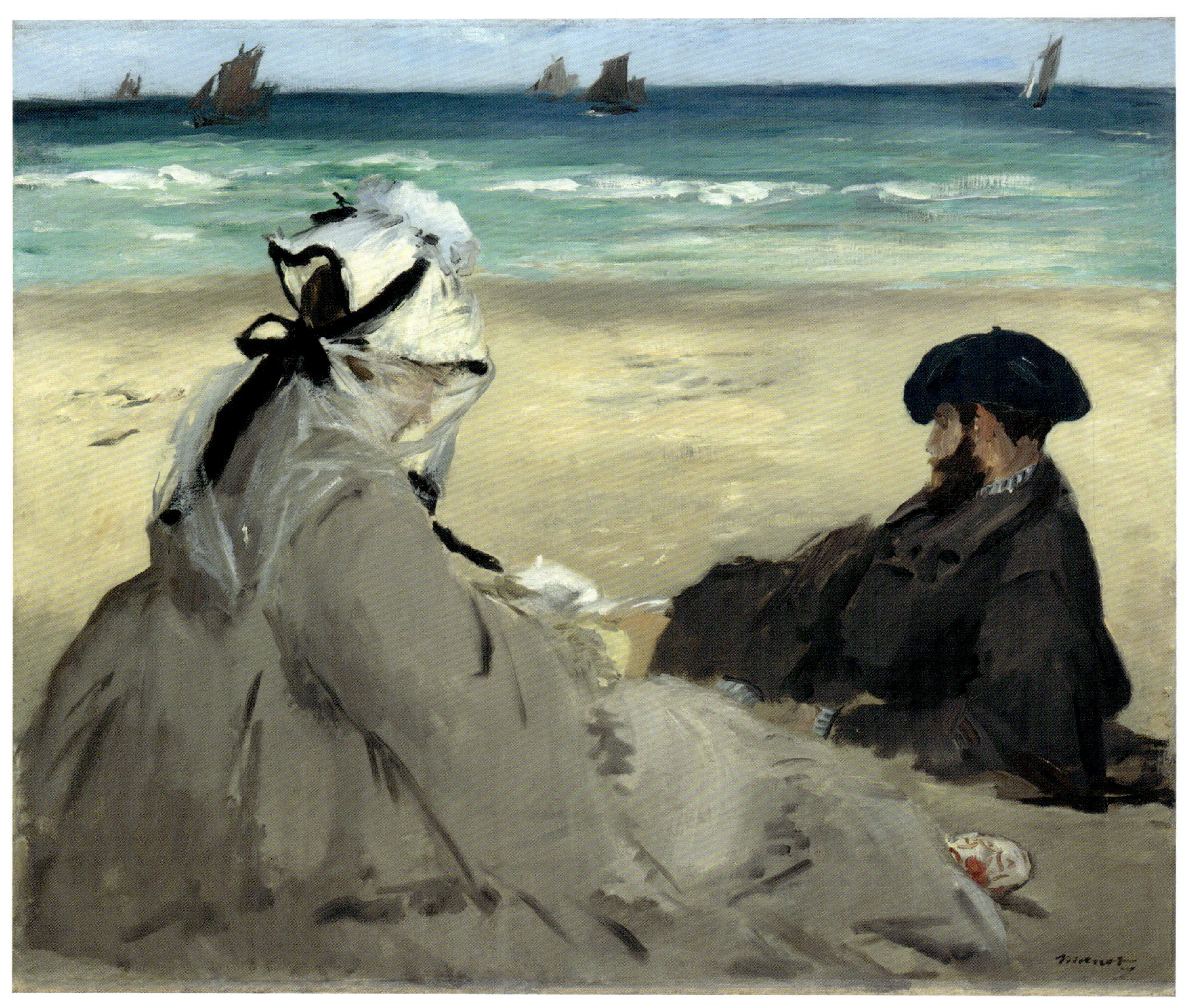

12

On the Beach

1873
Oil on canvas,
23 ½ × 29 in. (60 × 73.5 cm)
Paris, Musée d'Orsay,
RF 1953 24

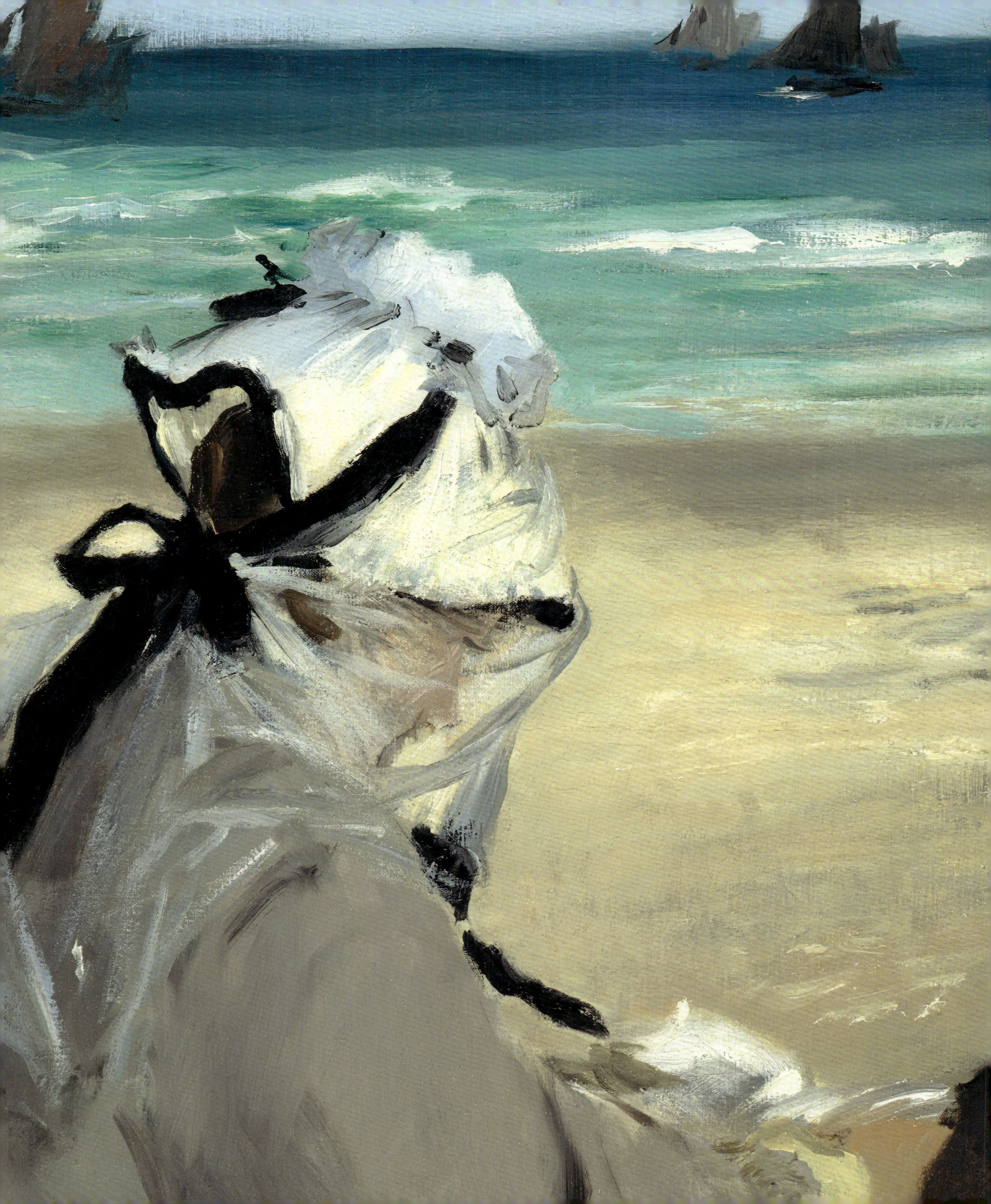

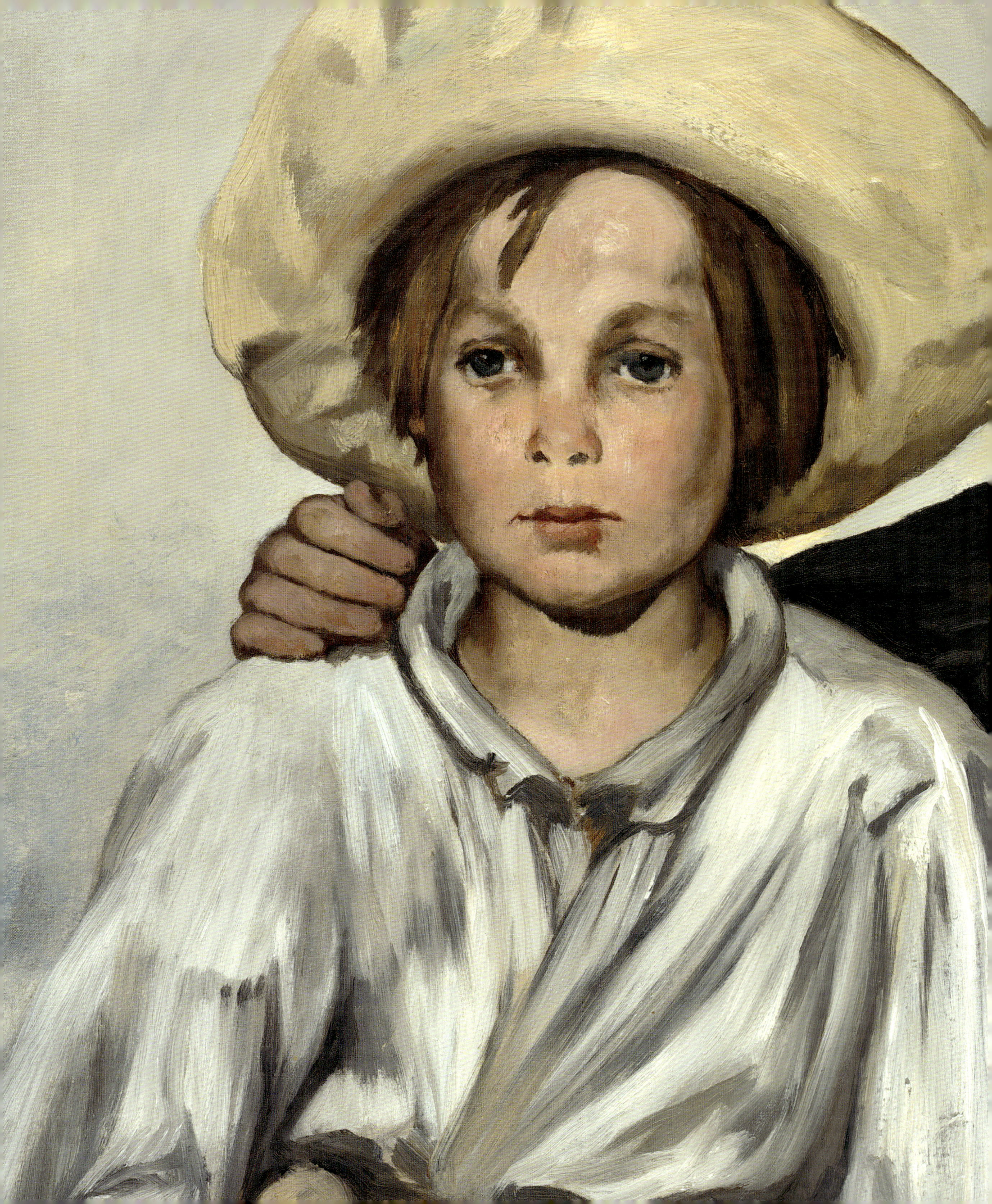

Past Made Present

Manet's coming of age as an artist coincided with a renewed interest in the art of the past in mid-nineteenth-century France. The Louvre Museum, open since 1793, offered aspiring artists the opportunity to copy works by the Old Masters as part of their training. Formerly private art collections became public, including King Louis-Philippe's collection of some four hundred Spanish paintings, displayed from 1838 to 1848 at the Galerie Espagnole at the Louvre, which a teenaged Manet regularly visited with his uncle.[1] In 1860, the Galerie Martinet in Paris held an exhibition of works by seventeenth- and eighteenth-century French artists, while a trove of works by eighteenth-century French masters, including Jean Siméon Chardin, entered the Louvre in 1869 through the La Caze bequest. Critics, notably Théophile Thoré and Jules Champfleury, also fueled this phenomenon, promoting the work of earlier artists ranging from the seventeenth-century Dutch master Johannes Vermeer to the Le Nain brothers, seventeenth-century French painters known for their realistic portrayal of peasant life. In 1849, Charles Blanc published the first volume of his influential *Histoire des peintres de toutes les écoles*, whose engraved illustrations became an essential resource for Manet. Throughout his career, Manet engaged in an ongoing dialogue with art-historical tradition, drawing from a broad range of sources and variously adapting them to suit his own artistic ends. As his friend Antonin Proust recalled, Manet believed that in art, "everything that has a sense of humanity, a sense of modernity, is interesting, everything that lacks these is worthless."[2] Manet's innovative repurposing of the art of the past lies at the heart of his modernity.[3]

Manet entered the studio of Thomas Couture in September 1850, where he would study for six years. Couture encouraged his students to paint historical subjects, which were accorded the highest status at the Salon, a state-sponsored, juried art exhibition held in Paris, where artists' reputations were made or destroyed. Manet, however, ultimately rejected Couture's teaching. As a student, he chafed at the academic practice of painting nude models in poses emulating antique sculpture, exclaiming to a recalcitrant model: "We're not in Rome. We do not

Detail of fig. 18

want to go there. We're in Paris. We intend to stay here."[4] As part of his training, Manet also honed his skills in the galleries of the Louvre by copying works by artists ranging from the Flemish artist Peter Paul Rubens to the French eighteenth-century painter François Boucher and the Romantic painter Eugène Delacroix (who was still alive when Manet copied his *Barque of Dante*). It was the influence of the seventeenth-century Spanish painter Diego Velázquez, whose work Manet first requested permission to copy in 1850, which proved both seminal and enduring.

The Absinthe Drinker (fig. 13) reveals Manet's assimilation of Velázquez's example. Its composition—an almost life-size figure swathed in a ragged-edged cloak and silhouetted against a neutral background—recalls the Spanish artist's imagined portraits of ancient Greek philosophers, which Manet would have known through reproductions. However, Manet transformed Velázquez's antique models into a contemporary urban type emblematic of the dark underbelly of nineteenth-century Paris: a ragpicker, impoverished and living on the margins of society, with a discarded bottle at his feet (Manet added the glass of green-hued absinthe after 1867). Further subverting convention, the figure is portrayed in the heroic scale traditionally associated with royal or noble subjects. Couture dismissed *The Absinthe Drinker* as a "crazy piece," leading Manet to break with his former teacher.[5] Manet intended to make his Salon debut in 1859 with this painting of a Parisian type in the style of Velázquez, but he was rejected by the conservative Salon jury. Manet complained to his friend Proust: "People don't understand. Perhaps they will understand better if I do a Spanish character."[6]

Two years later, Manet submitted a "Spanish character" to the Salon of 1861. The 1860 canvas, now known as *The Spanish Singer*, marked his first public success; awarded an honorable mention by the jury, the painting also signals a new direction in his art (fig. 14). It has been suggested that its bright colors and formal clarity reflect the influence of a painting at the Louvre then attributed to Velázquez, which Manet copied around 1860. Manet's copy, *The Little Cavaliers* (fig. 15), reveals a new, freer handling of paint that is absent from the original.[7] Similarly, Manet painted the head of the figure of the Spanish singer directly, in just two hours, using a "wet-on-wet" technique, that is, applying paint on a surface that has not yet dried, as he later told Proust. Manet added that he was thinking of "the Spanish masters and Franz [*sic.*] Hals" while painting the work.[8] Even at this early date in his career, Manet did not hesitate to draw from multiple sources in a single painting, here fusing seventeenth-century Spanish and Dutch influences. Contemporary critics recognized its affinity with Spanish art, as Théophile Gautier declared: "Velázquez would have greeted him with a friendly wink, and Goya would have asked him for a light for his *papelito*." Yet, Manet did not hide the work's artifice: the figure, a costumed model, clad in props from his studio, recalling *Boy with a Sword* (fig. 6), unconvincingly strums a guitar strung to be played right-handed with his left hand. An 1863 article in the

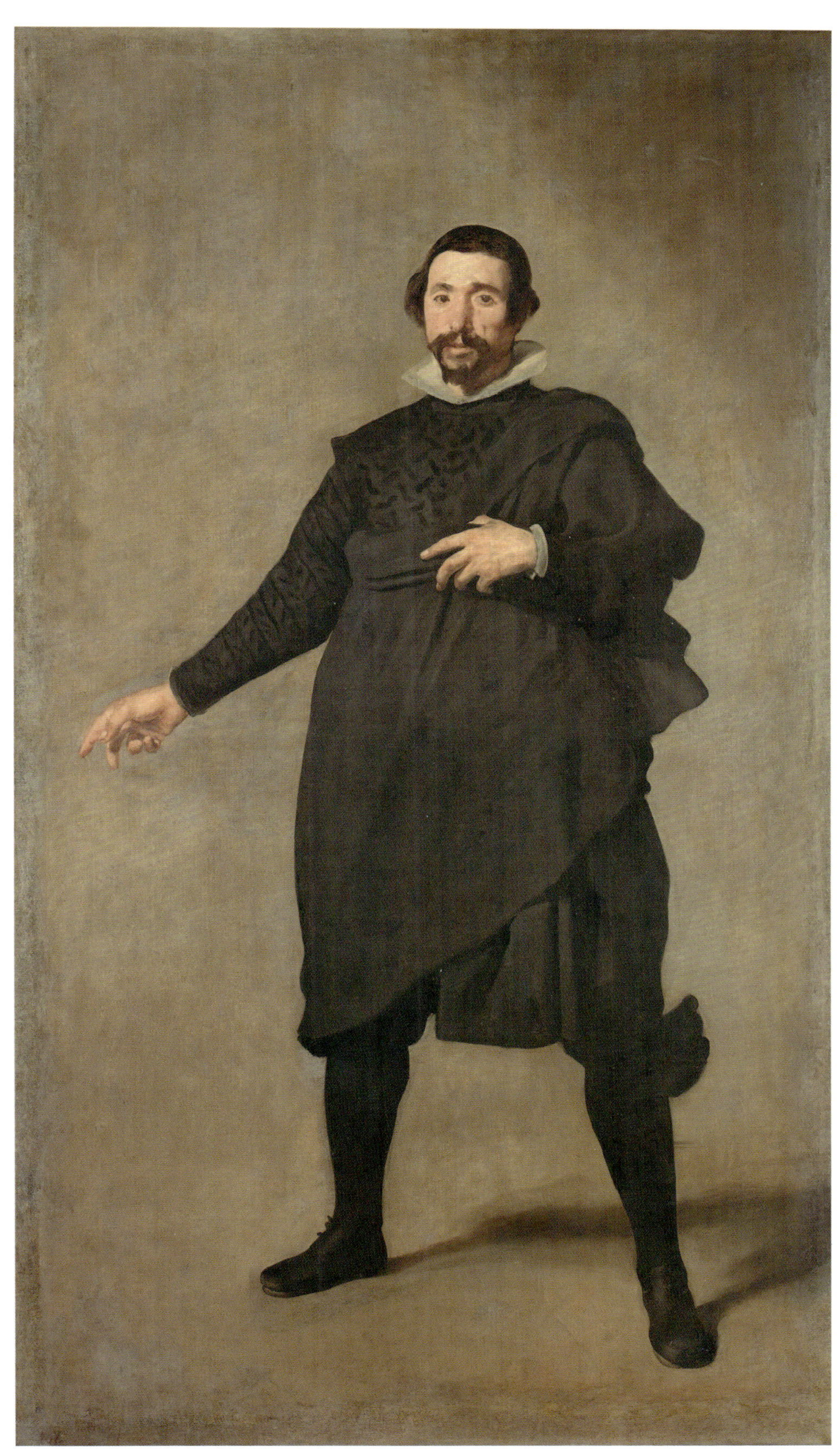

Diego Velázquez,
Pablo de Valladolid,
ca. 1635,
oil on canvas,
82 ¼ × 48 ⅓ in.
(209 × 123 cm). Madrid,
Museo Nacional del Prado,
P1198

French press recalled that the originality of *The Spanish Singer*, "painted in a certain new, *strange* way," attracted a group of emerging artists, who sought him out. These artists, among them Henri Fantin-Latour and Alphonse Legros, figure alongside Manet in a group portrait painted in 1864 by Fantin-Latour, *Homage to Delacroix* (Musée d'Orsay, Paris).[9]

Buoyed by the success of *The Spanish Singer*, Manet responded to the fascination with Spain in mid-nineteenth-century French culture with a group of paintings displayed in 1863 at the Galerie Martinet, a new exhibition venue run by Louis Martinet that showed both contemporary art and art of the past. Manet's works featured members of a troupe of dancers from the Royal Theatre of Madrid who had performed in Paris the year before; Manet probably attended one of their performances at the Hippodrome. The frieze-like arrangement of figures in *The Spanish Ballet* (fig. 16), reflects the influence of Velázquez by way of Manet's *Little Cavaliers,* which is signed "Manet d'après Vélasquez."[10] Like Manet's earlier Spanish-inspired figures, the dancers and musicians, posed as if performing, are set against a neutral background, here evocative of a bare stage save for a bouquet of flowers, which reads as a tribute from the unseen audience (perhaps intended for the troupe's star dancer, Lola Melea, who is seated in the center of the scene). At the same time, its artifice, like that of *The Spanish Singer*, is underscored by a pair of male figures shrouded in shadow in the background, who are modeled on another Spanish source: a print from *The Art of Bullfighting* by Francisco de Goya y Lucientes, published in 1816. Manet also alluded to his own recent work: the green bench used by the model in *The Spanish Singer*, a studio prop, can be glimpsed both behind the central dancers and in the lower right corner, which situates the troupe of dancers in the artist's studio on rue Guyot.

Manet also executed a portrait of the dancer Lola Melea, whose celebrity inspired poetry and even a popular song during her time in Paris (fig. 17). Manet's portrait, known as *Lola de Valence*, figured among the Spanish-themed works he exhibited at the Galerie Martinet in 1863. The dancer was originally portrayed standing against a neutral background, a format favored by Velázquez in his figure paintings; after 1867, Manet reworked the canvas, adding a backdrop of stage scenery and, beyond, a view of the audience. Her pose, one hand on her hip, a fan in the other and her feet in dancer's fourth position, has been likened to that of the Duchess of Alba, as portrayed by Goya in a 1797 painting then in Paris (The Hispanic Society of America, New York).[11]

Among the Hispanicizing subjects on view at Martinet's gallery was *The Old Musician* (fig. 18), an 1862 canvas whose overall composition recalls a work by Velázquez known as *Los Borrachos* (*The Drinkers, or The Triumph of Bacchus*, ca. 1628–29, Museo Nacional del Prado, Madrid), which Manet likely knew from Goya's etched copy.[12] A print after Velázquez's work also appears in the background of Manet's 1868 portrait of Émile Zola (fig. 39), attesting to its currency in the 1860s. With *The Old Musician*, Manet transformed his Spanish prototype into a contemporary Parisian subject, signaling his increased engagement with modern life by this date. Set in a barren landscape, the gathering of figures evokes the marginalized urban types who were displaced by the ongoing modernization of the capital under Baron Georges-Eugène Haussmann, begun in 1853, from the central figure of the old musician, an itinerant street performer, to the impoverished children and ragpickers. The figure of Manet's *Absinthe Drinker*, also inspired by Velázquez, reappears in this gathering, reinforcing the scene's artifice as a studio construct.

In 1863 *The Old Musician* was largely overshadowed by another view of modern Paris informed by the precedent of Velázquez on display in Martinet's gallery. A group portrait set outdoors, *Music in the Tuileries Gardens* (fig. 19), evokes the Spanish master by way of the *Gathering of Gentlemen* at the Louvre, which Manet had copied (now attributed to the workshop of Juan Bautista del Mazo, *Gathering of Fourteen Figures*, 1645/1650, Paris, Musée du Louvre). An 1858 Louvre catalogue noted of the work, then attributed to Velázquez: "The figures, thirteen in number, are thought to represent famous artists, contemporaries of Velázquez. He has placed himself, dressed in black, at the left, and Murillo, hardly more than his head visible, stands near him."[13] In *Music in the Tuileries Gardens*, Manet depicted himself at far left, in the place of the Spanish master, dressed in black and holding a cane; standing in front of him, à la Murillo, is the artist and Manet's former studio mate Comte Albert de Balleroy. Rhythmically distributed across the canvas, Manet's other modern "Gentlemen" include his friends and other artists and writers, identifiable by their portrait likenesses. Among them are the poet and critic Charles Baudelaire, standing with a trio of men directly behind the woman seated at far left, and Manet's brother, Eugène, shown conversing with a seated woman near the center, and, seated behind him, the composer Jacques Offenbach. Manet transformed a scene of modern Parisian leisure, then the realm of popular illustrators such as Constantin Guys, into a contemporary group portrait rooted in art-historical tradition.

Although *Music in the Tuileries Gardens* was painted the same year as *The Old Musician*, its looser, more sketch-like handling reflects a radical new approach, one that marks a transformative moment in Manet's art. The figures are rendered in varying degrees of finish, while the visible brushwork and the absence of half-tones signal Manet's rejection of the polished surface finish and three-dimensional modeling associated with contemporary Academic art, as propagated at the Salon. In some areas of the canvas, Manet's brushwork verges on abstraction, particularly in the treatment of the hats worn by the two seated women in the center. In 1983, art historian Françoise Cachin cited this work as "the earliest true example of modern painting, in both subject matter and technique."[14] However, when it was first shown in 1863, critics assailed Manet's innovative handling of paint and his palette, with one complaining that the work "hurts the eye as carnival music assaults the ear." When Manet reexhibited the canvas at his 1867 retrospective, another reviewer, describing the portraits within the scene, accused Manet of possessing a "mania for seeing things in patches."[15]

During the 1860s, Manet's ongoing dialogue with the art of Velázquez and, by extension, Spain infused such works as *Incident in a Bullfight*, an imagined scene exhibited at the Salon of 1864 to overwhelmingly hostile reviews. Sometime before 1867, Manet cut apart the large canvas, preserving two fragments that he reworked as independent works of art. One of these, *The Dead Torreador* (fig. 20), recalls the composition of a painting of a dead soldier then thought to be by Velázquez, which was housed in a private collection in Paris.[16] In reworking this canvas, Manet painted over the bull in the upper right corner, masterfully condensing the work's narrative to the small pool of blood by the fallen bullfighter's left shoulder, a barely visible sign of his violent death in the bullring.

The following year, Manet boarded a train from Paris to Madrid where he spent seven days, intent on seeking "advice" from Velázquez, as he told his friend Zacharie Astruc. Manet was not alone in making such a pilgrimage, as the Manet scholar Juliet Wilson-Bareau notes: "By 1865, every alert young artist who was drawn to Velázquez understood that the only place to really see his work was Madrid."[17] In the only letter Manet wrote from Spain, he extolled the Spanish master to fellow artist Henri Fantin-Latour: "Velázquez, who all by himself makes the journey worthwhile; the artists of all the other schools around him in the museum at Madrid, who are extremely well represented, all look like shams. He is the

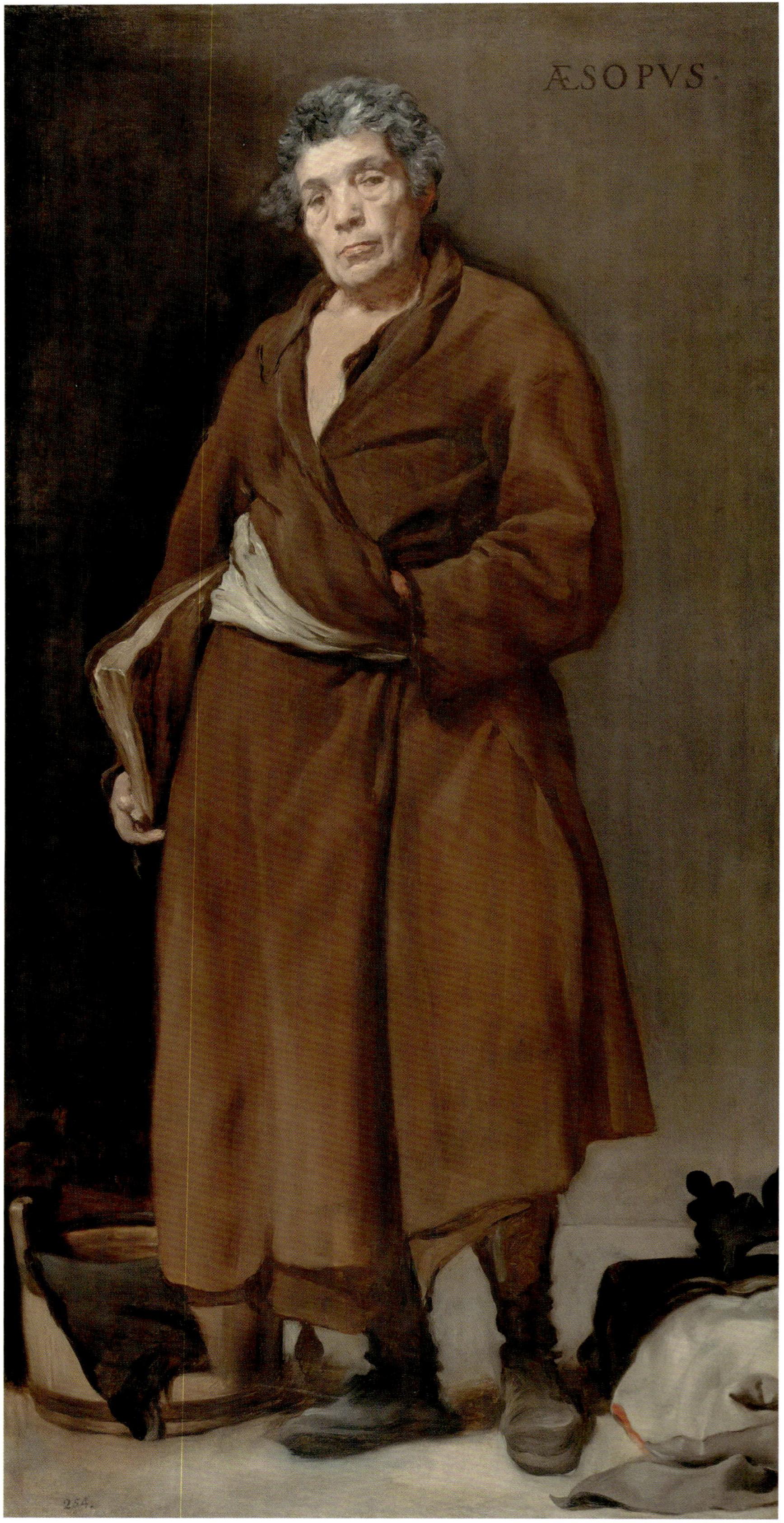

supreme artist; he didn't surprise me, he enchanted me." He was especially captivated by a portrait of a jester in the court of Philip IV of Spain, set in an indeterminate space with only the slightest shadow suggestive of depth, exclaiming, "there's nothing but air surrounding the fellow, who is all in black and appears alive." He called the portrait, thought at the time to represent a famous actor, "possibly the most extraordinary piece of painting that has ever been done."[18]

Upon his return to Paris, Manet painted his rejoinder: a portrait of the actor Philibert Rouvière as Hamlet, the role for which he was best known (fig. 21). Manet's extraordinary response was painted from memory, as Velázquez's portrait had not yet been reproduced.[19] Working from photographs of Rouvière, who had recently died, and using his friends as models, Manet emulated Velázquez's neutral background—"nothing but air"—and his limited palette, dominated by subtly modulated shades of black. However, Manet's thickly applied paint, as well as the figure's self-contained pose and inward air, depart from Velázquez's precedent. He submitted the work for exhibition at the Salon of 1866, calling it *The Tragic Actor* "to escape criticism from people who may not find it a good likeness," as he explained to his friend Baudelaire. Rejected by the Salon jury, the work appeared in Manet's 1867 solo exhibition, where the artist's overt debt to Spanish art prompted one critic to dub him a "*Velasquez of the boulevards* or a Spaniard of Paris."[20]

That characterization was reinforced by the presence of two other life-size figure paintings on view in 1867, both of which Manet titled "Philosopher" (figs. 22 and 23). These works reflect the influence of Velázquez's paintings of the ancient Greek fabulist, Aesop, and Menippus, the Greek philosopher—"astounding pieces," as Manet wrote to Fantin-Latour from Madrid.[21] However, Manet likely first knew them through Goya's etchings after Velázquez. In fact, art historian Juliet Wilson-Bareau suggests that Manet began at least one of the canvases, known as *Beggar with a Duffle Coat*, before his 1865 trip to Spain.[22] Manet's paintings transform Velázquez's ancient philosophers into modern urban types, beggars from the margins of Parisian society, recalling his *Absinthe Drinker* of 1859. In a guide to Paris published the same year as Manet exhibited his *Philosophers*, author Charles Yriarte cited the disappearance of the "philosopher-ragpicker" among the regrettable effects of the ongoing urban renewal projects in Paris: "No more colorful rags, no more extravagant songs or extraordinary speeches . . . the strolling musicians, the philosopher-ragpickers . . . have departed . . ."[23]

After Velázquez, the Spanish artist who most interested Manet was Goya. Writing to Fantin-Latour from Madrid, Manet observed that Goya was "the most original next to the master [Velázquez] whom he imitated too closely in the most servile sense of imitation. But still he's immensely spirited."[24] During his return journey, Manet wrote to his friend Baudelaire, "I saw some interesting things by Goya, some of them very fine, including an incredibly charming

Diego Velázquez, *Aesop*, ca. 1638, oil on canvas, 70 ½ × 37 in. (179 × 94 cm). Madrid, Museo Nacional del Prado, P1206

portrait of the Duchess of Alba dressed as a majo [*sic*]."[25] Baudelaire had seen a copy of this work, *The Clothed Maja*, and one of its pendant, *The Naked Maja*, in an art gallery in Paris in 1859, and he asked Félix Nadar to photograph the paintings. Whether Manet also saw the copies remains unknown; however, around 1862–63, before his trip to Spain, he painted *Reclining Young Woman in Spanish Costume* (fig. 24), in which the pose and attire of the model suggestively mirror Goya's *Clothed Maja* of 1800–7.[26] In Goya's Spain, the *maja* was a popular type of urban, working-class woman, who cultivated a flamboyant personal style based on exaggerated interpretations of traditional dress. Manet's unknown model is provocatively dressed *en travestie*, wearing a bolero jacket and the form-fitting satin breeches of a bullfighter, just as Victorine Meurent would do when she posed in the artist's studio around the same time (fig. 32). Manet later dedicated his Goyaesque work to Nadar, inscribing the canvas "to my friend Nadar."

A few years after his trip to Spain, Manet revisited the theme of Goya's *majas* in a Parisian update of one of the Spanish master's paintings of *Majas on a Balcony* (private collection), which Manet could have seen at the Galerie Espagnole of the Louvre when he was a teenager or, later, reproduced in Yriarte's 1867 publication on Goya.[27] In *The Balcony*, exhibited at the Salon of 1869, Manet's friends, the artist Berthe Morisot, Antoine Guillemet, a landscape painter, and Fanny Claus, a violinist and friend of Manet's wife, conjure Goya's fashionable *Madrileños* observing the city from a balcony (fig. 25). The prominent wrought-iron railing and green shutters emphatically assert Haussmann's modern Paris: one Salon critic dismissed "this uncouth art, where, as in the green shutters of *The Balcony*, [Manet] lowers himself to engaging in competition with house painters."[28] No less modern is the psychological isolation of each of the figures, who, unlike Goya's *majas*, do not interact with one another. Perhaps in another nod to Goya's balcony scenes, Manet depicted a shadowy background figure carrying a ewer, which is based on one of his own earlier images of Léon Leenhoff, Suzanne Manet's young son. Manet's models recalled the work's protracted execution in 1868–69 and the repeated, lengthy sittings required by the artist. *The Balcony* was among the works Manet exhibited at the 1869 Salon, which Morisot memorably characterized in a letter to her sister, Edma: "His paintings, as always, create the impression of some wild fruit, a bit unripe even. I am far from disliking them . . . I look strange rather than ugly. It seems that the term *femme fatale* has been circulated among the curious."[29] Following the Salon, Manet kept this painting in his studio, where it hung next to *Olympia* until his death.

Manet's 1868 portrait of the art critic Théodore Duret (fig. 26) more subtly alludes to Goya's precedent. The allusion to Goya is apt, as the two men first met during Manet's 1865 trip to Madrid, where they became travel companions. Duret later recounted, "Naturally we went every day to stand for a long time in front of the Velázquez at the Prado."[30] Three years later,

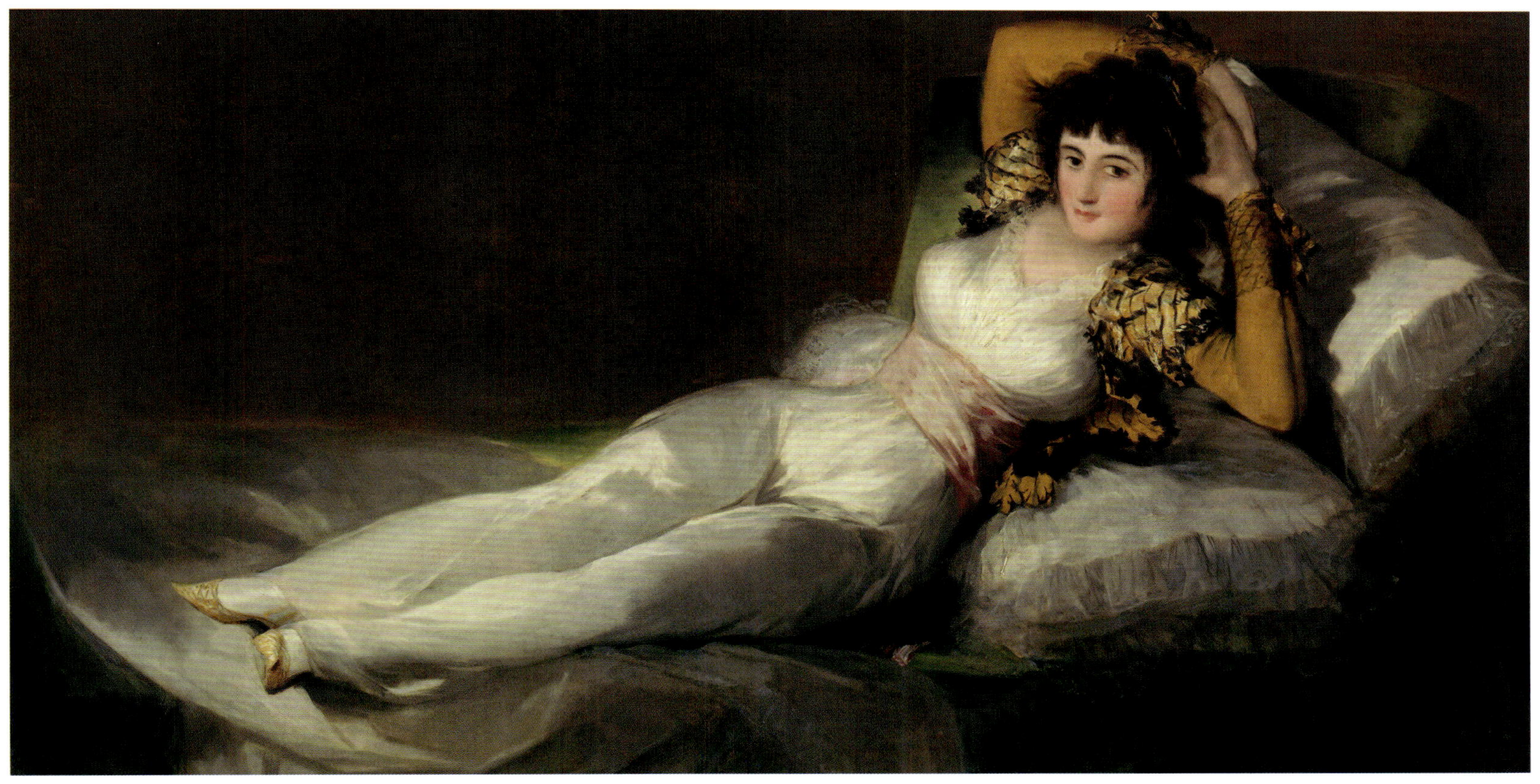

Francisco de Goya y Lucientes, *Clothed Maja*, 1800–7, oil on canvas, 37 ¼ × 74 in. (94.7 × 188 cm). Madrid, Museo Nacional del Prado, P741

Duret asked Manet to paint his portrait. One hand partially tucked into his vest, Duret projects the cultivated elegance for which he was known, sporting a cane that is more stylish accessory than support. His pose recalls Goya's portrayals of fashionably dressed men.[31] In what is perhaps another, witty reference to Goya, Duret's cane points to Manet's signature, prominently inscribed upside down, as if intended for the sitter to read it. In Goya's 1797 portrait of the Duchess of Alba, which Manet could have seen at the Galerie Espagnole, the sitter points downward with her right index figure toward the artist's signature, inscribed upside down in the sand at her feet: "*Solo Goya*."

While the influence of seventeenth- and eighteenth-century Spanish art infused Manet's art of the 1860s, his work from this period also reflects his assimilation of a wide range of other artistic sources, including earlier French painting. In 1867, he portrayed a teenaged Léon Leenhoff absorbed in the act of blowing a soap bubble in a work whose subject and composition nod to the French eighteenth-century painter Jean Siméon Chardin (fig. 27). Earlier that year, one of Chardin's three known paintings of a young man blowing soap bubbles (*Soap Bubbles*, probably 1733/1734, National Gallery of Art, Washington, D.C.) had been sold at auction in Paris, no doubt prompting Manet's painted response. Manet might also have been responding to the same subject as painted by his former teacher, Couture (*Soap Bubbles*, ca. 1859, The Metropolitan Museum of Art, New York). Couture's image of a young boy contemplatively gazing upon soap bubbles invites a reading of the subject as an allegory of life's transience, as popularized in seventeenth-century Dutch genre painting. Art historian Françoise Cachin has convincingly argued that Manet deliberately rejected Couture's moralizing approach in favor of a scene based on naturalistic observation.[32] Indeed, Chardin was among the French artists whom Manet admired for his "sense of truth."[33]

Chardin also figures in relation to Manet's sustained engagement with still-life painting throughout his career. The genre, traditionally held in low esteem, gained in popularity during the middle decades of the nineteenth century, stimulated by the rediscovery of Chardin's still lifes.[34] Manet's repeated forays in the genre with a group of still lifes dating from 1862 to 1870 suggest his awareness of the eighteenth-century master's oeuvre; these works culminate with *The Brioche*, which directly engages with Chardin's precedent (fig. 28). It was painted in 1870, the year after Chardin's painting of a brioche surmounted by a sprig of orange blossom and flanked by a porcelain tureen and a glass decanter entered the Louvre as one of nearly a dozen still lifes by the artist as part of the bequest of Dr. Louis La Caze (*The Brioche*, 1763, Musée du Louvre, Paris). In Manet's canvas, a central brioche, decorated with a rose, is surrounded by other allusions to Chardin, from the peaches and plums, which recur in Chardin's paintings, to the knife whose handle projects over the edge of the table, a compositional device favored by Chardin. The eighteenth-century rococo-style table on which the objects are arrayed further reinforces Manet's tribute to Chardin.

Manet's wide-ranging dialogue with the art of the past definitively shaped the first decade of his career, from his response to Velázquez embodied in *The Absinthe Drinker* of 1859 to his Parisian variations on Goya's *majas* and his evocations of Chardin in his still-life paintings. His artistic borrowings are not simply pastiches of works by the Old Masters; rather, his engagement with earlier art elevates his modern-life subjects, whether it is the socially marginalized figure of a ragpicker, rendered in the heroic scale of one of Velázquez's *Philosophers*, or a scene of contemporary Parisian leisure, a subject then relegated to the realm of popular illustration but transformed through its allusion to the art of the past. Manet scholar Françoise Cachin aptly dubbed Manet "the Velázquez of the Tuileries,"[35] an epithet that captures the dual embrace of past and present that lies at the heart of Manet's innovative approach to painting modern life.

1 Proust 1988, 26.
2 Wilson-Bareau 1991, 302.
3 On this subject, see Michael Fried, *Manet's Modernism, or, The Face of Painting in the 1860s* (Chicago: The University of Chicago Press), 1996.
4 Proust 1988, 13.
5 Juliet Wilson-Bareau, "Manet and Spain," in Gary Tinterow et al. (ed.), *Manet/Velázquez, The French Taste for Spanish Painting* [exhibition catalogue], Paris, Musée d'Orsay and New York, The Metropolitan Museum of Art 2002–3, 209–13, 483.
6 Proust 1988, 89.
7 Paris and New York 2002–3, 483–84.
8 Proust 1988: 28.
9 Paris and New York 1983, 63, 67.
10 Paris and New York 2002–3, 488–89.
11 Paris and New York 1983, 146.
12 On Manet's sources for the work, see Juliet Wilson-Bareau, "Manet and Spain," in Paris and New York 2002–3, 213.
13 Paris and New York 1983, 126.
14 Ibid., 126.
15 Ibid., 126.
16 Ibid., 195–97; Italian, *A Dead Soldier*, seventeenth century, National Gallery, London.
17 Juliet Wilson-Bareau, "Manet and Spain," in Paris and New York 2002–3, 230.
18 Ibid., 231.
19 Ibid., 496.
20 Ibid., 236–37.
21 Paris and New York 1983, 234.
22 Juliet Wilson-Bareau, in Gloria Groom and Genevieve Westerby (eds.), *Manet Paintings and Works on Paper at the Art Institute of Chicago* (Chicago, Art Institute of Chicago, 2019), cats. 10–11, paras 17–20.
23 Paris and New York 1983, 236.
24 Juliet Wilson-Bareau, "Manet and Spain," in Paris and New York 2002–3, 231.
25 Paris and New York 2002–3, 392.
26 Ibid., 228.
27 Ibid., 499.
28 Paris and New York 1983, 307.
29 Letter to her sister Edma, cited in Paris and New York 1983, 304.
30 Kathleen Adler, *Manet* (Oxford: Phaidon, 1986), 71.
31 Paris and New York 1983, 288–89.
32 Ibid., 269–70.
33 Proust 1988, 31.
34 See John McCoubrey, "The Revival of Chardin in French Still-Life Painting, 1850–1870," *Art Bulletin* 46, no. 1 (March 1964), 39–53.
35 Paris and New York 1983, 126.

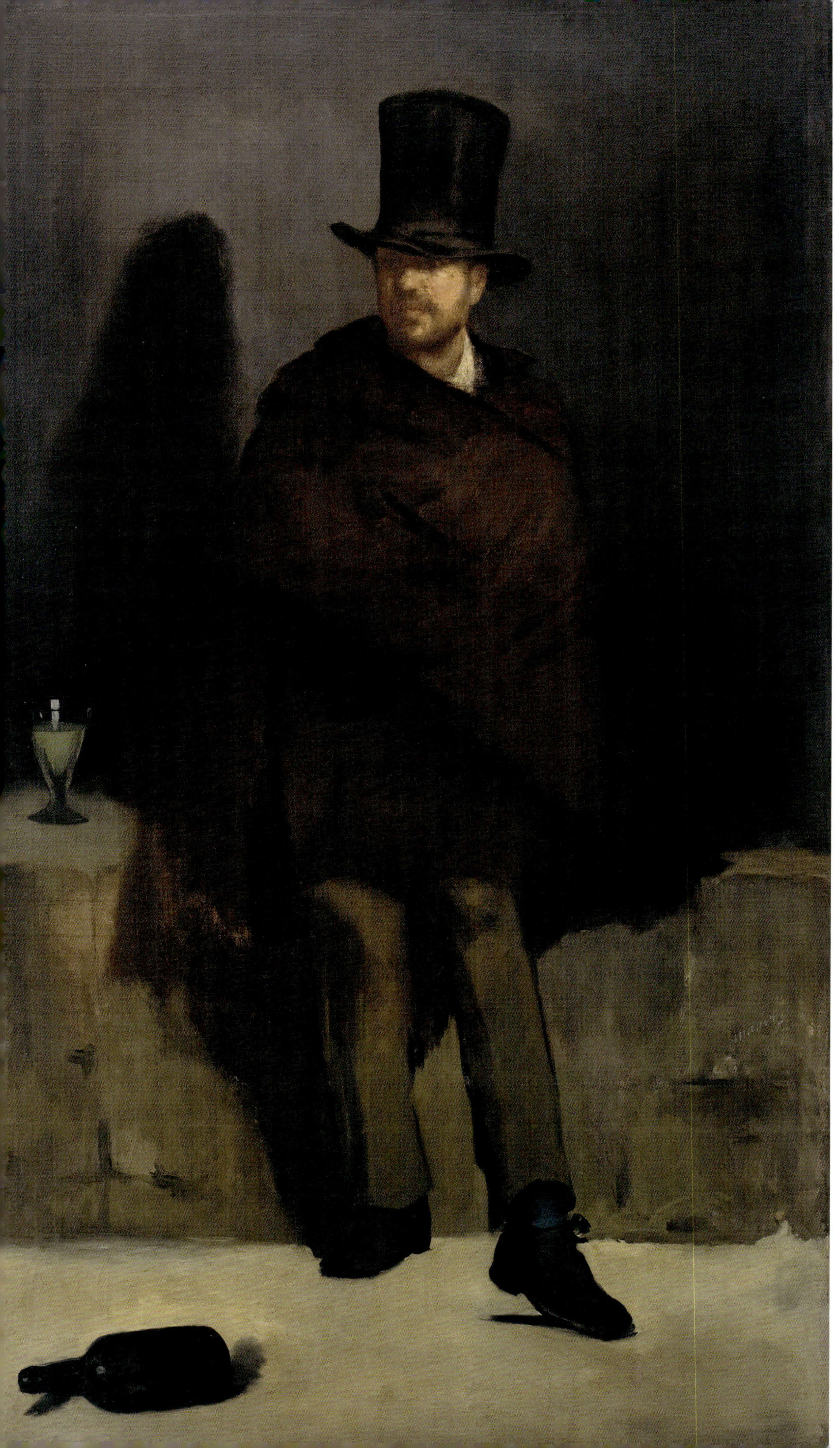

13

The Absinthe Drinker

1859
Oil on canvas,
71 × 41 ½ in.
(180.5 × 105.6 cm)
Copenhagen, Ny Carlsberg
Glyptotek

14

The Spanish Singer

1860
Oil on canvas, 58 × 45 in.
(147.3 × 114.3 cm)
New York, The Metropolitan
Museum of Art, Gift of
William Chirch Osborn, 1949,
49.58.2

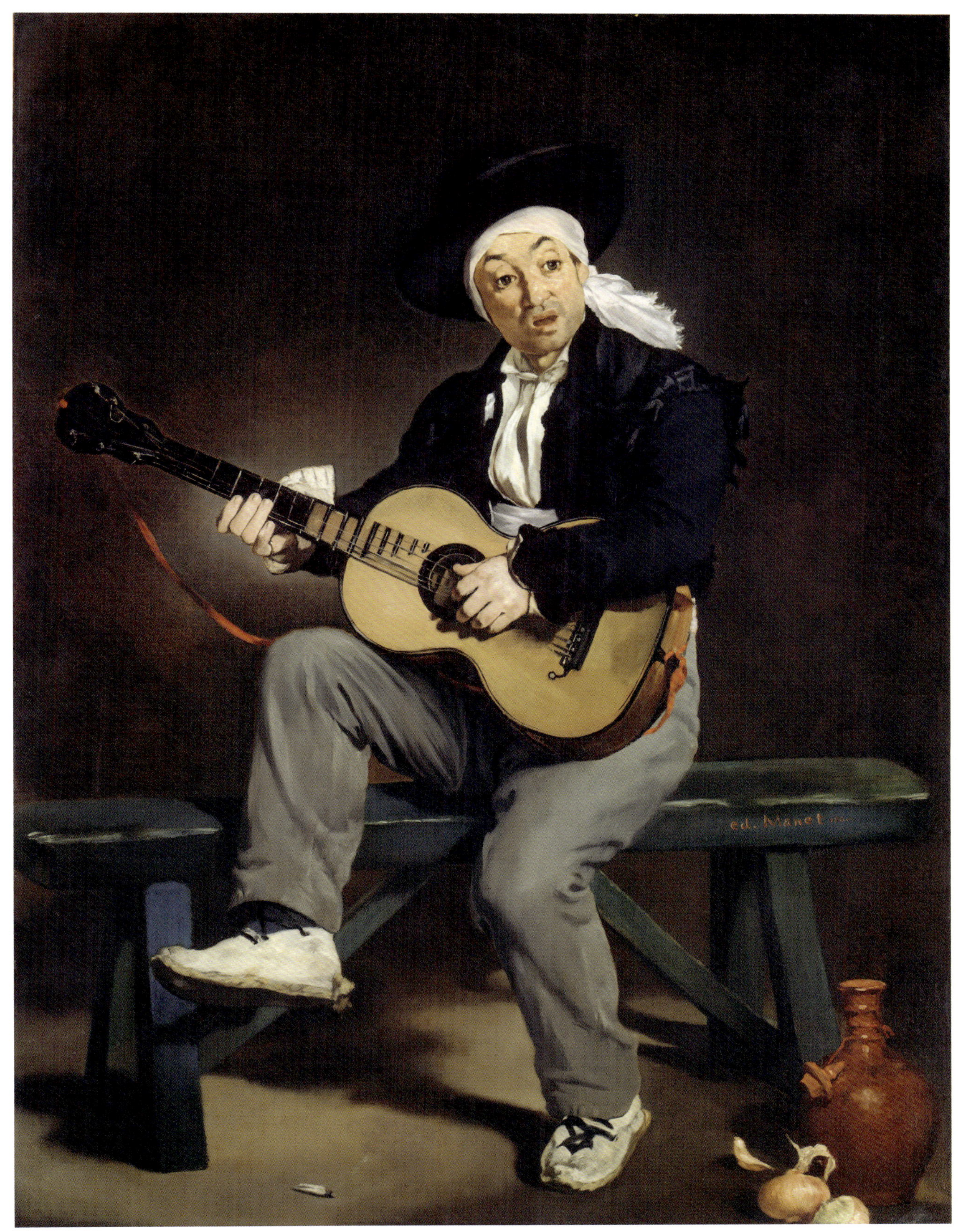
ed. Manet

15

The Little Cavaliers

ca. 1860
Oil on canvas, 18 × 29 ¾ in.
(45.7 × 75.6 cm)
Norfolk, Chrysler Museum of Art, Gift of Walter P. Chrysler, Jr., 71.679

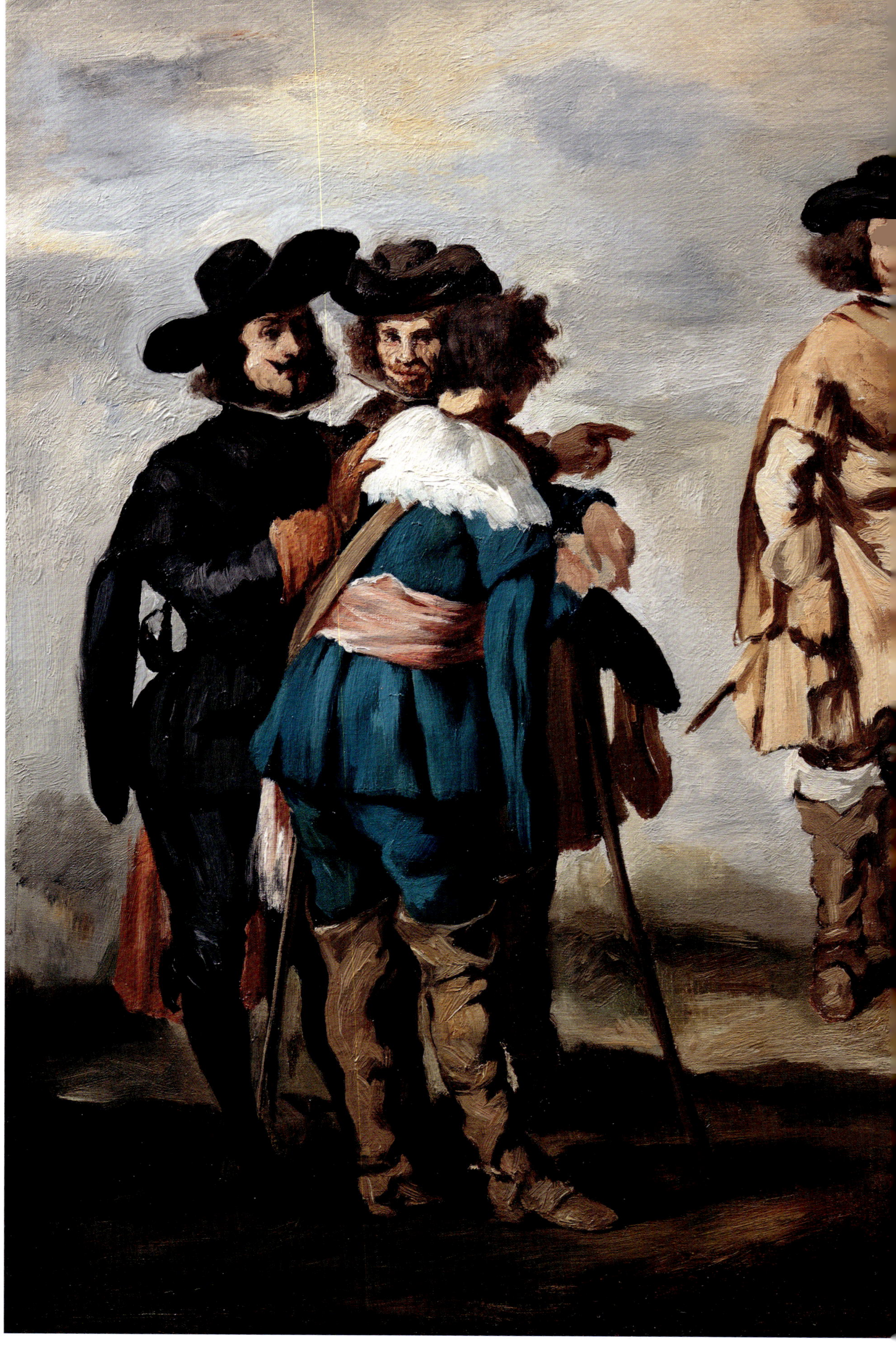

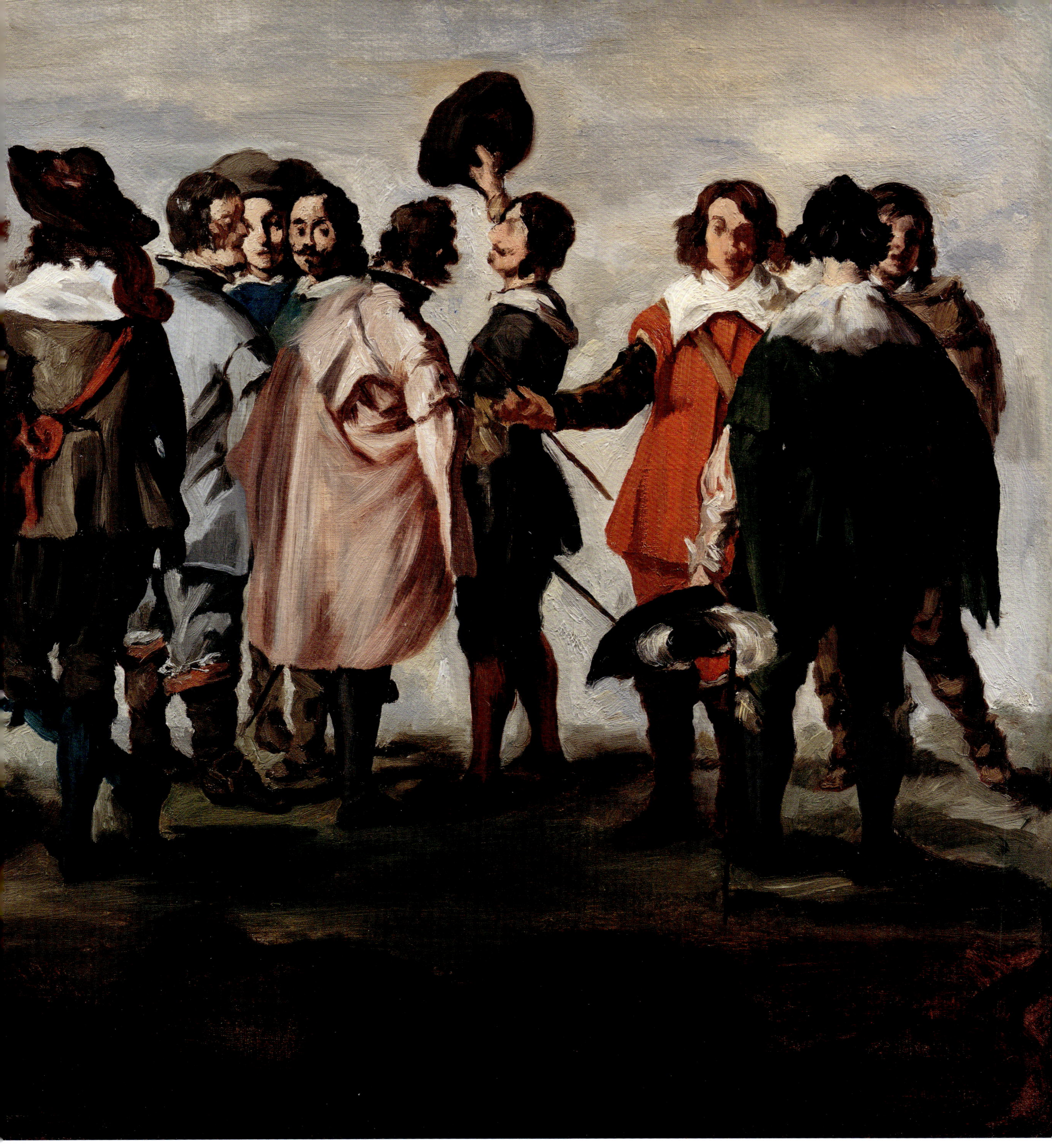

16

The Spanish Ballet

1862
Oil on canvas, 24 × 35 ⅝ in.
(60.96 × 90.48 cm)
Washington, D.C.,
The Phillips Collection,
acquired 1928, 1250

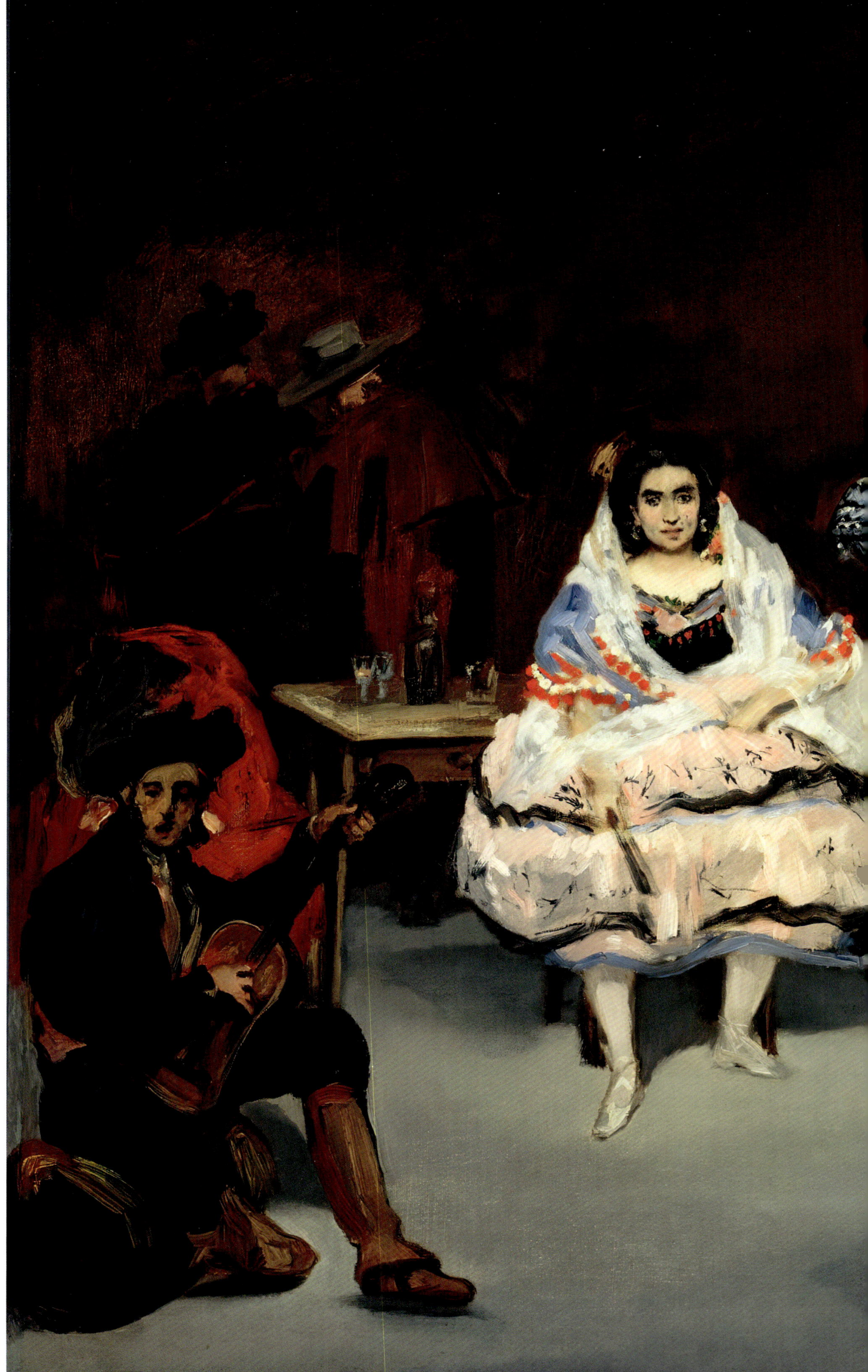

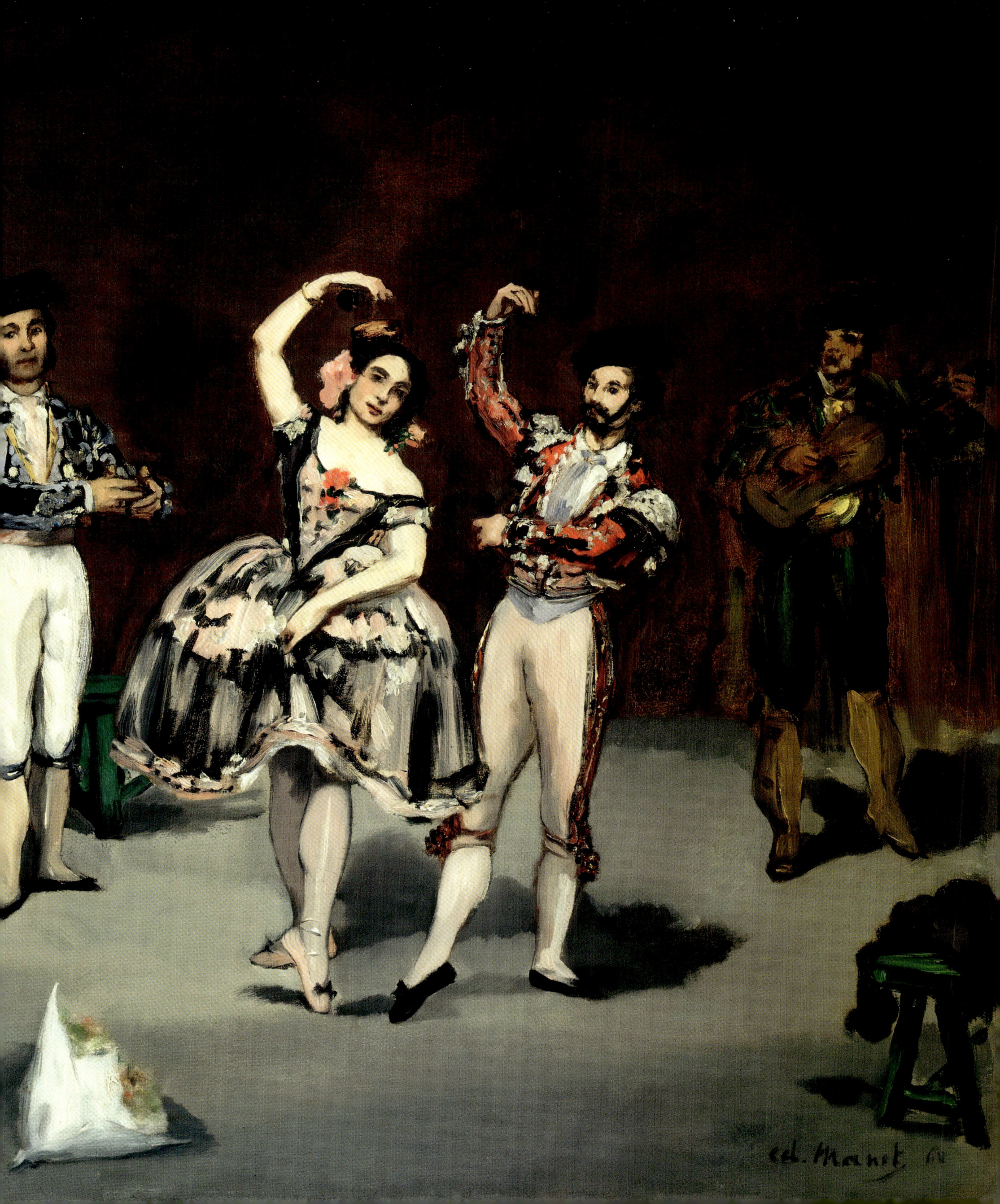
ed. Manet

17

Lola de Valence

1862
Oil on canvas,
48 7⁄16 × 36 ¼ in. (123 × 92 cm)
Paris, Musée d'Orsay, RF 1991

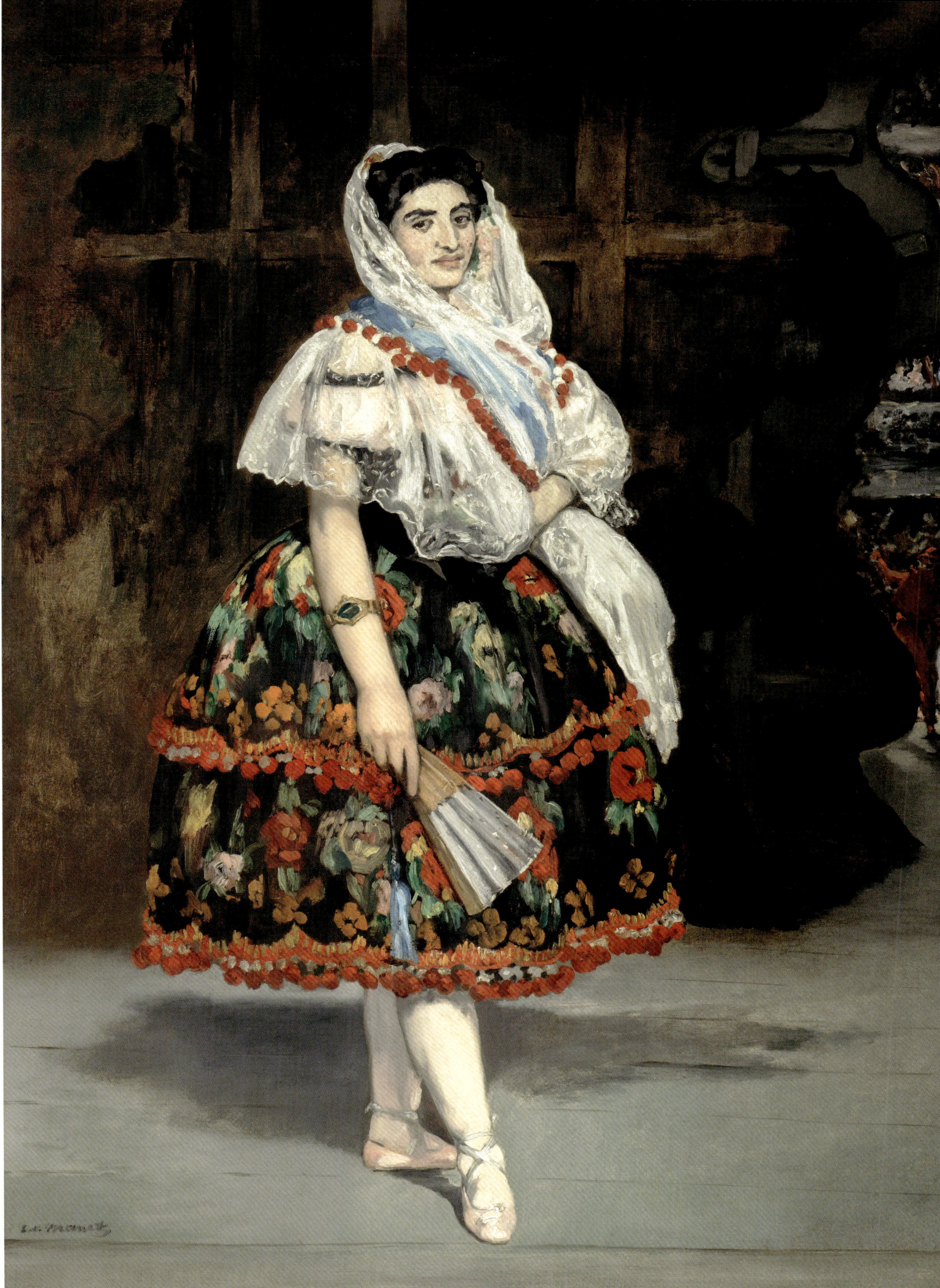

18

The Old Musician

1862
Oil on canvas, 73 ¾ × 97 11/16 in.
(187.4 × 248.2 cm)
Washington, D.C.,
The National Gallery of Art,
Chester Dale Collection,
1963.10.162

FOLLOWING PAGES

19

Music in the Tuileries Gardens

1862
Oil on canvas, 30 × 46 ½ in.
(76.2 × 118.1 cm)
Sir Hugh Lane Bequest, 1917,
London, The National Gallery.
In partnership with Dublin,
Hugh Lane Gallery, NG3260

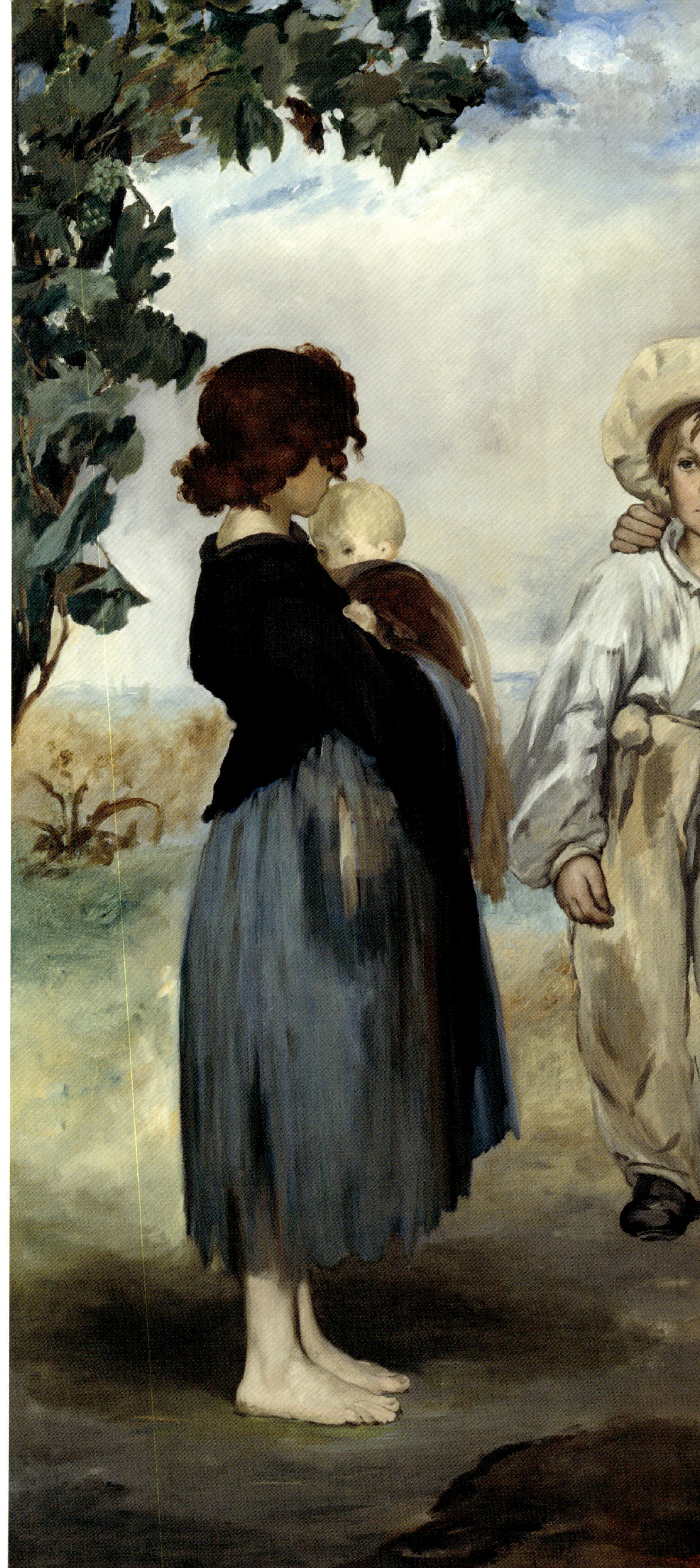

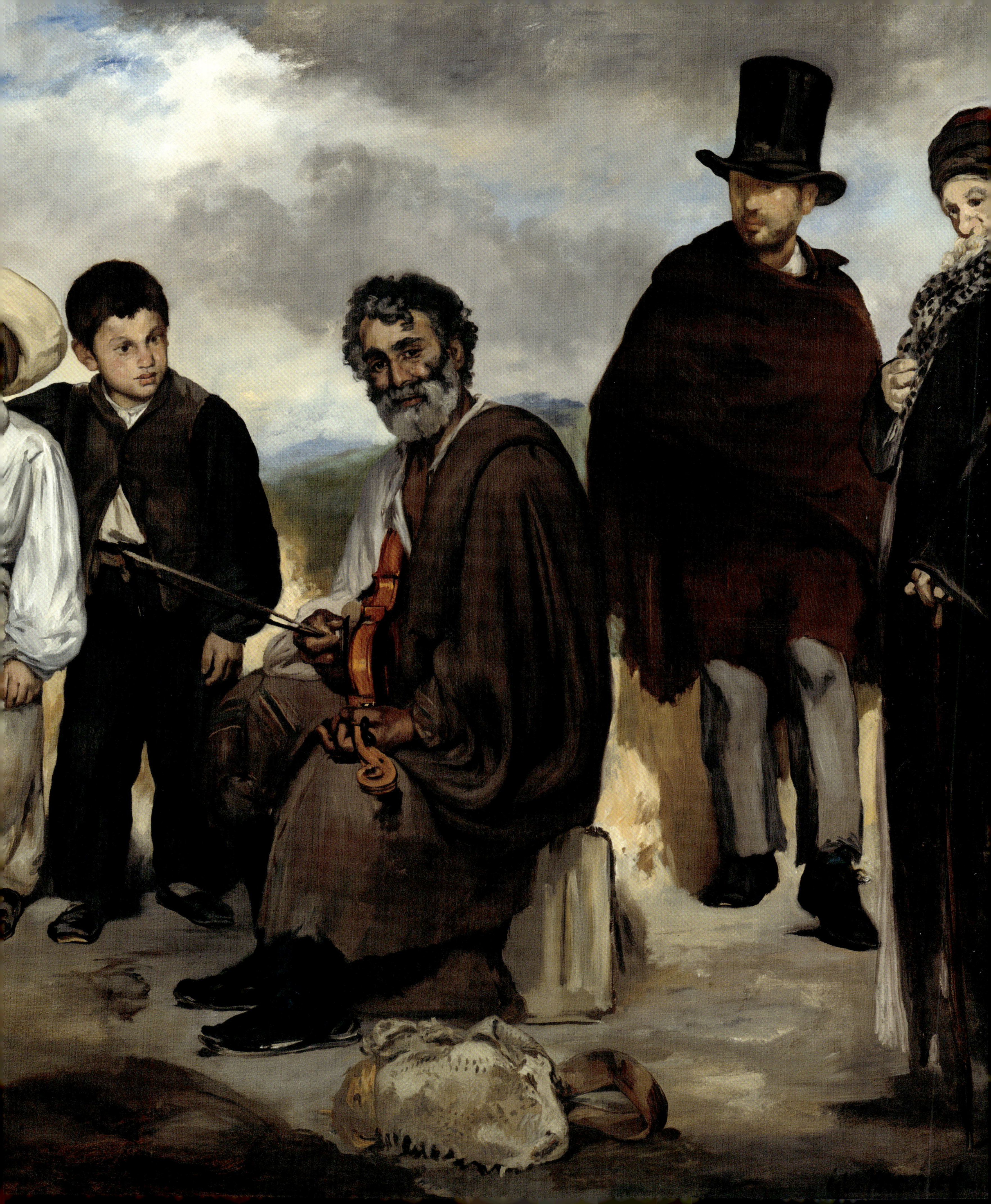

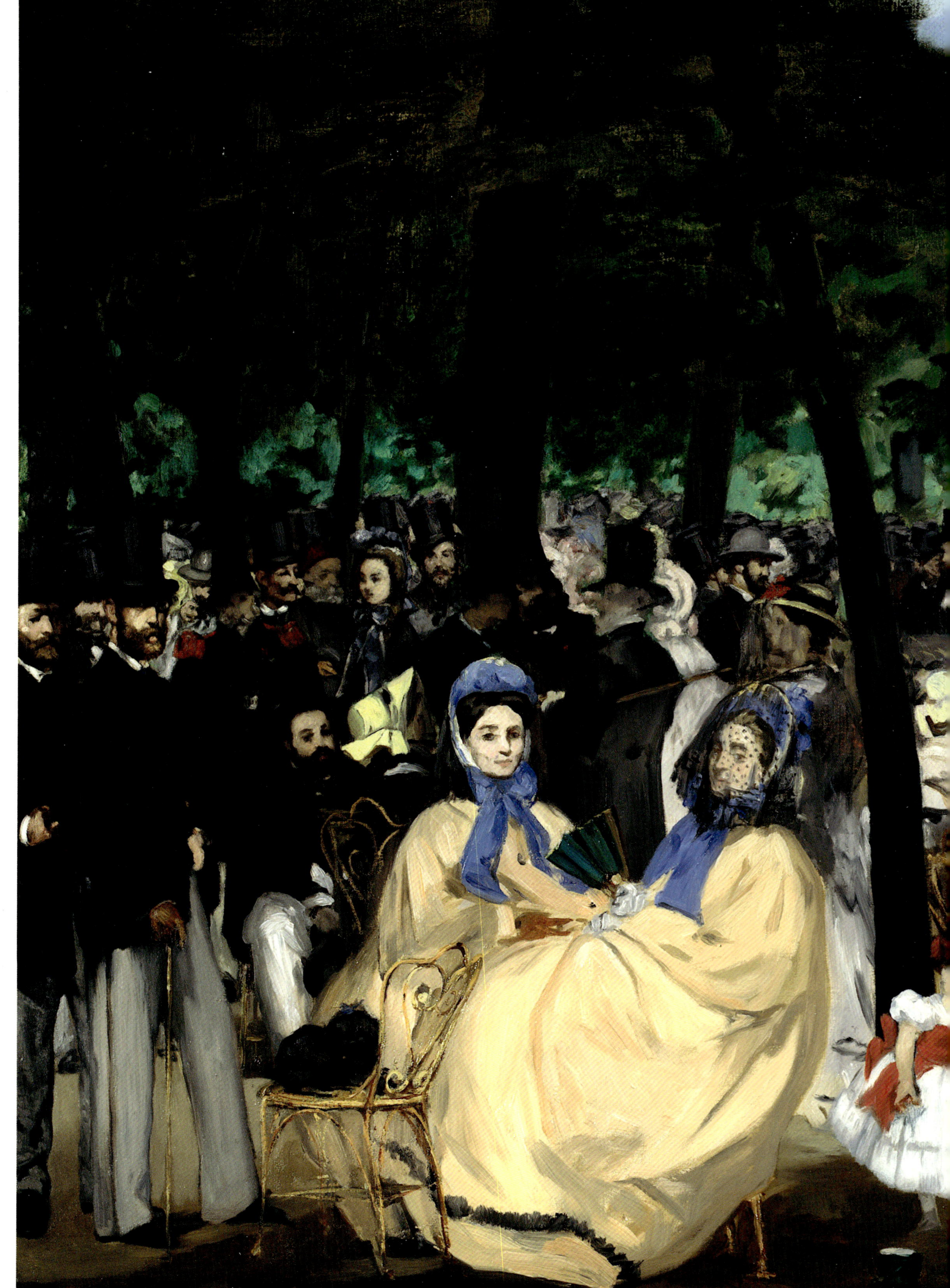

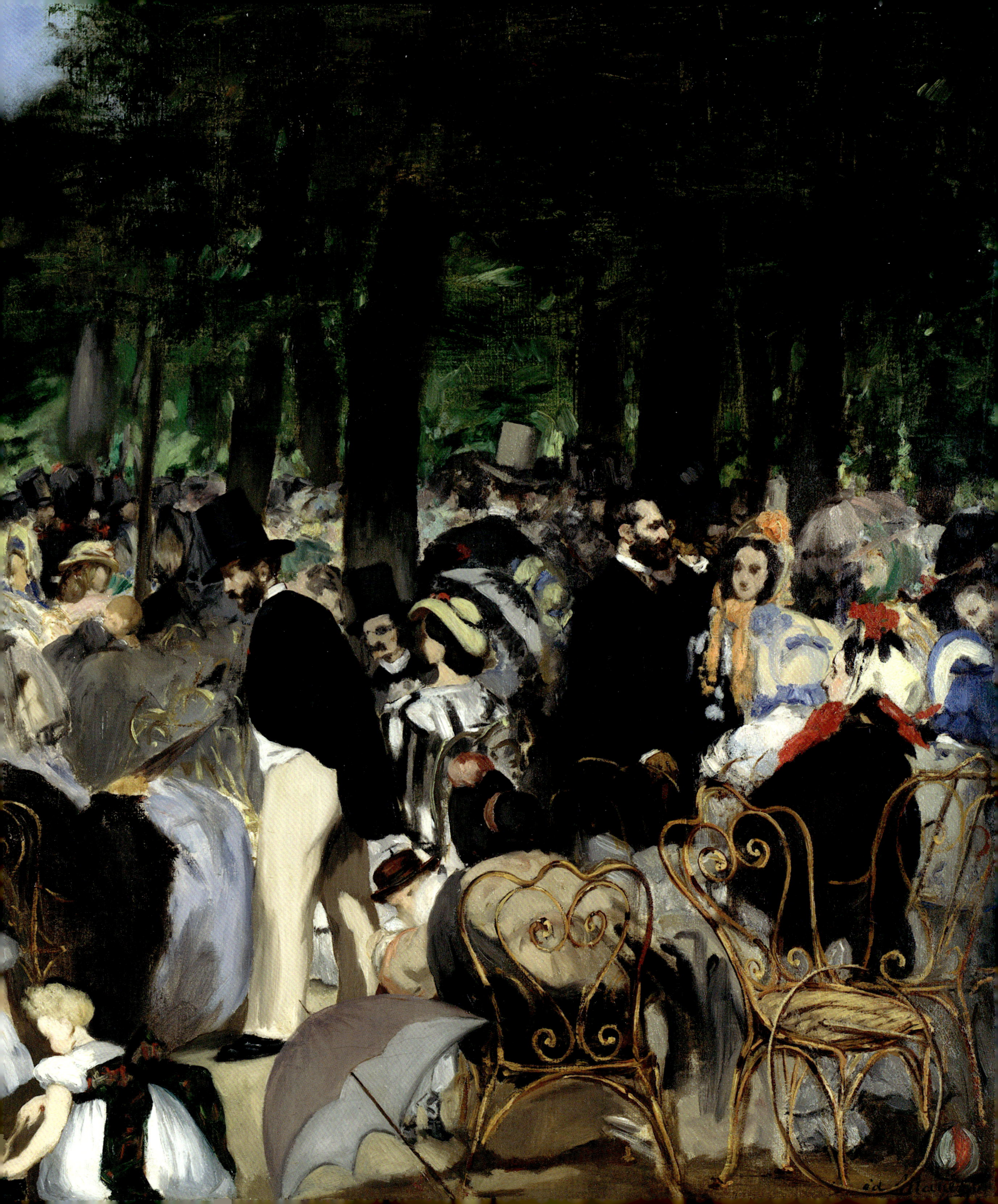

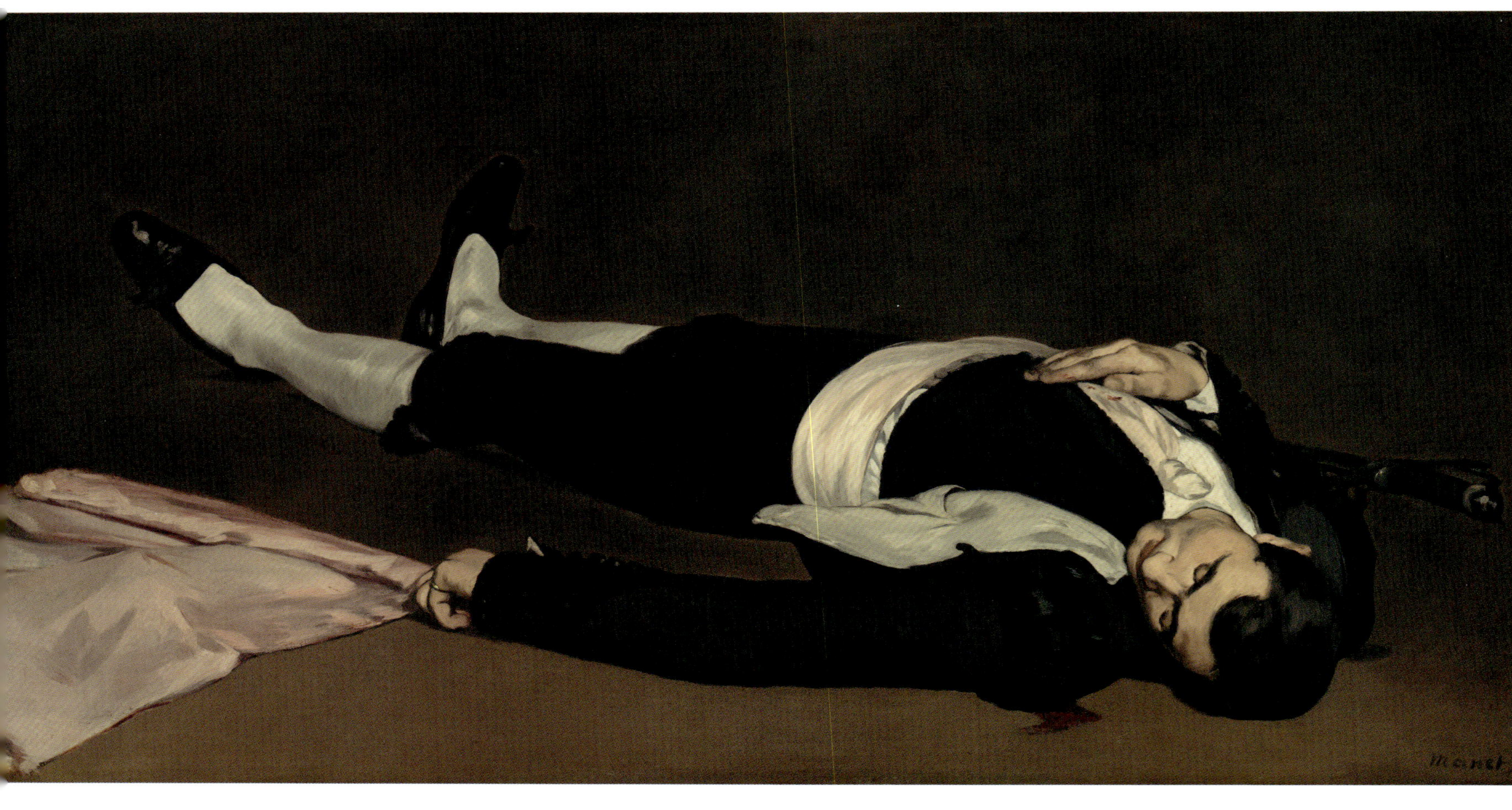

20

The Dead Toreador

probably 1864
Oil on canvas, 29 ⅞ × 60 ⅜ in.
(75.9 × 153.3 cm)
Washington, D.C.,
The National Gallery of Art,
Widener Collection, 1942.9.40

21

The Tragic Actor (Rouvière as Hamlet)

1886
Oil on canvas, 73 1/16 × 42 9/16 in.
(187.2 × 108.1 cm)
Washington, D.C.,
The National Gallery of Art,
Gift of Edith Stuyvesant
Gerry, 1959.3.1

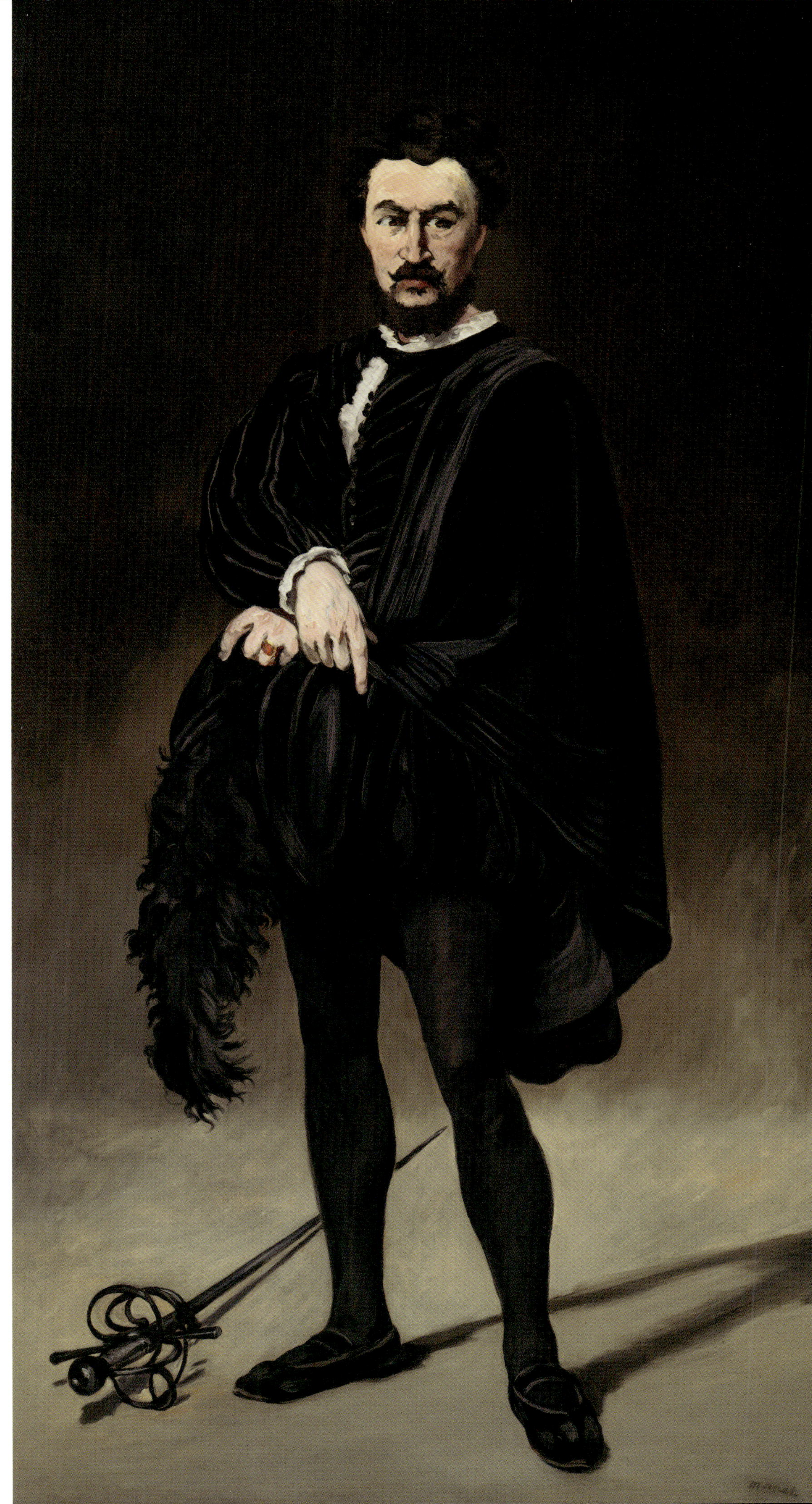

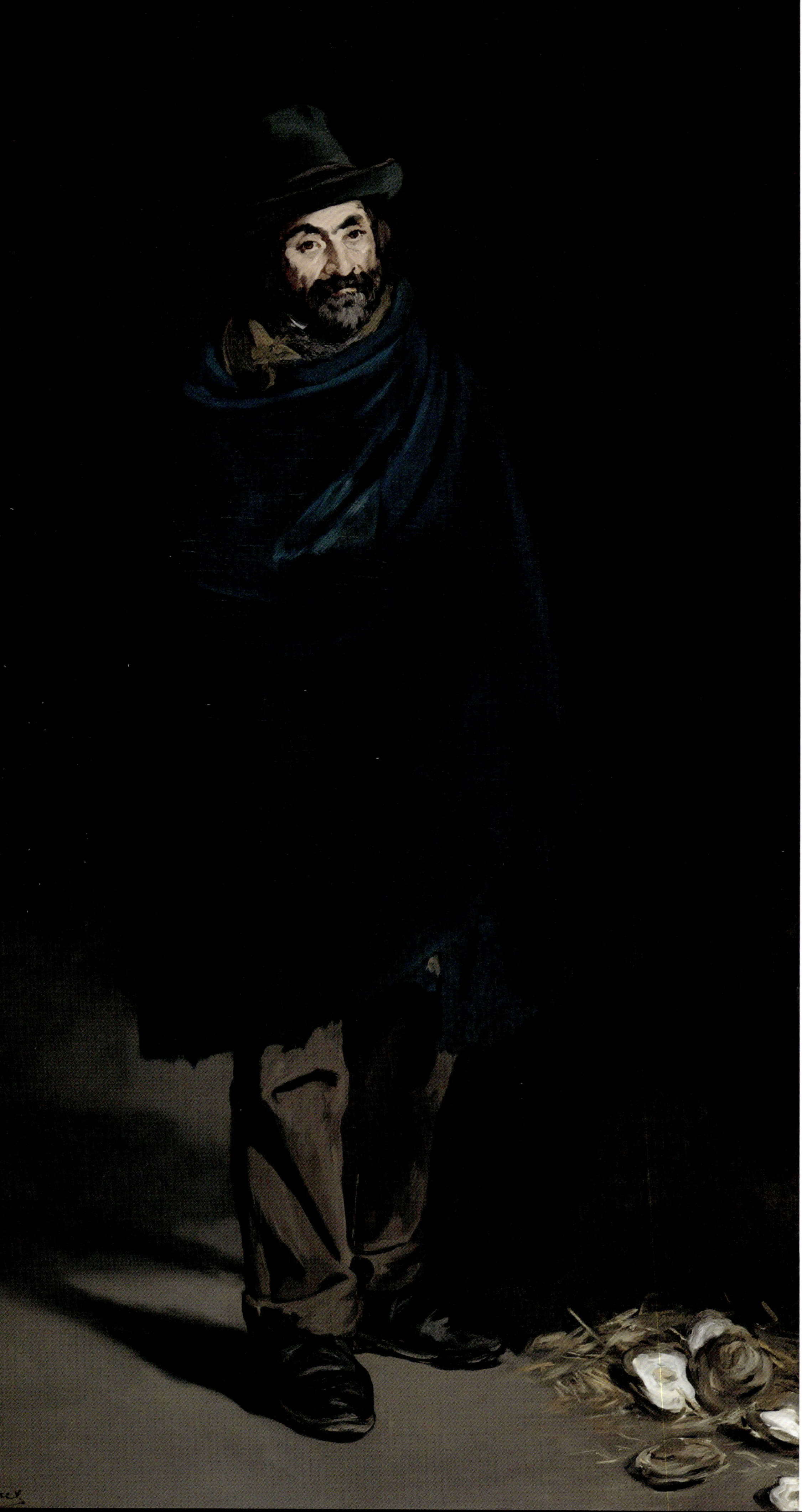

22

Beggar with Oysters (Philosopher)

1865–67
Oil on canvas, 74 × 43 ⅝ in.
(188 × 111 cm)
Williamstown, Clark Art Institute, Arthur Jerome Eddy Memorial Collection, 1931.504

23

Beggar with a Duffle Coat (Philosopher)

1865–67
Oil on canvas, 73 ⅞ × 43 ¼ in. (187.7 × 109.9 cm)
Chicago, The Art Institute of Chicago, 1910.304

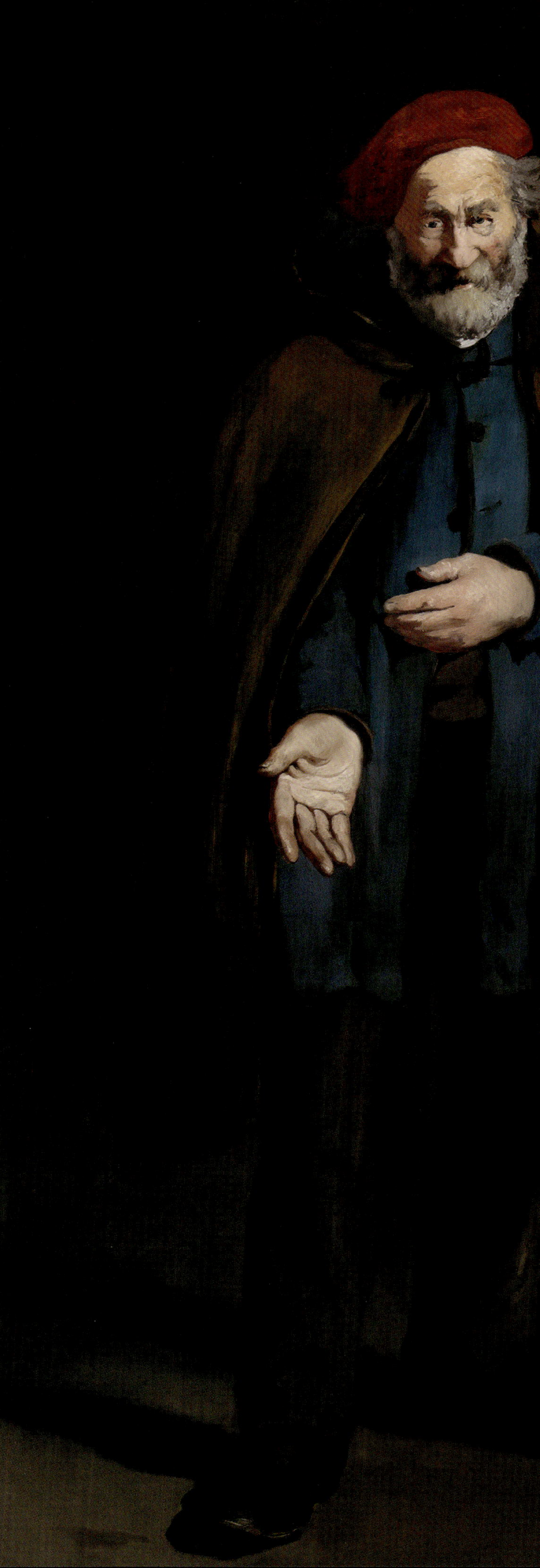

24

Reclining Young Woman in Spanish Costume

1862–63
Oil on canvas, 37 5⁄16 × 44 ¾ in.
(94.7 × 113.7 cm)
New Haven, Yale University Art Gallery, Bequest of Stephen Carlton Clark, B. A. 1903, 1961.18.33

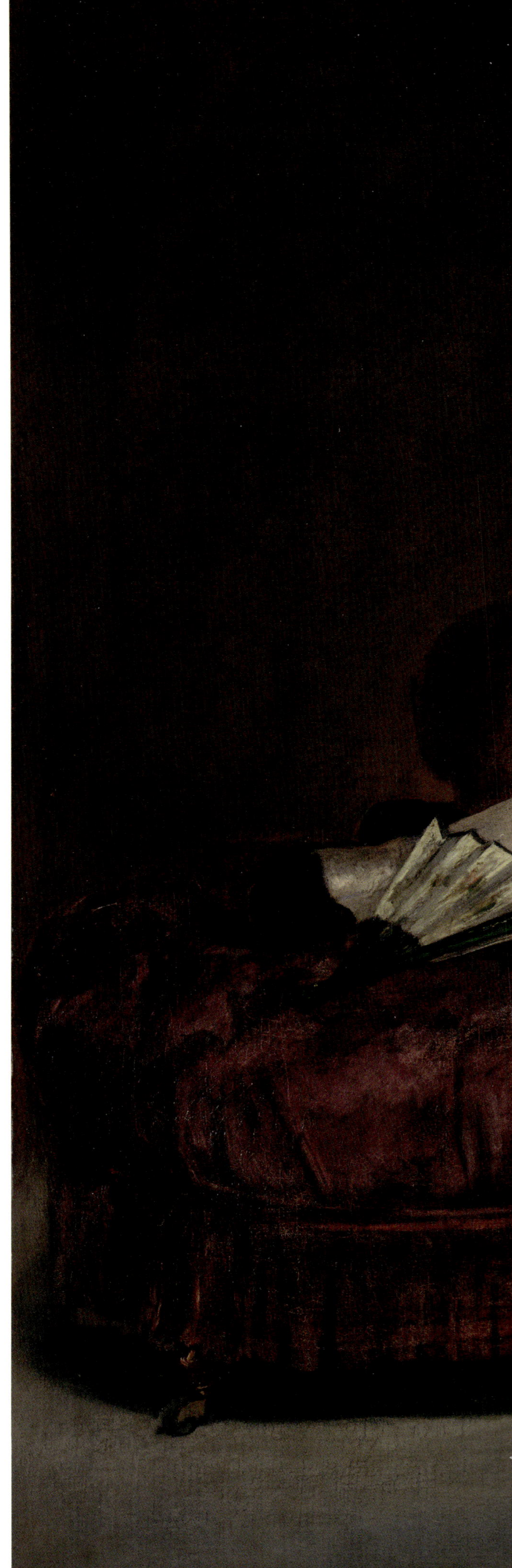

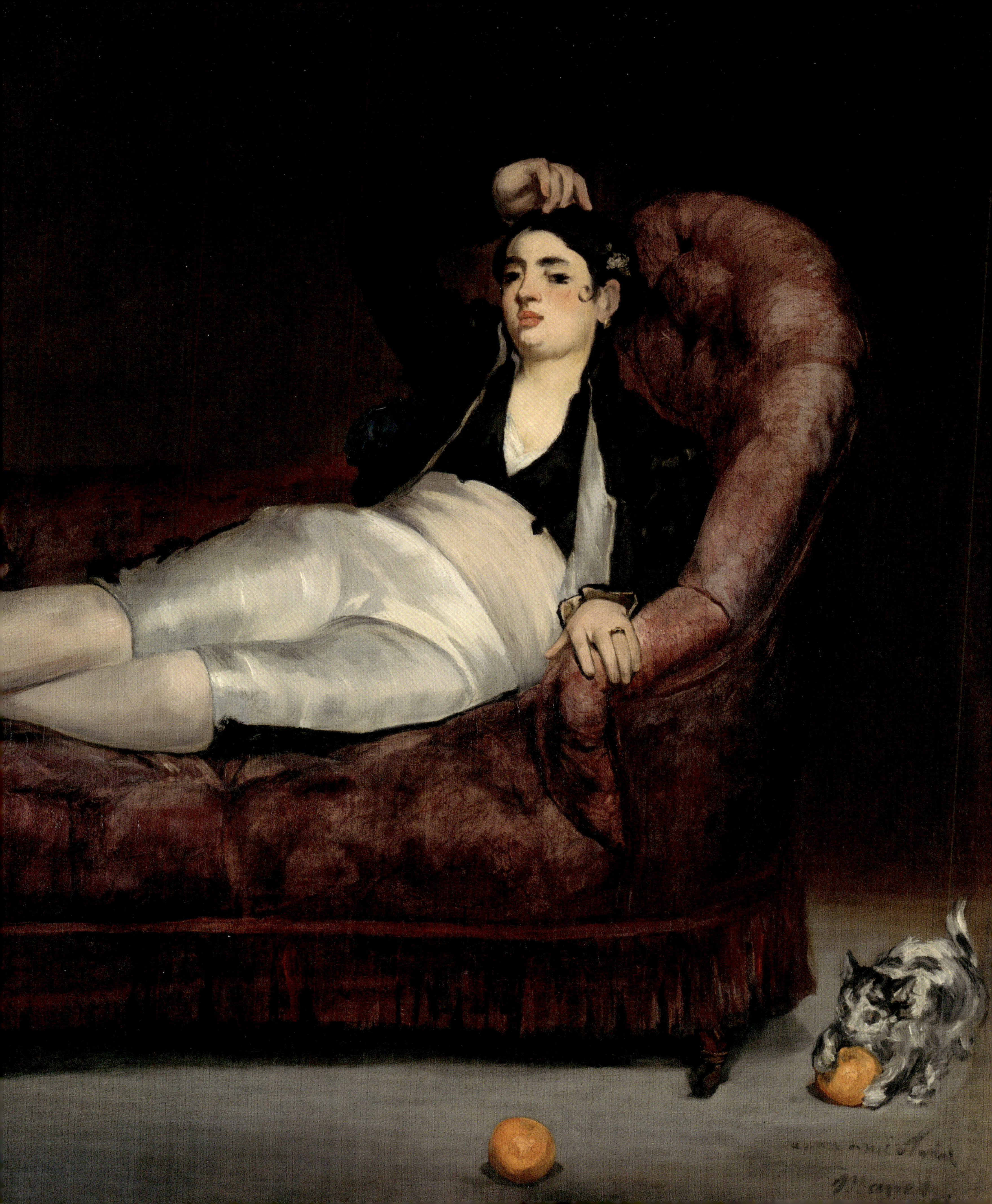
Manet

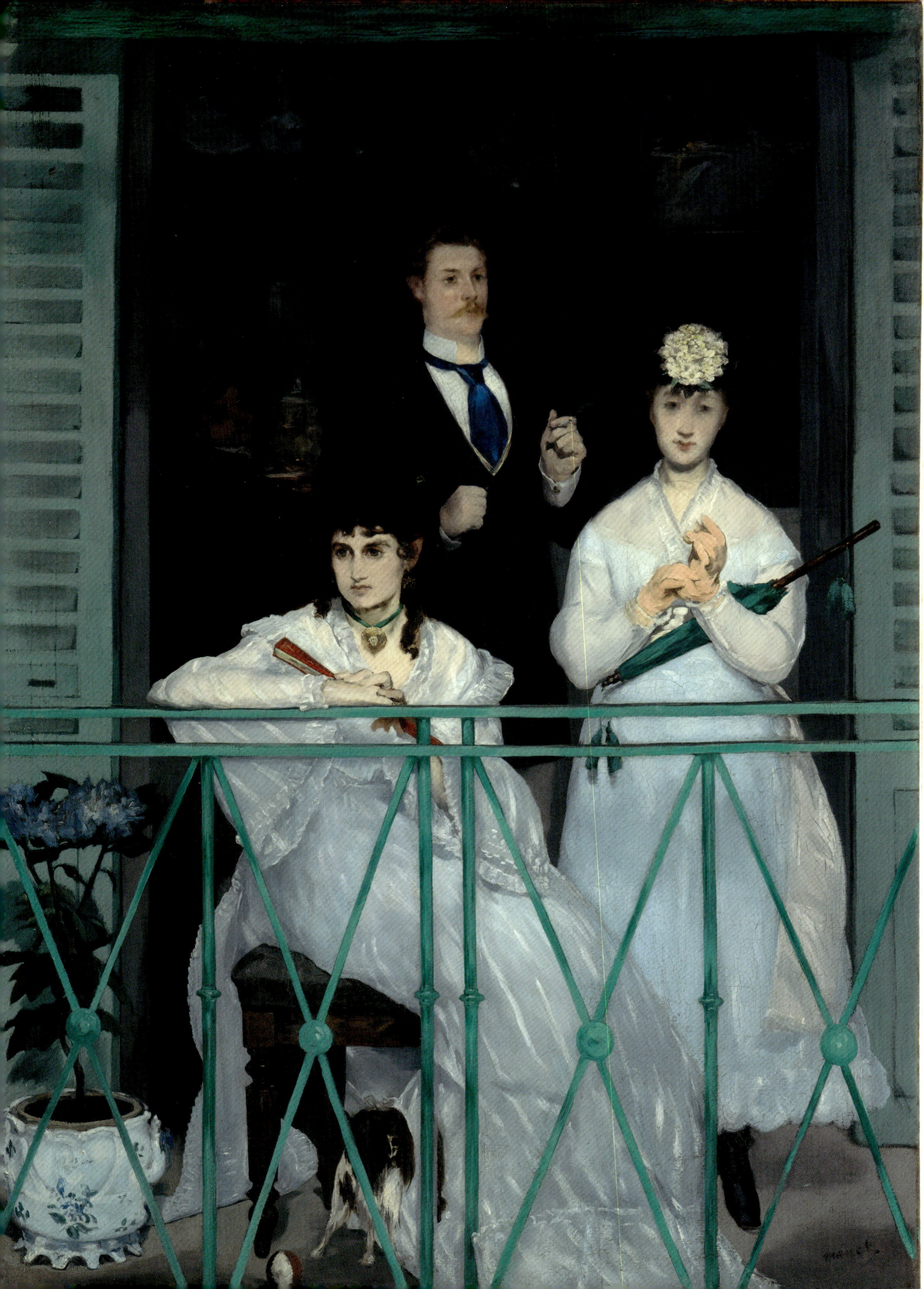
manet.

25

The Balcony

1868–69
Oil on canvas,
67 × 49 ¼ in.
(170 × 125 cm)
Paris, Musée d'Orsay,
RF 2772

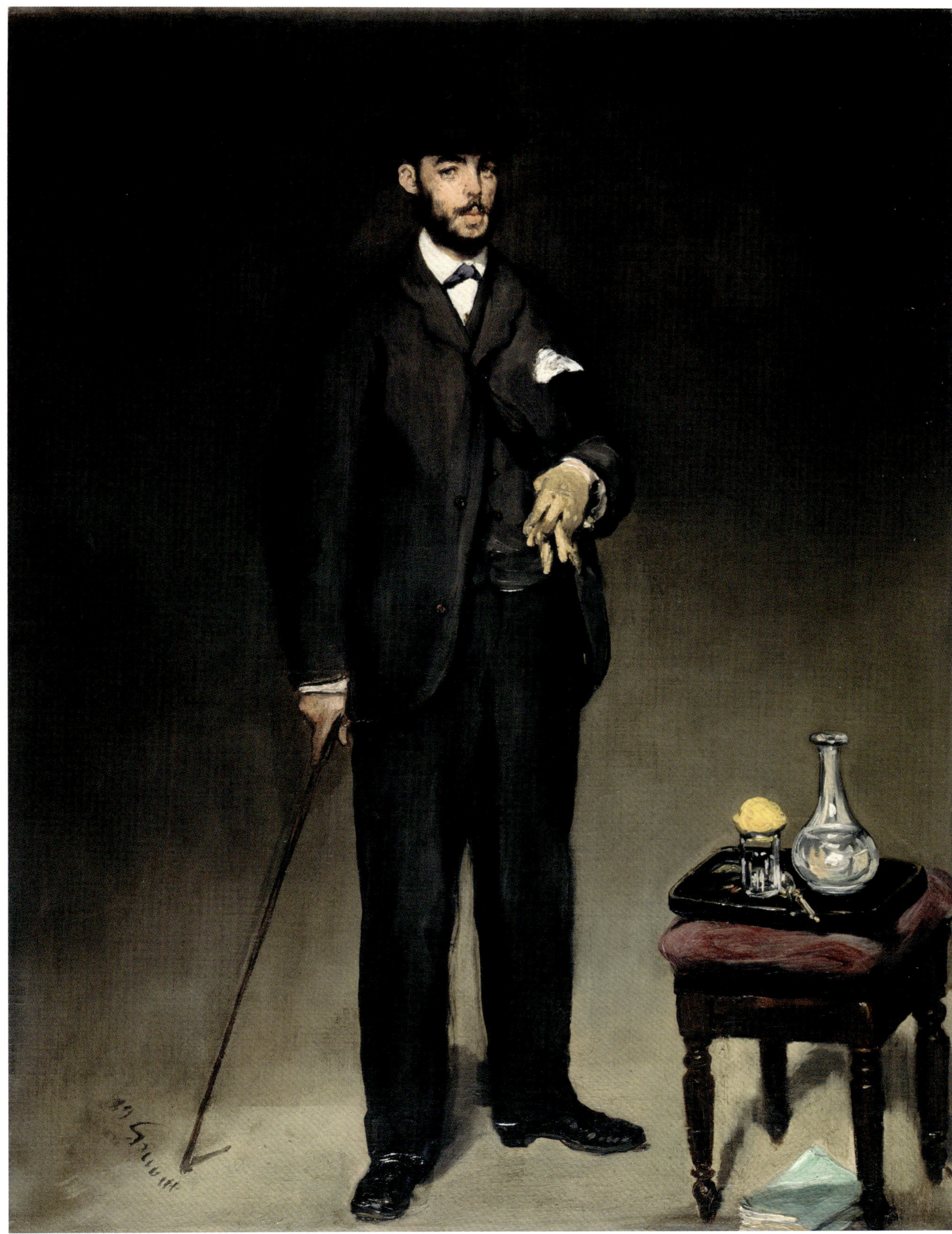

26

Portrait of Théodore Duret

1868
Oil on canvas,
18 ⅓ × 14 in.
(46.5 × 35.5 cm)
Paris, Petit Palais,
PPP485

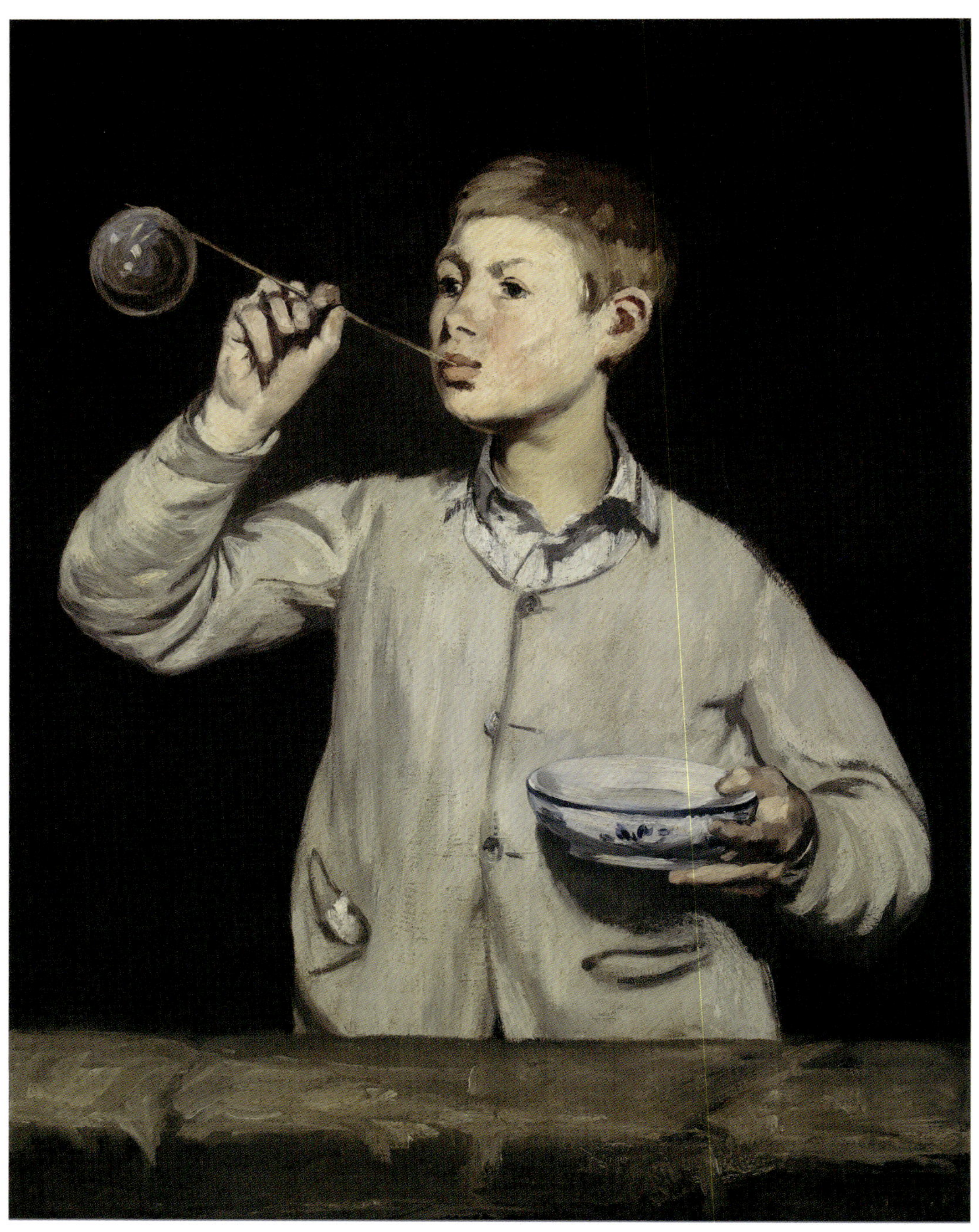

27

Boy Blowing Bubbles

1867
Oil on canvas,
39 ⅓ × 31 ⅔ in.
(100 × 81 cm)
Lisbon, Calouste Gulbenkian
Musuem, 2361

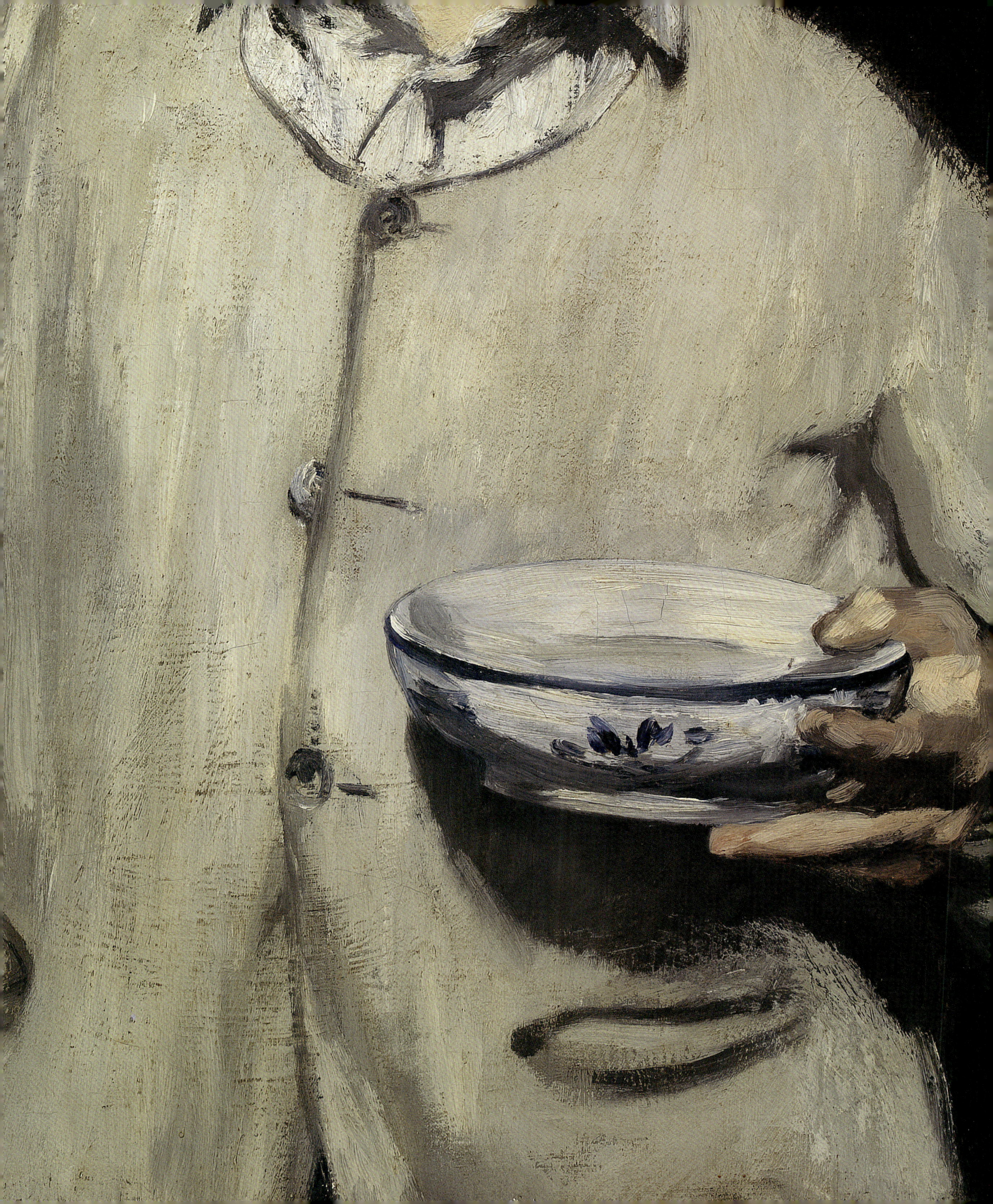

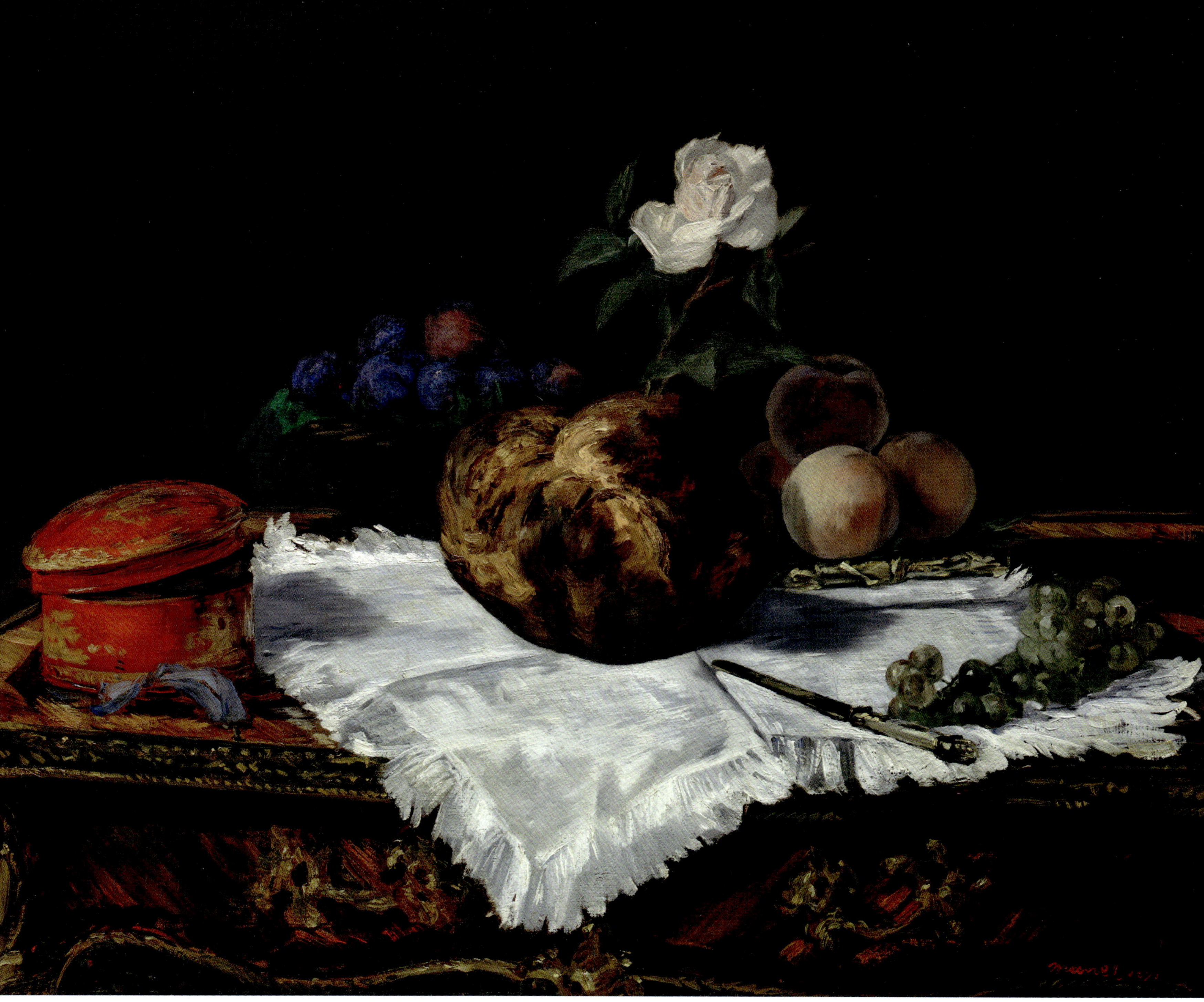

28

The Brioche

1870
Oil on canvas, 25 ⅝ × 31 ⅞ in.
(65.1 × 81 cm)
New York, The Metropolitan
Museum of Art, Gift and
Bequest of David and Peggy
Rockefeller, 1991, 2017,
1991.287

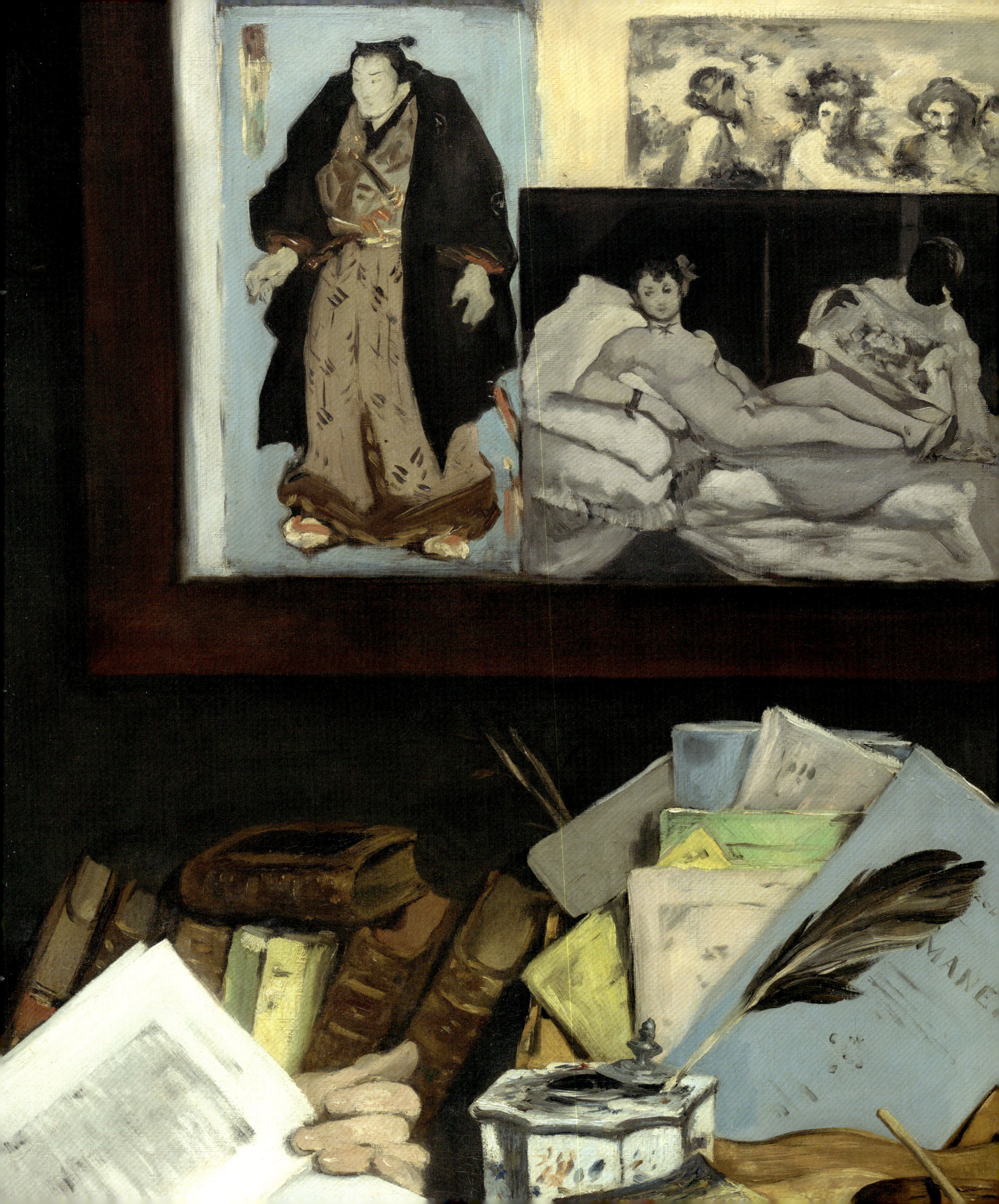

The 1860s: Scandals and Notoriety

Throughout his career, Manet sought official recognition as conferred by the French Academy of Fine Arts. Its members served on the jury of the state-sponsored Salon, an exhibition that attracted several hundred thousand visitors during its six-week run in the spring and generated widespread press coverage. An artist's reputation was at stake in the vast halls of the Salon, housed in the former Palais d'Industrie on the Champs-Élysées in Paris.[1] Manet called the Salon "the true field of battle."[2] By the 1860s, the Salon jury had become increasingly conservative, regularly rejecting works by Manet and other avant-garde artists, among them Claude Monet and Camille Pissarro, future founding members of the group that became known as the Impressionists. Despite a successful Salon debut with *The Spanish Singer* in 1861 (fig. 14), Manet endured repeated rejections and hostile criticism throughout the decade in a succession of scandals at the Salon that established him as the de facto leader of the avant-garde. Manet's rise to prominence at the Salon in the 1860s was inextricably linked to his revolutionary paintings in which Victorine Meurent served as model. These works became the embodiment of both modern art and modern life in nineteenth-century Paris.[3]

Accounts vary as to how Manet met Victorine in the early 1860s. Dismissing the suggestion that it was a chance encounter on the street, Manet's early biographer Adolphe Tabarant observed, "She was not some unknown on the left bank." He added, "She was barely twenty years old, in that year of sixty-two, but one would have said she was twenty-five, so marked with gravity were her features. It is true that if her profile was rather hard, her full face gave the lie to the impression of hardness, a face vivified by beautiful eyes and animated by a fresh and smiling mouth."[4] A small bust-length portrait, likely painted directly from life, is thought to be Manet's first painting of Victorine (fig. 29). The artist possibly gave it to her as a gift; the portrait was never exhibited in Manet's lifetime.[5] Rapid, visible brushwork, as seen on the chin and the folds of the dress, reveal Manet's painterly freedom. Her features are dramatically lit; the abrupt passage from light to shade without halftones became a hallmark of Manet's radical technique

Detail of fig. 39

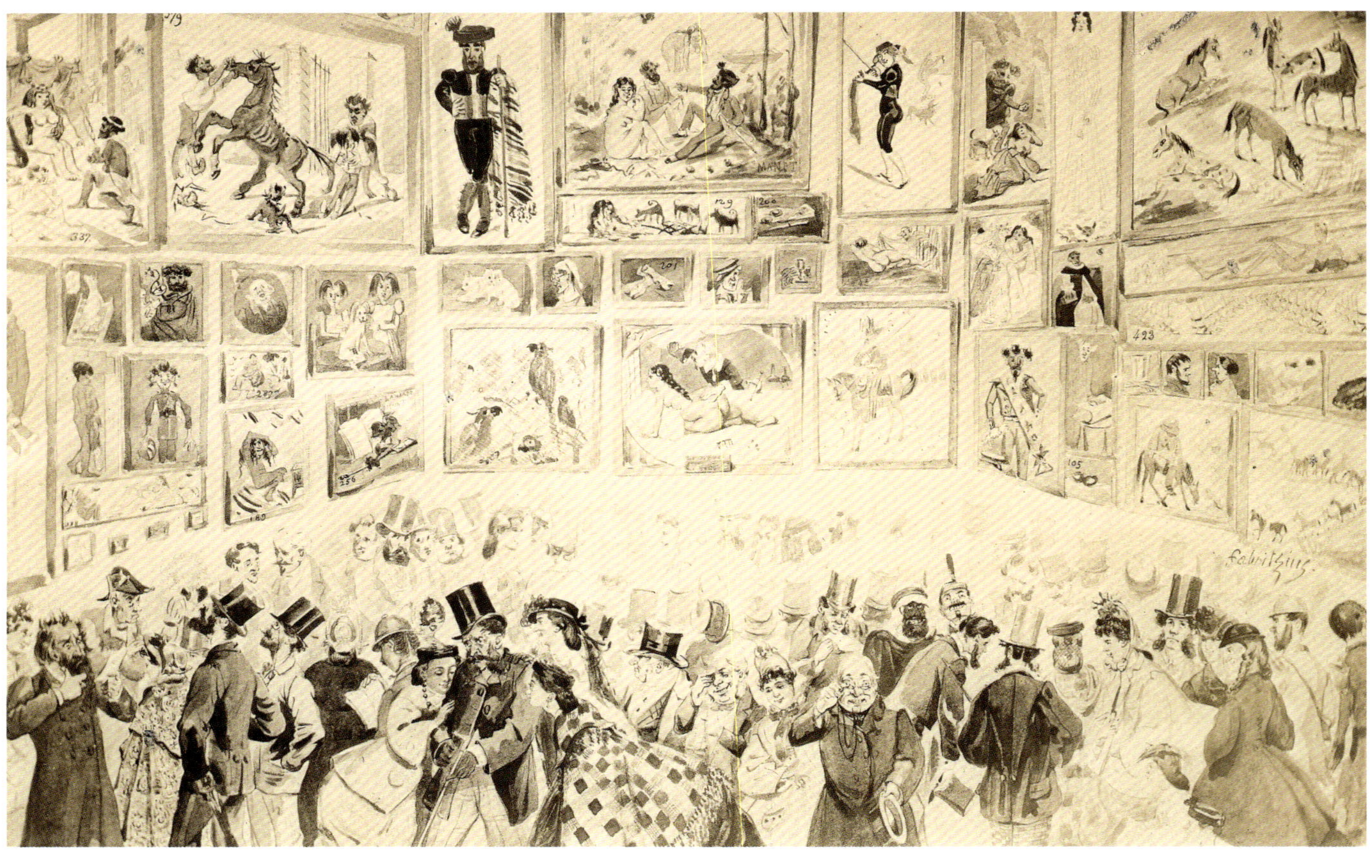

Caricature of the Salon des Refusés, 1863, albumen print by Photographie de la Madeleine of a drawing by Fabritzius, 5 ⅓ × 8 ⅞ in. (13.6 × 22.3 cm). Paris, Fondation Custodia

in the 1860s. The directness of Victorine's gaze conveys her presence, which Manet would exploit in the modern subjects for which she served as his model. Between 1862 and 1873, she modeled for six major paintings by Manet.

In a work painted around 1862, Victorine reenacts an encounter Manet had on the streets of Paris, as variously recounted by his contemporaries: "A woman came out of a sleazy cabaret, lifting up her skirt, clutching her guitar. [Manet] went straight up to her and asked her to come pose for him. She just laughed. 'I'll grab her again, he said, and then if she still doesn't want to come, I have Victorine."[6] His subsequent portrayal of Victorine in *The Street Singer* captures the fleeting moment that he experienced (fig. 30). The glimpse of petticoat beneath the figure's raised skirt and the two red cherries provocatively raised to her lips lend the work an erotic charge. In his biography of Manet, Tabarant observed of Victorine, "Manet represented her . . . just as she was, opening her eyes wide in her audacious, tired face."[7] Its ambitious, full-length format and modern subject align *The Street Singer* with Manet's contemporaneous portrayals of other Parisian types (figs. 22 and 23).

The Street Singer is the first painting of Victorine that Manet exhibited; it went on view in a show of his works that opened at the Galerie Martinet on March 1, 1863, which was possibly intended to pave the way for his acceptance by the Salon jury that spring. However, his paintings failed to garner the critics' favor. In *The Street Singer* "all form is lost," declared the reviewer for the *Gazette des Beaux-Arts*, adding, "we must ask to be excused from pleading M. Manet's case before the exhibition jury."[8] His remarks proved prescient.

In 1863, Manet submitted three other paintings to the Salon, all of which the jury rejected. That year, nearly half of the six thousand works submitted were refused, and a protest by artists led to the establishment of the Salon des Refusés, which represented the first significant challenge to the Salon monopoly. Held at the same venue and at the same time as the official Salon, this "counter-exhibition," as its organizers called it, displayed some eight hundred paintings that had been refused by the Salon jury, among them Manet's trio of *refusés*, which were installed in the last gallery of the exhibition on the far wall. *Luncheon on the Grass* was in the center, flanked by two Spanish-themed works: *Young Man in the Costume of a Majo*, on the left, and *Mademoiselle V . . . in the Costume of an Espada*.[9] One of Manet's more sympathetic critics likened the effect of his works to "blowing a hole in the wall."[10] The tenor of this remark is in keeping with the public reaction to the Salon des Refusés: "This exhibition, at once sad and grotesque, is one of the oddest you could see . . . There is even something cruel about this exhibition; people laugh as they do at a farce."[11]

Manet would claim that *Luncheon on the Grass* (fig. 31) was born of his desire to "do a nude" and that he set out to "redo" and make modern a celebrated work of the Italian Renaissance, Titian's *Pastoral Concert*, then attributed to Giorgione, as his friend Proust recalled.[12] As an art student, Manet had copied the painting in the galleries of the Louvre. At least one critic cited Giorgione as Manet's inspiration in 1863.[13] However, the overt modernity of Manet's outdoor picnic departs from this pastoral ideal; Manet's female nude, "dressed only in the shadow of leaves," her discarded clothing prominently displayed in the foreground, was seen as a prostitute.[14] Manet further flouted convention by rendering a scene from modern life on the scale of history painting.

Victorine posed for the nude figure in *Luncheon on the Grass*; she was joined by Manet's future brother-in-law Ferdinand Leenhoff, seated next to her, and, opposite, a figure modeled by the artist's brothers Eugène and Gustave, who took turns posing in Manet's studio, where the work was painted. The identity of the woman shown bathing in the background is not known. The arrangement of the central trio is based on a group of river gods and a naiad in the lower right of an early sixteenth-century engraving by Marcantonio Raimondi after Raphael's *Judgment of Paris* (ca. 1510–20, The Metropolitan Museum of Art, New York). Although this engraving was well known among artists at this time, only one contemporary reviewer identified Manet's Renaissance source.[15]

Instead, Salon critics focused on Manet's technique, which departed from the realistic tonal modeling of forms and polished surface finish espoused as the Academic ideal. Objecting to his broad handling of paint, one reviewer suggested that Manet painted with "a floor polishing brush," adding, "It is a decoration to see from a distance of a kilometer."[16] The absence of conventional modeling and the use of bold, visible brushwork prompted another critic to ask, "Is this drawing? Is this painting?"[17] The critics described Manet's painting as unfinished and sketch-like, their language prefiguring that used to describe Impressionist paintings a decade later in the 1870s. The radical fusion of the art of the past with a subject from modern life in this work went unmentioned in 1863. Even today the painting defies a clear narrative reading. Manet first called the painting *Le Bain* (*The Bath*) in reference to the mysterious bather in the background; critics called it *Déjeuner sur l'herbe* (*Luncheon on the Grass*), the title that Manet adapted when he next exhibited the work in his 1867 one-man show.

The controversy generated by *Luncheon on the Grass* in 1863 largely overshadowed Manet's other two paintings on view at the Salon des Refusés, both of which featured models dressed in Spanish costume. In one, Victorine reappears, dressed as a man in the costume of an *espada*, or matador (fig. 32); Manet's youngest brother, Gustave, poses as an Andalusian *majo*, or dandy, in the other (fig. 33). Victorine and Gustave wear the same bolero jacket, satin cummerbund, and sombrero—all props from the artist's studio, underscoring the works' artifice. Critics were flummoxed by Manet's figures: "under these dashing costumes, something of the personality of the figure is missing; the heads ought to be painted differently from the fabrics, with more life and more profundity."[18] Both works blur the distinction between individual and social type, the latter characteristic of genre painting, and embody what the art historian Carol Armstrong has described as Manet "making the portrait strange."[19]

The painting of Victorine as an *espada* seemingly draws from an eclectic range of sources. The figure of Victorine evokes both Renaissance engravings of allegorical figures and *carte-de-visite*, or calling-card, photographic portraits of actresses and dancers cross-dressing as matadors, which were then in wide circulation, while the background conflates two of Goya's prints of bullfighting.[20] Recently discovered details of Victorine's biography also lend the work a portrait-like aspect: Manet's model was a popular cancan dancer whose stage name was "Mademoiselle Victorine"; she performed in an 1861 production at the Hippodrome in Paris that included a parody of bullfighting, although it is not known if she or another member of the all-female troupe danced in that scene.[21] Thus, when he painted Victorine as a matador in his studio the following year, Manet might well have been alluding to that performance if not to an actual role played by his model. Moreover, this work is the only one of Manet's staged images of Victorine in which it could be said that she appears as herself, albeit in character as Mademoiselle Victorine. *Mademoiselle V . . . in the Costume of an Espada* thus acquires a new dimension in the context of Manet's other portraits of performers (fig. 17).

Titian, *Pastoral Concert*, 1500–25, oil on canvas, 41 ⅓ × 54 in. (105 × 137.5 cm). Paris, Musée du Louvre, 71

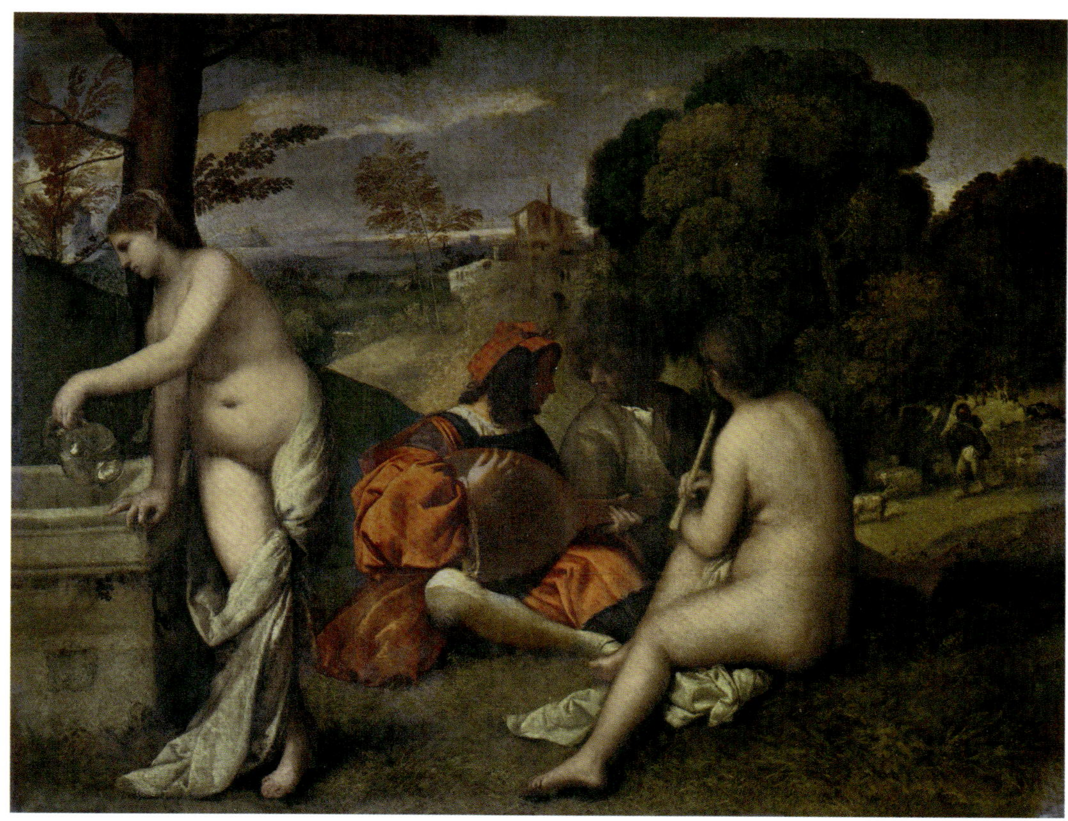

In 1863, Manet emerged as the uncontested *succès de scandale* with his emphatically modern subjects and his convention-defying technique. However, not all the reviews were negative; the critic for *L'Artiste* commented of Manet, "all took note of the bold one's name."[22] The following year, Manet's choice to submit a history painting to the jury, the genre most esteemed by the conservative art establishment, attested to his ambition to succeed at the Salon. He submitted a religious subject, which he titled *Angels at the Tomb of Christ* (fig. 34). It was shown along with *Incident in a Bullfight* (fig. 20)—two images of death, one sacred and the other secular.

In Manet's religious picture, the suffering endured by Christ is made explicit, the wounds visible on his lifeless body in contrast to the seemingly unmarred figure of the dead toreador. The unvarnished realism of Manet's image of a dead Christ flanked by angels was widely denounced by a public accustomed to idealized imagery in history painting. The harshly lit figure of Christ was variously described as dirty and "filthy" and likened to a cadaver.[23] Critics also faulted Manet for what was then believed to be the incorrect placement of Christ's chest wound on the left side; the artist was said to have ignored Baudelaire's advice to correct his error before the opening of the Salon. Salon commentators also objected to the blue color of the birdlike wings of one of the angels. Manet's naturalistically rendered angels might well represent the artist's rejoinder to the celebrated Realist artist, Gustave Courbet, who in 1861

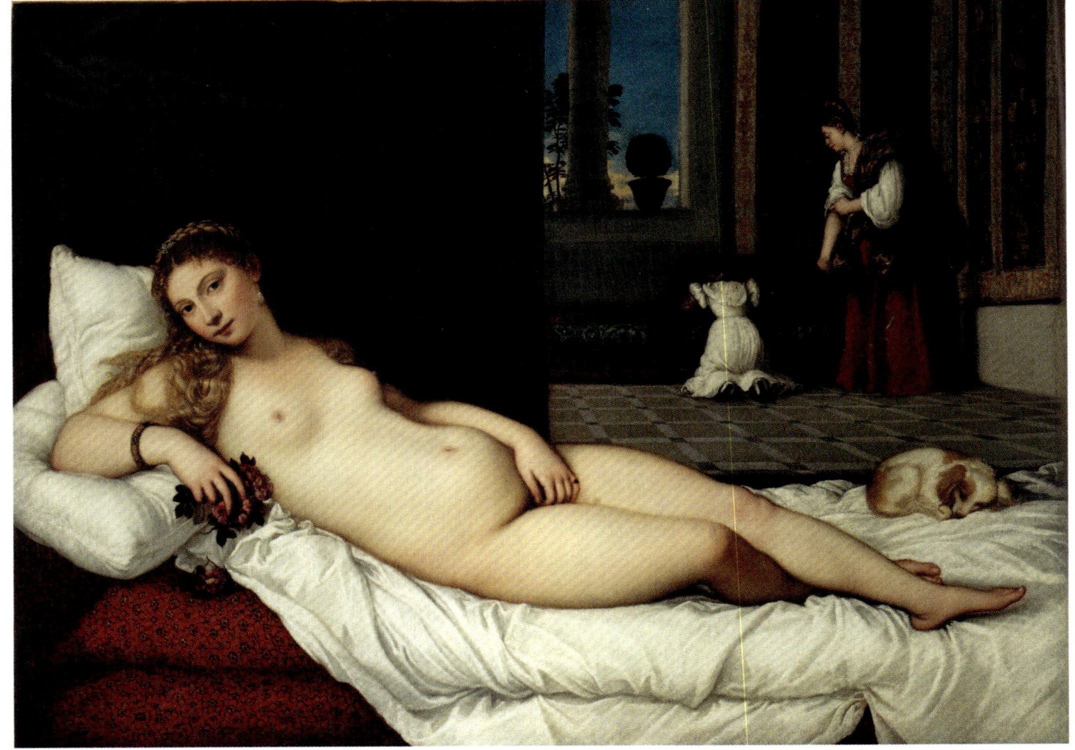

Titian, *Venus of Urbino*, 1538, oil on canvas, 46 ⅔ × 65 in. (119 × 165 cm). Florence, Uffizi Galleries, 1890 no. 1437

publicly proclaimed, "Painting is essentially a *concrete* art and consists only of representations of *real* and *existing* things." Courbet himself was quick to respond to Manet's work, mockingly asking him, "So you have seen angels then and know they have backsides?"[24]

Manet realized another episode from the Passion of Christ, *Jesus Mocked by the Soldiers*, which he exhibited at the Salon of 1865 (fig. 35).[25] Manet's interest in this subject might have been stimulated by the publication of Ernest Renan's *Life of Jesus*, a widely read biography published in 1863, which controversially presented Christ as human. In 1864, one Salon reviewer mockingly wrote, "Do not miss Manet's *Christ, or The Poor Miner Raised from the Coal Mine*, painted for Renan."[26] The emphatic naturalism of Manet's style in both paintings of Christ accords with Renan's approach; Manet's works also read as modern reimaginings of history painting, the pictorial genre most bound by tradition.

At the Salon of 1865, *Jesus Mocked by the Soldiers* was exhibited along with a contemporary subject Manet had painted two years earlier, *Olympia* (fig. 36). Once again, Victorine Meurent posed nude for Manet, this time in a composition modeled on Titian's celebrated *Venus of Urbino*, which Manet had copied during an 1853 trip to Florence. She is paired with Laure, a Black model whose presence in the scene recalls the two servants in the background of Titian's painting.[27] Manet's modern nude, though, is starkly rendered, her flesh depicted without halftones, and the outlines of her body are pronounced and angular in contrast to the softened contours and sensuous flesh of Titian's Renaissance goddess. Olympia's outspread hand, simultaneously covering and drawing attention to her sex, further underscores Manet's departure from Titian's idealized Venus.

Olympia also reads as Manet's pointed rejection of the female nudes that began populating the Salon at mid-century. Dubbed the "Salon of the Venuses," the Salon of 1863 witnessed the triumph of a trio of Venuses, painted by the Academic painters Amaury-Duval, Paul Baudry, and Alexandre Cabanel. All display a sense of three-dimensionality in the modeling of the figures and the polished surface finish that conform to the painterly idiom espoused by the Academy of Fine Arts. Manet's visible brushwork and the absence of tonal modeling in the nudes of Victorine were antithetical to the Academic ideal. The Salon "Venuses" were also safely couched in the guise of history painting, the genre prized by the conservative Academy—timeless, mythological goddesses rather than the contemporary Parisian who occupies center stage in both *Luncheon on the Grass* and *Olympia*.

Olympia scandalized the public at the Salon of 1865. In the words of one Salon reviewer, Manet's painting was "the scapegoat of the salon, the victim of Parisian Lynch law. Each

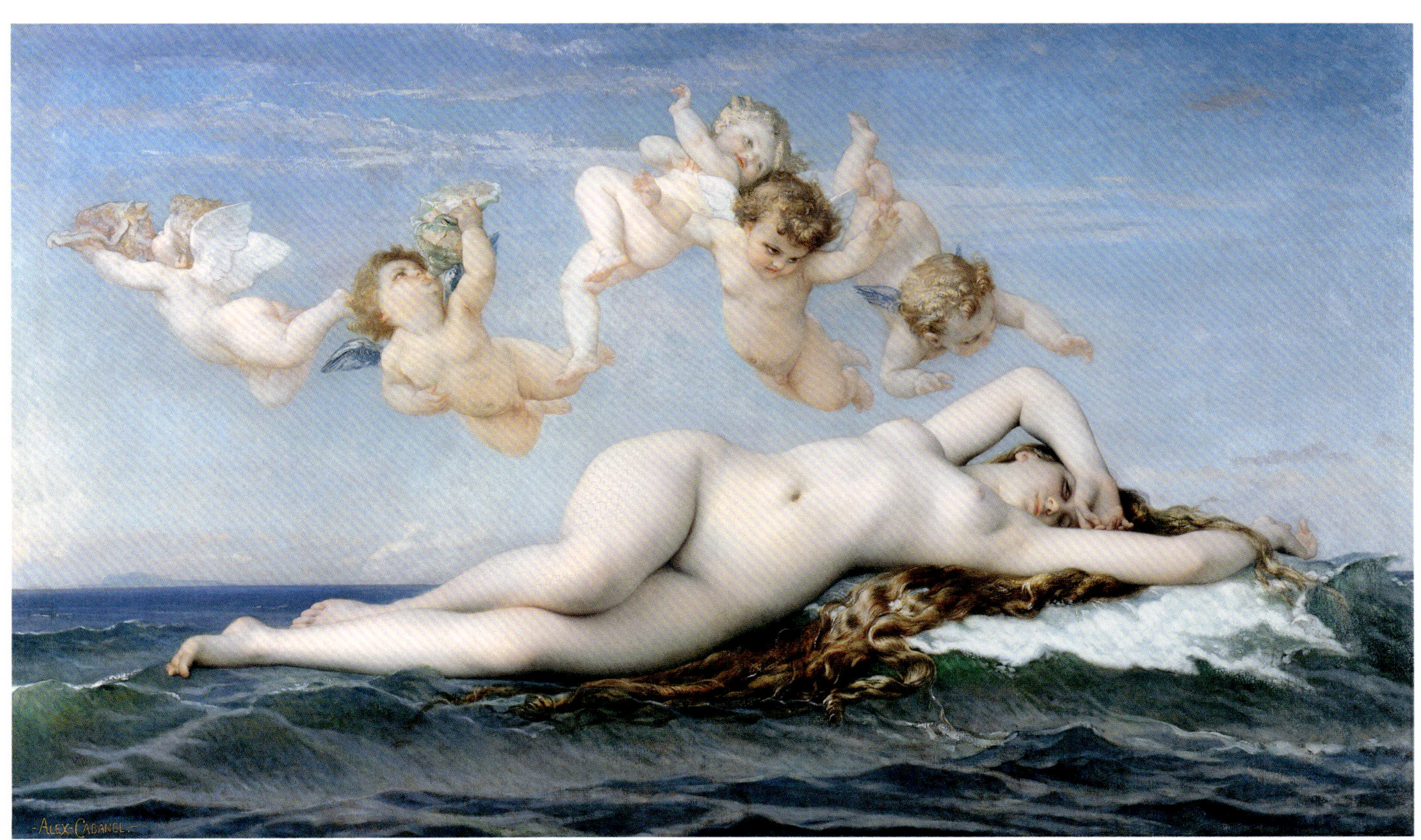

Alexandre Cabanel, *The Birth of Venus*, 1863, oil on canvas, 51 ¼ × 88 ½ in. (130 × 225 cm). Paris, Musée d'Orsay, RF 273

passerby takes a stone and throws it at her face."[28] Nearly every review was hostile, if not vitriolic; laughing and jeering crowds gathered around the work. In response, the Salon organizers removed the painting from its original location in the "M" gallery (works were grouped according to the artist's last name) and placed it in the last gallery, colloquially known as "the garbage dump" ("*le dépotoir*"). There it hung above a door "at a height where even the worst daubs had never been hung . . . where you scarcely knew whether you were looking at a parcel of nude flesh or a bundle of laundry," according to *Le Figaro*.[29] Another critic added, "She cannot even be laughed at any more, which has quite disappointed everyone."[30]

The name Manet gave his nude, "Olympia," was a common pseudonym for prostitutes, a reference not lost on the artist's contemporaries. In the 1860s, prostitution was embedded in the fabric of modern life in Paris; however, it was increasingly feared as a threat to morality and social order. Manet's nude was seen as a prostitute and the bouquet of flowers, a gift from a client. In the nineteenth century, Titian's *Venus* was also thought to depict a famous courtesan, but it was the kind of prostitute that Olympia represented, associated with her perceived lower social class, that unsettled Manet's audience in 1865, as art historian T. J. Clark has argued. The artist's contemporaries saw her as a working-class streetwalker rather than a high-end courtesan. This assumption, according to Clark, was embedded in multiple references to her dirtiness when critics wrote about her body: the figure of Olympia was described as an unwashed "coal lady," "drawn in charcoal," and her body was likened to a cadaver.[31] Similar language was used to describe the dead body of Christ in Manet's other exhibited painting.

Manet seemingly played into public fear by including at the foot of the bed a black cat, back arched and tail raised, in place of Titian's faithful, fluffy lapdog. The black cat, apparently a late addition to the work,[32] became a symbol of the painting's transgressive aspect. In the 1860s, cats were associated with promiscuous sexual behavior. Manet's black cat figured prominently in contemporary caricatures of the painting at the Salon, its raised tail often exaggeratedly emphasized. Manet was dubbed "the painter of the black cat," his identity irrevocably linked with the scandal generated by *Olympia*.

The fallout from *Olympia* was swift and harsh; about a week after the Salon opened on May 1, Manet wrote to his friend Baudelaire, who was in Brussels: "I wish I had you here, my dear Baudelaire, insults are beating down on me like hail, I've never been through anything like it . . . I wish I could have your sound judgment on my pictures because all this uproar has been upsetting, and obviously someone must be wrong."[33] At the end of August, Manet left Paris for Spain, intent on seeking the "advice" of "master Velázquez," as he wrote to his friend Zacharie Astruc the day before his departure.[34]

The influence of Velázquez is manifest in two full-length figure paintings that Manet realized in the months after his return to Paris, *The Tragic Actor* (fig. 21) and *The Fifer* (fig. 37). Set against neutral backgrounds and with only a hint of shadow to indicate depth, both works attest to Manet's admiration for Velázquez's portrait of Pablo de Valladolid (see p. 41), which he had seen on his visit to the Prado. *The Fifer*, set against a pale gray background, captures the sense of "nothing but air" surrounding the figure that so captivated Manet when he saw Velázquez's work in 1865. Silhouetted against a neutral ground and rendered in broad, flat areas of color, the figure appears two-dimensional, outlined in black like a cutout. The radical simplicity of its technique was without precedent in Manet's oeuvre.[35] Manet identified the subject of this work as "a fifer in the Light Infantry Guard" in a letter to Baudelaire, and his model was a boy trooper in the Imperial Guard, introduced to Manet by his friend and patron, Commandant Hippolyte Lejosne.[36] As in his portrait-like paintings of Victorine, Manet elided the boundaries between portrait and type, rendering a subject associated with small-format genre imagery on the large scale of a formal portrait.

Both *The Fifer* and *The Tragic Actor* were rejected by the Salon jury in 1866, although the same jurors accepted a figure painting by a young Claude Monet that was clearly indebted to Manet's precedent (*Camille*, 1866, Kunsthalle, Bremen). According to Manet's early biographer, Tabarant, it was not the works that offended the conservative jury; rather, it was the notorious artist himself. Almost immediately, Émile Zola, writing under the pseudonym of "Claude," sprang to the artist's defense in an article that appeared in *L'Événement* on May 7, 1866. He declared *The Fifer* to be his "favorite" work, adding, "I do not think it would be possible to obtain a stronger effect with less complicated means."[37] In turn, Manet responded to his rejection by organizing a private exhibition in his studio open to his friends that ran for two months; he displayed both rejected canvases along with a selection of other works, including a recent full-length figure painting for which Victorine modeled.

The work, *Young Lady in 1866*, which he exhibited without a title, featured his model intimately attired in a pink peignoir, holding a nosegay of violets while toying with a chain from which a man's monocle is suspended, both of which hint at an unseen male presence (fig. 38). The critic Théophile Thoré, not entirely disapproving, took note of Manet's "wild sketches," especially this work, but regretted its perceived lack of finish. In an article published on January 1, 1867, Zola observed that this canvas was "barely dry" and noted the parrot on its perch, which Thoré had not mentioned. More recently, Zola's commentary prompted art historian Henri Loyrette to suggest that Manet, with an eye to exhibiting the canvas at the next Salon, had reworked it and added the parrot on the stand in the second half of 1866.[38] The parrot was especially resonant at that moment: earlier in the year, Gustave Courbet exhibited at the Salon an erotically charged image of a female nude with a parrot, which elicited comparisons to *Olympia*. As a wild bird tamed, the parrot was associated with prostitutes in the nineteenth century, and Courbet's parrot, wings spread as it lands on the woman's raised hand, would have

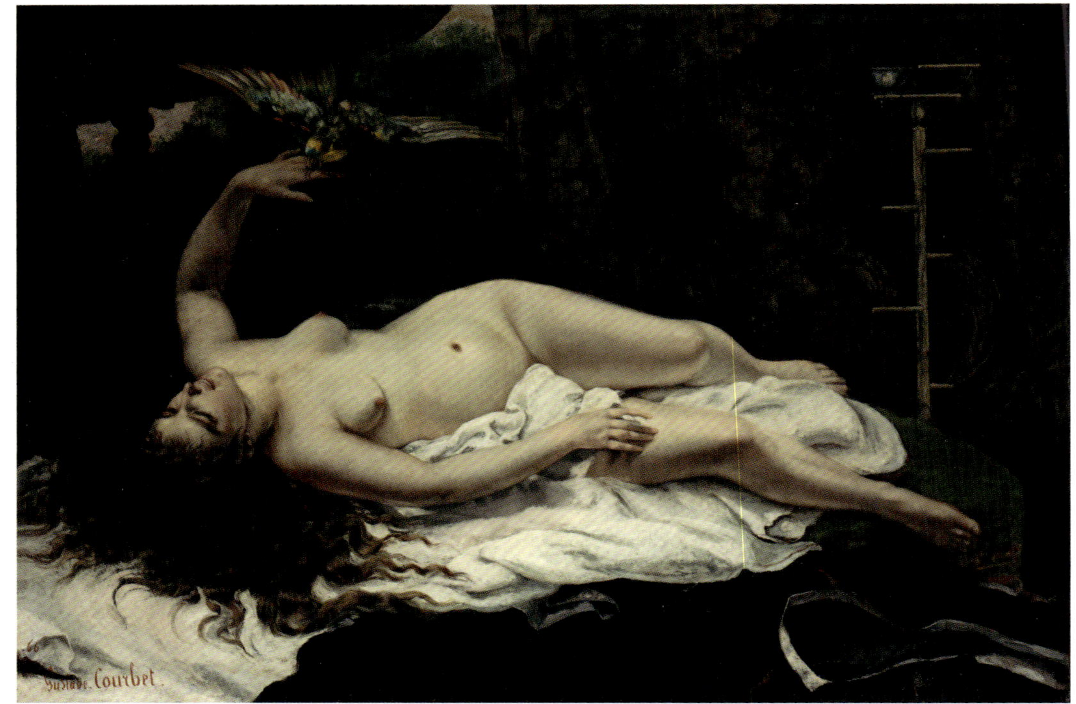

Gustave Courbet,
Woman with a Parrot, 1866,
oil on canvas, 51 × 77 in.
(129.5 × 195.6 cm).
New York, The Metropolitan Museum of Art,
H. O. Havemeyer Collection, Bequest of Mrs. H. O. Havemeyer,
1929, 29.100.57

been understood as a surrogate for an absent male. Victorine's avian companion explicitly links Manet's work with Courbet's Salon nude, a connection reinforced by the title Manet subsequently gave to his painting when he showed it in his 1867 solo exhibition: *Young Lady in 1866*. Manet translated the explicit sexuality of Courbet's *Woman with a Parrot* into a language of subtle erotic allusion, as embodied in the intimate way that he portrayed Victorine, paired with an African gray parrot, here safely contained on its perch. As a critic disapprovingly wrote in response to Manet's work when it was shown at the Salon of 1868, "Manet, who should not have forgotten the panic caused several years ago by the black cat in the painting [*Olympia*], has borrowed the parrot from his friend Courbet . . ."[39]

At the Salon of 1868, Manet's *Young Lady in 1866* was shown alongside his portrait of Zola "on the advice of Zola himself," according to Tabarant[40] (fig. 39). Their friendship dates to the time of Zola's groundbreaking defense of Manet in his review of the Salon of 1866, in which he predicted, "Manet will be one of tomorrow's masters," adding that his art was destined for the Louvre, which then housed works by living artists.[41] An expanded commentary followed in an article published in January 1867, which was reissued in the form of a pamphlet that May. Its publication coincided with the opening of Manet's solo show of fifty paintings in a purpose-built pavilion off the avenue de l'Alma, which the artist staged in response to his exclusion from the Exposition Universelle of 1867. Zola's pamphlet, with its light blue cover, stands out among the still life of artfully arranged objects on the desk in his portrait.

Zola recalled the long hours spent posing in Manet's studio on the rue Guyot, during which he observed the artist at work, standing at his easel: "He had forgotten me, he no longer knew I was there, he simply copied me, as if I were some human beast, with a concentration and artistic integrity that I have seen nowhere else." Manet, he added, explained his approach, "'I can do nothing without Nature. I do not know how to invent.'"[42] Manet portrayed Zola surrounded by the tools of his trade as a writer—inkwell and books. The Japanese screen and the woodblock print of a wrestler allude to the emerging taste for Japanese art in avant-garde circles.

It has been argued that this portrait is as much about Manet as Zola, if not more so.[43] Manet's name in the title of Zola's pamphlet is clearly legible, doubling as the artist's signature. Manet is writ large across this canvas, from the prominence accorded the prints showing his interest in Japonisme and his admiration of Velázquez, represented by a print after his *Borrachos* (*Drinkers*), to the significance of *Olympia* in his oeuvre. Manet had provided an etching of his work to illustrate Zola's pamphlet, in which the writer extolled the painting as a "masterpiece": "It will remain as the most characteristic example of his talent, his greatest achievement."[44] As if in acknowledgement of Zola's praise, this Olympia shifts her gaze to look at Zola. The artist gave the portrait as an expression of his gratitude to Zola, who kept it until his death.

The prominence of the still-life arrangement in Zola's portrait reflects Manet's ongoing engagement with this genre during the 1860s. He probably painted his first independent still life in 1862 (*Oysters*, National Gallery of Art, Washington, D.C.), and he exhibited still-life paintings in 1865 at Martinet's gallery and his 1867 solo exhibition. His work in this genre was acclaimed by critics, as Zola noted in 1867: "The most avowed enemies of Édouard Manet's talent admit that he paints inanimate objects well." Among the still lifes on view in 1867, Zola singled out for praise "a splendid bunch of peonies"[45] (fig. 40). Recently imported to Europe, the peony connoted luxury, and Manet grew the flower in his garden at Gennevillers.[46] Peonies serve as the subject of eight floral still lifes painted over the course of the decade, variously depicted in formal tabletop arrangements, as in the work Zola admired, or in pared-down compositions with nothing more than a flowering branch and a pair of pruning shears, whose apparent casualness is deceptive (fig. 41). The still lifes in this group share a painterly touch, evident in Manet's virtuoso rendering of the lush flowers, and a neutral backdrop that recalls his contemporaneous figure paintings.

Still lifes frame both sides of an ambitious multi-figure painting, *Luncheon in the Studio*, that Manet exhibited at the Salon of 1869 (fig. 43). On the left, an armored helmet and sword evoke the studio props Manet deployed in his earlier costumed figure paintings (fig. 6), while the black cat bathing itself on the same chair conjures Olympia's feline companion. Similarly, the white damask tablecloth recurs in Manet's tabletop still lifes from the 1860s, while on the right, the remains of the luncheon mirror the artist's early still-life paintings of fruit and fish (fig. 42).

Salon critics struggled to ascribe a narrative to the scene, which Manet exhibited alongside *The Balcony* (fig. 25). In the absence of a clear narrative in either work, reviewers resorted to likening the figures to still-life subjects, as Jules Castagnary wrote of Manet's *Luncheon*: "Just as Manet assembles, for the mere pleasure of astonishing, objects which should be mutually incompatible, in the same fashion he arranges his people at random without any reason or meaning for the composition."[47] Castagnary's words echo Zola's assessment of Manet's art, published in 1867: "He treats figure subjects in just the same way as still-life subjects are treated in art schools . . . he groups figures more or less fortuitously, and after that he has no other thought than to put them down on canvas as he sees them."[48]

The *Luncheon in the Studio* represents a culmination of the artistic interests that shaped the first decade of Manet's career. Its artifice as a studio construct is undisguised, from the scattered props to the lack of interaction among the figures. Manet's engagement with the art of the past resonates in the still life on the table, a nod to the seventeenth-century Dutch precedents that inspired his own works in the genre, and the muted palette of grays and blacks, evoking that of Velázquez.[49] The central figure, fashionably attired in a velvet jacket and straw boater, is Léon Leenhoff, now a young man of sixteen; his recurring role as a model in Manet's figure paintings during the 1860s reinforces the self-referential aspect of this work. It is also the most portrait-like of Manet's images of him, recalling the elision of portrait and genre imagery in Manet's paintings of Victorine. The work's ostensible subject—a luncheon—inevitably conjures Manet's 1863 *Luncheon on the Grass* with its similarly ambiguous narrative. Its composition, though, is less dependent on overt borrowings from the Old Masters than that of *Luncheon on the Grass* and represents what scholar Françoise Cachin has called Manet's "first true 'naturalist' scene."[50]

As the decade drew to a close, Manet had distanced himself from the scandals and notoriety generated by his work since the Salon des Refusés of 1863. In his review of the Salon of 1869, Théophile Gautier acknowledged Manet's influence on contemporary painting and added, "Manet's exhibition is comparatively prudent and won't create a scandal. If he wanted to take the trouble, he could become a good painter. He has the temperament for it."[51] As to Manet's standing in relation to the conservative Salon jury, the artist Frédéric Bazille reported to his father on the eve of the Salon of 1869 that its members "no longer dare reject" Manet.[52]

1 On the Salon in the 1860s, see Jane Mayo Roos, *Early Impressionism and the French State (1866–1874)* (New York, Cambridge University Press, 1996), 33–48.
2 John House, "Face to Face with *Le déjeuner* and *Un bar aux Folies-Bergère*," in James Cuno and Joachim Kaak (eds.), *Manet Face to Face* [exhibition catalogue], London, Courtauld Institute of Art and Munich Pinakothek-Dumont, 2004–5, 62.
3 On Manet's paintings of Victorine Meurent, see Carol Armstrong, *Manet Manette* (New Haven and London, Yale University Press, 2002), 135–72.
4 Cited in Armstrong 2002, 137.
5 On this work see Paris and New York 1994, 400.
6 Proust 1988, 28.
7 Cited in Armstrong 2002, 137.
8 Paris and New York 1983, 106–108.
9 On the display of Manet's works in 1863, see Juliet Wilson-Bareau, "The Salon des Refusés of 1863: A New View," *The Burlington Magazine* 145, 1250 (May 2007): 309–19.
10 Alan Krell, "Manet's *Déjeuner sur l'herbe* in the *Salon des Refusés*: A Re-appraisal," *The Art Bulletin*, vol. 65, 2 (June 1983), 318.
11 Maxime Du Camp, cited in George Heard Hamilton, *Manet and His Critics* (New Haven, Yale University Press, 1954), 42–43.
12 Proust 1988, 30.
13 Krell 1983, 319.
14 Ernest Chesneau, cited in Krell 1983, 317.
15 Hamilton 1954, 44.
16 Krell 1983, 318.
17 Castagnary, cited in Paris and New York 1983, 166.
18 Paris and New York 1983, 192.
19 Carol M. Armstrong, "Manet at the Intersection of Portraits and Personalities," in Toledo and London 2012–13, 42–49.
20 On Manet's sources, see Armstrong 2012, 48, and Paris and New York 1983, 113.
21 James Fairhead, "Victorine Meurent: New Evidence from America and Paris," in *The Burlington Magazine*, 165 (August 2023): 817–27.
22 Cited in Krell 1983, 320.
23 Paris and New York 1994, 403.
24 Anecdote as told by Auguste Renoir, cited in Henri Loyrette, "History Painting," in Paris and New York 1994, 47.
25 On this work, see Juliet Wilson-Bareau in Groom and Westerby 2019, cat. 5.
26 Paris and New York 1983, 199.
27 On the model Laure, see Denise Murrell, *Posing Modernity: The Black Model from Manet and Matisse to Today* (New Haven and London, Yale University Press, 2018), 53–70.
28 T. J. Clark, *The Painting of Modern Life, Paris in the Art of Manet and His Followers* (Princeton, Princeton University Press, 1984), 139.
29 Hamilton 1954, 73.
30 Clark 1984, 85.
31 Ibid., "Olympia's Choice," 79–146.
32 Paris and New York 1983, 180: Cachin cites Baudelaire's surprised reaction from Brussels in a letter of May 11, 1865 to Manet: "the cat (is it definitely a cat?)."
33 Juliet Wilson-Bareau, ed., *Manet by Himself* (London, Macdonald & Co Ltd., 1991), 33.
34 Paris and New York 2003, 392.
35 Paris and New York 1983, 246.
36 Ibid., 243.
37 Paris and New York 1994, 408.
38 Ibid., 409.
39 Marius Chaumelin, cited in Paris and New York 1983, 256.
40 Paris and New York 1994, 409.
41 Ibid., 413.
42 Émile Zola, "My portrait by Édouard Manet: memories of the sitting," *L'Événement Illustré*, May 10, 1868, reproduced in *Looking at Manet, Émile Zola* (Los Angeles, J. Paul Getty Museum, 2013), 110–11.
43 Paris and New York 1983, 282–84; Toledo and London 2012–13, 187.
44 Émile Zola, "A new way to paint: Édouard Manet," 1867, reproduced in Los Angeles 2013, 74–76.
45 Émile Zola, Los Angeles 2013, 86.
46 Paris and New York 1983, 208–9.
47 Hamilton 1954, 138.
48 Émile Zola, Los Angeles 2013, 53–54
49 Paris and New York 1983, 294.
50 Ibid., 294.
51 Hamilton 1954, 134–35.
52 Stéphane Guégan (ed.), *Manet: The Man Who Invented Modernity* [exhibition catalogue], Paris, Musée d'Orsay, 2011, 38.

29

Victorine Meurent

ca. 1862
Oil on canvas, 16 ⅞ × 17 ¼ in.
(42.9 × 43.8 cm)
Boston, Museum of Fine Arts, Gift of Richard C. Paine in memory of his father, Robert Treat Paine II, 46.846

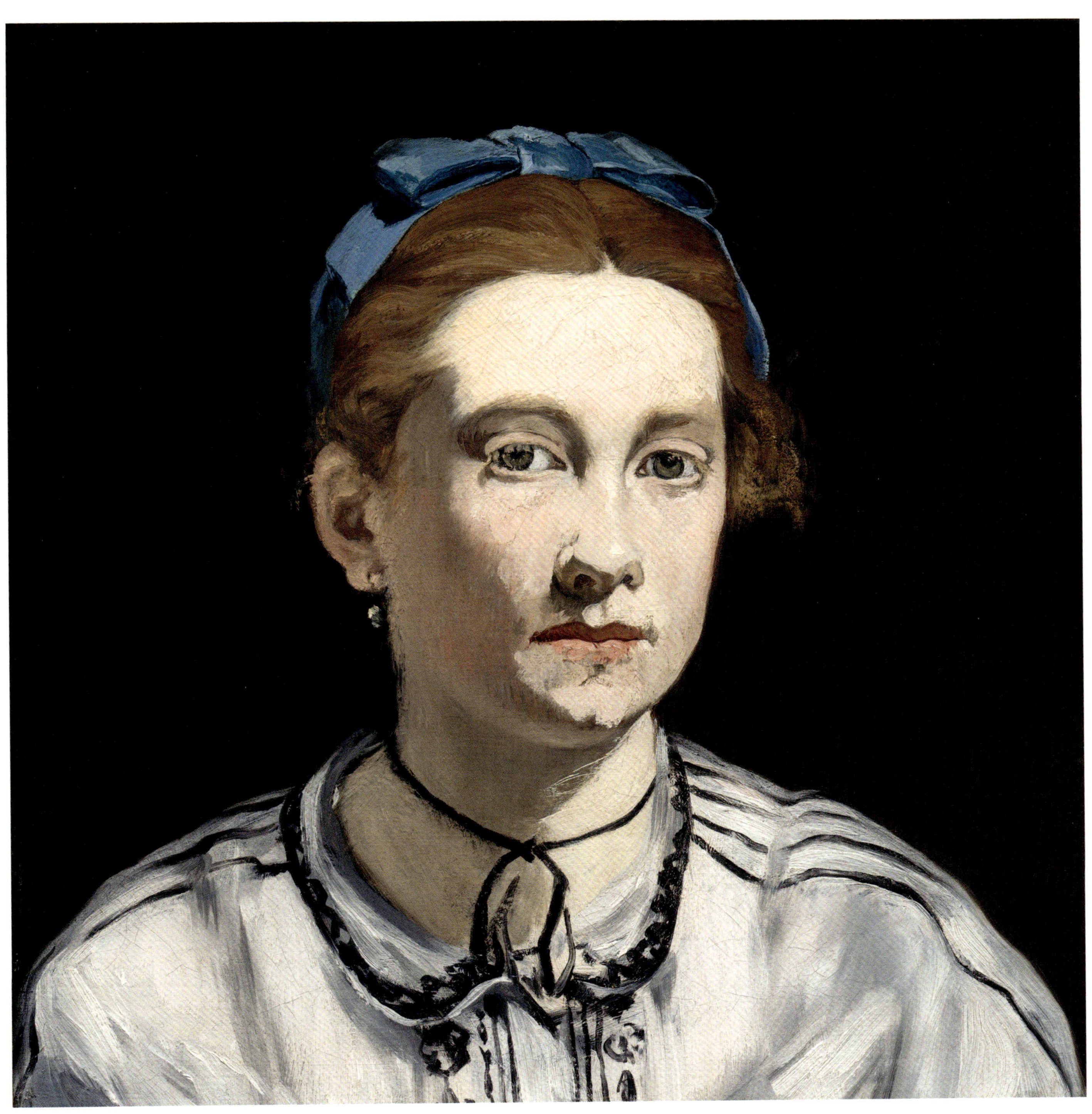

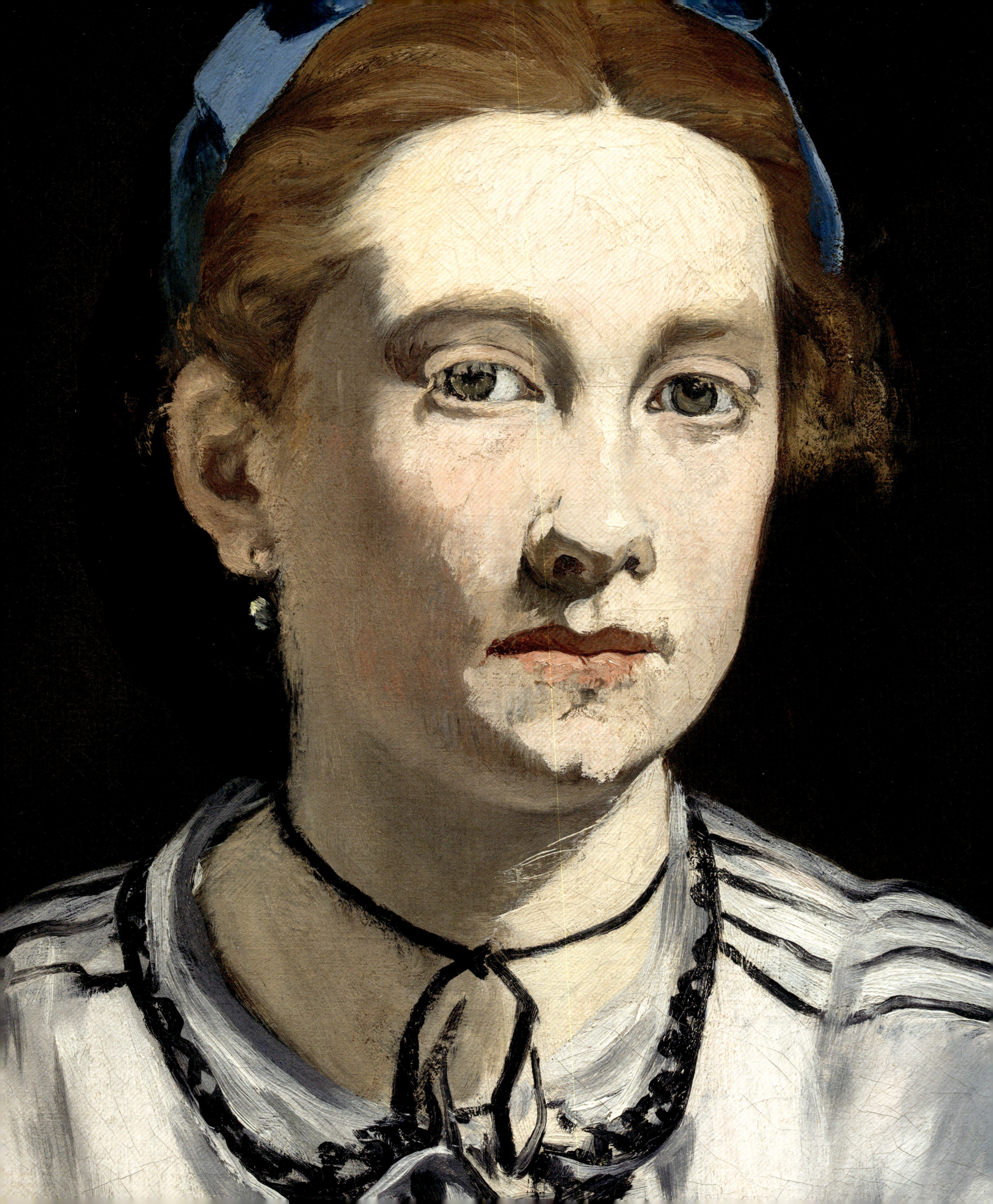

30

The Street Singer

ca. 1862
Oil on canvas, 67 ⅜ × 41 ⅝ in.
(171.1 × 105.8 cm)
Boston, Museum of Fine Arts, Bequest of Sarah Choate Sears in memory of her husband, Joshua Montgomery Sears, 66.304

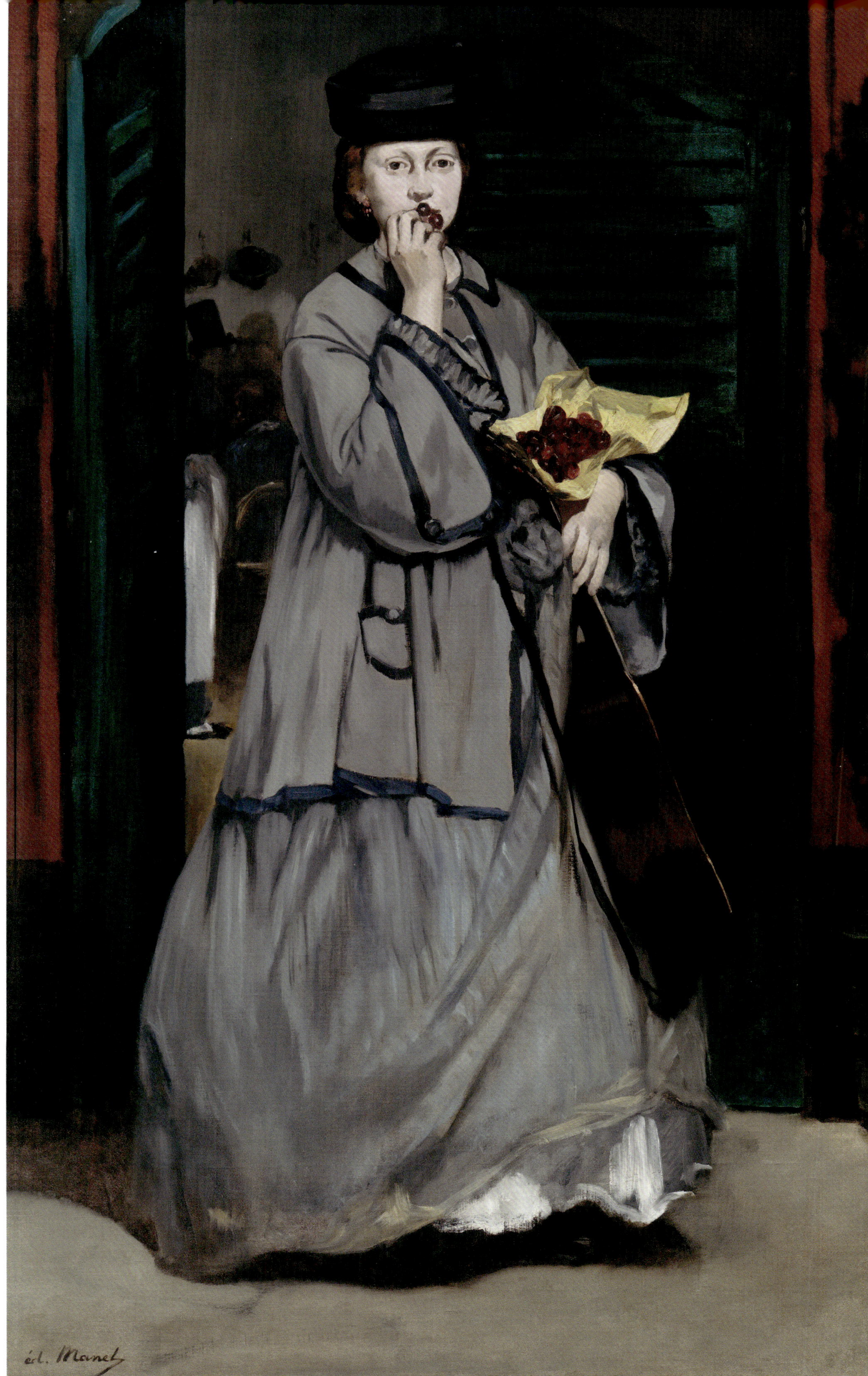

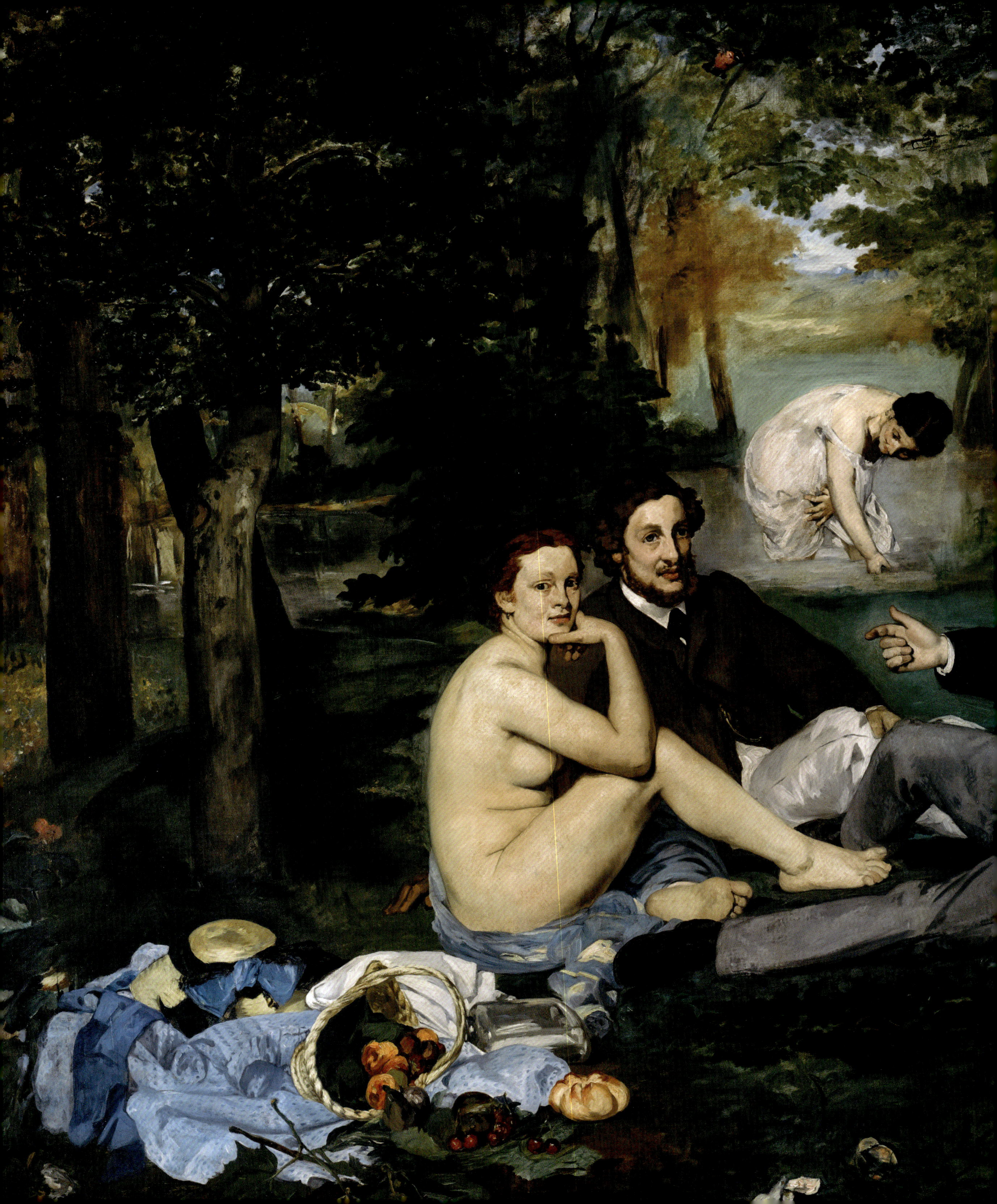

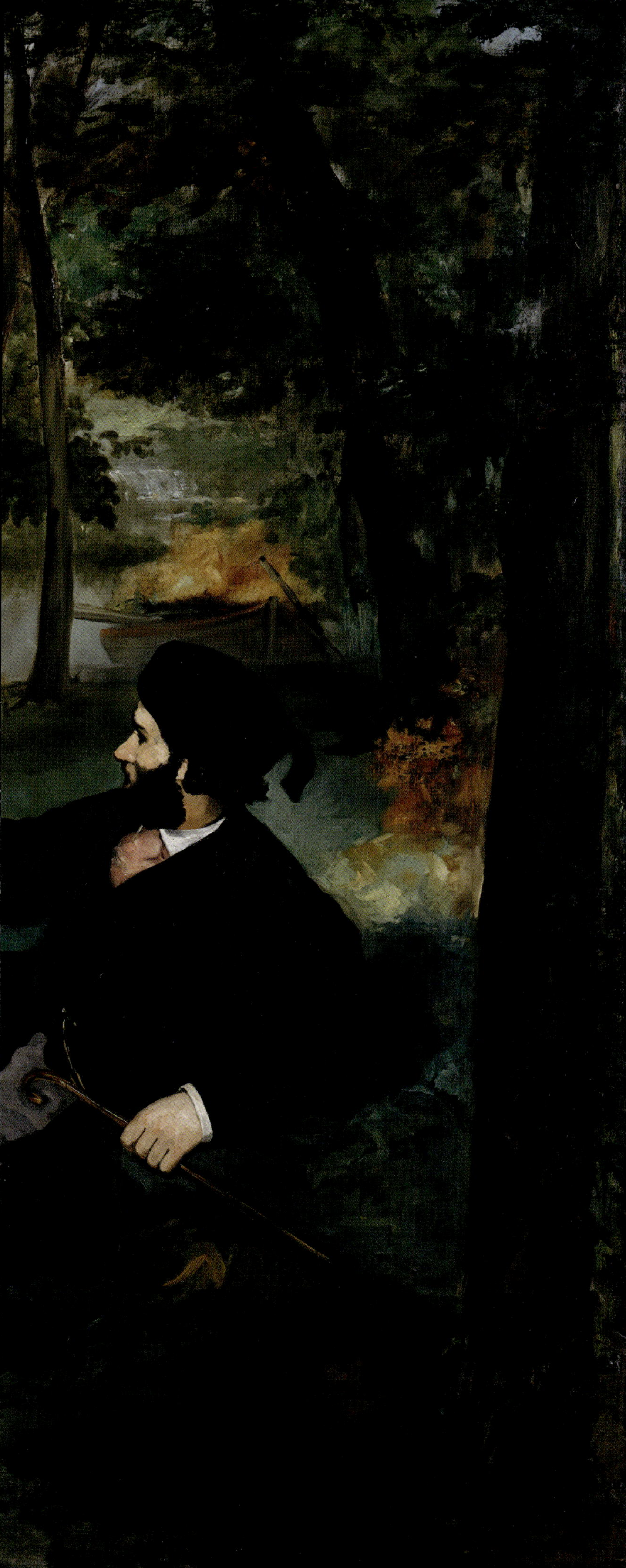

31

Luncheon on the Grass

1863
Oil on canvas,
81 ⅕ × 104 ⅓ in.
(207 × 265 cm)
Paris, Musée d'Orsay, RF1668

FOLLOWING PAGES

32

Mademoiselle V… in the Costume of an Espada

1862
Oil on canvas, 65 × 50 ¼ in.
(165.1 × 127.6 cm)
New York, The Metropolitan Museum of Art, H. O. Havemeyer Collection, Bequest of Mrs. H. O. Havemeyer, 1929, 29.100.53

33

Young Man in the Costume of a Majo

1863
Oil on canvas, 74 × 49 ⅛ in.
(188 × 124.8 cm)
New York, The Metropolitan Museum of Art, H. O. Havemeyer Collection, Bequest of Mrs. H. O. Havemeyer, 1929, 29.100.54

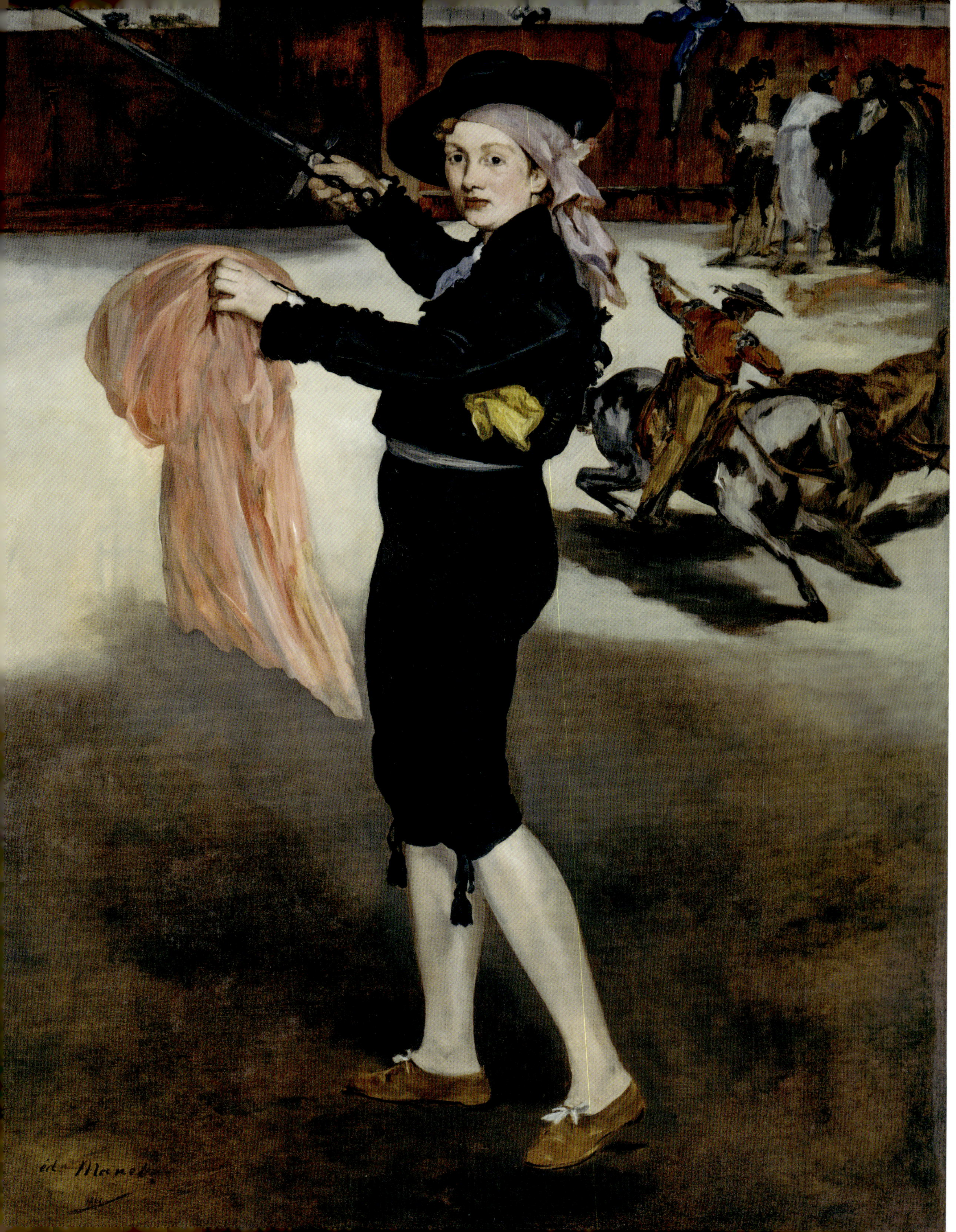

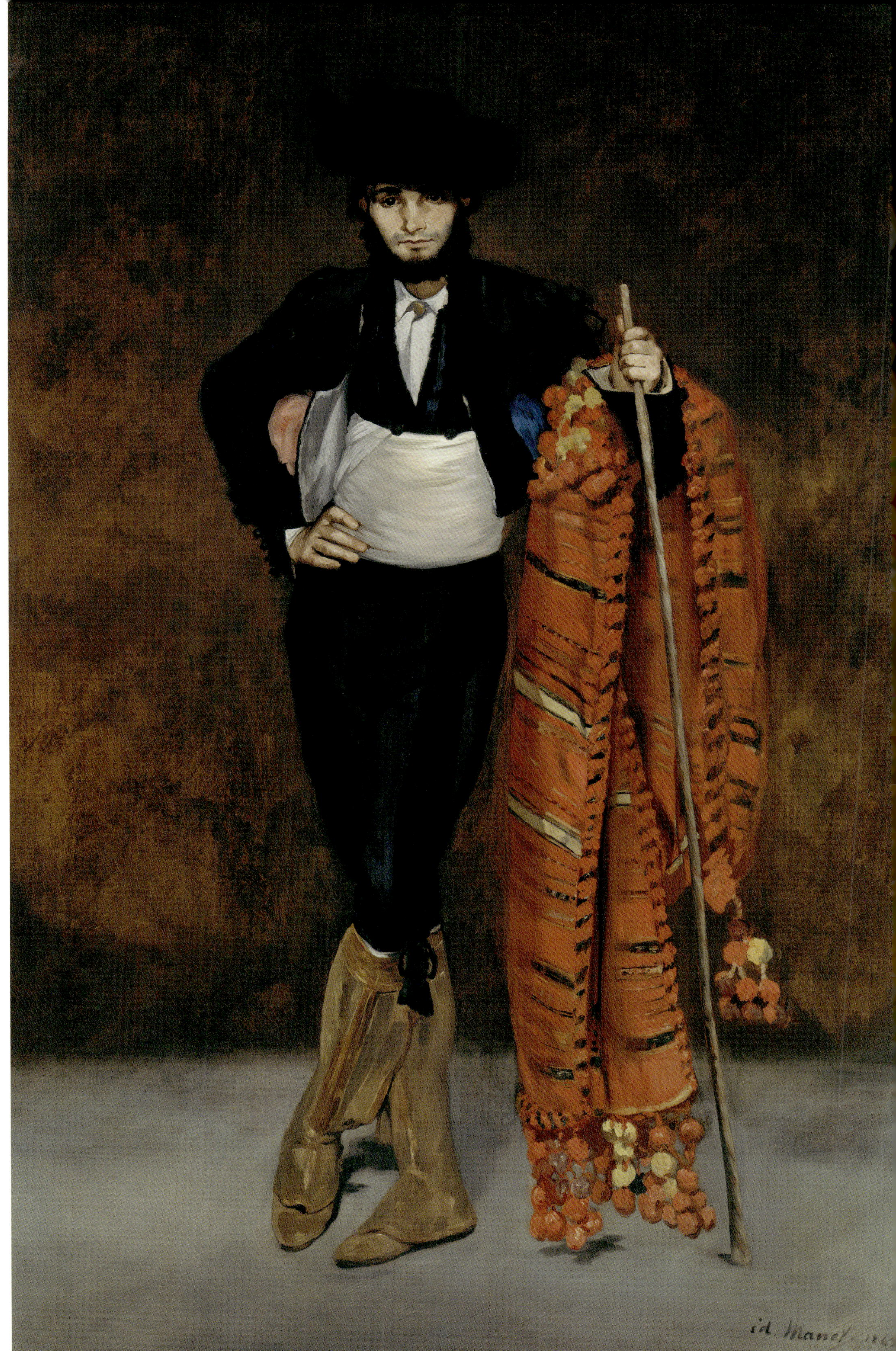
éd. Manet.

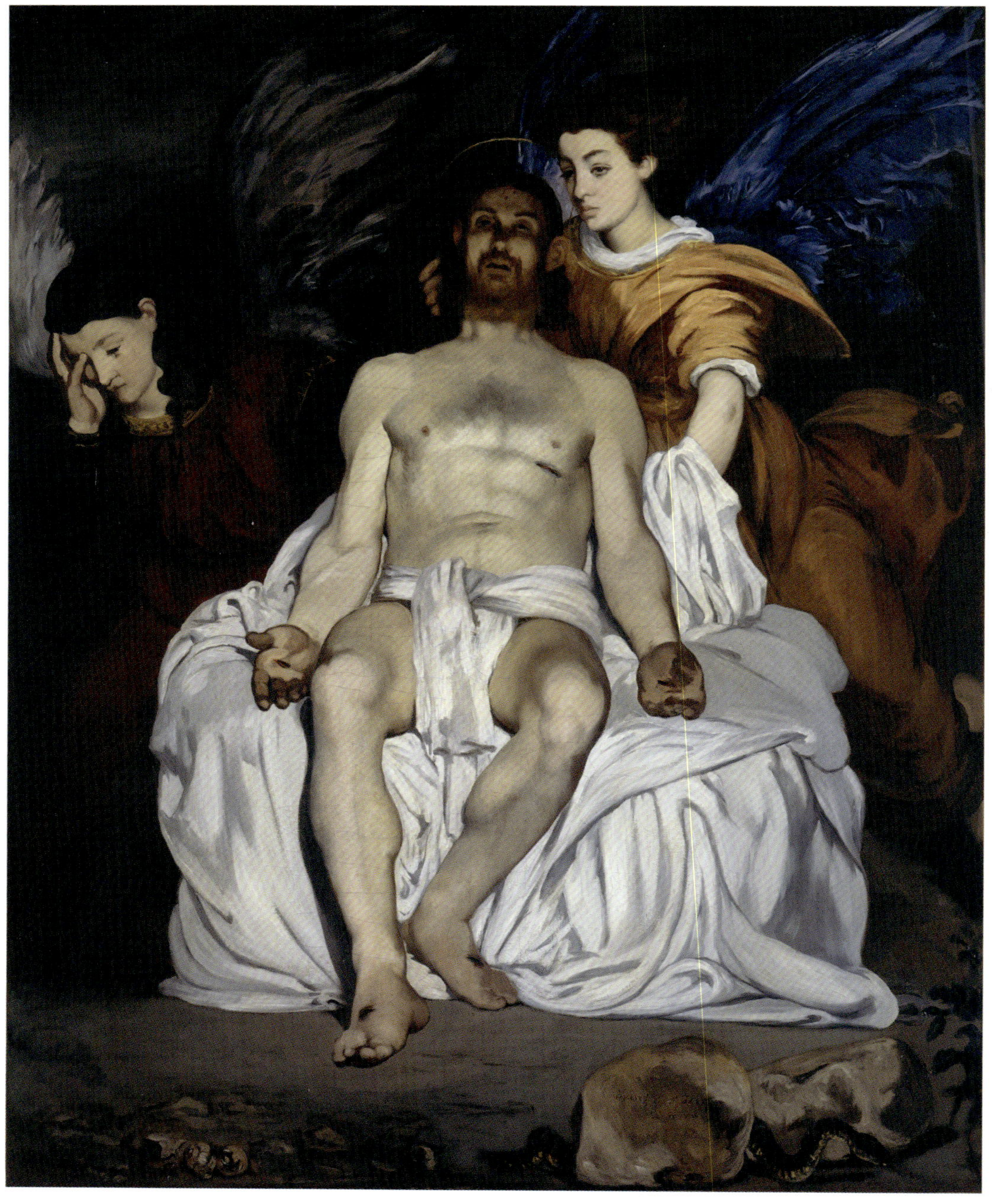

34

The Dead Christ with Angels

1864
Oil on canvas, 70 ⅝ × 59 in. (179.4 × 149.9 cm)
New York, The Metropolitan Museum of Art, H. O. Havemeyer Collection, Bequest of Mrs. H. O. Havemeyer, 1929, 29.100.51

35

Jesus Mocked by the Soldiers

1865
Oil on canvas, 74 ⅞ × 58 ⅜ in. (190.8 × 148.3 cm)
Chicago, The Art Institute of Chicago, Gift of James Deering, 1925.703

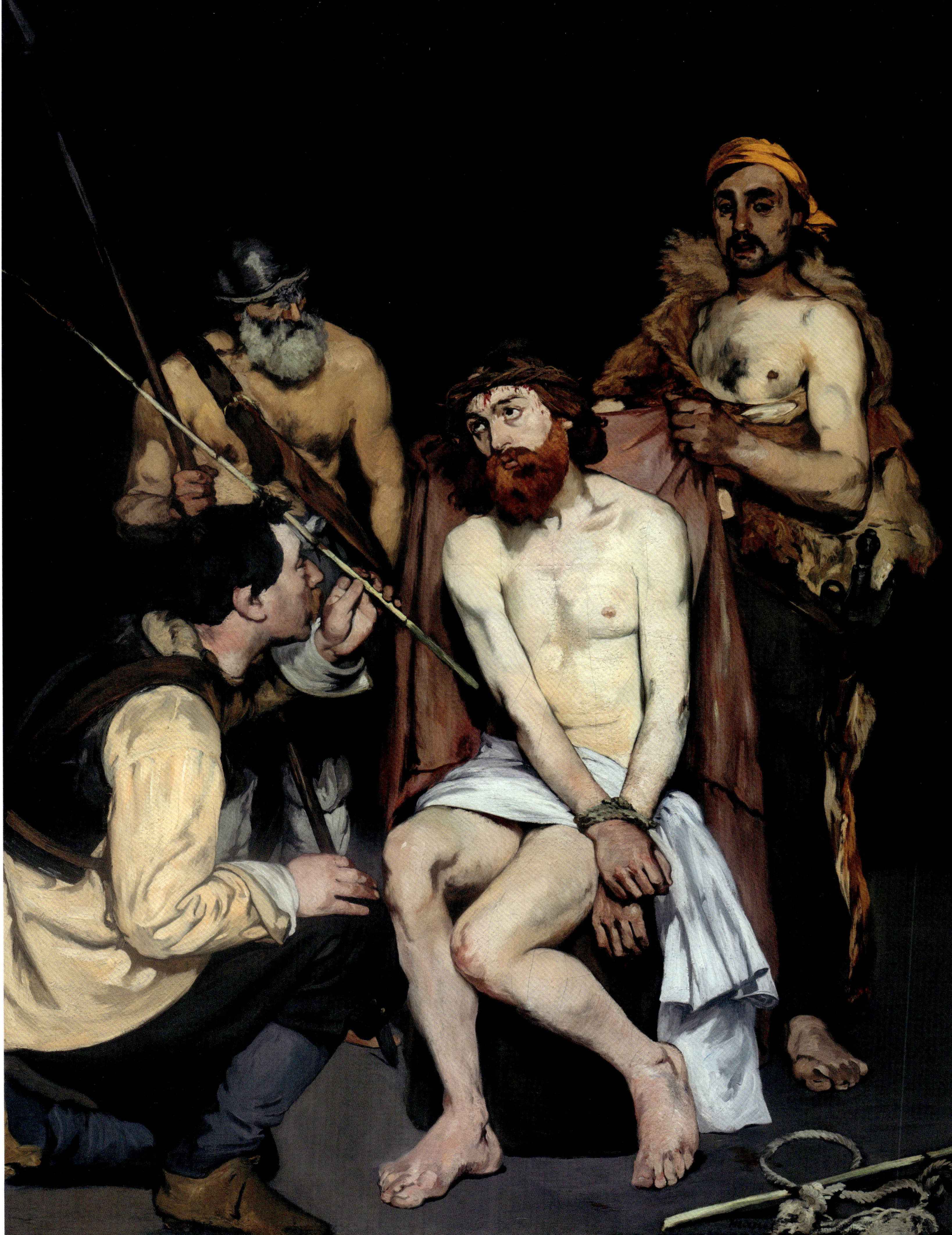

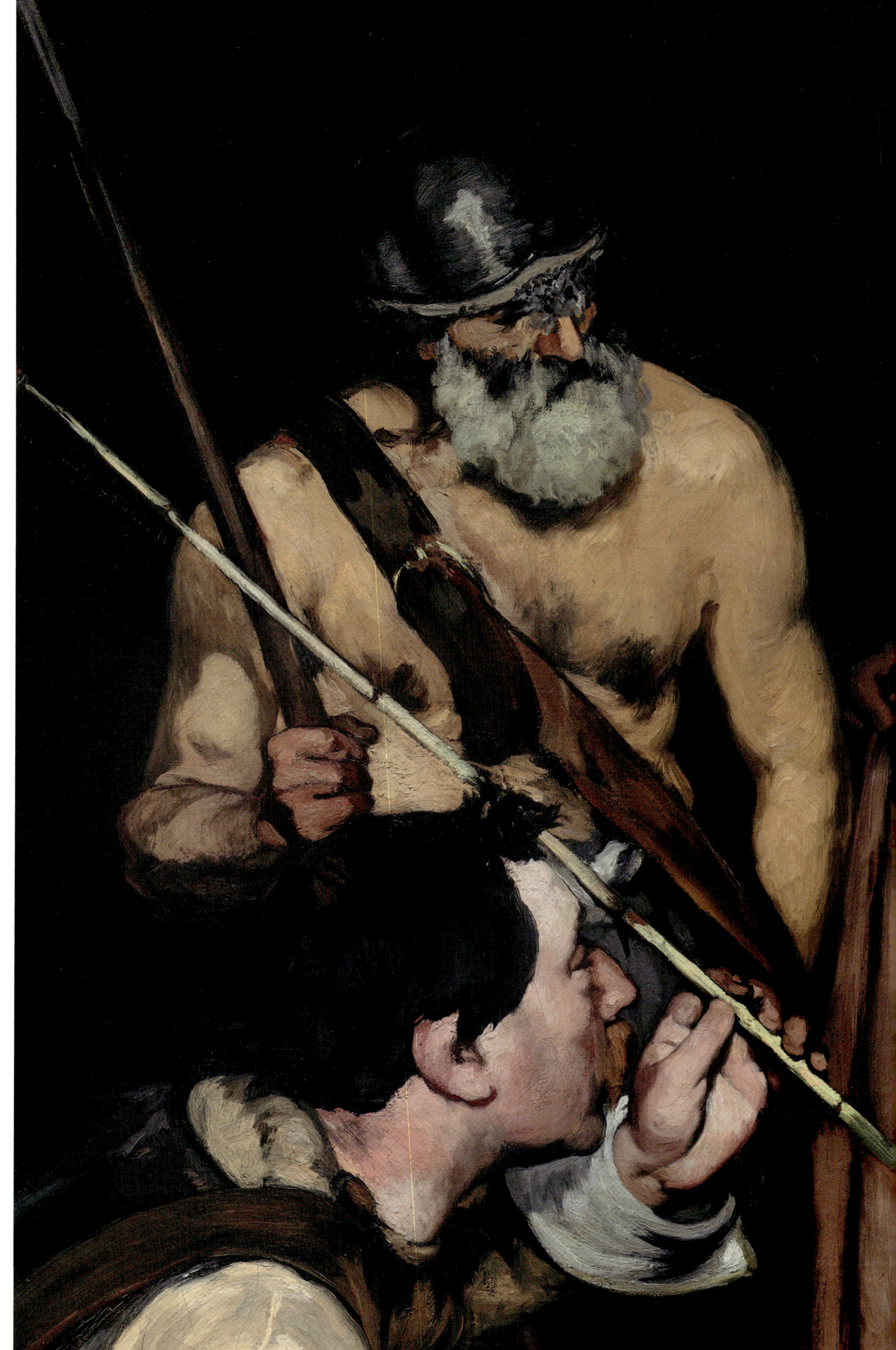

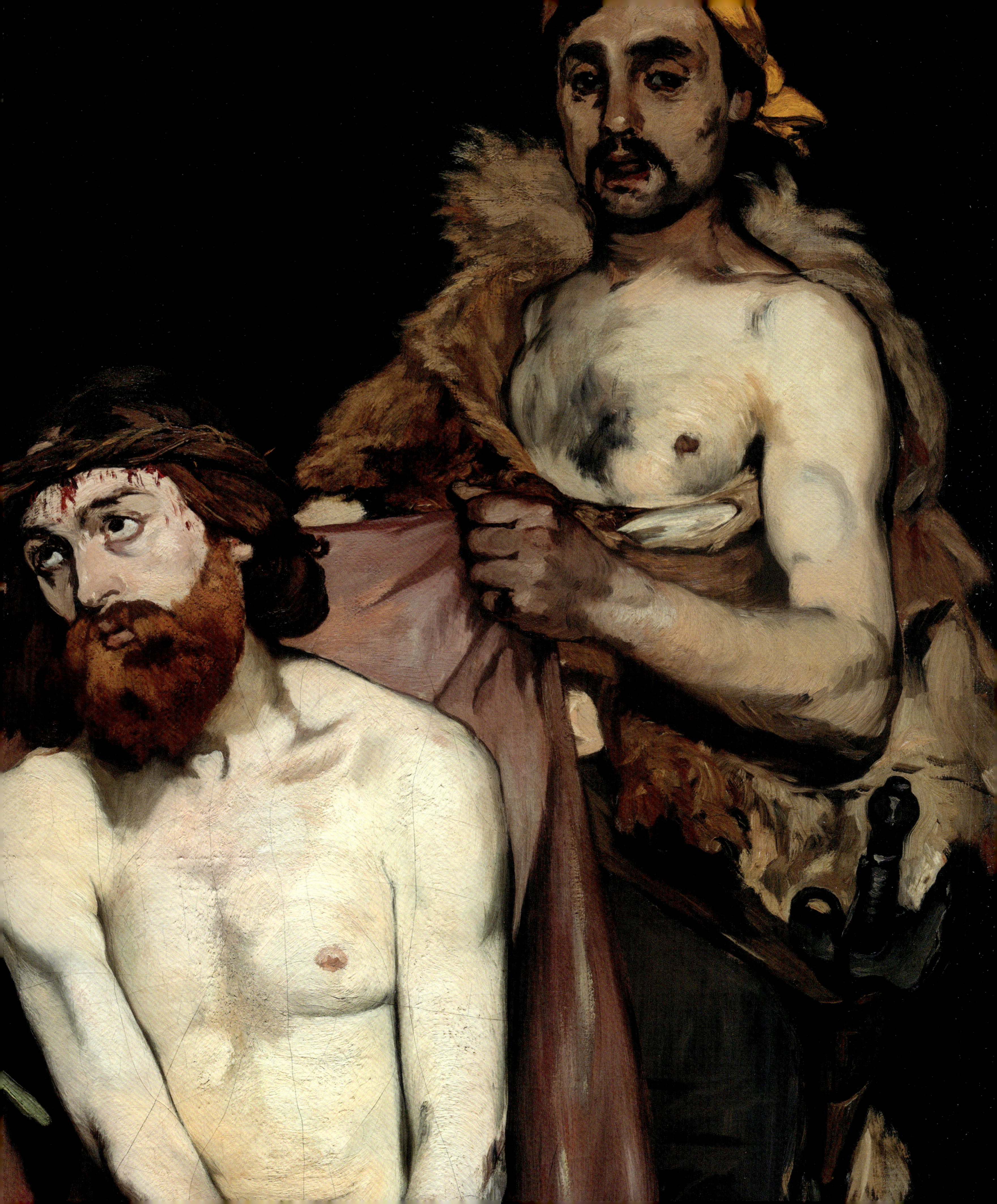

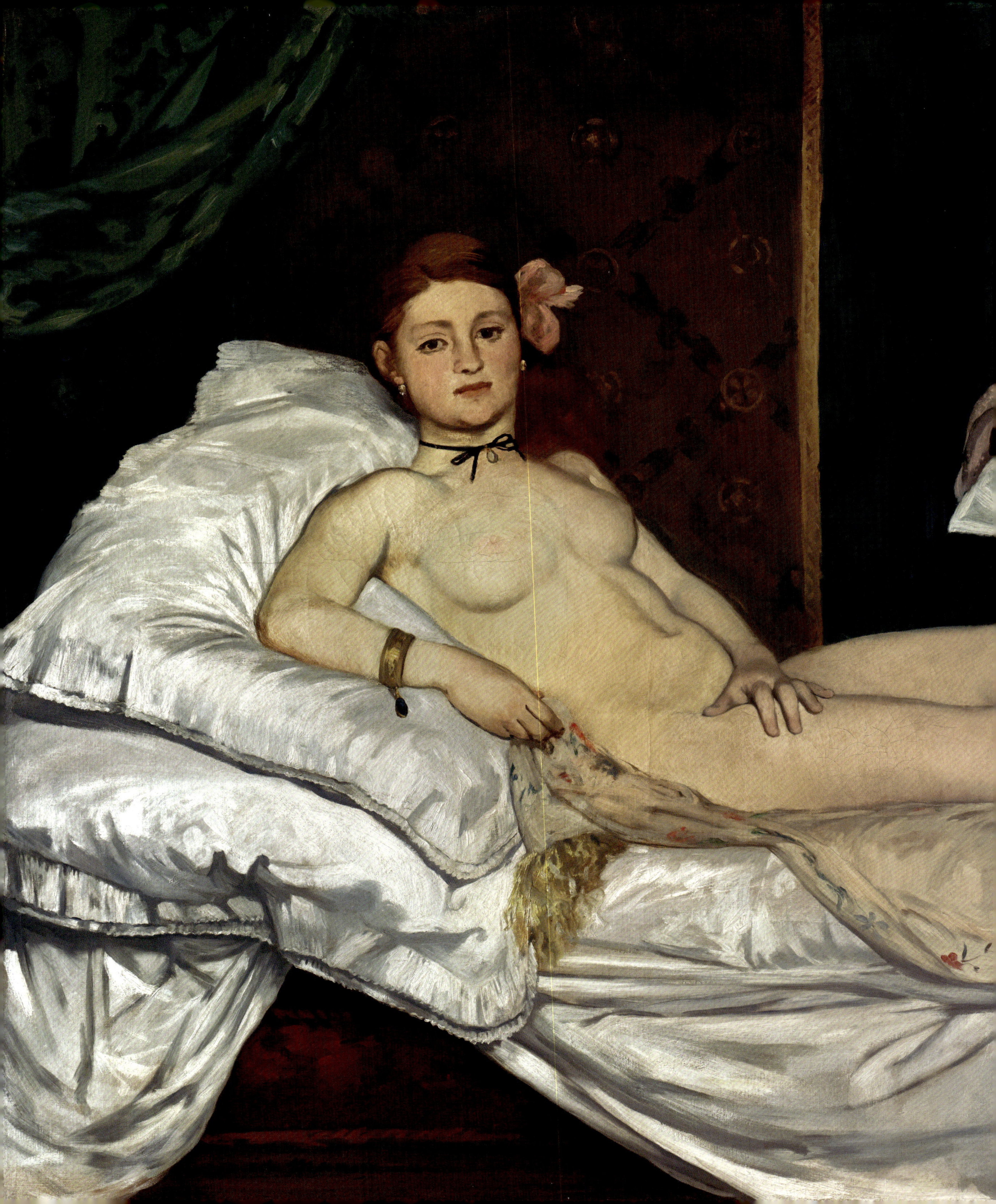

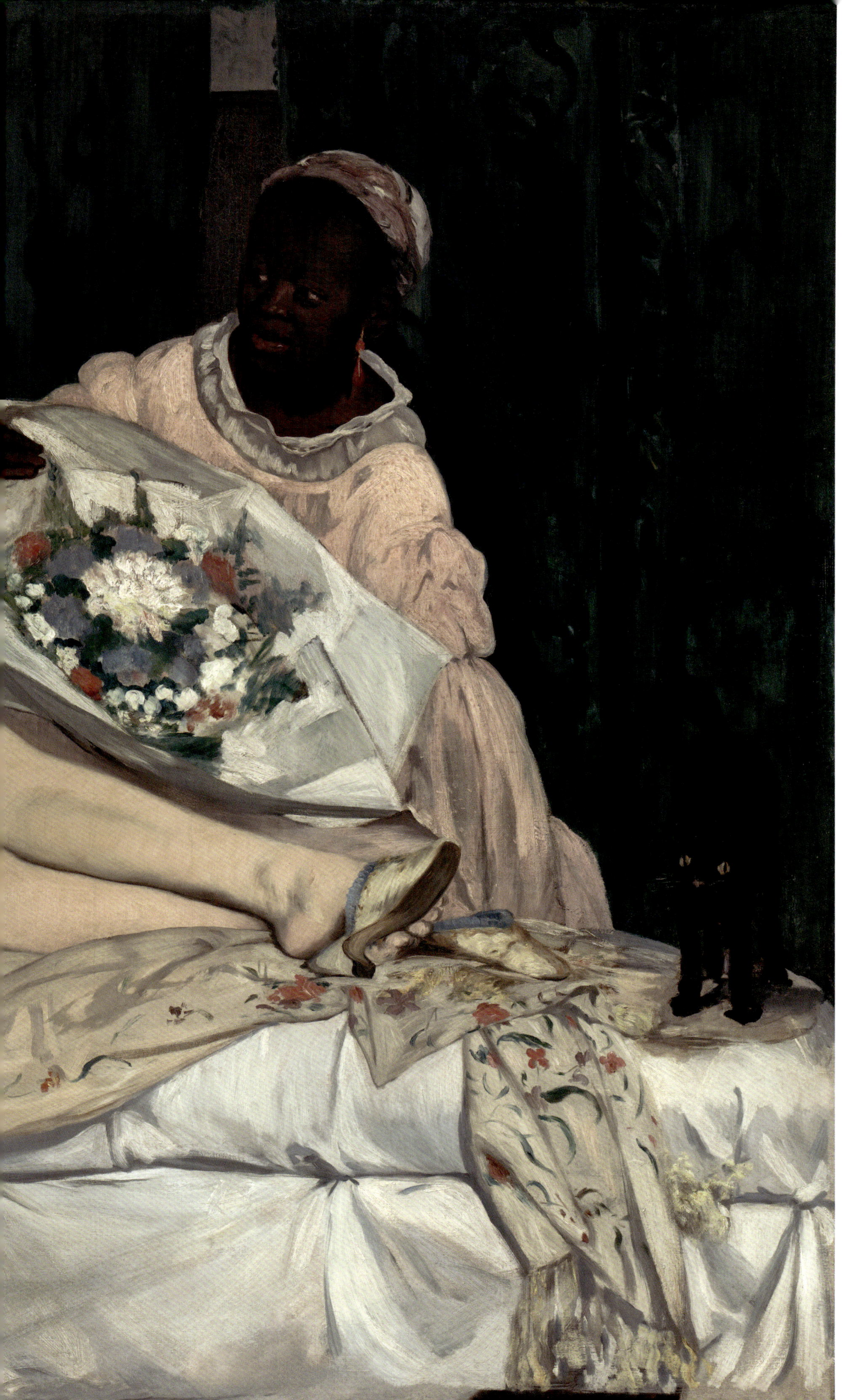

36

Olympia

1863
Oil on canvas,
40 ½ × 75 ¼ in.
(130.5 × 191 cm)
Paris, Musée d'Orsay,
RF 644

37

The Fifer

1866
Oil on canvas,
63 ¼ × 38 ¼ in.
(160.5 × 97 cm)
Paris, Musée d'Orsay,
RF 1992

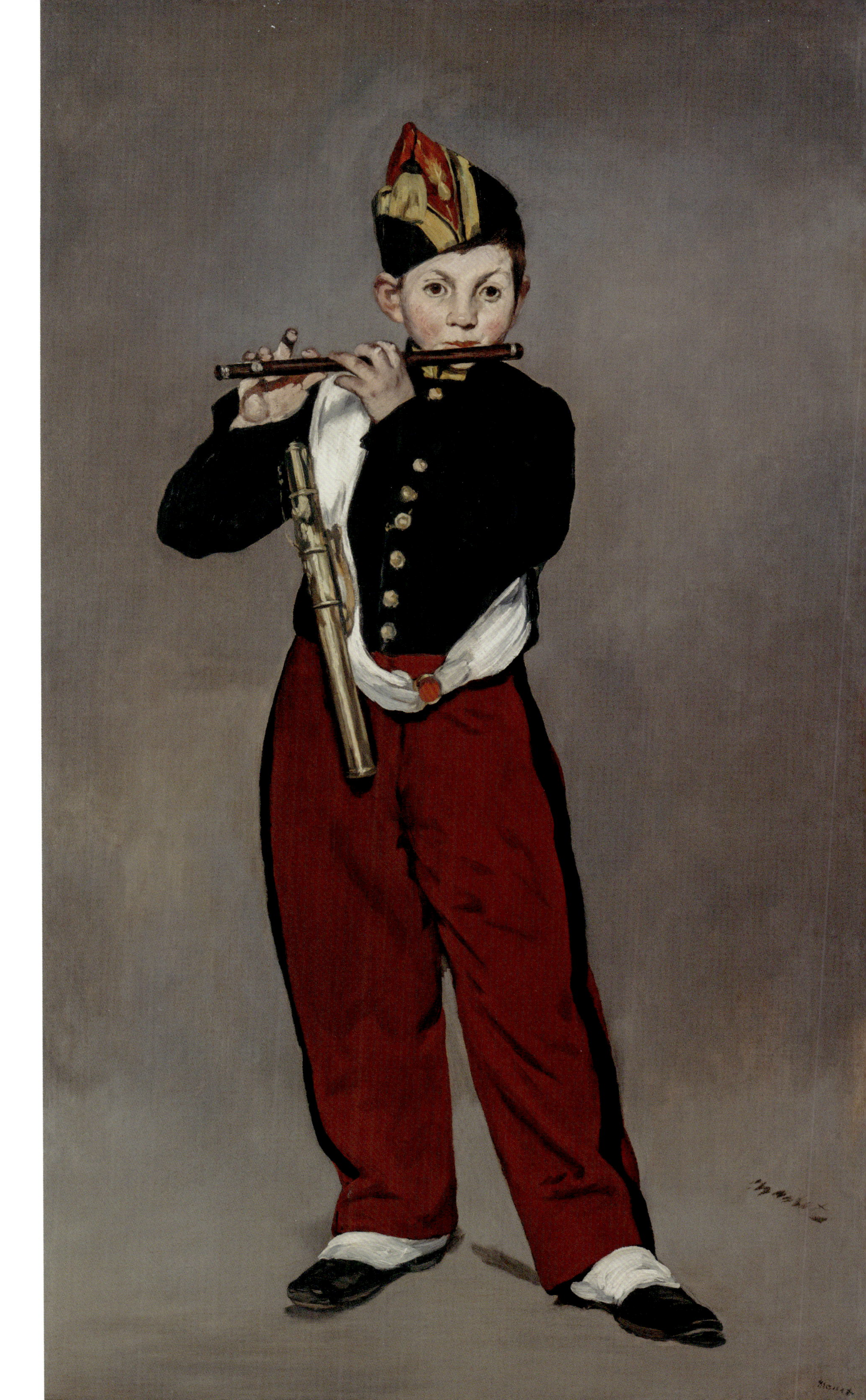

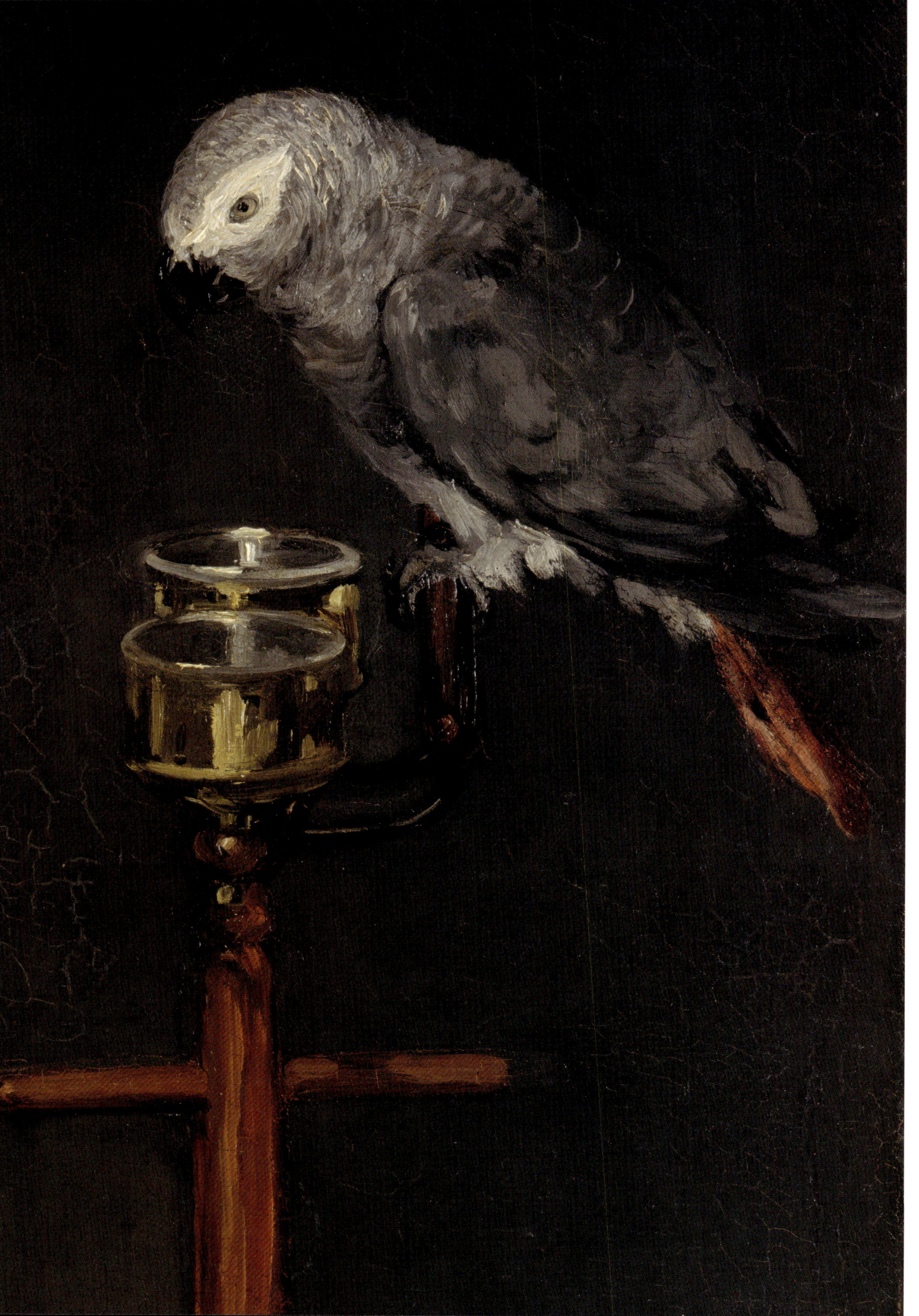

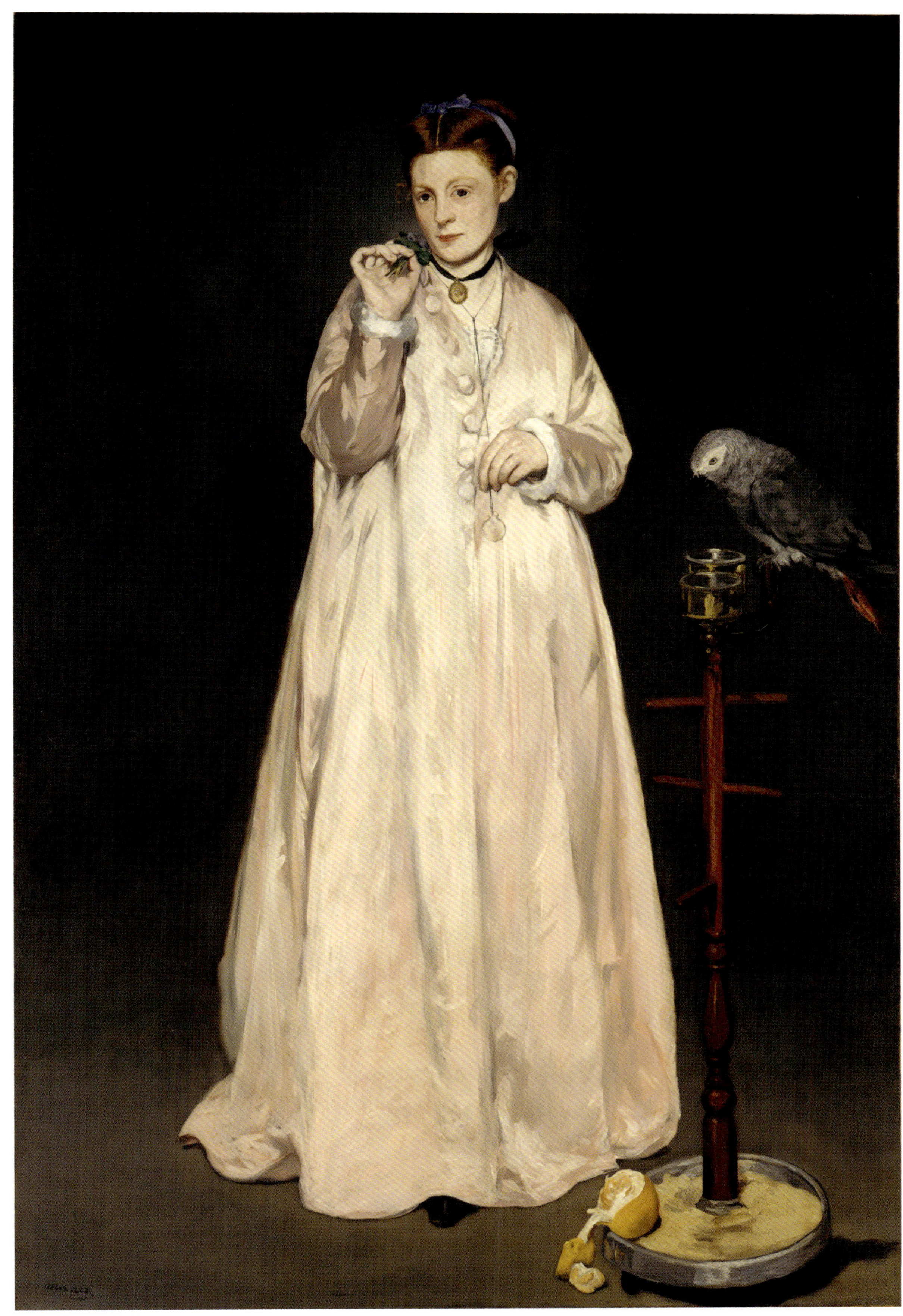

38

Young Lady in 1866

1866
Oil on canvas,
72 ⅞ × 50 ⅝ in.
(185.1 × 128.6 cm)
New York, The Metropolitan Museum of Art, Gift of Erwin Davis, 1889, 89.21.3

39

Émile Zola

1868
Oil on canvas, 57 ½ × 45 in.
(146 × 114 cm)
Paris, Musée d'Orsay,
RF 2205

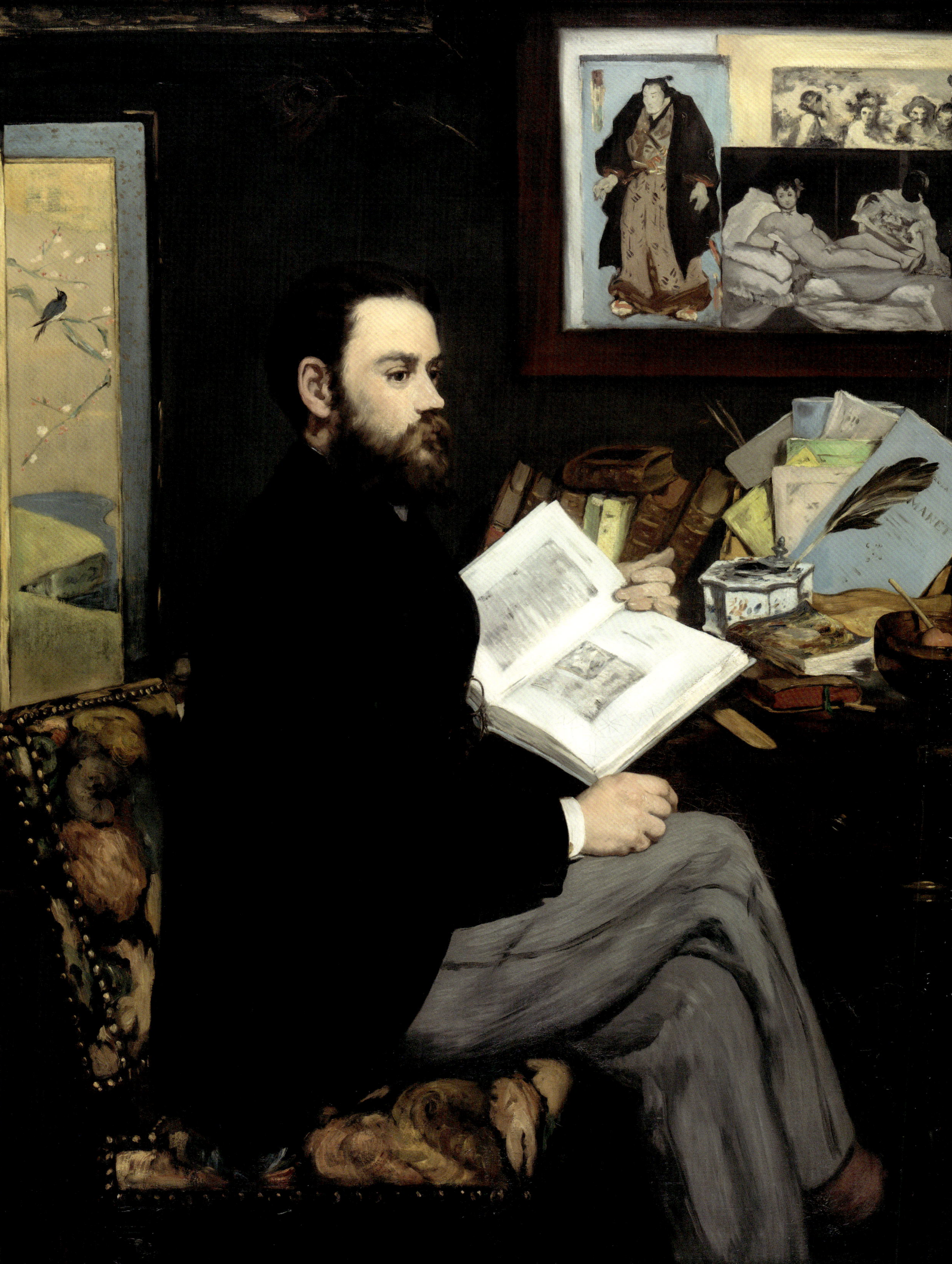

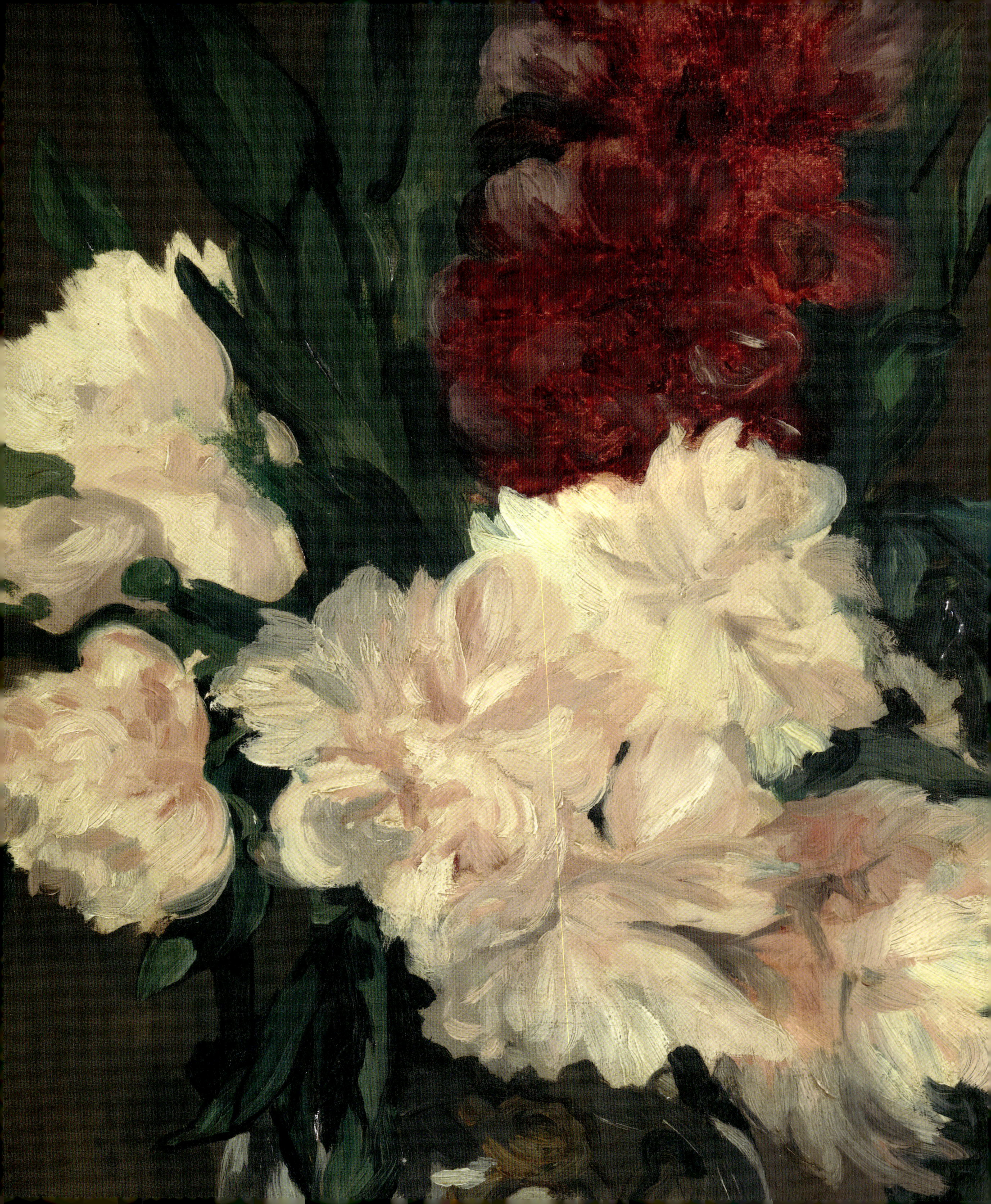

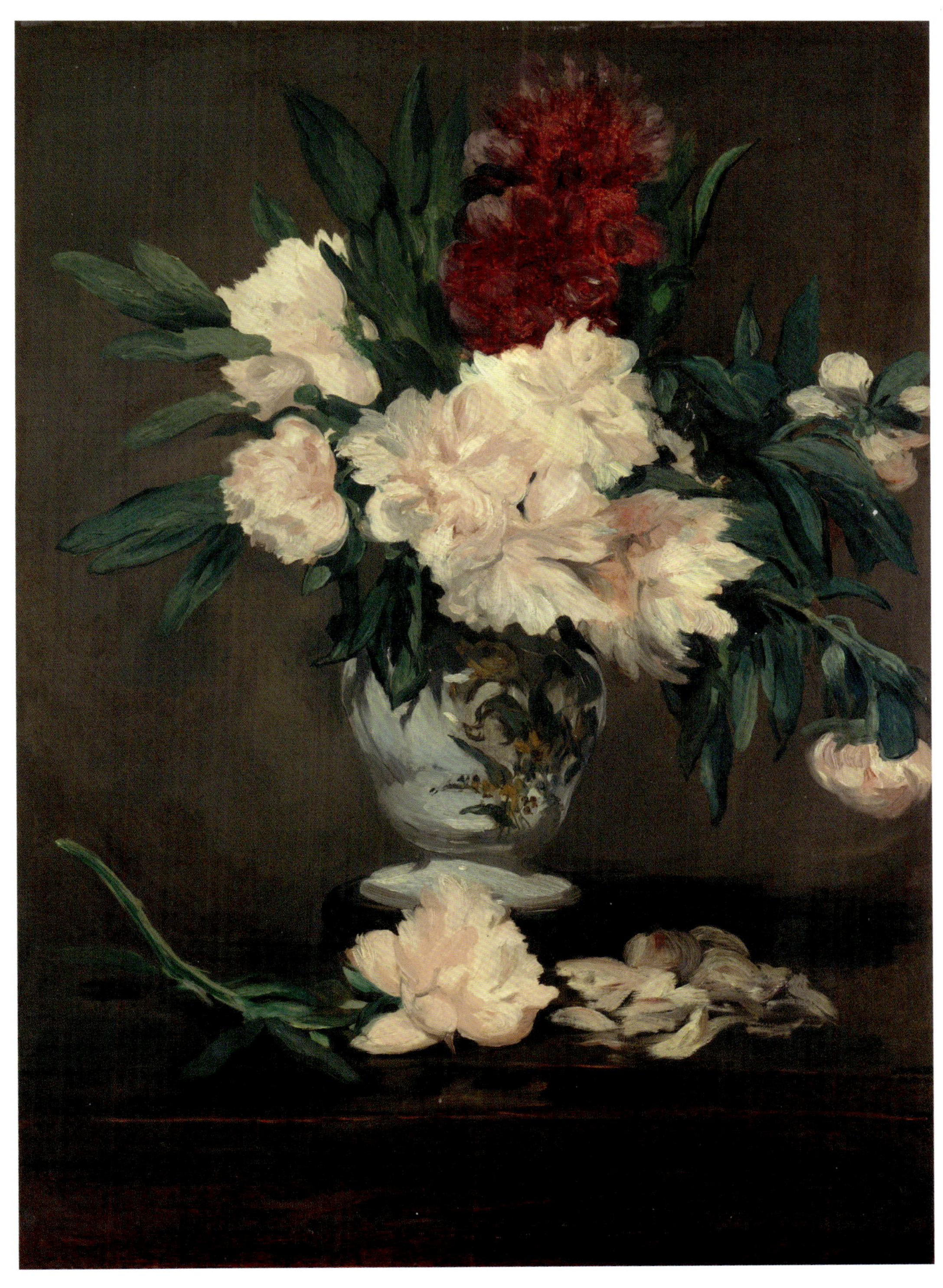

40

Peonies in a Vase on a Stand

1864
Oil on canvas, 36 ½ × 27 ⅛ in.
(93.3 × 70 cm)
Paris, Musée d'Orsay,
RF 1669

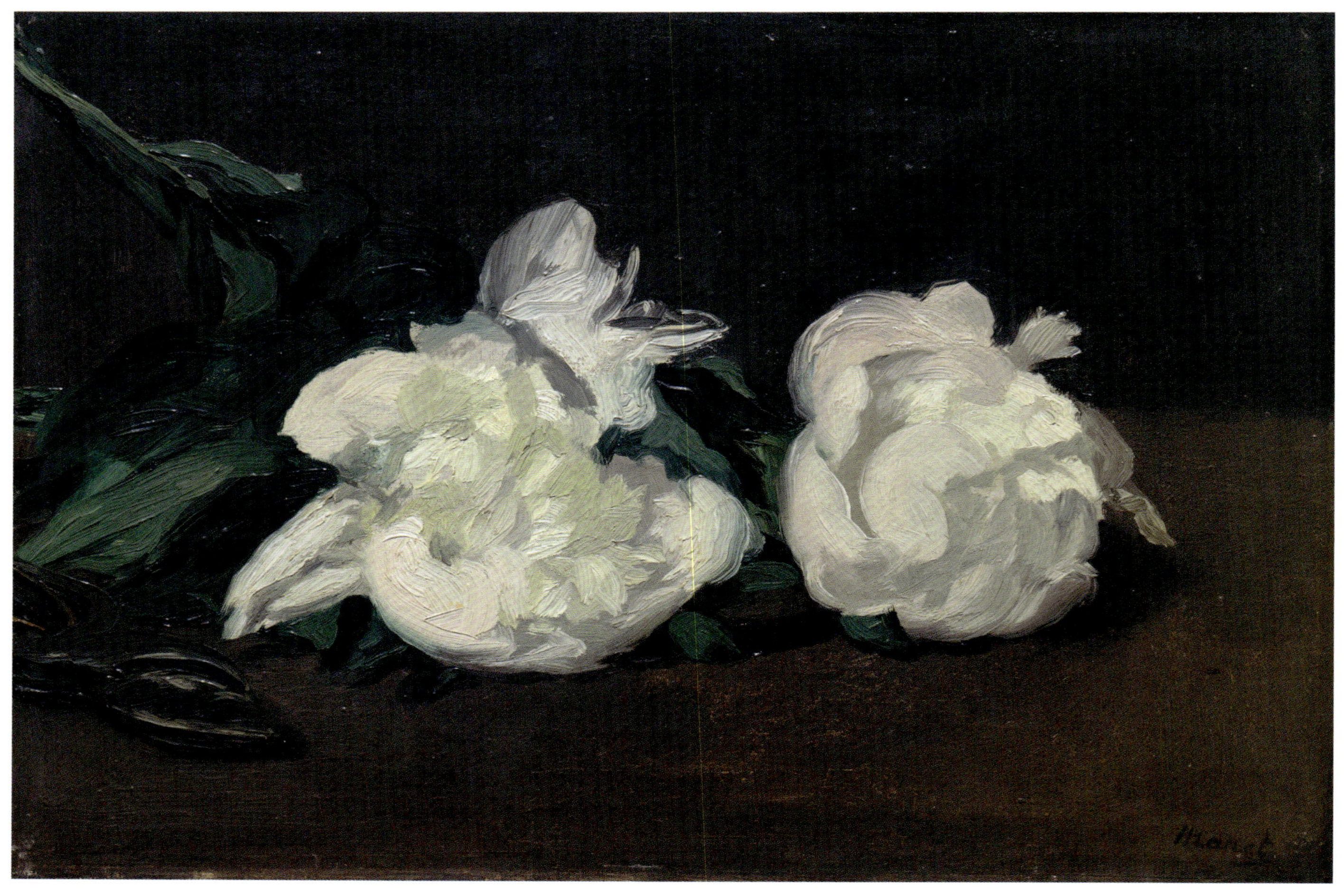

41

Bunch of White Peonies with Pruning Shears

1864
Oil on canvas, 12 × 18 ⅓ in.
(30.5 × 46.5 cm)
Paris, Musée d'Orsay, RF 1995

42

Still Life with Fish

1864
Oil on canvas, 28 15/16 × 36 ⅜ in.
(73.5 × 92.4 cm)
Chicago, The Art Institute of Chicago, Mr. and Mrs. Lewis Larned Coburn Memorial Collection, 1942.311

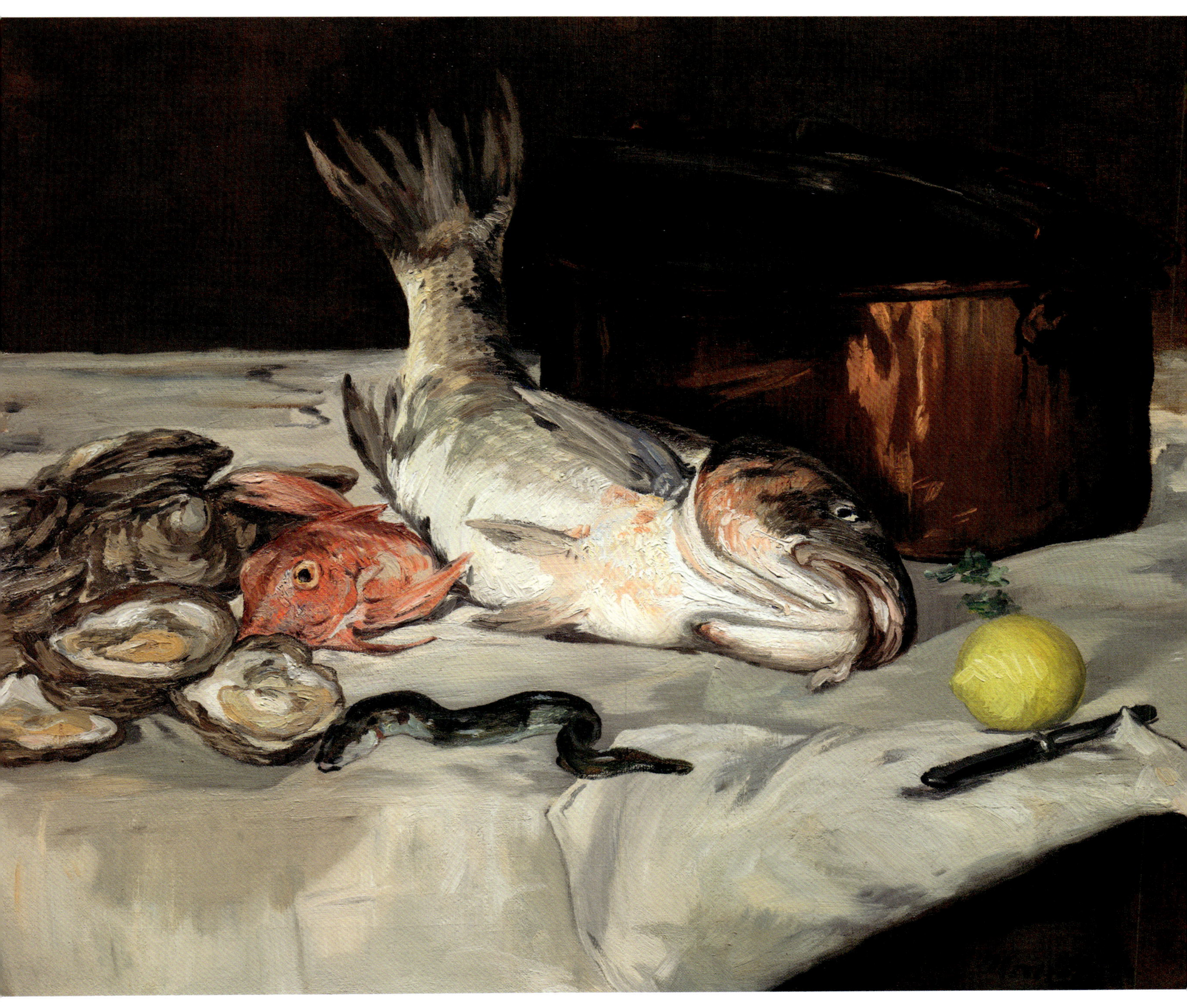

43

Luncheon in the Studio

1868
Oil on canvas, 46 ⅓ × 60 ⅔ in.
(118.3 × 154 cm)
Munich, Bayerische Staatsgemäldesammlungen – Neue Pinakothek München, 8638

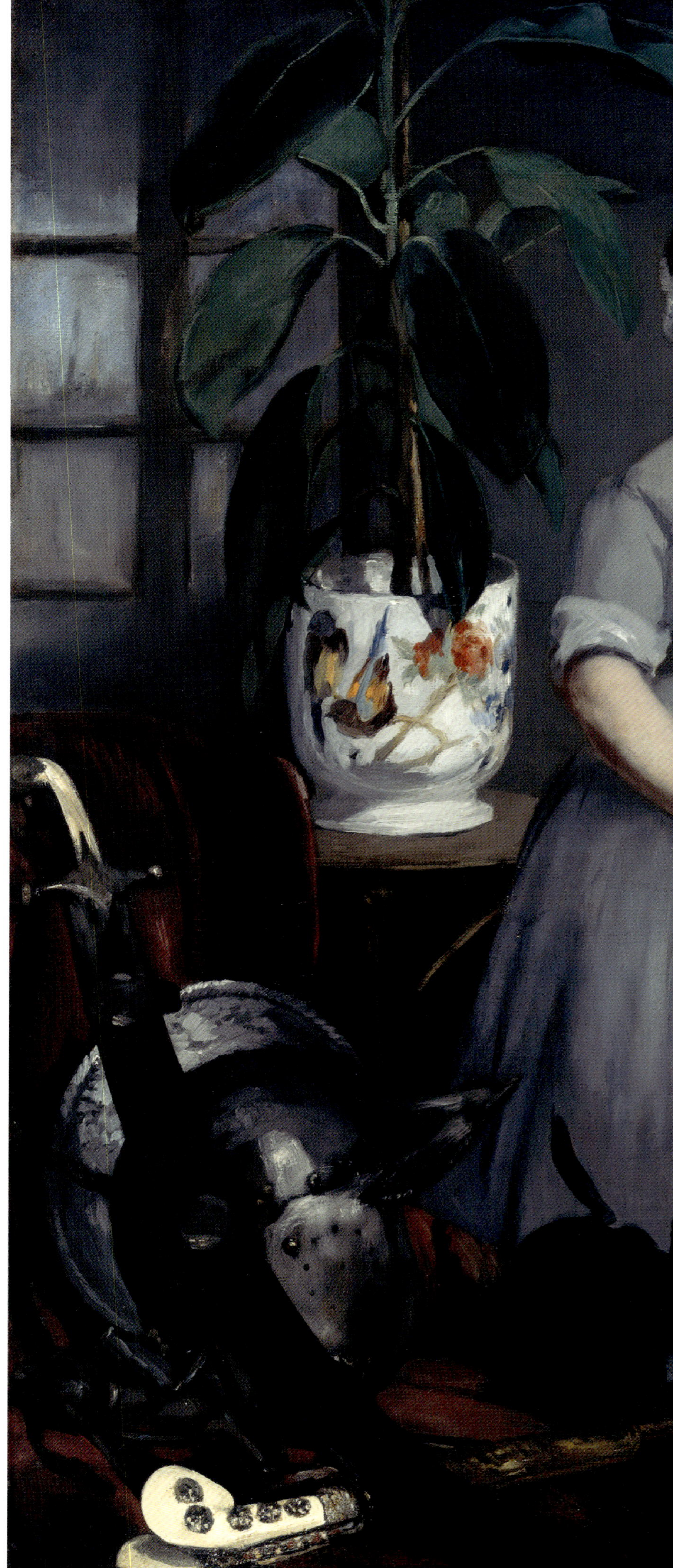

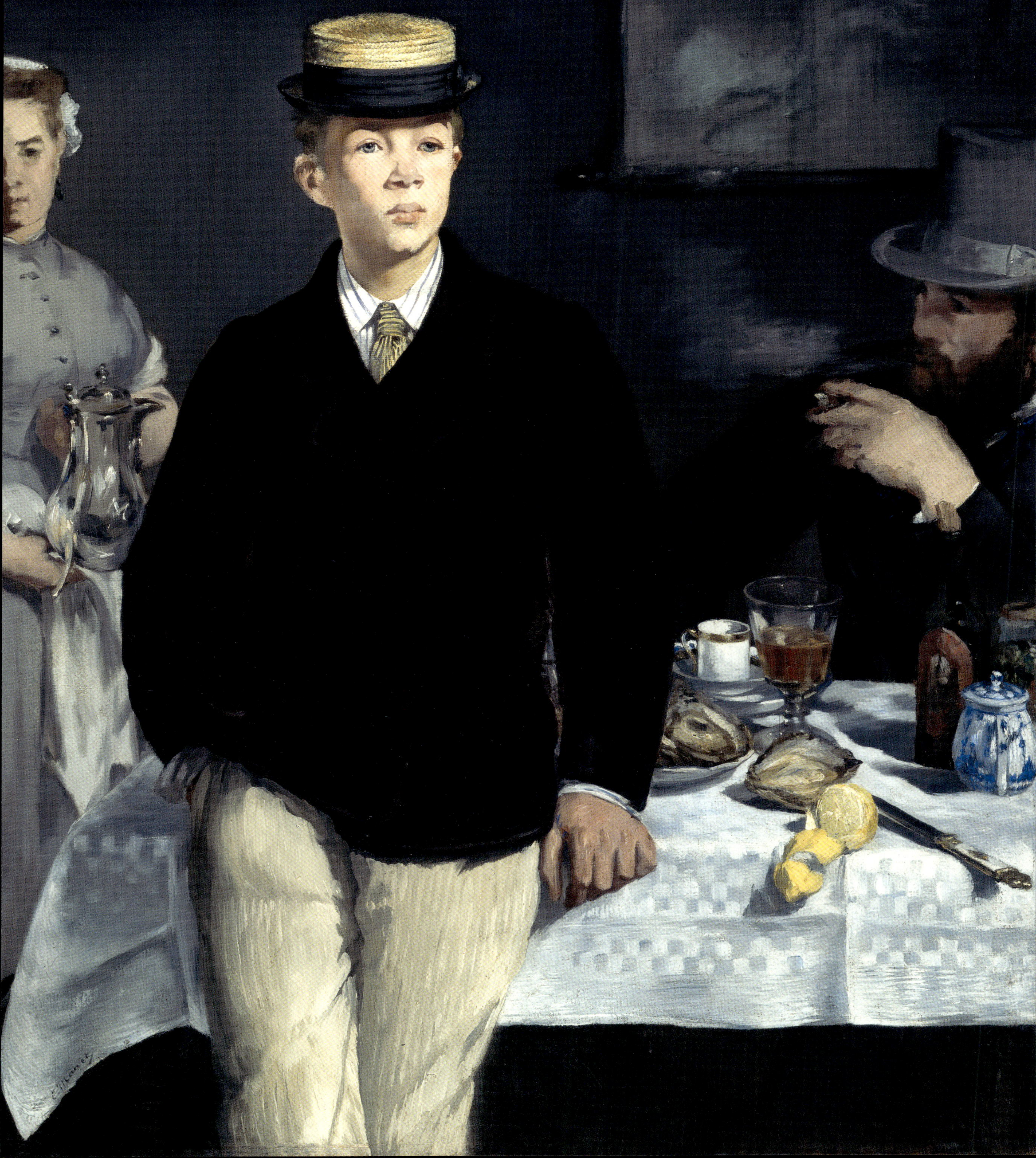

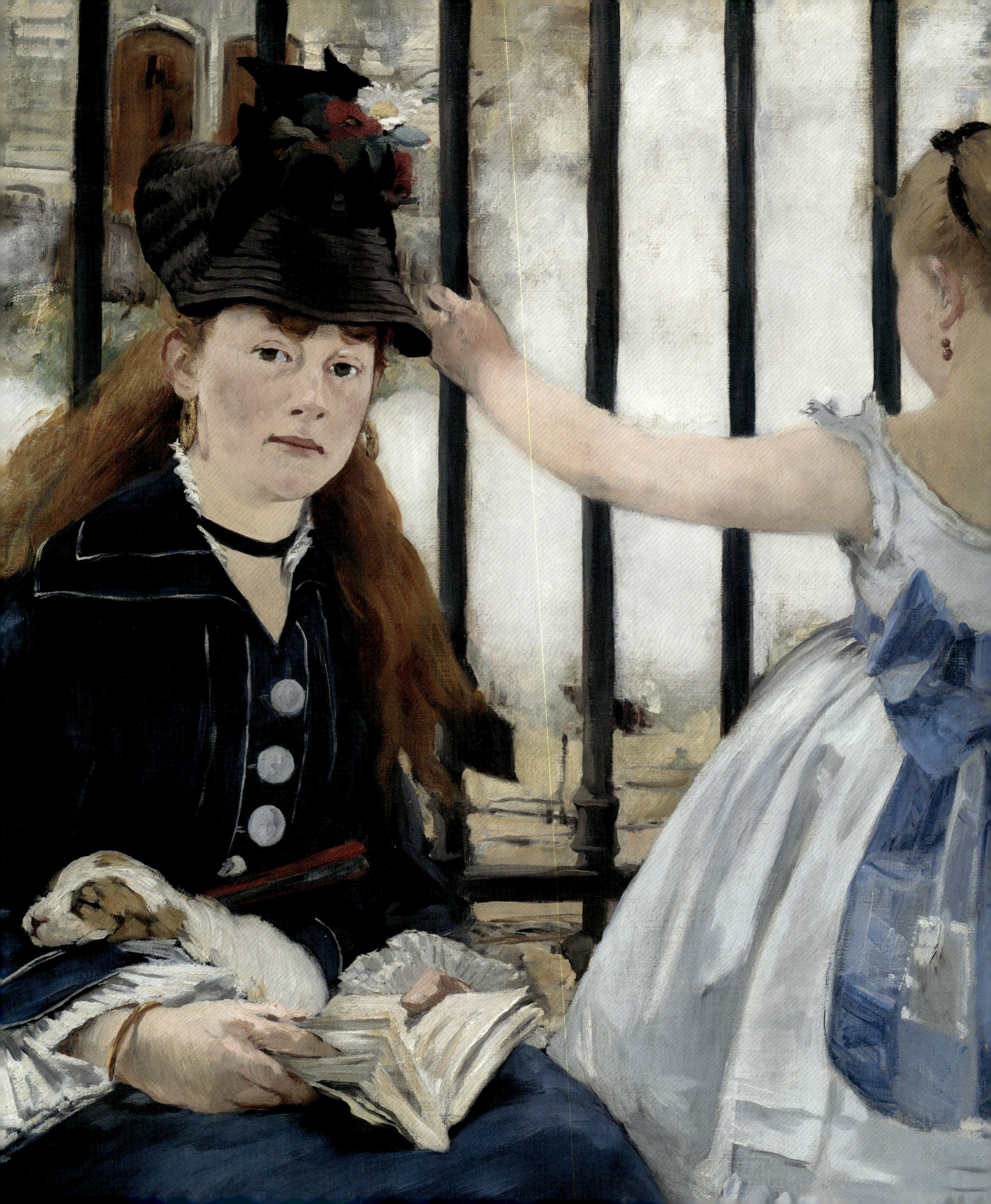

Painting Modern Life

The city of Paris was radically transformed during the Second Empire (1852–70). Between 1853 and 1870, Baron Georges-Eugène Haussmann, as prefect of the Seine, oversaw a vast urban-renewal project that changed the face of the French capital: narrow, medieval streets gave way to broad, gaslit boulevards lined with uniform rows of white stone buildings embellished with wrought-iron balconies to house the city's rapidly growing population. A culture of leisure flourished in its cafés, entertainment venues, and new public parks, where different social classes mixed freely. At the same time, the urban poor were displaced and marginalized on the outskirts of the city, and prostitution was on the rise. Haussmann designed modern Paris, and his Paris became Manet's Paris.

At the end of 1863 Manet's friend Charles Baudelaire published the first installment of "The Painter of Modern Life," which appeared in serial form in the pages of *Le Figaro*. Written some three years earlier, Baudelaire's work expands on his belief in "the heroism of modern life," first expressed in his little-known review of the Salon of 1845. In "The Painter of Modern Life," Baudelaire defined modernity as "the transitory, the fleeting, the contingent, the half of art whose other half is the eternal and the immutable."[1] His words were intended as a rallying cry to artists to paint contemporary life instead of the historical subjects prized by the Academy of Fine Arts. While a student at the Collège Rollin, Manet similarly proclaimed, "it is necessary to be of one's time," as his friend Proust recalled.[2] Although Baudelaire's call for modern subjects in art coincided with Manet's first forays into contemporary imagery in the early 1860s, his ideal "painter of modern life" was not Manet but rather Constantin Guys (1802–92), known for his illustrations of life in Paris during the Second Empire. Baudelaire himself figures among Manet's friends and supporters in the throng of Parisians enjoying an afternoon concert in the Tuileries Gardens, as painted by Manet in 1862, but this modern group portrait allegedly "failed to seduce" him when he saw it, according to Manet's early biographer (see fig. 19).[3] Nonetheless, their contemporaries recognized the two men's shared interests; Salon reviewers invoked

Detail of fig. 57

Baudelaire in their discussions of Manet's work throughout the decade. In 1865, a critic characterized *Olympia* [fig. 36] as a "painting of the Baudelaire school, freely executed by a pupil of Goya."[4]

Baudelaire's untimely death from syphilis in 1867 brought an end to their brief friendship. Manet attended the poet's funeral on September 2; an unfinished view of a funeral procession in the outskirts of Paris, painted around this date, is thought to represent that of Baudelaire (fig. 44). Its sky, darkened by looming storm clouds, and the small number of mourners behind the carriage mirror contemporary accounts of Baudelaire's funeral.[5] A few brushstrokes summarily render each of the black-clad figures, while the Parisian landmarks silhouetted against the sky are identifiable, including the domes of the Observatory, on the left, and that of the Panthéon—perhaps in a tribute to Baudelaire's Paris, as art historian Henri Loyrette has suggested.[6]

Stylistically, *The Funeral* is closely related to another panoramic view of Paris, which Manet painted on location in June 1867, according to Léon Leenhoff (fig. 45).[7] From a vantage point overlooking the Champ-de-Mars, Manet captured the site transformed by the temporary structures built for the Exposition Universelle, which had opened in April. The Palais de l'Industrie, which housed the annual Salon, appears in the distance on the right, encircled by flags. Manet's works had been excluded from the Fine Arts pavilion of the Exposition; in response, the artist mounted his own exhibition of fifty paintings outside the exhibition grounds near the Pont de l'Alma. In his view of the Exposition Universelle, Félix Nadar's celebrated balloon, emblematic of modernity, floats above the scene; such balloons were a popular form of entertainment, and in 1862, Manet had produced a lithograph of another balloon about to ascend, surrounded by a crowd of onlookers on the Esplanade des Invalides (*The Balloon*, 1862, Bibliothèque Nationale, Paris). Manet's canvas is freely brushed, and the loosely sketched figures depict a range of Parisian types, from soldiers and a gardener at work to elegantly dressed Parisiennes. The young dandy shown walking a dog on the lower right has been identified as Léon Leenhoff,[8] embodying another Baudelairian type and prefiguring his appearance in Manet's *Luncheon in the Studio* painted in Boulogne-sur-mer the following summer (see fig. 43). The canvas remains unfinished; it has been suggested that Manet abandoned the work when reports of the execution of Maximilian I, emperor of Mexico, on June 19, 1867, reached Paris the following month[9] (fig. 74).

A woman on horseback, dressed *en amazone* (in a riding habit), occupies the center of Manet's view of the Exposition Universelle. Riding as well as horse racing were then in vogue. Fashionably attired women riders figure in contemporaneous illustrations by Constantin Guys, and Baudelaire expressed admiration for women "expertly controlling their exquisitely graceful steeds, themselves no less dazzling and dainty than their mistresses."[10] Manet's early notebooks include sketches of the crowd at horse races, and Manet appears as a spectator at one such event, riding crop in hand, in a drawing by Edgar Degas (*Édouard Manet at the Races*, ca. 1868–69, The Metropolitan Museum of Art, New York). Both Manet and Degas depicted horse races; Manet first exhibited a picture of this subject in 1864.

Two years later, Manet captured the thrilling finish of a race at the popular Longchamp racecourse in the Bois de Boulogne, which had opened in 1857 (fig. 46). The canvas, a fragment of a larger composition, belongs to a group of works from the 1860s related to a large-scale painting of a horse race, now unknown. Its unconventional head-on view, probably modeled on British sporting prints, signals the modernity of Manet's vision.[11] So too does its handling of paint, which accords with Baudelaire's call for artists to adapt a technique that mirrors the fleeting moments of modern life, as the poet wrote: "there is a rapidity of movement which calls for an equal speed of execution from the artist."[12] Manet rendered the crowd of onlookers lining both sides of the track in a flurry of loose brushwork that verges on abstraction, underscoring the dynamism of his subject. His handling of the crowd also recalls the scattered "patches" of color used to represent some of the figures in *Music in the Tuileries Gardens* (fig. 19).

In addition to the subjects that he painted, Manet himself embodied Baudelaire's ideal *flâneur*—the passionate observer of urban life. Whether he was holding court in the fashionable Tuileries Gardens on summer afternoons, strolling the new boulevards of Baron Haussmann's Paris, or frequenting the city's cafés, Manet was very much a man of his time. An 1867 portrait by Henri Fantin-Latour captures his innate elegance, expressed through the tailored fit of his frock coat and the walking cane suitable for urban promenades (see p. 13). Shown at the Salon of 1867, the portrait projects an image of haute bourgeois ease, as if to disprove the artist's detractors, who equated "the painter of the black cat" with his radical subject matter and treated him as a "slovenly dauber," as Émile Zola wrote that same year.[13]

Two portraits from 1870 confirm Manet's rising status among the avant-garde. Manet figures in a view of a light-filled artist's studio on the rue de la Condamine shared by Frédéric Bazille and Auguste Renoir, painted by the former. In this informal gathering, Manet, wearing a top hat, studies a painting displayed on Bazille's easel. The tall figure standing next to the easel is Bazille, who proudly wrote to his father, "Manet did me himself."[14] Manet's presence and his hand in the realization of Bazille's portrait in this studio scene attest to his influence among the artists who would be acknowledged as leading figures in the Impressionist movement. Manet's own studio, in the Batignolles quarter, also attracted emerging artists and progressive critics; it served as the setting for a group portrait by Fantin-Latour that celebrates Manet as their leader, which was exhibited at the Salon of 1870. Among the men in black suits surrounding Manet at work on a portrait of the critic Zacharie Astruc are the artists Renoir, Bazille, and Monet, as well as Zola. This sober image emanates bourgeois respectability, underscoring the seriousness of the men's shared enterprise. Nonetheless, the portrait was lampooned in an 1870 caricature that

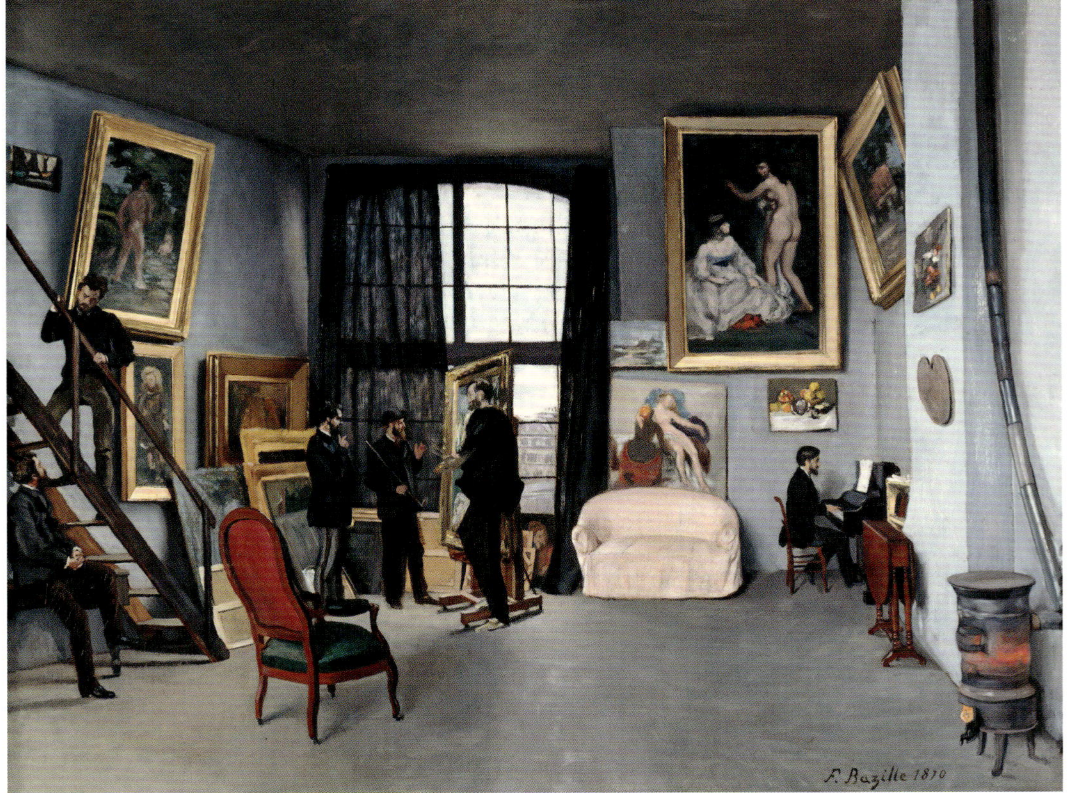

Frédéric Bazille, *Bazille's Studio*, 1870, oil on canvas, 38 ½ × 50 ⅓ in. (98 × 128 cm). Paris, Musée d'Orsay, RF 2449

appeared in the *Journal amusant*, entitled "Jesus Painting in the Midst of His Disciples, or the Divine School of Manet."[15]

Manet's portrait of the artist Eva Gonzalès was also on view at the Salon of 1870 (fig. 47). She is shown at work, seated before an easel in a pose mirroring that of Manet in Fantin-Latour's contemporaneous group portrait. Manet began the portrait in the summer of 1869, not long after Gonzalès became his first and only formal student. That August, Berthe Morisot reported Manet's progress on the work in a letter to her sister, Edma: "he has begun her portrait over again for the twenty–fifth time. She poses every day, and every night (in the evening) the head is washed out with soft soap." A month later, Manet's struggles continued, as Morisot wrote: "her portrait does not progress; he says that he is at the fortieth sitting and that the head is again effaced." Indeed, the visibly thicker application of paint and evidence of overpainting in the face betray Manet's repeated reworkings.[16] The portrait was painted in Manet's studio in the Batignolles, and Manet himself is felt throughout, from the white peony lying on the floor beside her, as if borrowed from one of his 1864 still-life paintings of his favorite flower (fig. 41), to the partially rolled print lying next to it, signed and dated "Manet 1870," which serves as his signature. A portfolio of drawings, if intended as a reference to Gonazalès's work as an artist, is relegated to the background of the scene. The still life on the easel has been identified as a painted version of an engraving after a work by the seventeenth-century French floral painter, Jean-Baptiste Monnoyer, published in the first volume of Charles Blanc's *Histoire des Peintres de toutes les écoles* in 1862, a copy of which Manet owned.[17] Blanc's publication was an essential reference for Manet during the 1860s; moreover, Gonzalès was not known for her paintings of still-life subjects. The portrait's self-referential aspect recalls Manet's 1868 portrait of Zola (fig. 39).

Clad in a fashionable white muslin dress, Gonzalès mirrors Manet's earlier portrayal of Suzanne Manet in *Reading*, begun in 1865 (fig. 11), and the figures of Berthe Morisot and Fanny Claus in *The Balcony*, painted in 1868–69 (fig. 25). Manet's depictions of fashionably attired women in white accord with Baudelaire's notion of fashion as an essential element of modern beauty.[18] Morisot's appearance in a white peignoir in Manet's reimagining of Goya's *Majas on a Balcony* led

Henri Fantin-Latour, *Studio in the Batignolles*, 1870, oil on canvas, 80 ⅓ × 107 ⅔ in. (204 × 273.5 cm). Paris, Musée d'Orsay, RF 729

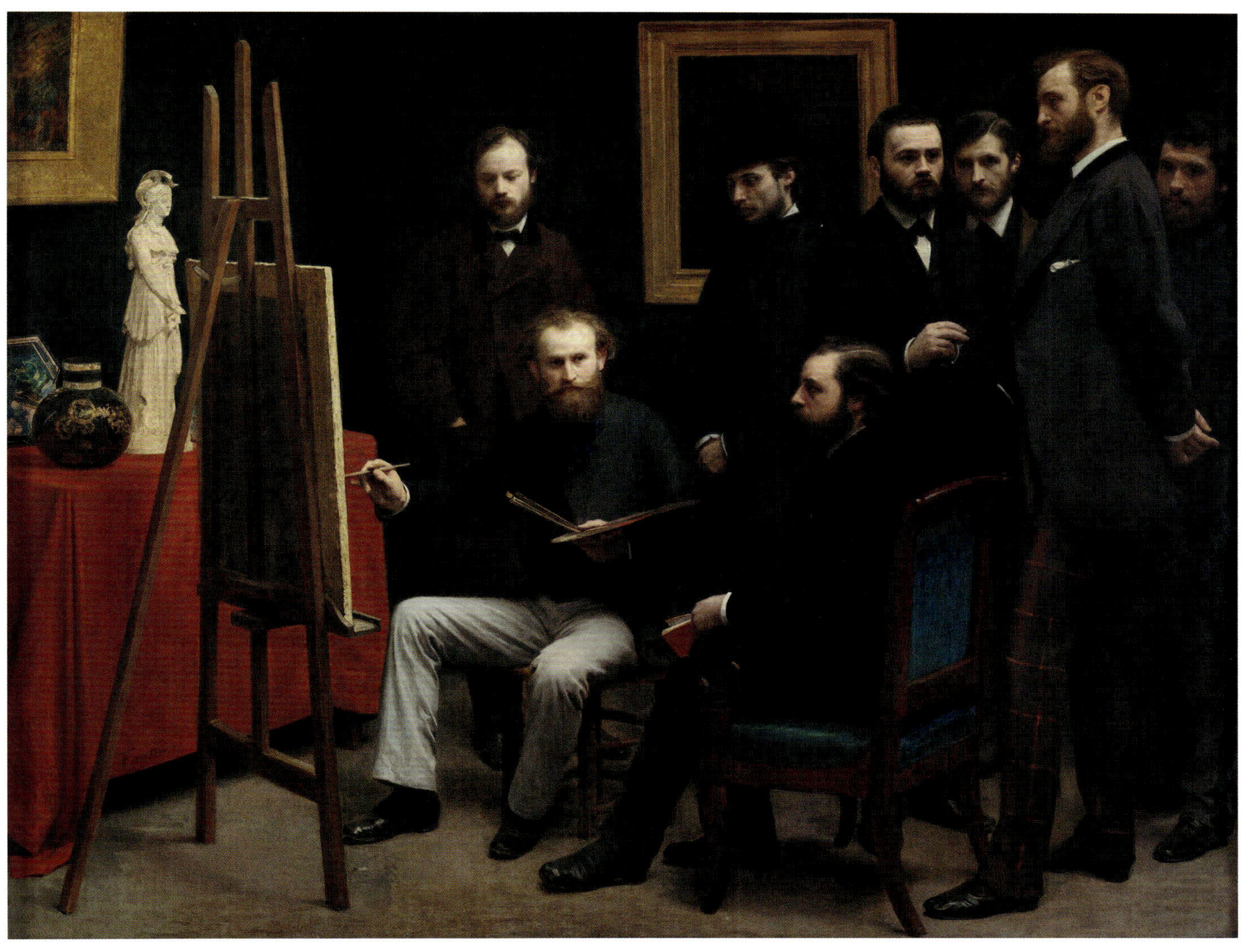

some Salon-goers to describe her as a "femme fatale" when the work was exhibited in 1869, as Morisot wrote to her sister, Edma.[19] That this term had only recently been coined to refer to a dangerously seductive woman attests to the modernity of Manet's vision.

The Balcony was the first of eleven paintings that Manet made of Morisot between 1868 and 1874, a period marked by their deepening friendship and artistic dialogue. It was followed by *Repose*, another large-scale work, intended for the Salon, that reflects Manet's ongoing engagement with modernity[20] (fig. 48). This time Morisot was his sole subject, clad in a white muslin day dress, its top button undone, and holding a red lacquer fan, as she did in *The Balcony*. Manet began the painting in the summer of 1870 in Morisot's studio, identified by its red sofa and the Japanese *ukiyo-e*, or color woodblock print, prominently displayed directly above Morisot's head, although he subsequently finished the canvas in his own studio.[21] Despite its setting, Manet did not depict Morisot at work in this or any other painting for which she posed, and he excluded any reference to her identity as an artist. Its large scale, like that of Manet's portrait of Gonzalès, is associated with the tradition of formal portraiture; however, Morisot's pose—"neither standing nor seated" in the words of a contemporary critic[22]—subverts artistic convention in its informality and suggests Manet's familiarity with his subject. Manet himself distinguished the work from traditional portraits, writing to Morisot's mother in 1871 that it was "not at all in the character of a portrait."[23] Its atmospheric quality was later invoked by the poet and critic Stéphane Mallarmé, who recalled that Manet "justly called [it] a 'Rêverie,'" adding "This work is altogether exceptional and sympathetic."[24] In its elision of the boundaries between portraiture and modern-life subjects, *Repose* recalls Manet's images of Victorine Meurent from the 1860s (fig. 30).

When *Repose* was shown at the Salon of 1873, the modernity of Manet's portrait-like image of Morisot polarized critics.[25] The majority of reviews were hostile; the painting was variously described as "neither painted nor drawn," "a confusion defying all description," and, even, a "horror." Tellingly, though, Baudelaire's name was invoked more than once in association with Manet's modern subjects. The conservative critic Théophile Silvestre noted the late poet's "extreme and extravagant taste for the painting of Édouard Manet," and added, "Manet has a taste for modern life and the cult of realism; perhaps his intuitions are good, but he seldom realizes them." The lone voice in support of Manet's work was the critic for *Le National*, who called *Repose* "an engaging portrait which holds our attention and which imposes itself on our imagination by an intense character of *modernity* . . ." He added, "Baudelaire was indeed right to esteem Manet's painting, for this patient and sensitive artist is perhaps the only one in whose work one discovers that subtle feeling for modern life which was the exquisite originality of the *Fleurs du mal*."[26]

Morisot also appears in a series of intimate portraits by Manet that were not intended for public exhibition. In these works, Manet explored modern womanhood and, at the same time, challenged the boundaries of traditional portraiture. Morisot is often dressed in black, a color she herself favored and one that Manet privileged in his palette.[27] While the sitter's innate sense of style is evident, Manet also plumbed a range of emotions in these images of Morisot, signaling the modernity of his approach to portraiture. A portrait of 1872 depicts her side-lit, an unusual choice for Manet, with one side of her face shrouded in shadow (fig. 49). The directness of her gaze calls to mind the portrait of Victorine Meurent (fig. 29). Around the time she sat for her portrait, Morisot confided her unhappiness to her sister, Edma, "I'm sad as sad can be . . . what I see most clearly is that my state is unbearable from any point of view."[28] Painted quickly "in one or two sittings," as Morisot's daughter recalled,[29] the work is striking in both its psychological intensity and technical virtuosity. Writing about this portrait in 1932, the poet Paul Valéry, who was Morisot's nephew, was struck by "the *black*—the absolute black . . . it is a black that could only be Manet's." He likened the effect of Manet's portrait to "*poetry*."[30] The work's significance to Manet is attested by the fact that he reproduced it in two lithographs and an etching, none of which were published in his lifetime. Morisot's expression differs slightly in each.

Against the rich black of Morisot's fashionable dress in the 1872 portrait is a small bunch of violets, pinned to the bodice, recalling the nosegay of the same flower that Victorine Meurent coyly holds in *Young Lady in 1866* (fig. 38). In the painting of Victorine, Manet played on its amorous association—a gift from a male admirer, not unlike the large bouquet being delivered to Olympia (fig. 36). Violets reappear in an intimate still life of 1872, which Manet presented as a gift to Morisot (fig. 50). In it, a small bouquet of violets lies next to a red-lacquer fan—another allusion to Manet's portraits of Morisot—and a partially folded note, which serves both as the artist's dedication to the work's recipient, "A Mlle Berthe," and his signature, "E Manet."[31] The work invites a reading as a symbolic double portrait of Manet and Morisot in the guise of still life. Manet never again painted this flower.

In an 1874 portrait, Morisot again wears black but this time it is the black of mourning following the death of her father in January 1874 (fig. 51). Wearing a long black veil, she leans forward, resting her face on her gloved hand in a traditional gesture of mourning.[32] Manet's rapid, slashing brushwork expressively captures Morisot's anguish in this intimate record of deeply felt emotion. In another portrait from 1874, Morisot toys with her fan as if distracted (fig. 52). She averts her gaze, and her hand stands out against the black of her dress, revealing what appears to be an engagement or wedding ring. On December 22, 1874, Morisot married Manet's brother Eugène. Manet would never paint her again.

Manet's portrayals of Morisot embody modernity in their rejection of conventional modes of portraiture, not unlike the role-playing images of Victorine from the 1860s. Victorine herself was a performer, as were other artists' models at this time, among them the actress Ellen Andrée, who modeled for Manet and Degas as well as other painters in the 1870s.[33]

In a work of around 1876, Andrée posed for Manet as a popular type known as "La Parisienne," a young and fashionable woman who embodied the modern city (fig. 53).[34] She wears a bluish-black walking dress (*robe de promenade*) that evokes the riding habits worn by stylish horsewomen.[35] Manet rendered the ensemble with bravura brushwork. The tailored elegance of the model for *La Parisienne* mirrors that of the fashionable *flâneur*. Long after her career as an artist's model was over, Andrée recalled her sittings with Manet, "Of all those painters he was the only one I looked up to . . . He was engrossed, courteous, distant. He was so high class!"[36] The portrayal of Andrée playing the role of "La Parisienne" sets the stage for a series of portraits of fashionable women that he realized in the final years of his career (fig. 86).

Manet's modern Paris was a world recreated in his studio. In contrast, his younger contemporaries sought to capture the spontaneity of Baudelaire's "fleeting moment" outdoors as they experienced it, and this commitment to plein air painting would become a hallmark of Impressionism. Manet's *Luncheon on the Grass* of 1863, which was also a studio construct, led Monet to embark on his own version of the same subject but realized en plein air with an eye to capturing the fleeting effect of natural light on figures outdoors. Another large-scale figure painting done outdoors, Bazille's *View of the Village* (Musée Fabre, Montpellier), was accepted by the jury of the 1869 Salon; it is this canvas, displayed on an easel, that Manet contemplates in Bazille's painting of his studio, realized the following year.

Responding to the innovations of the rising generation of artists, Manet executed a figure painting en plein air in 1870, possibly his first such work (fig. 54). Manet's models and the setting of *In the Garden* remain uncertain, although it has been suggested that his subjects are Morisot's sister, Edma, her infant daughter, and Morisot's brother, posing in the garden of the Morisot house on 16, rue Franklin. The freely brushed patches of sunlight on the garden path and the scattering of bright white highlights on the woman's muslin dress record the effect of fleeting light outdoors. Manet's loose handling of paint also accords with the emerging Impressionist style, which its critics faulted as sketch-like and unfinished. Its composition is equally modern in the way that the central figure of the seated woman audaciously bisects the reclining male figure behind her. In 1889, the modernity of Manet's work struck Theo van Gogh, who wrote to his brother Vincent, "This is certainly not only one of the most modern paintings, but also one in which there is the most advanced art."[37]

The Croquet Party of 1871 (fig. 55) represents another scene of outdoor leisure although preliminary sketches that Manet made for some of the figures suggest that the work was painted in the studio rather than outdoors.[38] Nonetheless, the painting retains the freedom of handling of *In the Garden* and an emphasis on fleeting atmospheric effects, notably the stiff coastal breeze that carries the smoke from the distant ship on the horizon, unfurls the flags, and forces the woman in black to place a protective hand on her fashionable hat. The composition,

Claude Monet,
Luncheon on the Grass,
1865–66, oil on canvas,
98 × 86 in. (248.7 × 218 cm).
Paris, Musée d'Orsay,
RF 1987 12

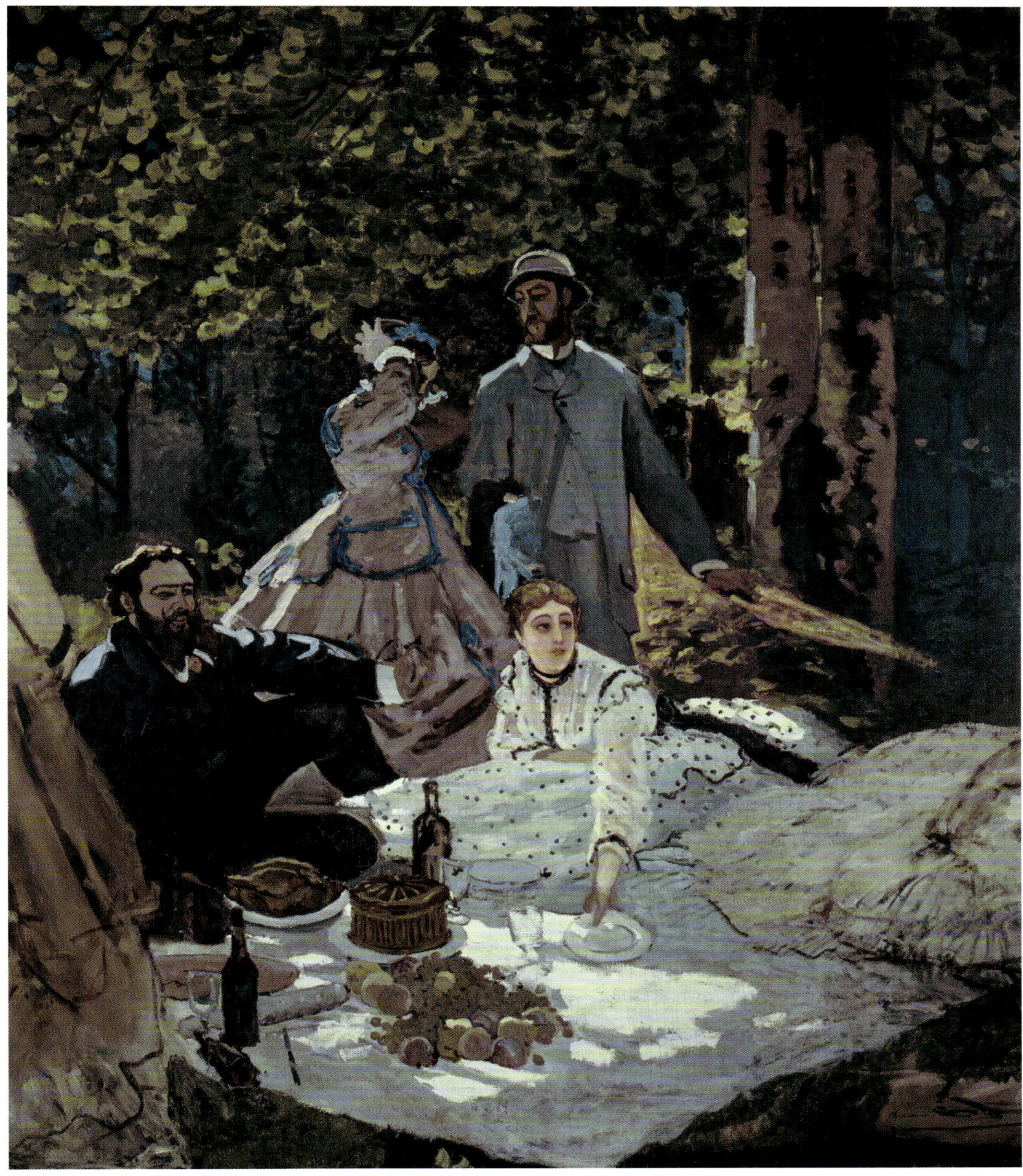

comprised of three horizontal bands of lawn, sea, and sky, bisected by a pair of flags, suggests that of Monet's *Garden at Sainte-Adresse* (The Metropolitan Museum of Art, New York), a work from 1867 that Manet admired in Bazille's studio around the time that it was painted. The setting of *The Croquet Party* has been identified as the croquet lawn of the casino in the seaside resort of Boulogne-sur-Mer, where Manet probably sojourned in the summer of 1871.[39] The figures are modeled by Manet's close friends and family, including his wife, Suzanne, wearing a gray dress, and, in the center, her son, Léon Leenhoff, holding a croquet mallet. The game of croquet, an English import, had recently become fashionable among the elite in France. Manet's choice of subject reflects his sustained interest in depicting modern leisure pursuits ranging from horse racing to boating, which he shared with the Impressionists (fig. 59).

In 1873, Manet's engagement with contemporary Parisian life inspired a painting set in the lobby of the old Paris Opéra on rue le Peletier (fig. 56). Its yearly masked balls, held during the pre-Lenten celebration known as the Paris Carnival, attracted throngs of revelers for "a scene recalling the ancient bacchanalia, and lasting from midnight until five in the morning," according to an account of the ball published in 1852.[40] In March 1873, Manet attended several balls, sketchbook in hand, as his early biographer noted: "From midnight until six in the morning, Manet did not tire of making sketches."[41] From April to November, he enlisted his friends to recreate the scene in his studio, which "some days was rumored to be a masquerade night." His friend Théodore Duret, among those who posed for Manet, recalled that the artist's desire for verisimilitude was such that "he varied his models, even for the actors in the background, of whom one would see only a detail of a head or shoulder."[42] Although most of the men who appear in the painting elude identification, the figure with the blond beard gazing outward on the far right is generally agreed to be Manet himself, who wittily signed the work on the dance card lying near his feet. Manet enlivened the scene with vignettes of flirtation and seduction, as women in masks and costumes, some *en travesti* (in drag), mingle among the crowd of men uniformly clad in black frock coats. An 1873 caricature of the ball by Charles Amédée Noé, known as Cham, parodies one such encounter in the halls of the Opéra, in which a male guest assures a costumed woman, "Madame, my intentions are pure."[43]

Manet submitted *Masked Ball at the Opera* to the Salon of 1874. Its subject was topical, as the old Opéra had been destroyed in an overnight fire in October 1873. However, the work was one of two of the artist's three paintings that were rejected by the conservative Salon jury—Manet's first refusal since 1867. The jury's decision prompted the young Stéphane Mallarmé, then an unknown poet and English teacher, to pen an ardent defense of Manet that was published on the eve of the opening of the Salon in the short-lived journal, *La Renaissance littéraire et artistique*. In language evocative of Baudelaire, Mallarmé defended Manet's choice of subject as "a rendezvous apt for showing the appeal of a modern crowd"; he added, "There is therefore nothing disorderly or scandalous about the painting, which seems to want to step out of its frame: it is, on the contrary, the heroic attempt to capture . . . a complete vision of contemporary life."[44] Manet acknowledged Mallarmé's support with this brief note: "Thanks, if I had a few more supporters like you, I wouldn't give a f . . . about the jury."[45]

The Salon jury did accept another scene of modern life by Manet in 1874, *The Railway* (fig. 57). The work is set in a private garden overlooking the Saint-Lazare train station, not far from Manet's new studio at 4, rue Saint-Pétersbourg, whose window and door are visible in the upper left corner of the canvas.[46] Manet's models are a fashionably attired Victorine Meurent, posing a final time for Manet after a seven-year hiatus, and the daughter of Manet's artist friend Alphonse Hirsch. Their relationship to each other in the scene is unclear. A cloud of billowing smoke and steam behind the figures offers the only sign of the train on the tracks below. Despite its plein air setting, it is thought to be a studio work.[47] Ambiguously straddling the boundary between portraiture and genre, the work challenged conservative Salon critics in 1874, who faulted Manet for his choice of subject. The writer for the *Revue Des deux Mondes* mockingly asked, "Is Manet's *Railway* a double portrait or a subject picture? . . . We lack information to solve this problem; we hesitate all the more concerning the young girl, which at least might be a portrait seen from the rear."[48]

Nearly all of the Salon reviews in 1874 were hostile and uncomprehending. Exceptionally, the critic Ernest Chesneau recognized the originality of Manet's vision, "M. Manet, whose summary methods may appear brutal at times . . . seems concerned above all to express modern life exactly as it is and to free his art from technical conventions."[49] Similarly, the future Impressionists, who claimed Manet as their leader, espoused modernity in both their choice of subjects and their technique. Manet, though, refused the invitation to participate in their inaugural exhibition, which opened in the former studio of the photographer Nadar on the boulevard des Capucines two weeks before Manet's *Railway* went on view at the Salon of 1874. Although Manet would seek recognition at the state-sponsored Salon throughout his career, he nevertheless engaged in a lively dialogue with Impressionist painting and its leading artists over the course of the 1870s.

1 Charles Baudelaire, "The Painter of Modern Life," in Jonathan Mayne, trans. and ed., *"The Painter of Modern Life" and Other Essays* (London, Phaidon Press Ltd., 1964), 27.
2 Proust 1988, 10.
3 Cited by Henri Loyrette, "Modern Life," in Paris and New York 1994, 266.
4 Paris 2011, 137.
5 Paris and New York 1983, 260–61.
6 Paris and New York 1994, 411.
7 Ibid., 413.
8 Locke 2001, 123.
9 Paris and New York 1994, 413.
10 Baudelaire 1964, 39.
11 For a detailed discussion of the work's evolution, see Juliet Wilson-Bareau with the assistance of Kathryn Kremnitzer and Genevieve Westerby in Groom and Westerby 2019, cat. 12, paras 23, 24, and 27.
12 Baudelaire 1964, 4.
13 Émile Zola, "A new way to paint: Édouard Manet," 1867, reproduced in Los Angeles 2013, 36.
14 Letter of January 1, 1870, cited in Michel Hilaire and Paul Perrin (eds.), *Frédéric Bazille (1841–1870) and the Birth of Impressionism* [exhibition catalogue], Montpellier, Musée Fabre, Paris, Musée d'Orsay, and Washington, D.C., National Gallery of Art, 2016–17, 165.
15 Hamilton 1954, 149.
16 https://www.nationalgallery.org.uk/paintings/catalogues/national-gallery-2024/eva-gonzales; cited under "Technical Notes."
17 https://www.nationalgallery.org.uk/paintings/catalogues/national-gallery-2024/eva-gonzales; cited under "Subject."
18 Baudelaire 1964, 12–13.
19 Paris and New York 1983, 304.

20 On the modernity of this work, see also Toledo and London 2012–13, 182.

21 Paris and New York 1983, p. 317, citing Tabarant 1947, 69.

22 Hamilton 1954, 164.

23 Bernice F. Davidson, "Le Repos. A Portrait of Berthe Morisot by Édouard Manet," *Bulletin of the Rhode Island School of Design, Museum Notes* 46, no. 2 (December 1959): 6. I am grateful to Maureen C. O'Brien, Curator of Painting and Sculpture, Museum of Art, Rhode Island School of Design, for providing this reference.

24 Stéphane Mallarmé, "The Impressionists and Édouard Manet," *The Art Monthly Review and Photographic Portfolio* 1, no. 9 (September 30, 1876), reprinted in Charles Moffett (ed.), *The New Painting, Impressionism 1874–1886* [exhibition catalogue], National Gallery of Art, Washington, D.C., and The Fine Arts Museums of San Francisco, 1986, 30.

25 For a summary of Salon criticism in 1873, see Hamilton 1954, 162–74.

26 Hamilton 1954, 172.

27 Gloria Groom, "The Social Network of Fashion," in Gloria Groom (ed.), *Impressionism, Fashion, & Modernity* [exhibition catalogue], Musée d'Orsay, Paris, The Metropolitan Museum of Art, New York, and the Art Institute of Chicago, 2012–13, 38–39.

28 Paris and New York 1983, 336.

29 Sylvie Patry (ed.), *Berthe Morisot, 1841–1895* [exhibition catalogue], Lille, Palais des Beaux-Arts and Martigny, Fondation Pierre Gianadda, 2002 460.

30 Cited in Armstrong 2002, 175.

31 Carol Armstrong, "Manet's Little Nothings," in Los Angeles and Chicago, 2019–20, 114–15.

32 Toledo and London 2012–13, 182.

33 On this subject, see Leah Lehmbeck, "All the World's a Stage: Manet's Images of Model-Actresses," in Chicago and Los Angeles 2019–20, 55–69.

34 On the Parisienne as a type, see Françoise Tétart-Vittu, "Édouard Manet, *The Parisienne*," in Paris–New York–Chicago 2012–13, 76–83.

35 Gloria Groom, "The Social Network of Fashion," in Paris–New York–Chicago 2012–13, p. 40.

36 Cited by Lehmbeck in Chicago and Los Angeles 2019–20, 58.

37 Paris and New York 1983, 318–20.

38 Simon Kelly, "Édouard Manet, *The Croquet Party*, 1871," catalogue entry in Aimee Marcereau DeGalan (ed.), *French Paintings and Pastels, 1600–1945: The Collections of the Nelson-Atkins Museum of Art* (Kansas City, The Nelson-Atkins Museum of Art, 2021).

39 Ibid.

40 Cited in Paris and New York 1983, 352.

41 Adolphe Tabarant, *Manet et ses oeuvres* (Paris, Gallimard, 1947), 204.

42 Ibid., 231.

43 "Revue comique du mois, par Cham," *L'Univers illustré* (March 15, 1873): 173.

44 Cited in Hamilton 1954, 183; Hamilton also notes its similarity to Baudelaire's 1845 call for painting that expresses "the heroism of modern life."

45 Wilson-Bareau 1991, 167.

46 See the discussion of the work and its setting in Juliet Wilson-Bareau, *Manet, Monet, and the Gare Saint-Lazare* [exhibition catalogue], Paris, Musée d'Orsay, and Washington, D.C., National Gallery of Art, 1998, 41–63.

47 Paris and Washington, D.C. 1998, 57.

48 Hamilton 1954, 179.

49 Cited Paris and Washington, D.C. 1998, 55.

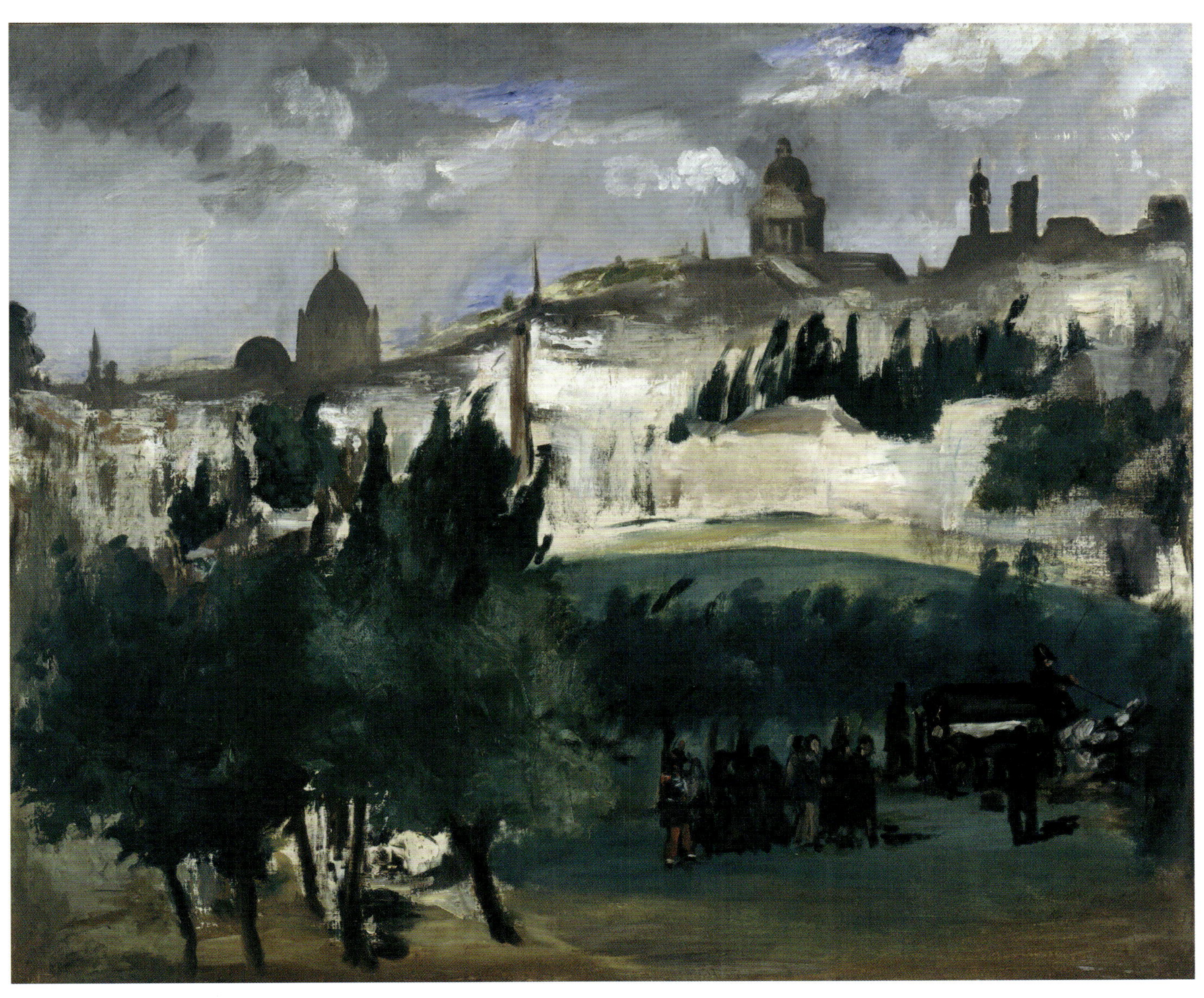

44

The Funeral

ca. 1867
Oil on canvas, 28 ⅝ × 35 ⅝ in.
(72.7 × 90.5 cm)
New York, The Metropolitan Museum of Art, Catharine Lorillard Wolfe Collection, Wolfe Fund, 1909, 10.36

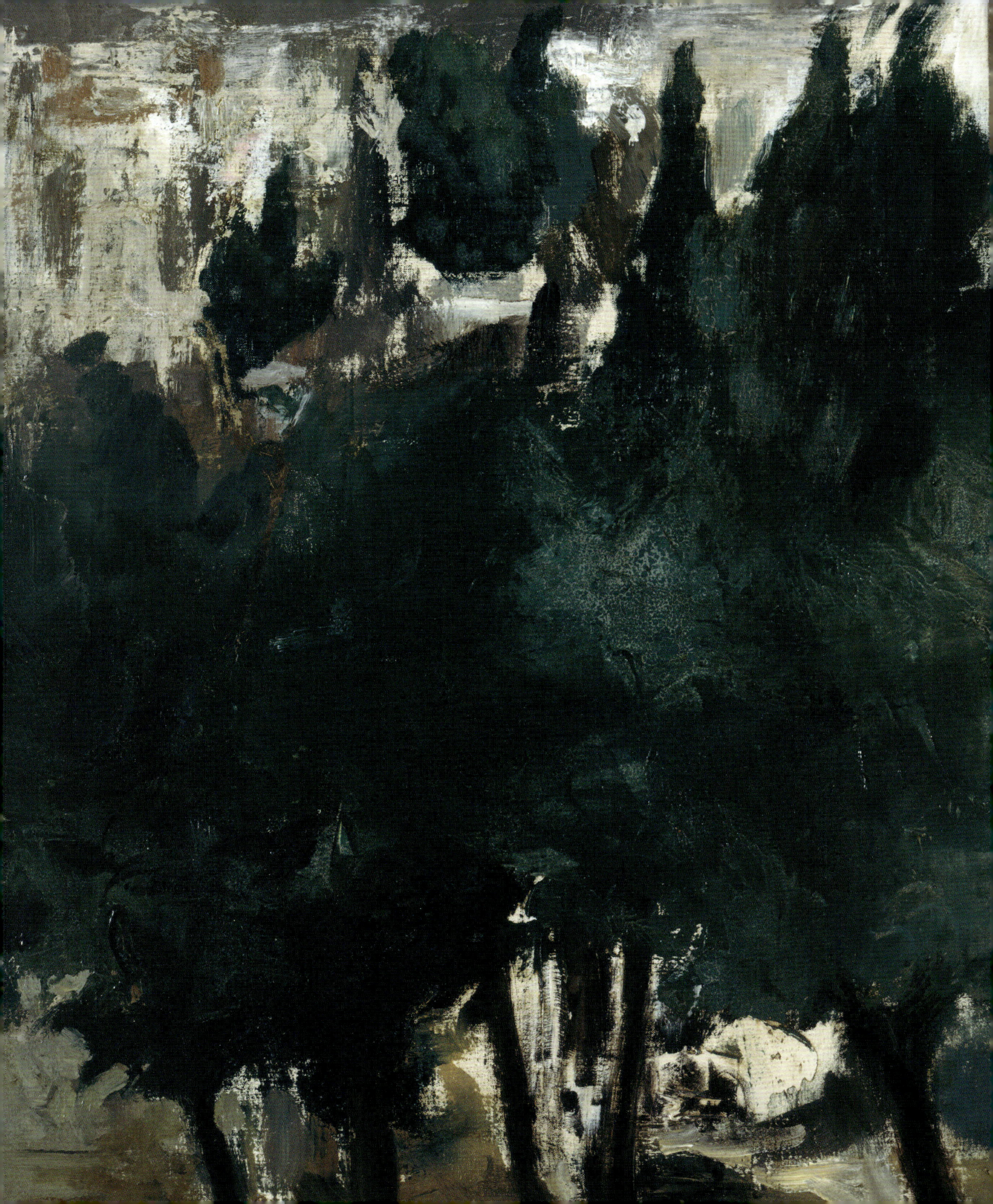

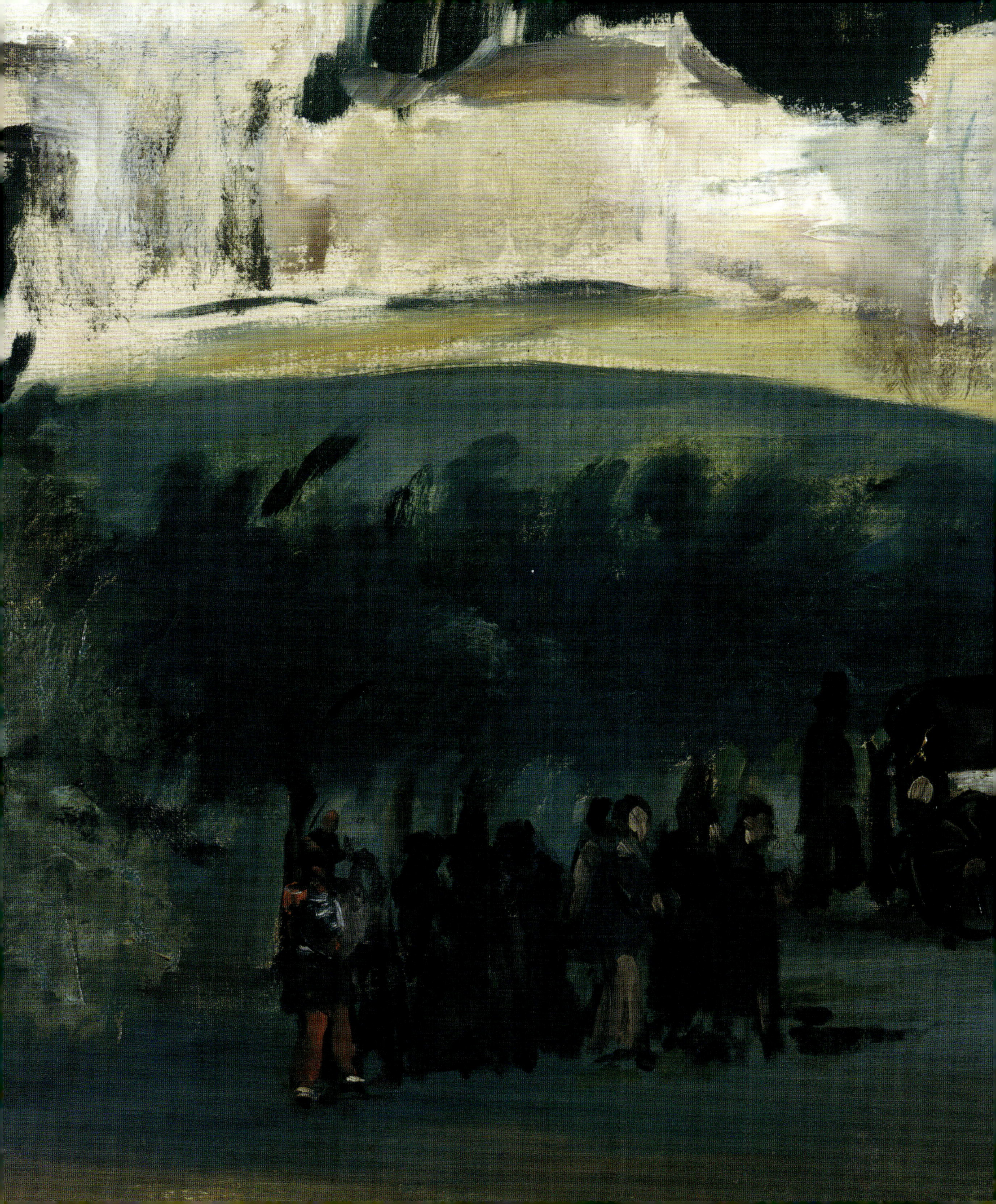

45

View of the 1867 Exposition Universelle

1867
Oil on canvas, 42 ½ × 77 in.
(108 × 196 cm)
Oslo, Nasjonalmuseet for kunst, arkitektur og design, The Fine Art Collections, NG.M.01293

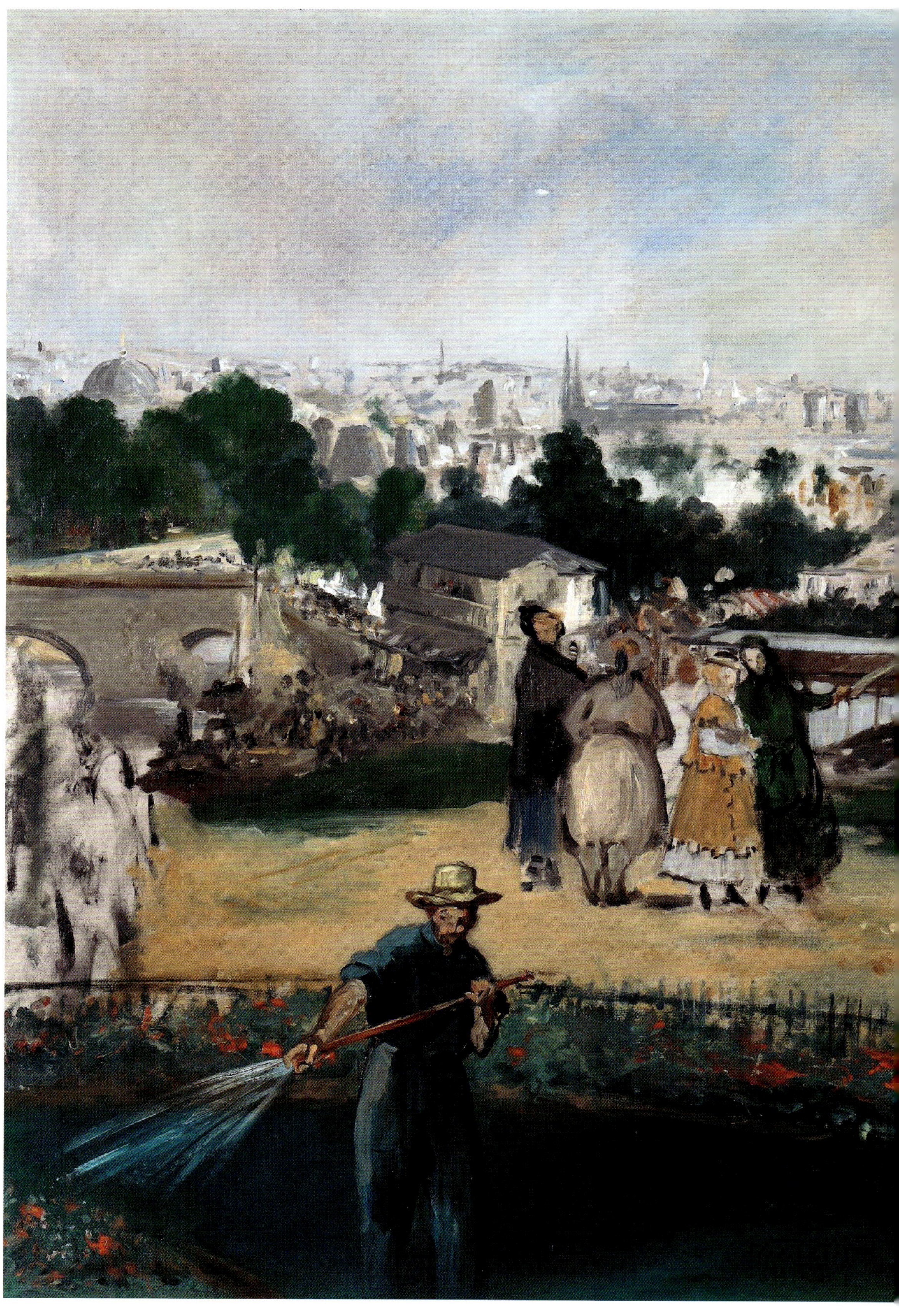

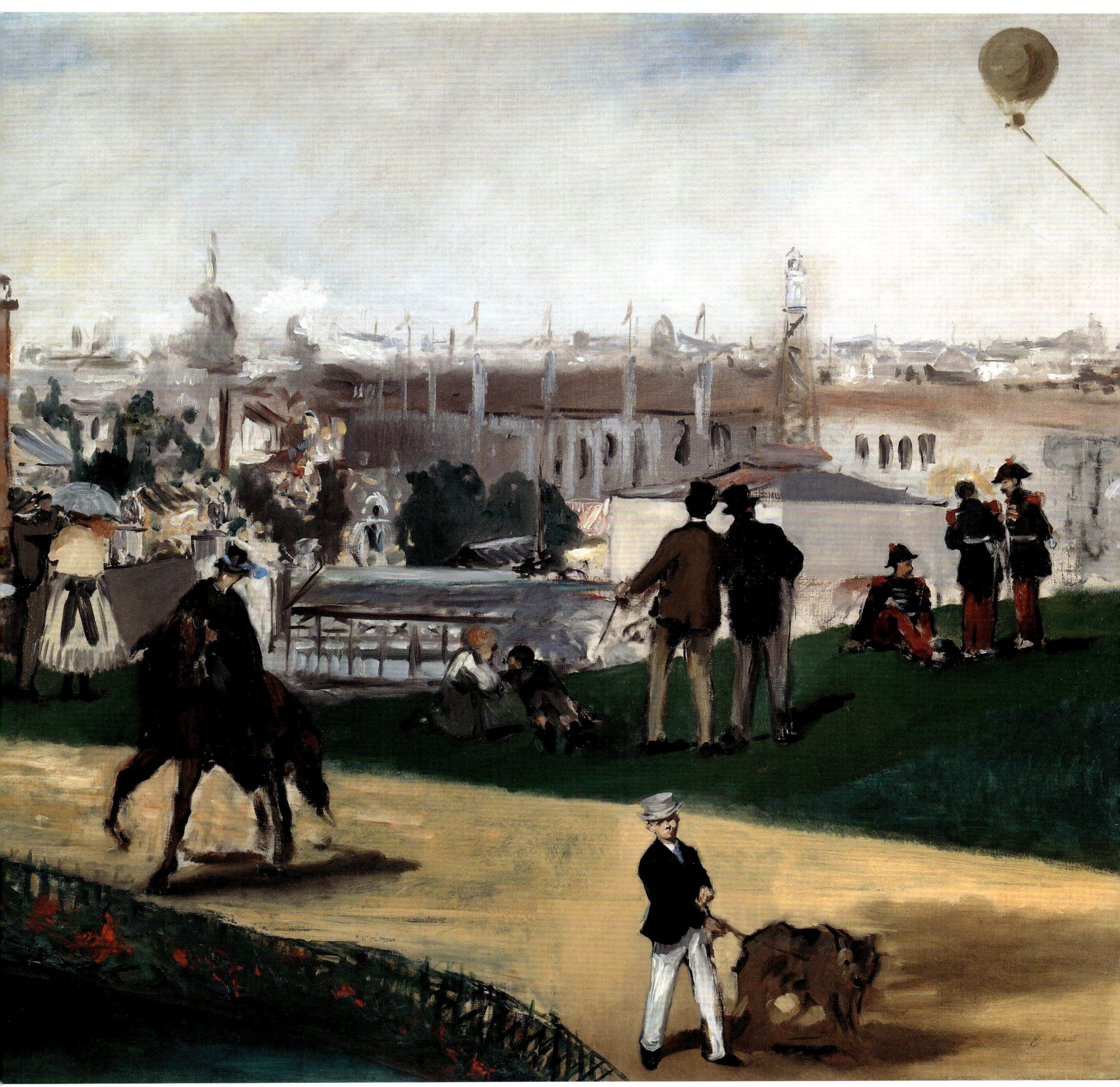
E. Manet

46

The Races at Longchamp

1866
Oil on canvas, 17 5⁄16 × 33 1⁄8 in.
(44 × 84.2 cm)
Chicago, The Art Institute of Chicago, Potter Palmer Collection, 1922.424

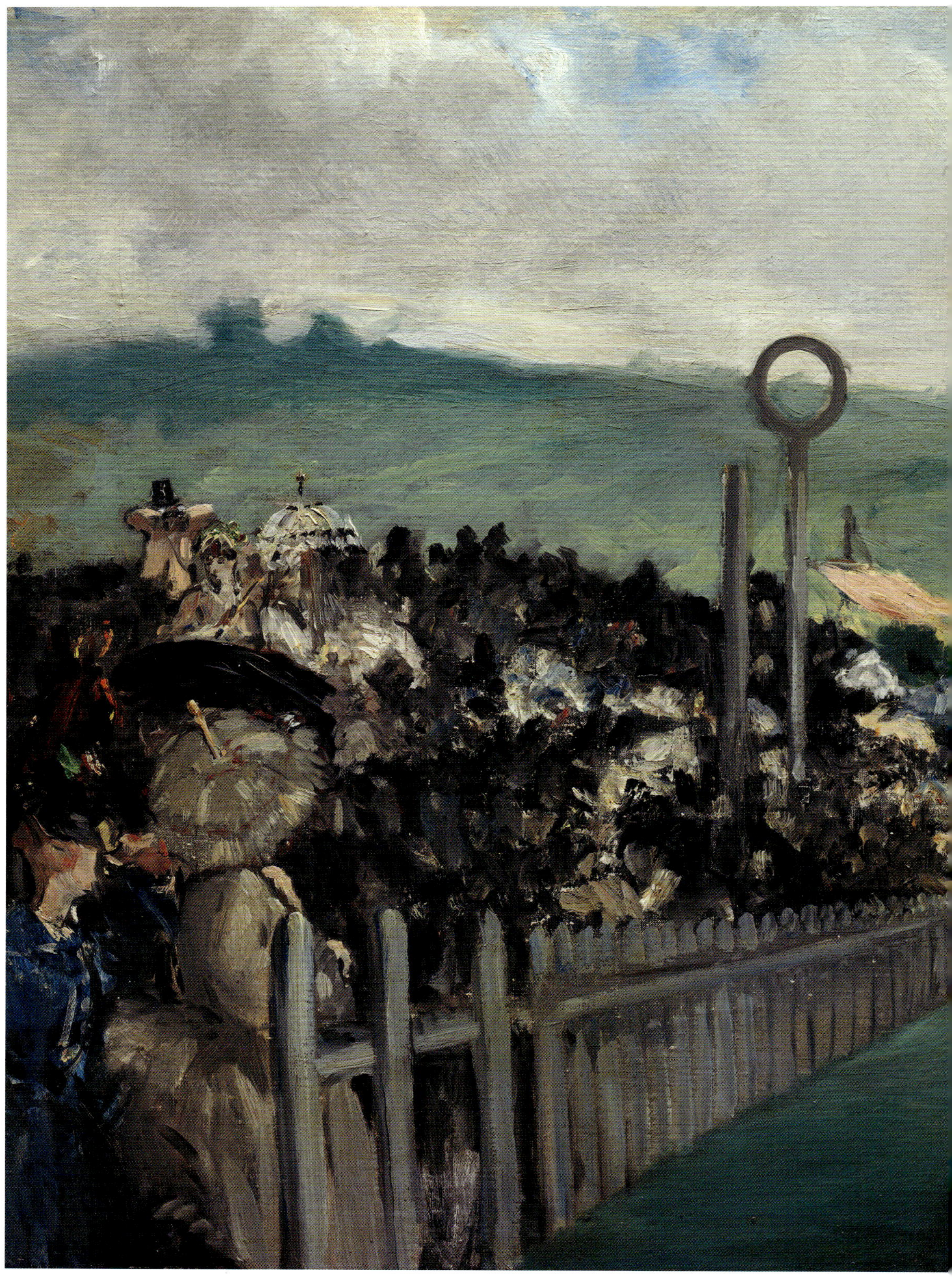

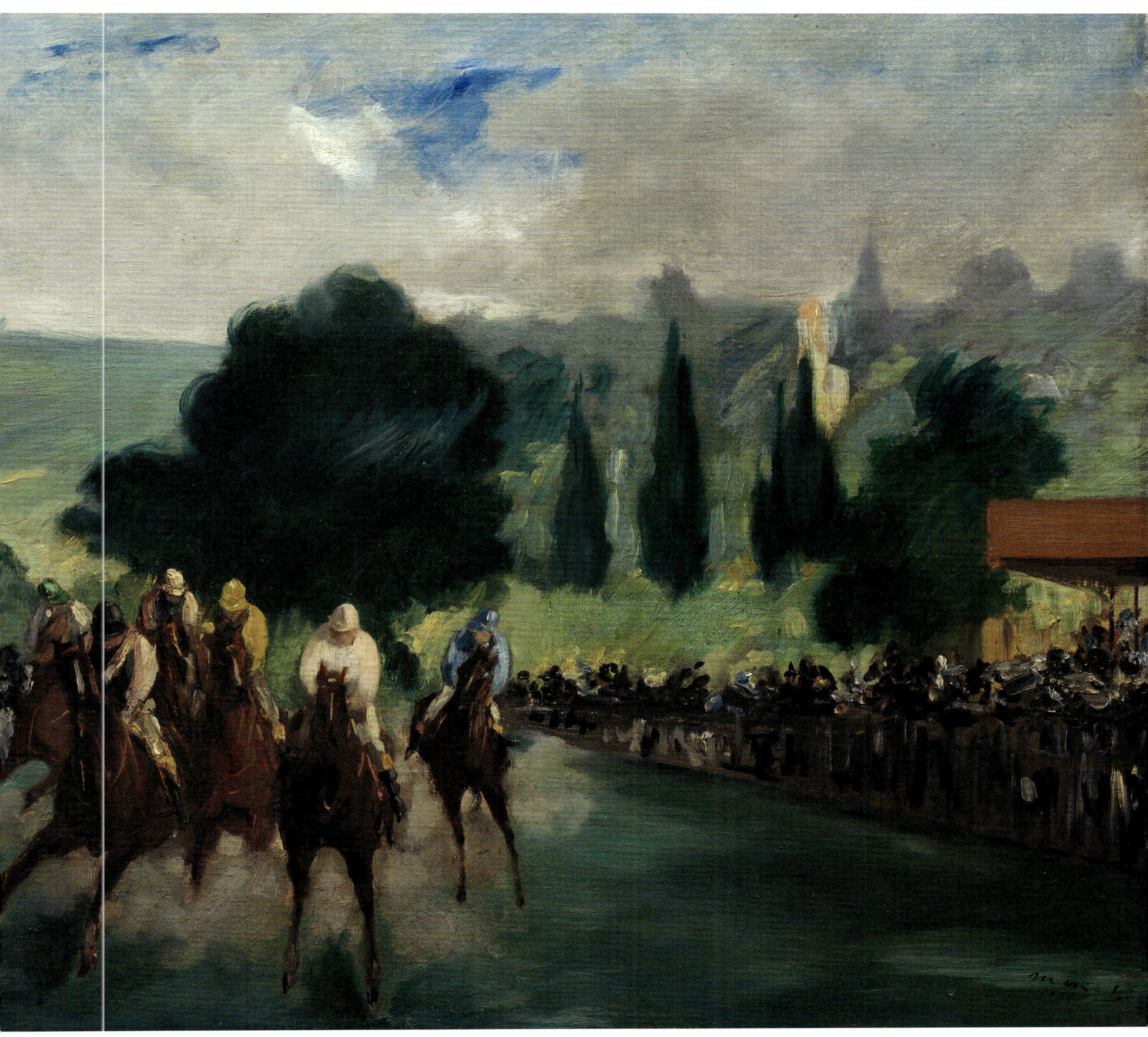

47

Eva Gonzalès

1870
Oil on canvas, 75 ¼ × 52 ½ in.
(191.1 × 133.4 cm)
Sir Hugh Lane Bequest, 1917,
London, The National Gallery.
In partnership with Dublin,
Hugh Lane Gallery, NG3259

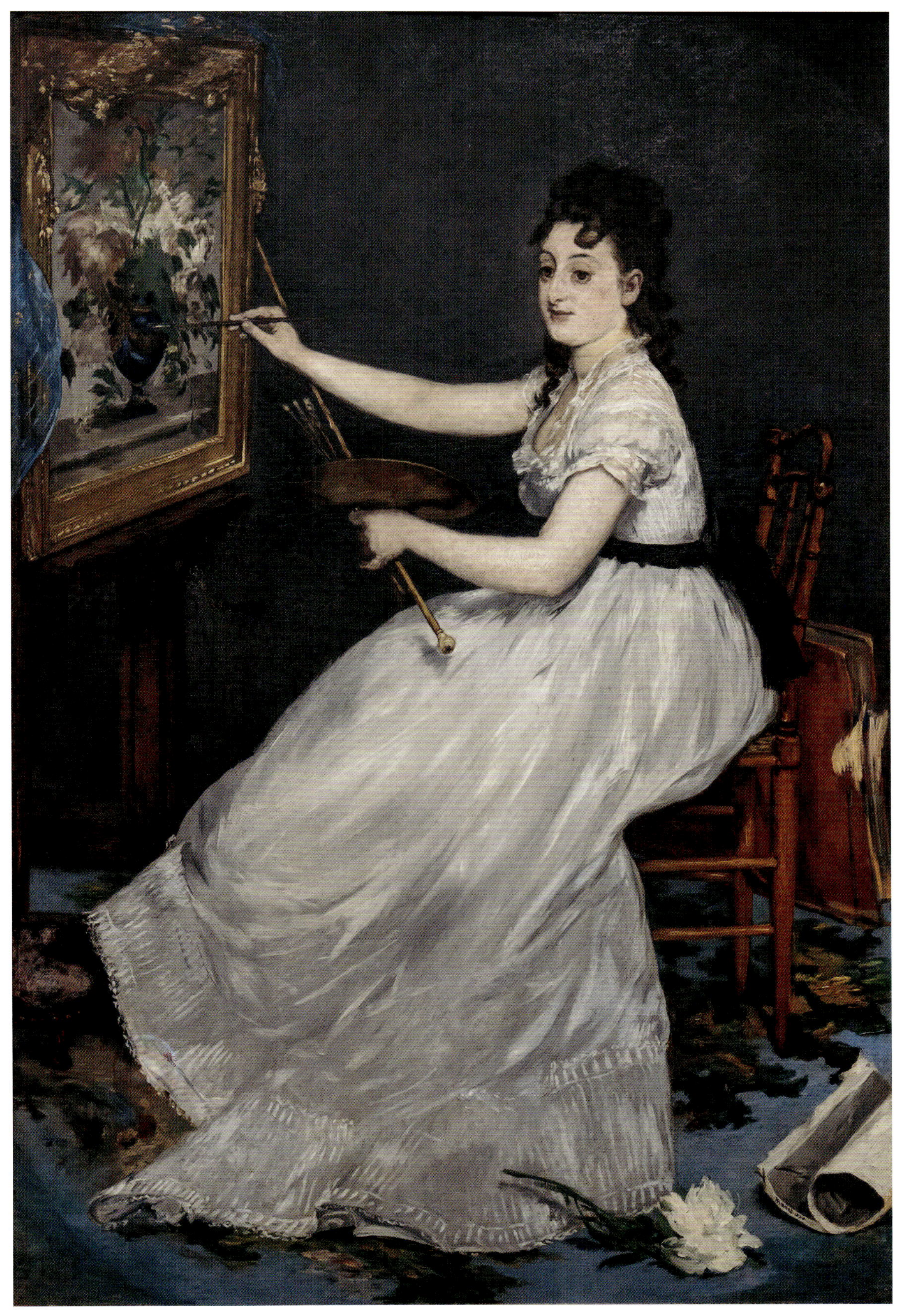

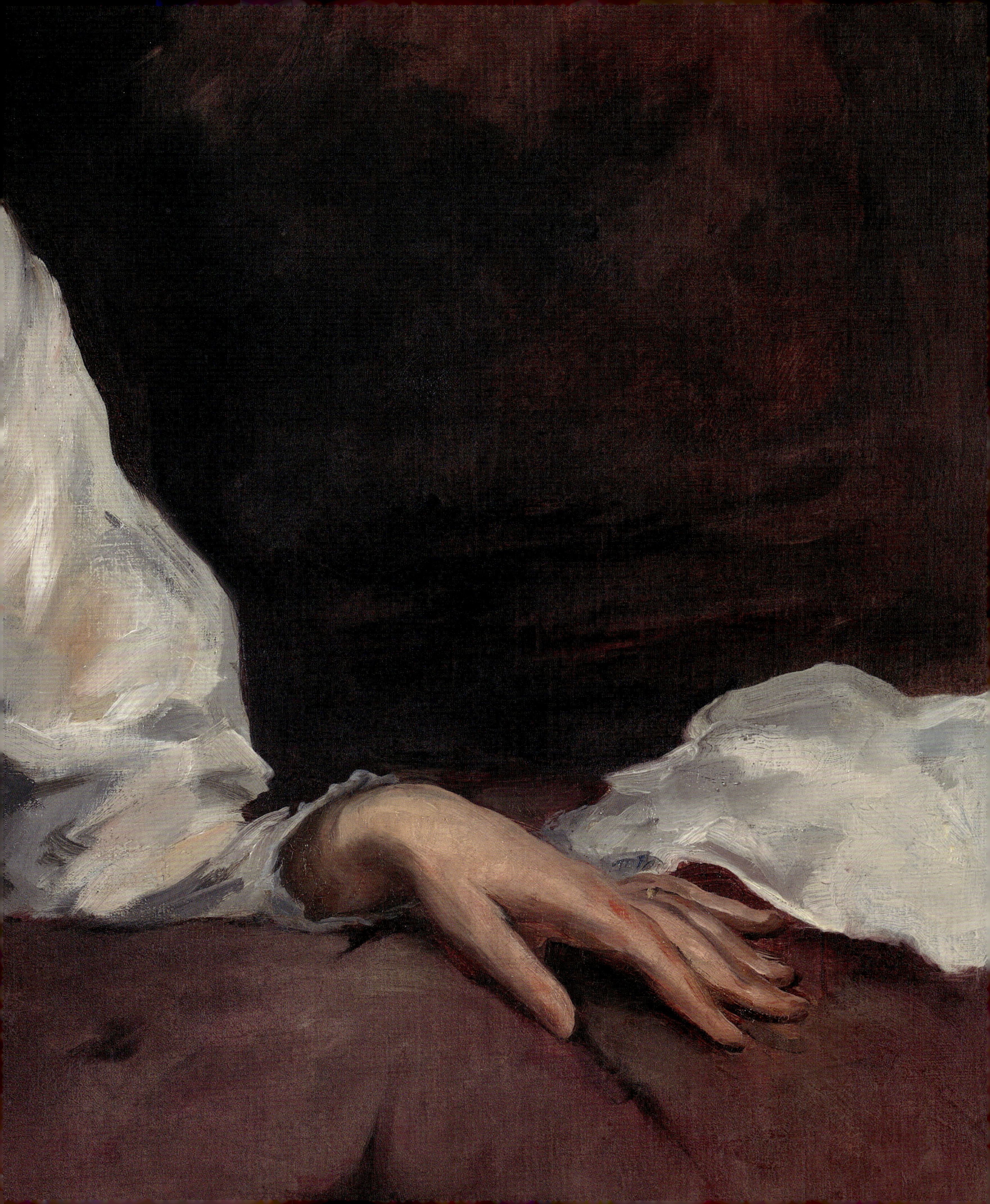

48

Repose

1870
Oil on canvas, 59 ⅛ × 44 ⅞ in.
(150.2 × 114 cm)
Providence, RISD Museum,
Bequest of Mrs. Edith
Stuyvesant Vanderbilt Gerry,
59.027

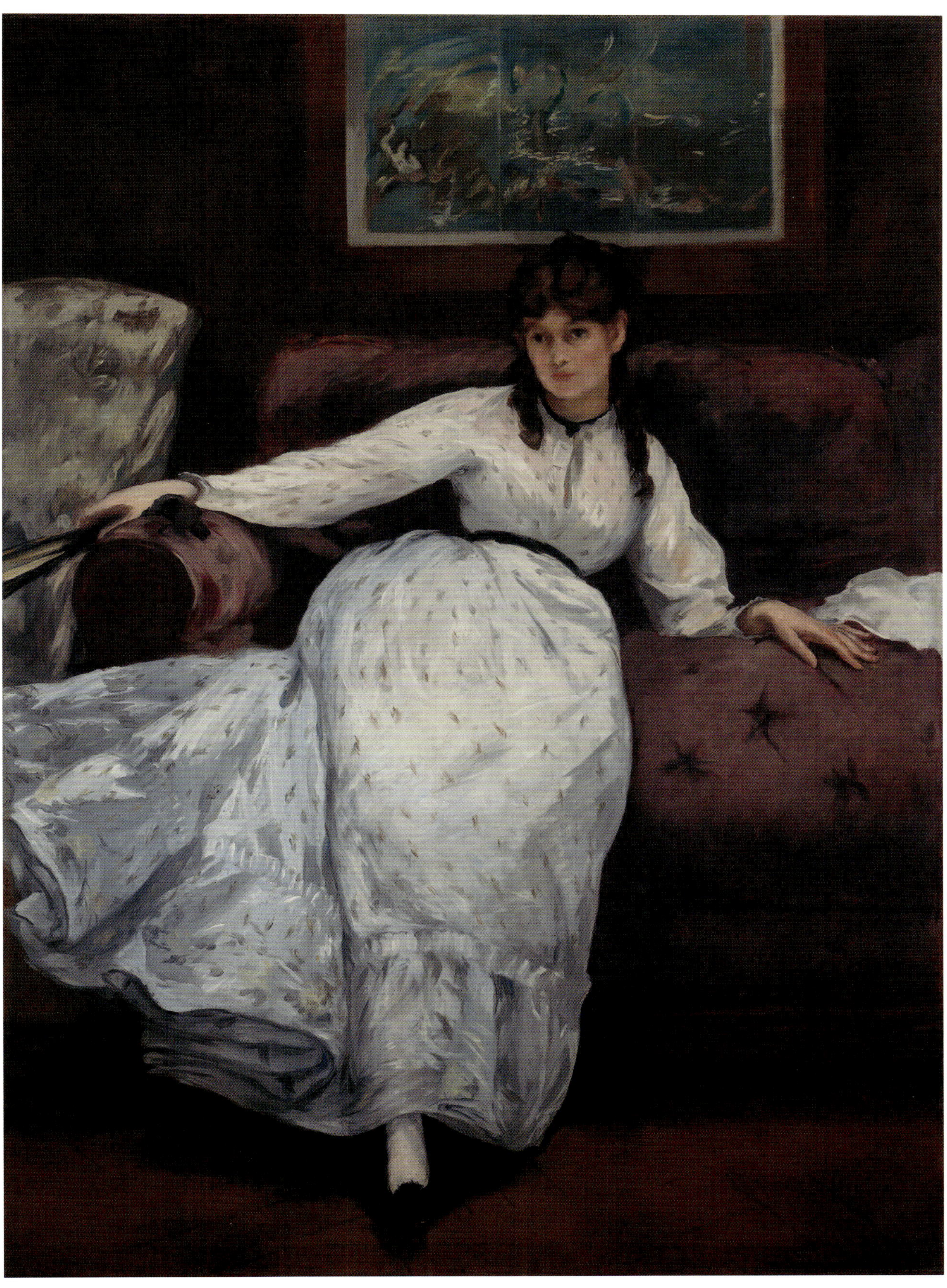

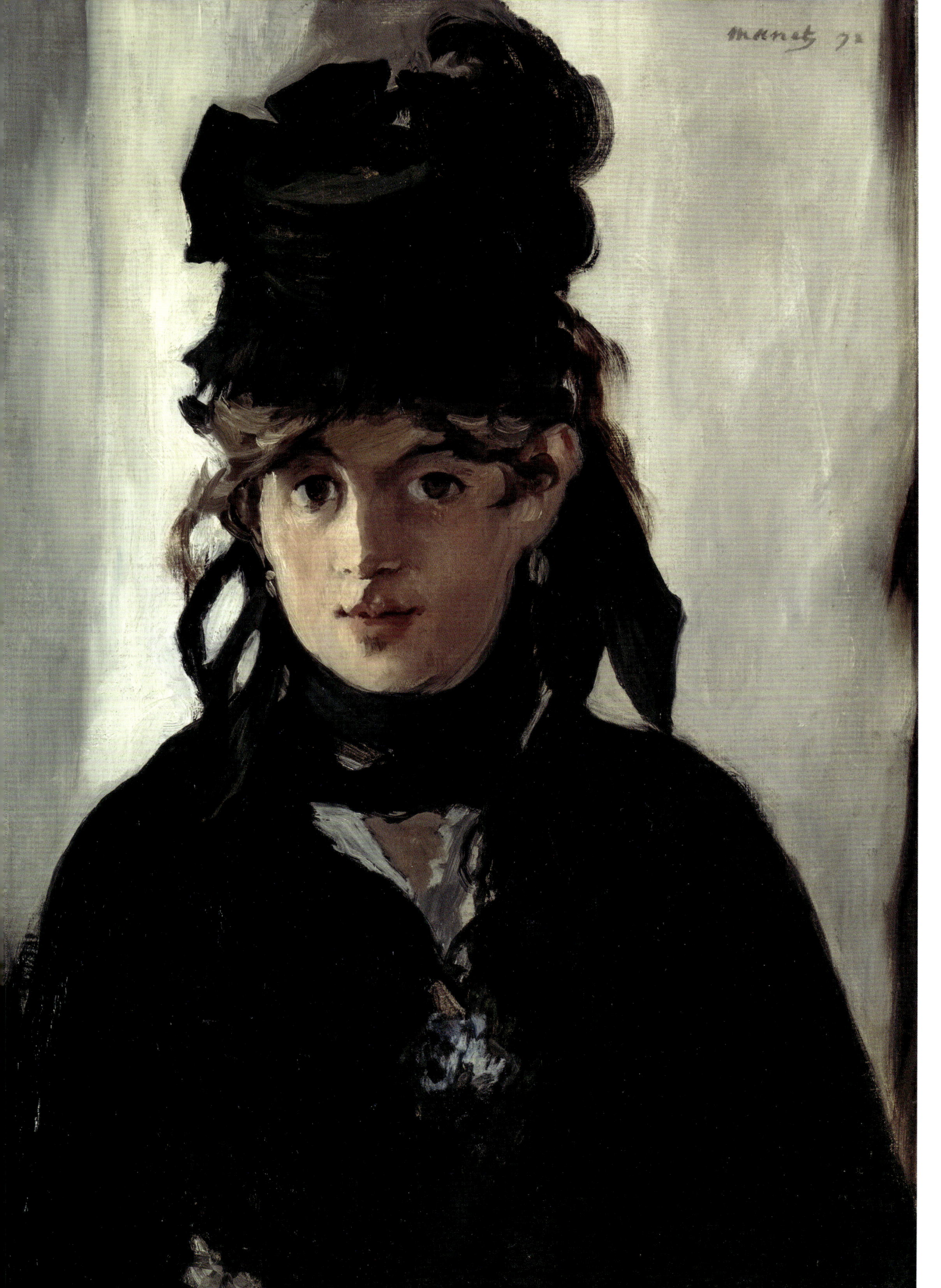
manet 72

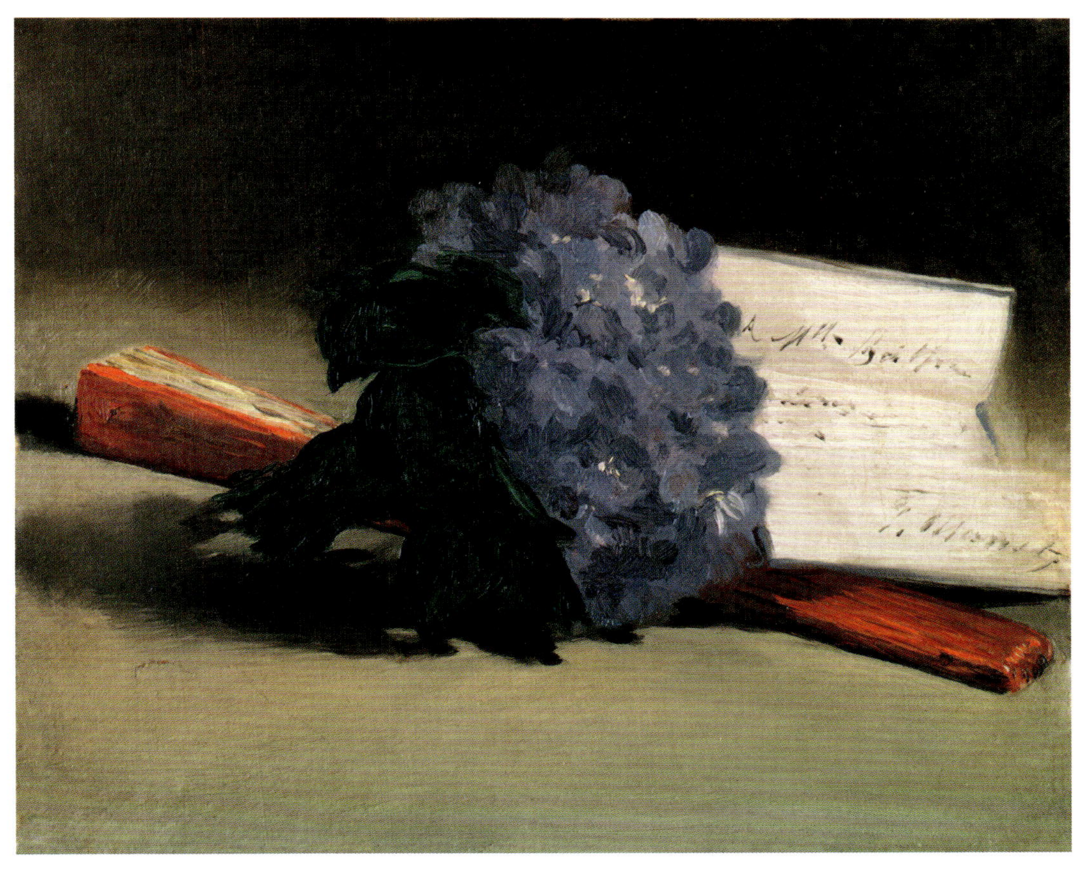

49

Berthe Morisot with a Bouquet of Violets

1872
Oil on canvas, 21 ⅔ × 16 in.
(55.5 × 40.5 cm)
Paris, Musée d'Orsay,
RF 1998 30

50

Bouquet of Violets

1872
Oil on canvas, 10 ⅔ × 8 ⅔ in.
(27 × 22 cm)
Private Collection

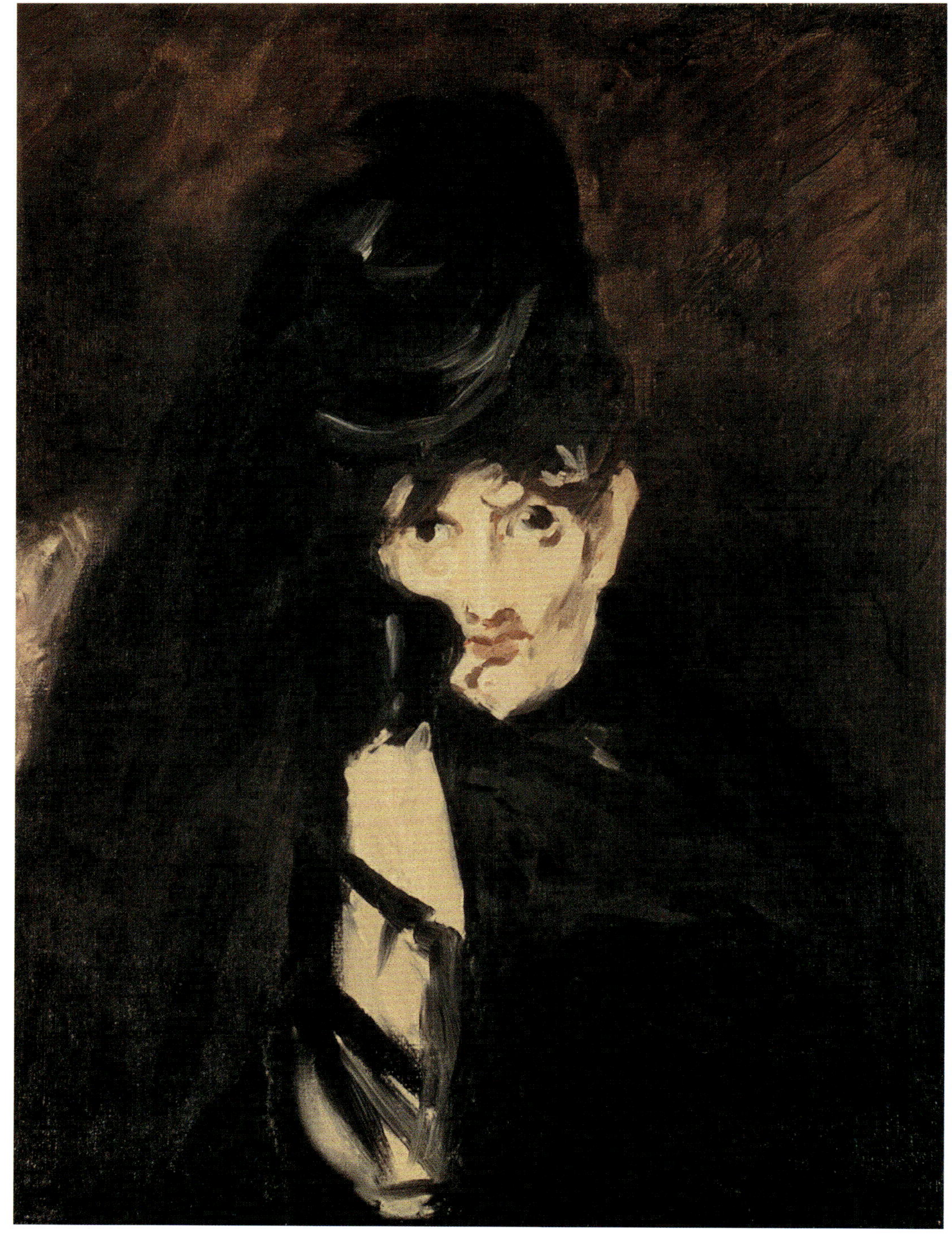

51

Berthe Morisot in Mourning

1874
Oil on canvas, 23 ⅝ × 18 ⅞ in.
(60 × 47.9 cm)
Switzerland, Private Collection

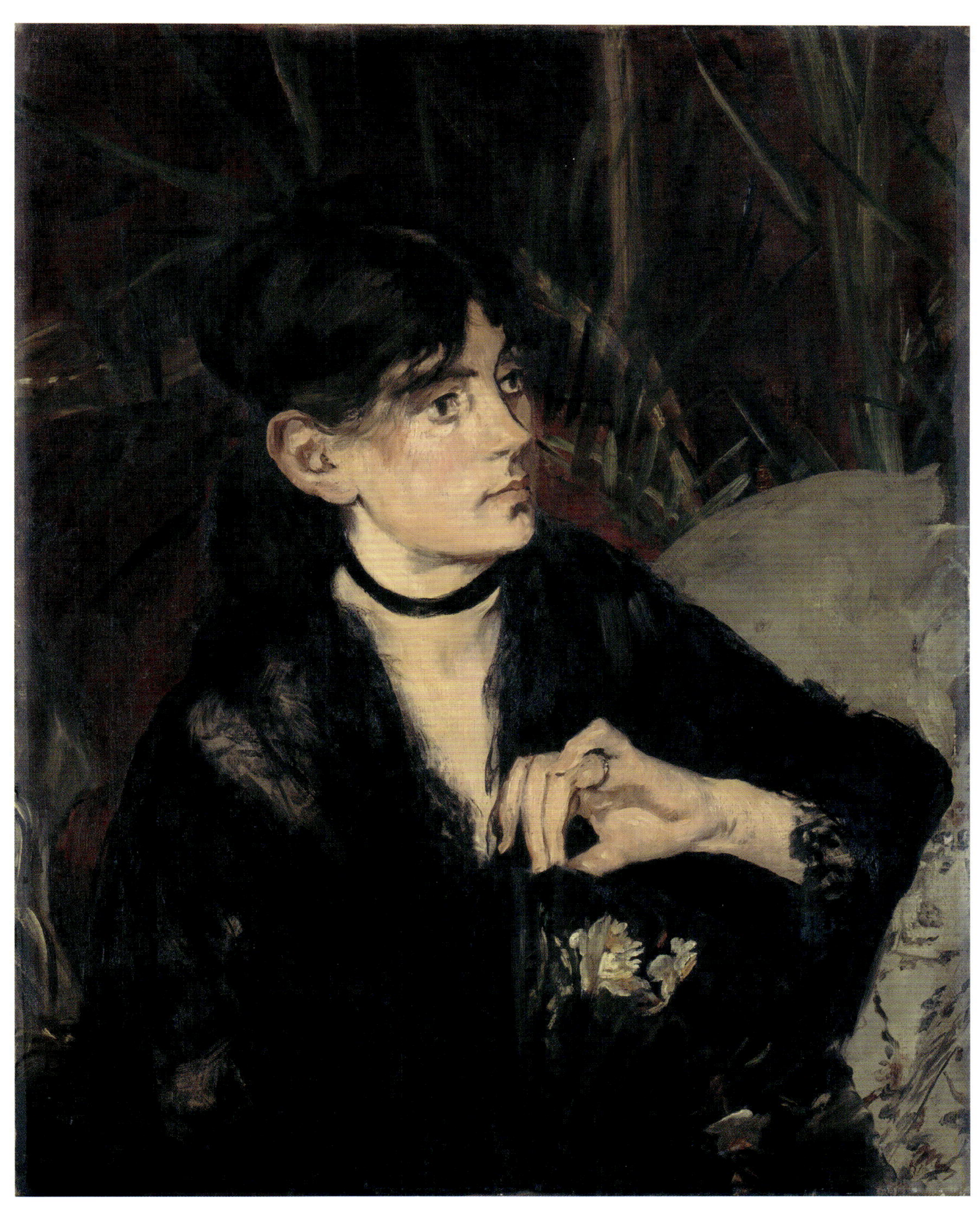

52

Berthe Morisot with a Fan

1874
Oil on canvas, 24 × 19 11/16 in.,
(61 × 50 cm)
Lille, Palais des Beaux-Arts
de Lille, inv. D 2000-1-1

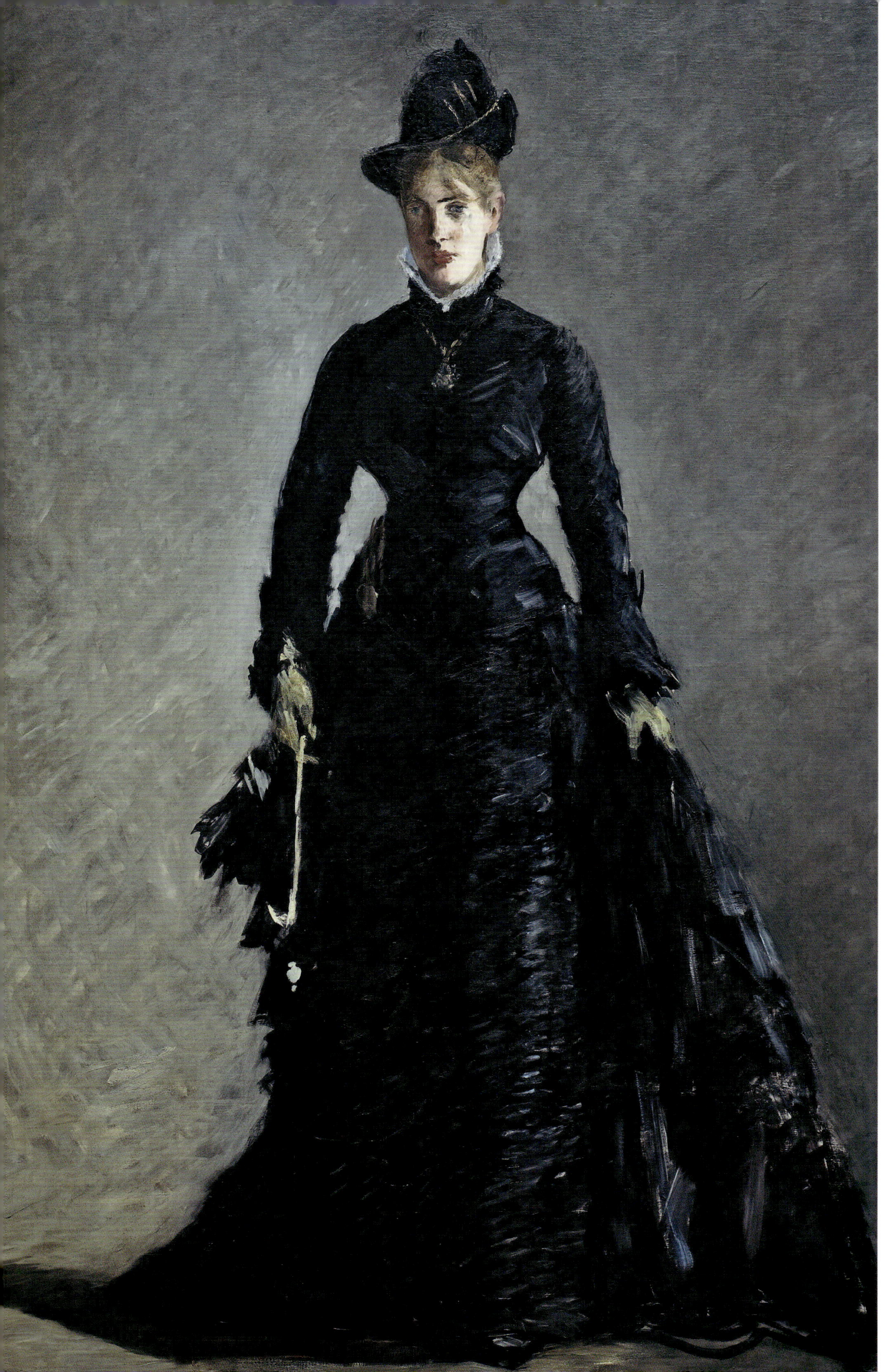

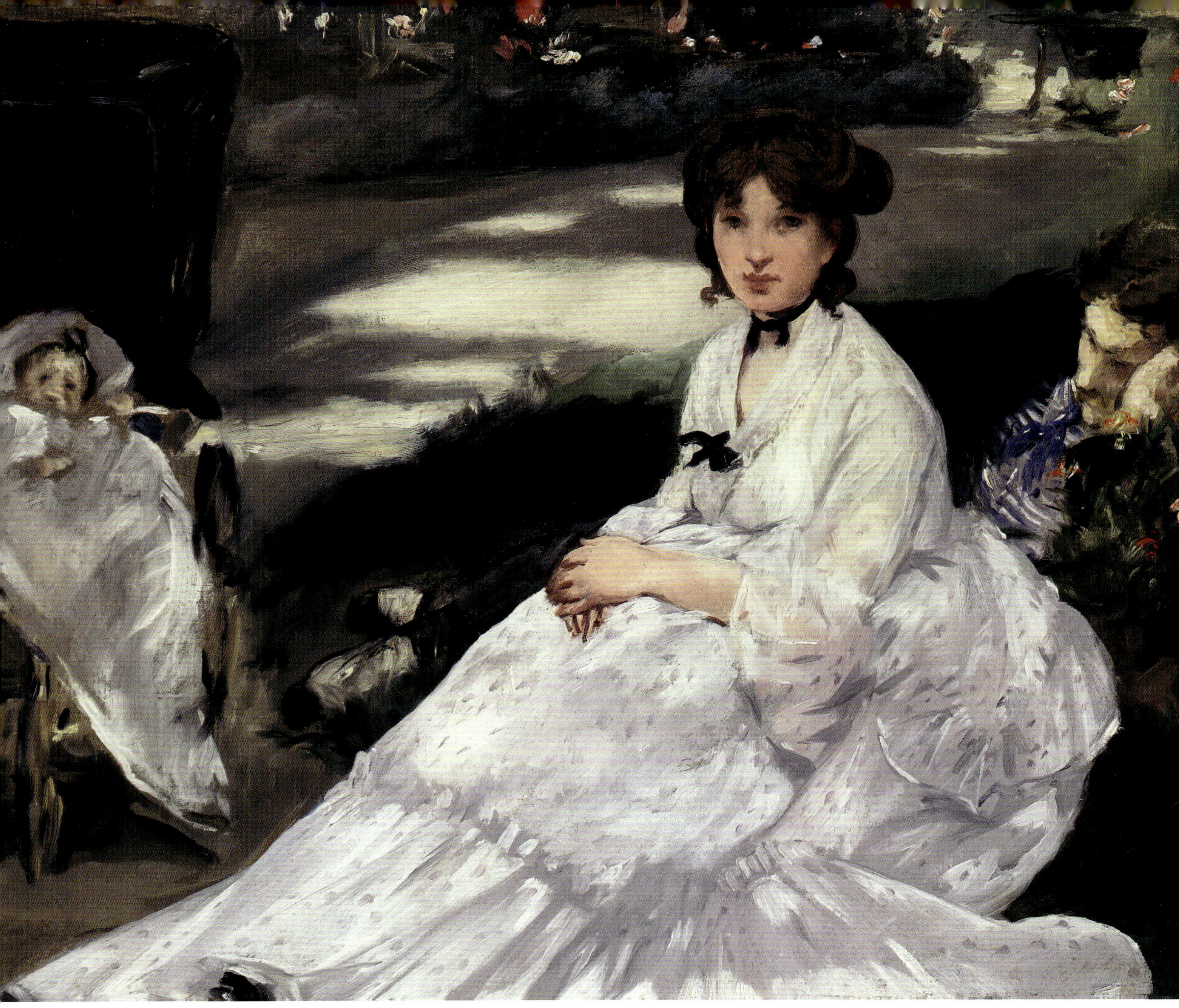

53

La Parisienne

ca. 1883
Oil on canvas, 75 ½ × 49 ¼ in.
(192 × 125 cm)
Stockholm, Nationalmuseum,
NM 2068

54

In the Garden

1870
Oil on canvas, 17 ½ × 21 ¼ in.
(44.5 × 54 cm)
Vermont, Shelburne
Museum, Shelburne, Gift
of Dunbar W. and Electra
Webb Bostwick, 1981-82
(27.1.1-200)

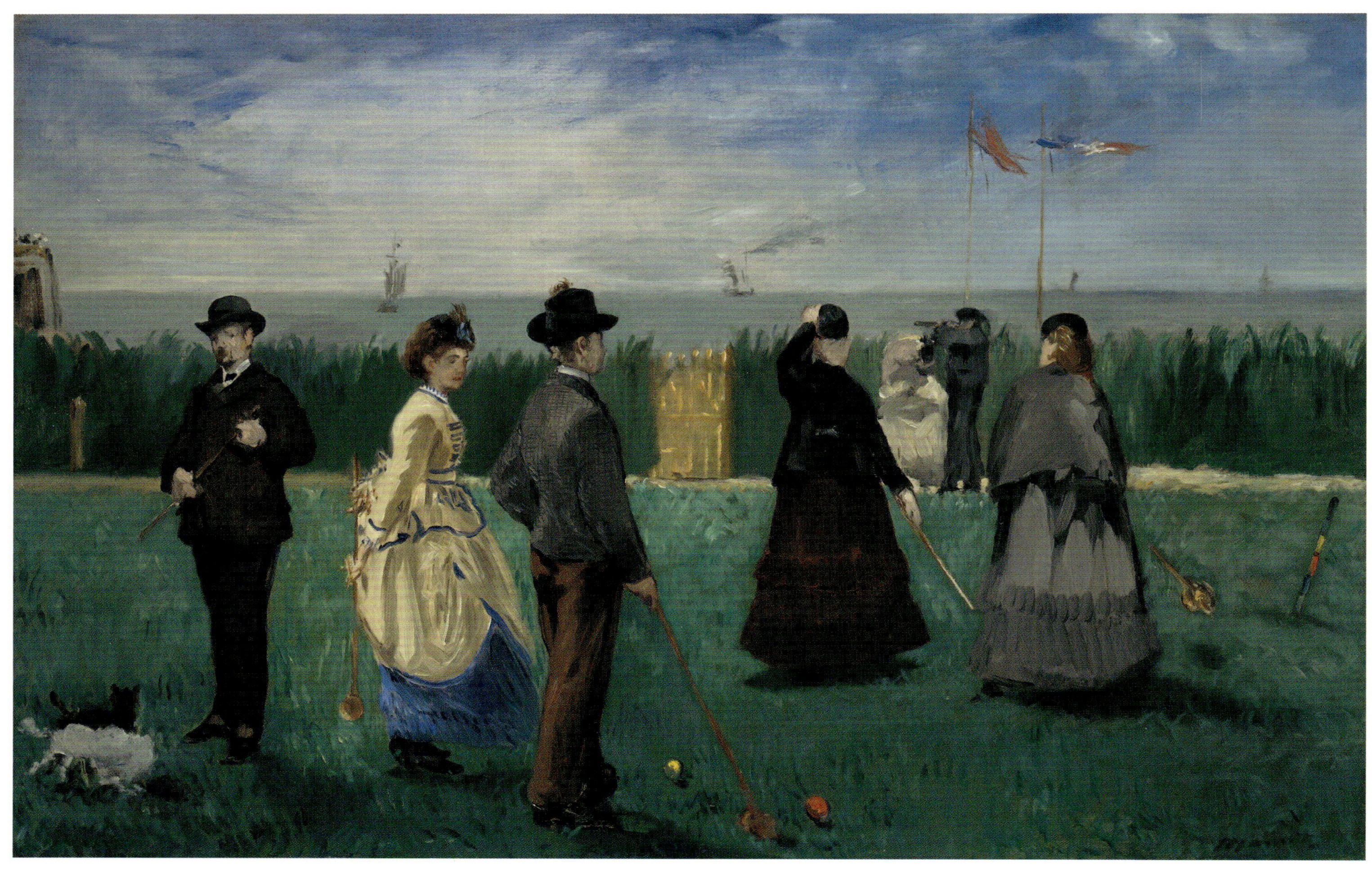

55

The Croquet Party

1871
Oil on canvas, 18 × 28 ¾ in.
(45.7 × 73 cm)
Kansas City, Nelson Atkins Museum of Art Gift of Henry W. and Marion H. Bloch, 2015.13.11

56

Masked Ball at the Opera

1873
Oil on canvas, 23 ¼ × 28 9/16 in.
(59.1 × 72.5 cm)
Washington, D.C.,
The National Gallery of Art, Gift of Mrs. Horace Havemeyer in memory of her mother-in-law, Louisine W. Havemeyer, 1982.75.1

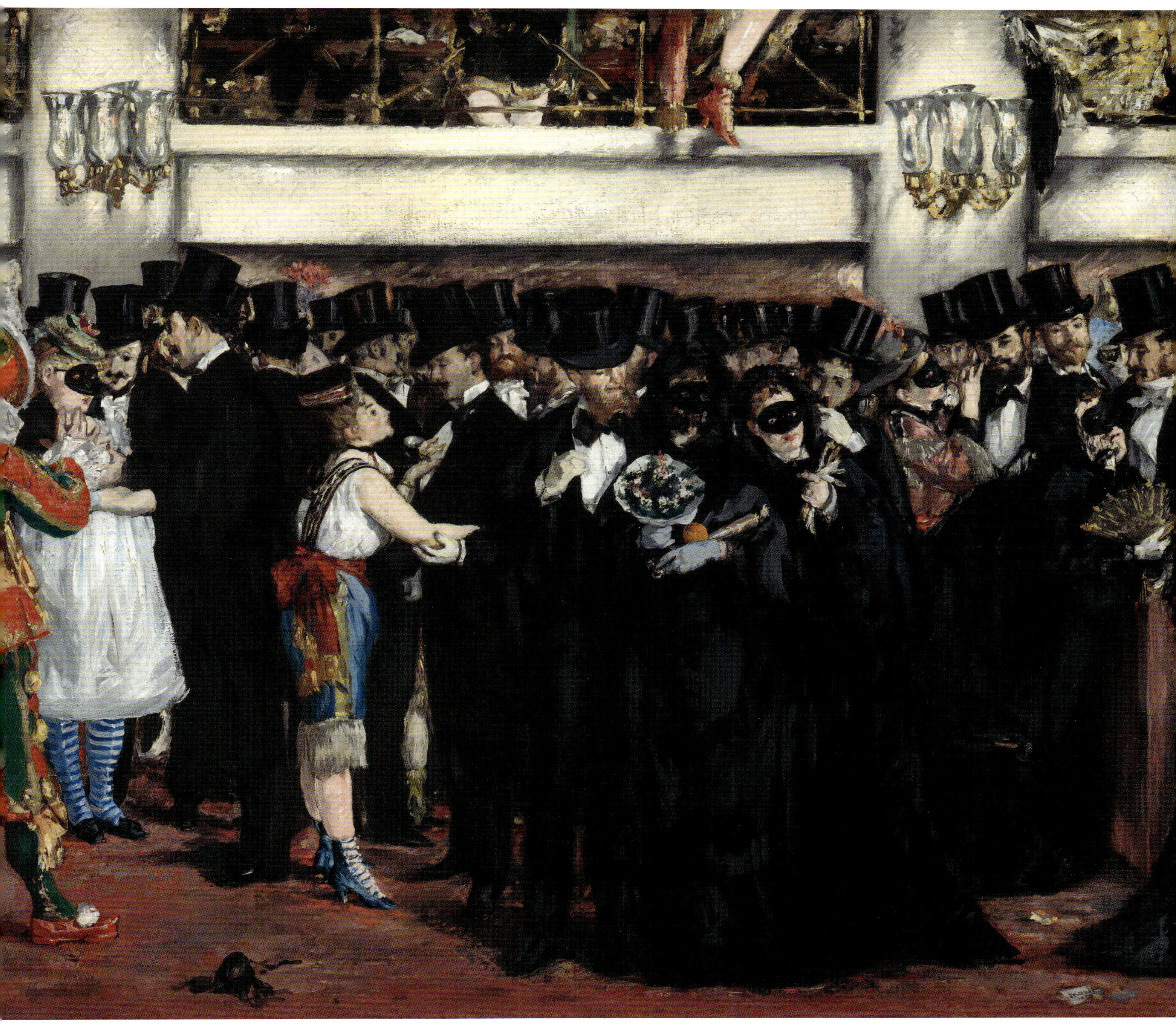

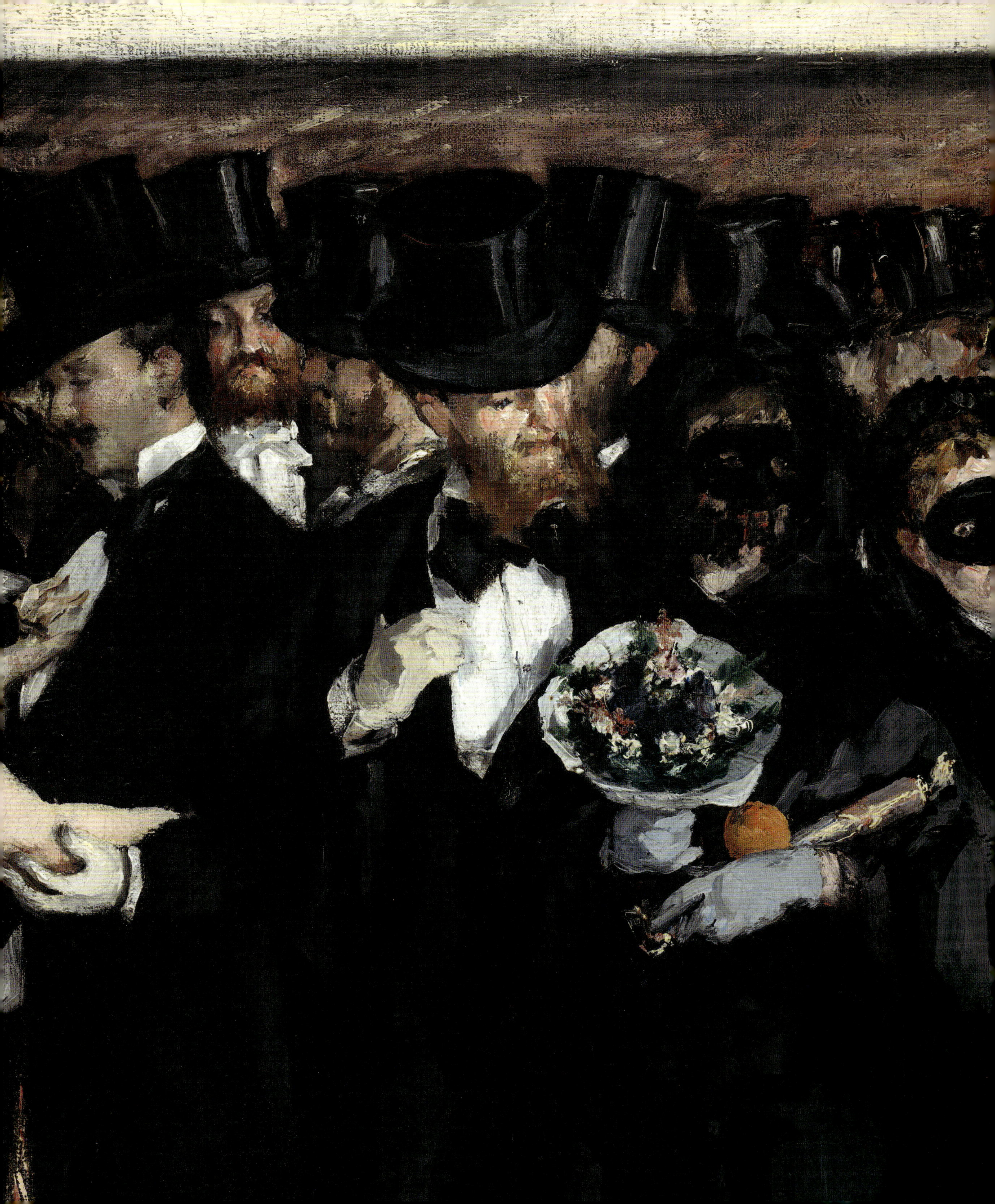

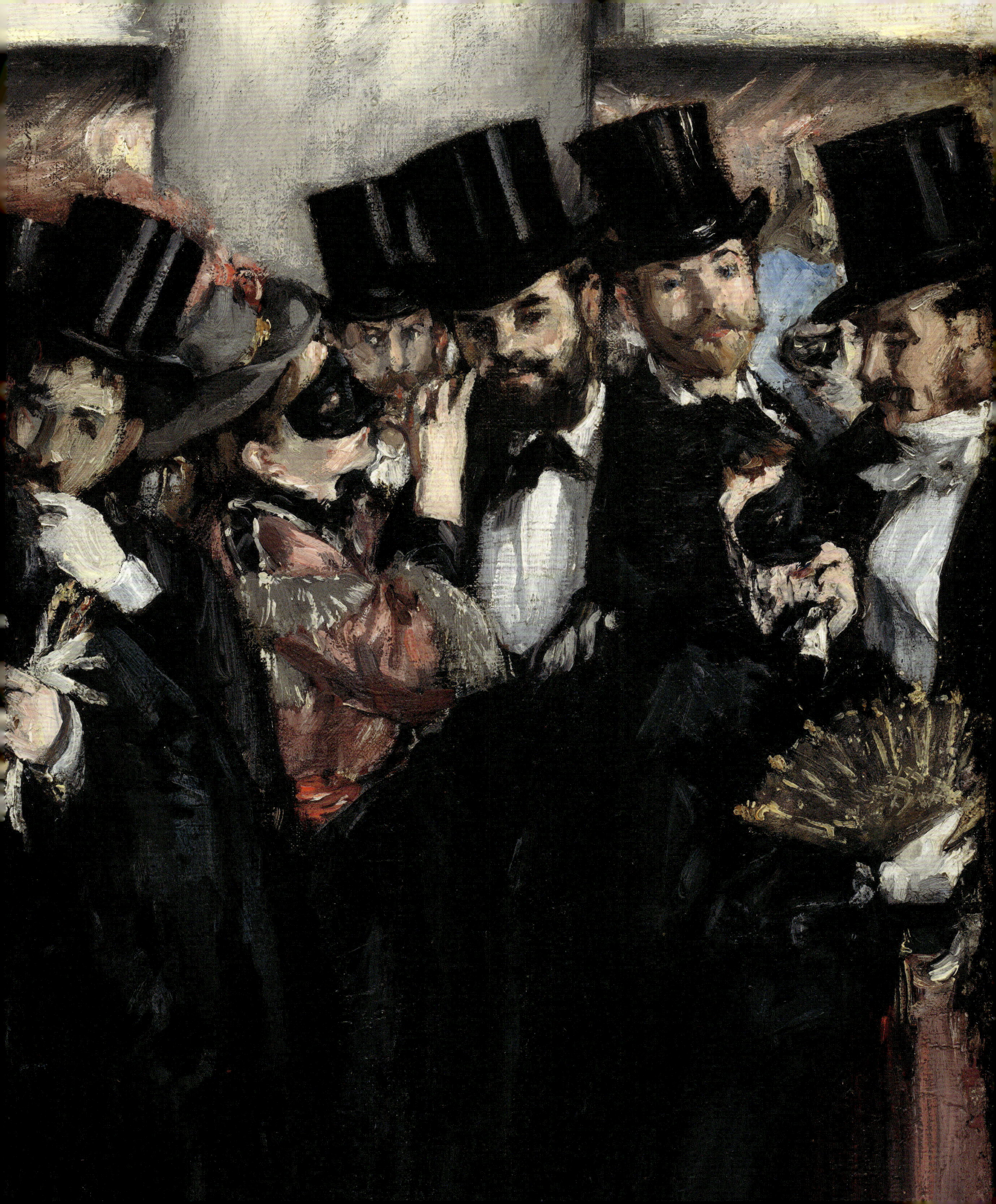

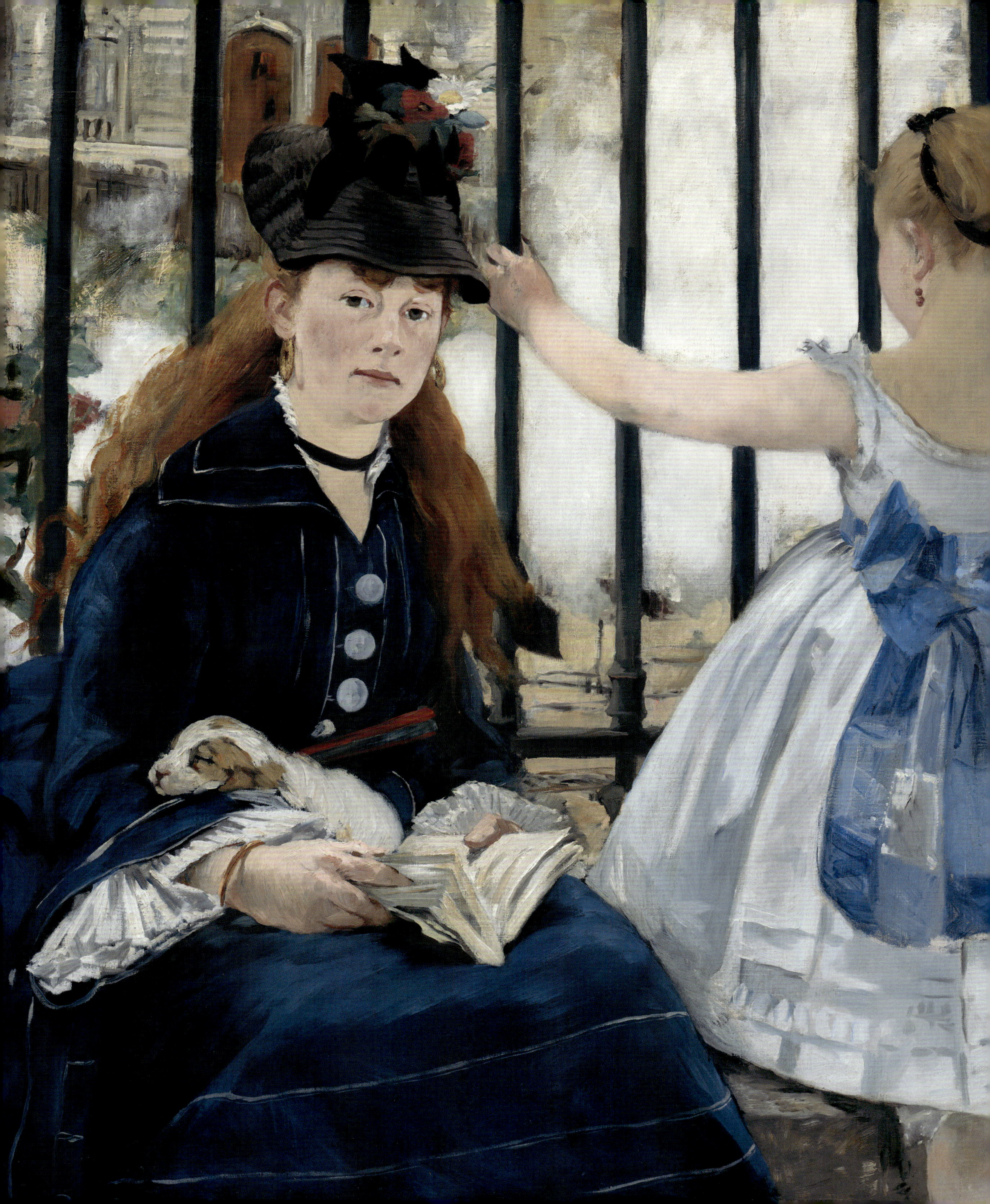

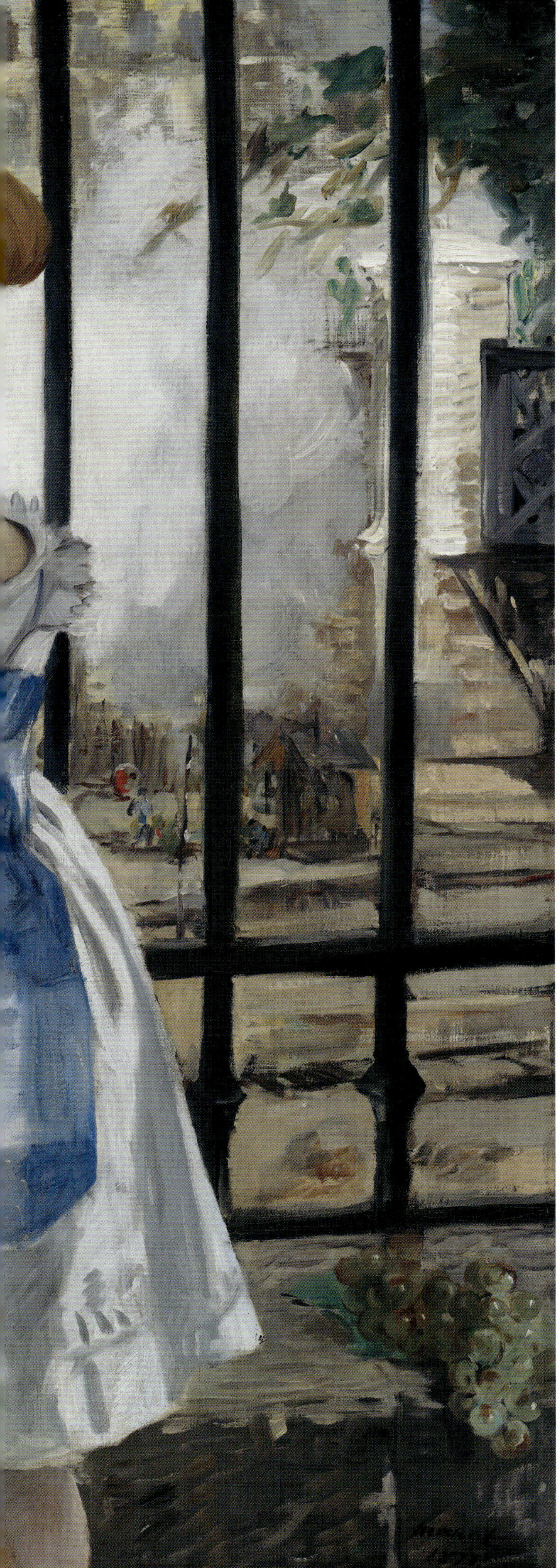

57

The Railway

1873
Oil on canvas, 36 ¾ × 43 ⅞ in.
(93.3 × 111.5 cm)
Washington, D.C., The
National Gallery of Art,
Gift of Horace Havemeyer
in memory of his mother,
Louisine W. Havemeyer,
1956.10.1

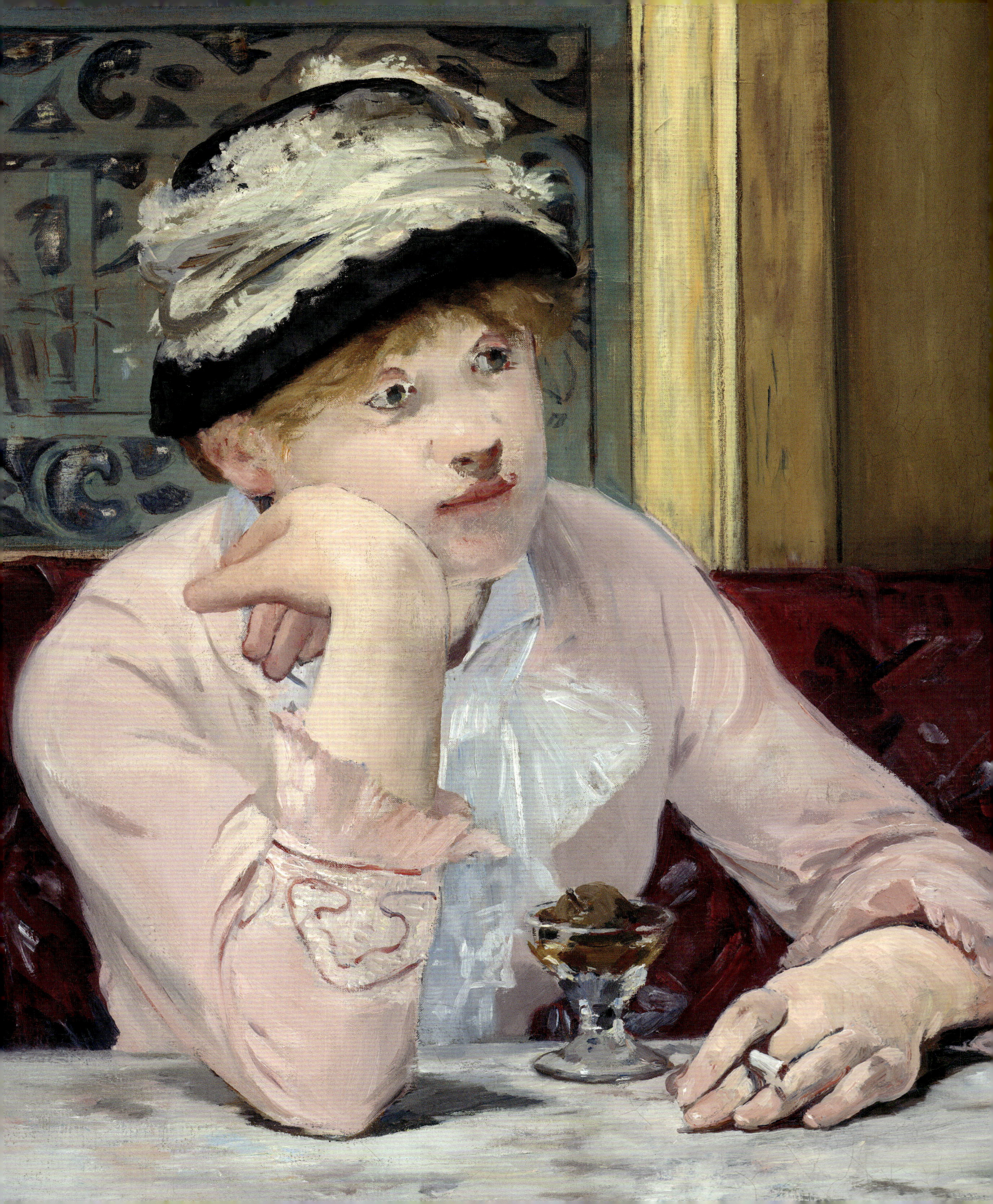

Manet and Impressionism

The radical nature of Manet's paintings from the 1860s galvanized a group of emerging artists, who were attracted by the modernity of their subjects and technique. By 1865, Claude Monet, eight years younger than Manet, was at work on a plein air response to Manet's *Luncheon on the Grass* (fig. 31). Although there is no evidence that Monet saw Manet's work at the Salon des Refusés in 1863, much later in his life Monet referred to his own work as "after Manet."[1] Similarly, by the end of the decade both Monet and Auguste Renoir were painting large-scale figure paintings that, like Manet's images of Victorine Meurent, elide the distinction between portraiture and genre subjects. These artists' presence in Fantin-Latour's 1870 group portrait set in Manet's studio in the Batignolles quarter of Paris declares their allegiance to Manet as the leader of the avant-garde (see p. 119). The artists and writers in this formal portrait gathered regularly at the nearby Café Guerbois, the site of lively discussions that stimulated their creativity, which Monet recalled in an interview in 1900: "They sharpened one's wits, encouraged frank and impartial inquiry, and provided enthusiasm that kept us going for weeks and weeks until our ideas took final shape."[2] By 1874, however, the locus of avant-garde art shifted from the Batignolles to the Parisian suburb of Argenteuil, a fifteen-minute train ride from the Saint-Lazare station.[3]

At the first Impressionist exhibition in April 1874, Monet exhibited a freely painted canvas of a sunrise over the port of Le Havre on the Normandy coast, whose title, *Impression, Sunrise*, would soon give rise to the name of this new movement in art (Musée Marmottan Monet, Paris). The painting also established Monet as the new face of avant-garde art, his notoriety eclipsing that of "the painter of the black cat." Manet's refusal of the group's invitation to join its first exhibition in 1874 did not escape the judgment of Edgar Degas, who wrote to a fellow artist, "Manet seems determined to keep aloof, he may well regret it . . . I definitely think he is more vain than intelligent."[4] Nonetheless, in the summer of 1874 Manet sought out Monet's company in Argenteuil, where the artist's family had been renting a house since 1871 (possibly secured with the assistance of Manet, whose family property was in the neighboring town of Gennevilliers).

Detail of fig. 64

Over the course of the summer, Manet realized a group of outdoor scenes set in Argenteuil and its environs. Although Manet, an inveterate studio painter, had experimented with outdoor painting before 1874 (fig. 54), his Argenteuil works reveal an unprecedented focus on this approach. As Monet scholar Paul Hayes Tucker has noted: "In a dramatic role reversal, Manet was in Argenteuil as a student—at least in terms of plein air painting, since that had not been a consistent part of his oeuvre in the 1860s."[5]

During his first visit, on July 23, Manet captured Monet's wife, Camille, and their young son Jean relaxing in their backyard as Monet tended to the garden (fig. 58). Manet painted the informal family portrait outdoors, adapting the loose, visible brushwork that Monet favored in the 1870s, perhaps in homage to his subject. Renoir, who arrived unexpectedly on the same day, produced two related works. One canvas, now lost, depicted Manet, seated at his easel in the garden and clad in a straw hat and painter's smock, painting his portrait of the Monet family; the other is a close variant of Manet's family portrait, painted alongside him and emulating his technique. Much later, Monet amusingly recounted Manet's response to Renoir's paintings that day: "He's a nice lad, but since he's your friend, you should encourage him to give up painting straight away; what he does is simply awful."[6]

Manet subsequently realized another portrait of Monet and his wife, portrayed in the boat that Monet had transformed into a floating studio, in which he plied the Seine in search of motifs to paint (fig. 61). Monet recalled, "What delightful hours I spent with Manet in that little boat! He painted my portrait there."[7] The portrait, painted from a vantage point on the dock overlooking the Argenteuil boat basin, shows Monet as a "painter-sailor," clad in an artist's blouse and straw boating hat. He is at work on a painting that has been identified as a view of the shore over his left shoulder, part of which Manet also replicated in the upper left corner of his own work.[8] In addition to the dual references to Monet's painting in his portrait, Manet also assimilated Monet's imagery and technique.[9] He foregrounded the Seine with the riverbank of Gennevilliers on the left and the smokestacks of Argenteuil's factories in the distance, motifs that recur in Monet's Argenteuil paintings. Manet later praised Monet as the "Raphael of water," adding, "He knows it in its movements, in all its depths, at all its hours."[10] Here, Manet adapted the broken brushstroke of Impressionism in painting the background landscape, especially evident in the treatment of the river and its reflective surface, which contrasts with the "Manet-like" broad, flat planes of color used to render the boat itself.[11]

Manet's engagement with Impressionism in the summer of 1874 continued in a pair of boating scenes (figs. 59 and 60). Argenteuil, located along the Seine River, was a mecca for boating, catering to avid sportsmen as well as day-tripping Parisians. In Manet's works the ostensible subject of boating serves as a pretext for a staged encounter between a man and a woman. His brother-in-law Rodolphe Leenhoff posed for both scenes, attired in the colors of the elite

Auguste Renoir, *Madame Monet and Her Son*, 1874, oil on canvas, 19 13⁄16 × 26 ¾ in. (50.4 × 68 cm). Washington, D.C., The National Gallery of Art, Ailsa Mellon Bruce Collection, 1970.17.60

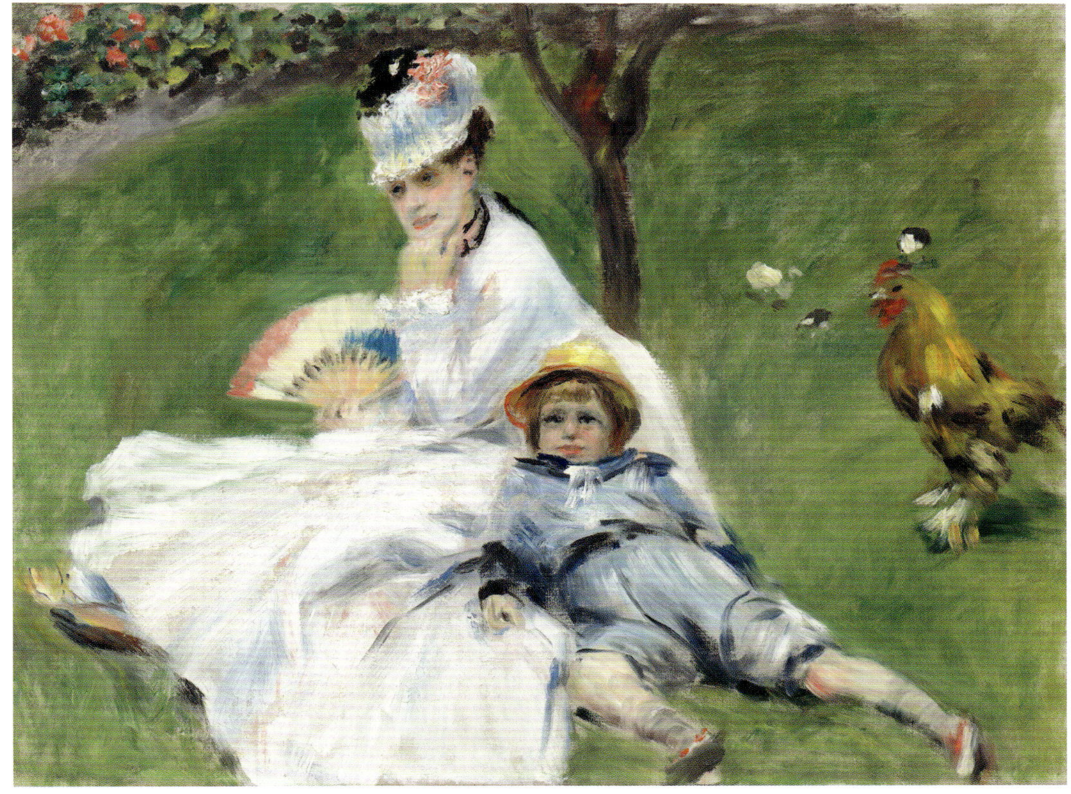

Asnières yachting club, *Cercle nautique*, in *Boating* and dressed as a boatman in the other work, known as *Argenteuil*. In *Boating*, his companion wears a fashionable striped dress and the same hat donned by Manet's wife in two beach scenes from 1873 (fig. 12), while her less elegant attire in the other scene suggests a woman of a lower social class.[12] The identity of the model who posed as Rodolphe's female companion is unknown, but she is alleged to have complained, "posing for M. Manet was no joke—some rough sessions."[13] In both, the narrative remains ambiguous, laced with sexual innuendo as conveyed by Rodolphe's body language and, in *Argenteuil*, emphasized by his suggestive gesture with the rolled parasol. This aspect of Manet's boating scenes was not lost on his contemporaries; his friend Théodore Duret later commented, "Boatmen come from various walks of life, but the women they brought with them all belong to the class of second-rate ladies of pleasure. Such is the one in *Argenteuil*."[14] Both works privilege the figure over the landscape, which sets his outdoor subjects apart from those of the Impressionists in the 1870s.

The following year Manet selected *Argenteuil* for exhibition at the Salon, where its loose handling and brightly hued palette, especially the vivid blue of the Seine, were widely lampooned. As the critic for *L'Illustration* complained, "Truly, Manet makes fun of the public and of the jury by sending them barely outlined sketches . . ." A year after the first Impressionist exhibition, Manet's overt borrowings from Impressionism prompted the critic Jules Castagnary, writing in *Le Siècle*, to proclaim, "He is the head of a school and exerts an indisputable influence on a certain group of artists." Although he regretted the absence of modeling in Manet's figures, Castagnary defended the Impressionist practice of "open air" painting as he saw it embodied in Manet's canvas: "In every case, each attempt at this is a step away from convention toward greater truth, naturalism, and life."[15] In the eyes of his contemporaries, *Argenteuil* established Manet as the leader of the Impressionists in 1875: "The Impressionists start from Baudelaire . . . M. Édouard Manet . . . sets the tone, marks the cadence. He is the drill sergeant." The same writer said of Manet's *Argenteuil*, "the *plein air* school loudly proclaims it a masterpiece."[16]

In September 1876, Manet's friend Stéphane Mallarmé, who had first defended the artist against the Salon jury two years earlier, published an article in an English journal that posited him as "the head of the school of Impressionists, or rather the initiator of the only effective movement in this direction."[17] Mallarmé's characterization captures Manet's influence on Impressionism but sets him apart from its artists.[18] As an expression of gratitude, Manet began Mallarmé's portrait less than a month after his article was published (fig. 62). In the work, the poet lounges on the couch in Manet's studio, smoking his signature cigar, its plume of smoke evoking Impressionism's fleeting moment. Its casual air contrasts with the formality of Manet's 1868 portrait of the writer Émile Zola (fig. 39) and reflects his close relationship with Mallarmé. The close-up vantage point adds to the portrait's intimacy and immediacy. In his article, Mallarmé wrote admiringly of Manet's innovative "manner of cutting down the pictures," which the framing of his own portrait would subsequently reflect.[19] After Manet's death in 1883, the poet recalled the daily visits to his studio on the rue de Saint-Pétersbourg over the course of their ten-year friendship.[20]

Manet's forays into Impressionism during the 1870s were not limited to plein air painting and outdoor scenes. His ongoing exploration of subjects drawn from modern urban life align his work with the similar Impressionist imagery of Degas, his friend and artistic rival from the time the two first met in the early 1860s, reportedly in the galleries of the Louvre.[21] In an 1877 painting Manet depicted a courtesan at her toilette, modeled by the notorious actress and demimondaine, Henriette Hausser, provocatively clad only in her undergarments (fig. 63). The elegantly attired male figure who observes her was a late addition to the composition.[22] A comment by Manet captures the erotic charge of his image—"The satin corset may be the nude of our era."[23] The work's vivid palette and loose brushwork reflect Manet's ongoing dialogue with Impressionism. Unanimously rejected by the Salon jury, Manet's painting was put on display in a shop window on the boulevard des Capucines on the opening day of the Salon. The critic Joris-Karl Huysmans observed the public's reaction: "From morning to night, crowds gather before this canvas, and . . . it draws screams of indignation and derision . . ."[24] In his discussion of the work, Huysmans was the first to posit Manet's subject as Nana, a character that Zola had recently introduced in his novel *L'Assommoir*, published serially from April 1876 to January 1877.[25] Manet reported to Zola in the summer of 1876, "I've just read the latest installment of *L'Assommoir* in *La République des lettres*—marvelous!"[26] Manet began work on his canvas late that same year, but he would disavow the author's fictional character as the subject of his painting, asserting in 1880, "I never intended to do Zola's *Nana*."[27]

Despite Manet's denial, the painting's association with Zola's literary creation persisted, and it has been known as *Nana* ever since. That identification has only recently been called into question.[28] Both Manet's painting and Zola's novel play on the currency of prostitution in the popular imagination. The nickname "Nana," like that of "Olympia" in the 1860s, was then fashionable among the demimondaines of Paris, the type embodied by Manet's model for *Nana*.[29] The model herself was nicknamed "Citron" (Lemon) in a playful nod to her then-lover the Prince of Orange. The allusion to prostitution in Manet's work is reinforced by the presence of the male figure, who conjures the men in top hats and black suits populating Degas's contemporaneous brothel scenes. Unlike Degas's small-scale prints, which were intended for private consumption, Manet's *Nana*—an image of a Parisian prostitute—is rendered on the large scale traditionally reserved for history painting, an overt transgression not lost on his contemporaries. As one reviewer observed in 1877, "M. Manet's high crime is not so much that he paints modern life as that he paints it *life size* . . ."[30]

Nana launched what the artist's early biographer termed his "'naturalist' series," a trio of paintings with female protagonists from 1877 that capture the changing face of Parisian life in the early years of the Third Republic.[31] Manet was a regular at the Café de la Nouvelle Athènes, which was frequented by the avant-garde; both he and Degas each had a reserved table there in the 1870s. The site has been linked to Manet's first café subject, made around 1877, for which the actress Ellen Andrée again served as his model (fig. 64). Its title, *Plum Brandy*, refers to the brandied plum on the table before her, a popular Parisian specialty mentioned in the pages of Zola's *L'Assommoir*. In fact, Manet's scene was a studio construct, the marble table a prop that would reappear in subsequent works (fig. 88) and the background décor his creation.[32] The work recalls a similar café scene by Degas, exhibited in the 1876 Impressionist exhibition, which also features Ellen Andrée, shown nursing a glass of absinthe seated next to the artist Marcellin Desboutin.

Continuing his exploration of Parisian café culture, in 1878 Manet undertook a large-scale, multi-figure scene set at the Brasserie de Reichshoffen in Montmartre, perhaps with an eye to exhibiting it later that year at the Exposition Universelle. A small sketch of top-hatted man and a waitress facing each other across a café table, drawn from life in one of his pocket sketchbooks, may have served as the basis for the work, which he painted in his studio.[33] Manet ultimately abandoned the large canvas, cutting it in two sections, both of which he reworked as independent paintings. *Au Café* (fig. 66) represents what was the left two-thirds of the original canvas. Its angled marble countertop aligns with that in *Corner of a Café Concert* (fig. 67), the remaining portion of the original canvas. In addition, cast shadows that appear on the counter of *Au Café* accord with the placement of glasses on the bar of the latter work. The pair of canvases record the mix of social classes that the brasserie attracted, from elegantly attired *flâneurs* and Parisiennes to workers in blue smocks, there to partake of the Alsatian beer for which it was known and, in this instance, the entertainment on offer. The background of *Corner of a Café Concert* reveals a female performer on a stage accompanied by musicians below. Despite their close proximity, the figures in Manet's two café scenes do not interact with one another. Manet enlisted his friends, the actress Ellen Andrée and the artist Henri Guérard, to model for the fashionably dressed pair of figures along with a waitress from the Brasserie de Reichshoffen whom he admired for her "skill" at carrying multiple glasses of beer without spilling any while serving her customers.[34] Before the Second Empire, servers in cafés and brasseries were usually men; the modernity of the waitress in Parisian café culture likely appealed to Manet as well.[35]

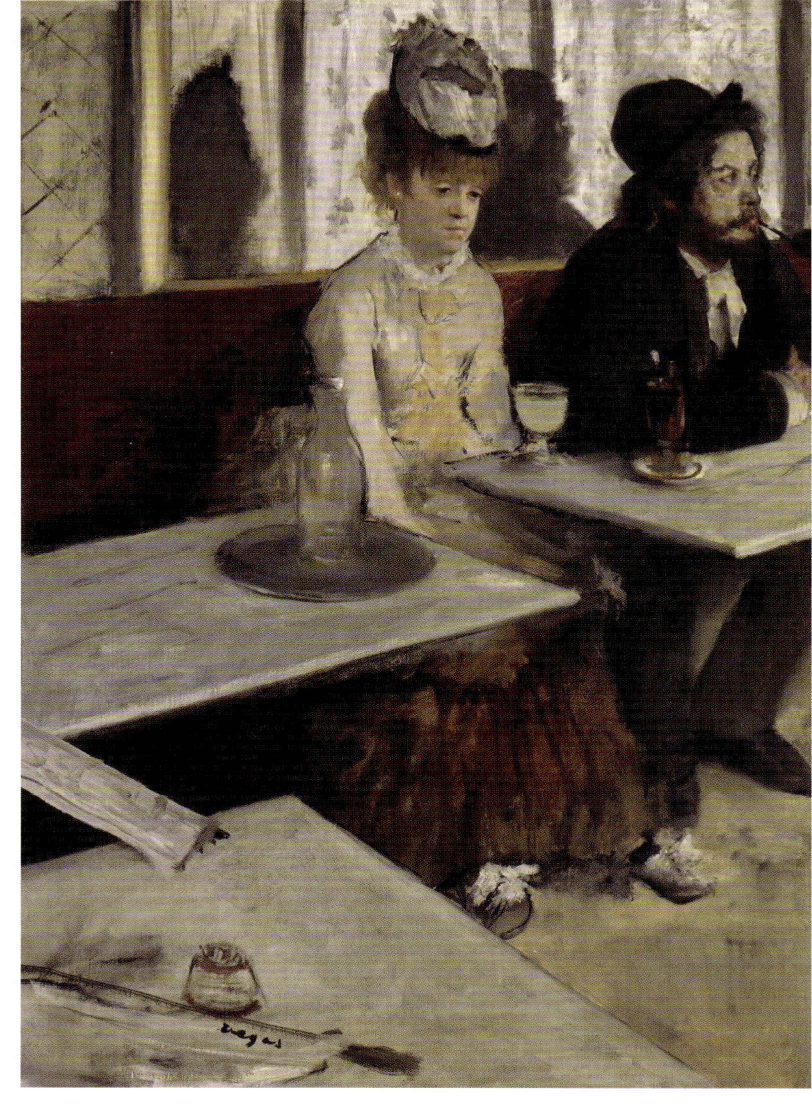

Edgar Degas, *In a Café*, 1875-76, oil on canvas, 26 ¼ × 27 in. (92 × 68.5 cm). Paris, Musée d'Orsay, RF 1984

Manet's café scenes also represent some of his most innovative compositions. Their boldly cropped forms and compressed spaces embody the fleeting aspect of modern urban life that lies at the heart of Impressionist imagery. In *The Café Concert*, painted around 1879–80 (fig. 65), the three principal figures look in different directions, disconnected from one another. At a late stage in the work, Manet added the background mirror and its reflection of the performer known as Elsa La Polonaise, which provides a pretext for the gaze of the top-hatted gentleman in the direction of the unseen stage. The lack of a central focus point further heightens the effect of the scene as glimpsed in a fleeting moment, emphasized by the seemingly rapid brushwork.[36] In April 1880, Manet exhibited café scenes in oil and pastel, including this work and *Plum Brandy*, in a solo show at the gallery of the illustrated journal *La Vie Moderne*. The exhibition marked the first time his café subjects were shown to the public. Critics variously derided Manet's imagery as "life's most vulgar and least appealing scenes" and "subjects drawn from a disreputable Parisian bohemia."[37] The critic for *L'Artiste* mockingly asked, "Why this series of women drinking beer, these clients of the cafés-concerts?"[38]

As the decade neared its end, Manet continued to engage in a dialogue with Impressionism as he mined modern life for subjects to paint. The conservatory had recently been popularized as an amenity in Parisian town homes; in the 1870s, the enclosed garden figured in contemporary art and Naturalist novels as a site for clandestine encounters and scenes of seduction. An 1877 acccount of a visit to Manet's studio describes a painting set in a conservatory as a work in progress: "against a garden bench leans a man of the world . . . he leans over the green-painted rail of the seat, resting on his crossed arms, while he speaks to his young wife seated on the bench . . ." (fig. 68). The conservatory setting, like that of Manet's *Balcony* in 1869, is emblematic of modern Paris (fig. 25). Manet's friends Jules and Jeanne Guillemet posed in the artist's studio for *In the Conservatory*; Manet reportedly had a green bench as a studio prop, and he painted husband and wife against a backdrop of exotic flowers, rendered with uncharacteristic precision of detail. The compositional prominence accorded their wedding bands is at odds with the figures' apparent detachment from each other. The work hovers between portrait and genre subject, and the ambiguous nature of the figures' relationship seemingly confounded Manet's contemporaries. In his review of the Salon of 1879, where the work was exhibited, the critic Huysmans described the scene simply as "a woman seated on a green bench, listening to a gentleman."[39] At the other extreme, a caricature of the painting in *Le Journal Amusant* was captioned, "An innocent young person cornered in the conservatory by an infamous seducer."[40]

The composition of *In the Conservatory* suggestively recalls an earlier plein air painting by Monet, set in the artist's garden at Argenteuil, for which Camille Monet and an unidentified male model posed. Manet could have seen Monet's garden scene during the summer of 1874 when he was painting with Monet in Argenteuil. Its affinity with Monet's genre scene is reinforced by Manet's choice to exhibit it alongside an earlier work, *Boating*, at the Salon of 1879. *Boating* was a product of his 1874 "Impressionist" interlude in Argenteuil, where he absorbed the lesson of Monet, as is manifest in its outdoor subject and bright palette. Manet reportedly made his decision after contemplating *Boating* on his easel in his studio for fifteen days.[41]

In 1879, Manet's pairing of *In the Conservatory* and *Boating*, both of which represent variations on Monet's Impressionist imagery, might well have been a strategic move, reasserting his continued relevance among the avant-garde while capitalizing on the embrace of Impressionist plein air painting by more mainstream Salon artists.[42] The Salon opened the day after the fourth Impressionist exhibition closed, from which Manet had again abstained. A review of this exhibition suggested that Manet's influence in the movement was waning: "The formerly uncontested leader has shoved away the boat containing his disciples, and it continues nonetheless to sail without him in its noble independence."[43] Around the time that the Salon opened its doors in May, the artist Gustave Caillebotte, one of the organizers of the 1879 Impressionist exhibition, reported to Monet, "Manet himself is beginning to see that he has taken the wrong road."[44] The Salon reviews of Manet's work were mostly unfavorable with Zola faulting him for failing to live up to his artistic potential: "In short, during the last fifteen years we have seen no other painter with greater subjective ability. If his technical side equaled the correctness of his perception, he would be the great painter of the second half of the nineteenth century."[45]

The Salon jury was also becoming more tolerant of plein air painting, especially the work of such Academic painters as Jules-Bastien Lepage and Ernest-Ange Duez, whose modified Impressionist style has been described as "*juste milieu*" ("happy medium"). By 1880, Manet was credited with having paved the way for these artists and their "lukewarm Impressionism," in the words of one contemporary critic.[46] Thus Manet's avowed desire, confided to his friend Proust in 1879—"to paint a plein air picture, but completely outdoors where the figures' features would dissolve, as he put it, into the vibrations of the atmosphere"—reflects his ongoing engagement with both contemporary Salon art as well as the work of the Impressionists.[47] The following year, Manet exhibited another plein air painting at the Salon.

Chez le Père Lathuille, en plein air (fig. 69) was painted in 1879 on the terrace of a restaurant of the same name not far from Manet's studio in the Batignolles quarter. By appending "en plein air" to the work's title, Manet unequivocally aligned his work with trends in contemporary painting. Its subject signals Manet's ongoing interest in café subjects, complementing those that were just featured in the artist's exhibition in the gallery of *La Vie Moderne*. The models for his outdoor luncheon were Louis Gauthier-Lathuille *fils*, the eldest son of the restaurant's owner, and the actress Ellen Andrée, who was replaced after a few sittings by Judith French. Gauthier-Lathuille recalled the scenario that Manet staged for his models: "You, you're a volunteer flirting with a pretty woman. Place yourselves like this and like that and chat with each other while I'm working . . ." Manet first asked him to pose in his military uniform but then changed his mind: "Take off your tunic . . . Put on my jacket!"[48] The scene captures the dynamic of a younger man making overtures to an attractive older woman dining alone, which in itself contravened accepted social codes for women of her social standing. The impropriety of Manet's subject offended conservative critics such as Paul Mantz, who decried the work as "a scene 'in the open air' of the most disturbing character." Salon critics also balked at the work's overtly Impressionist

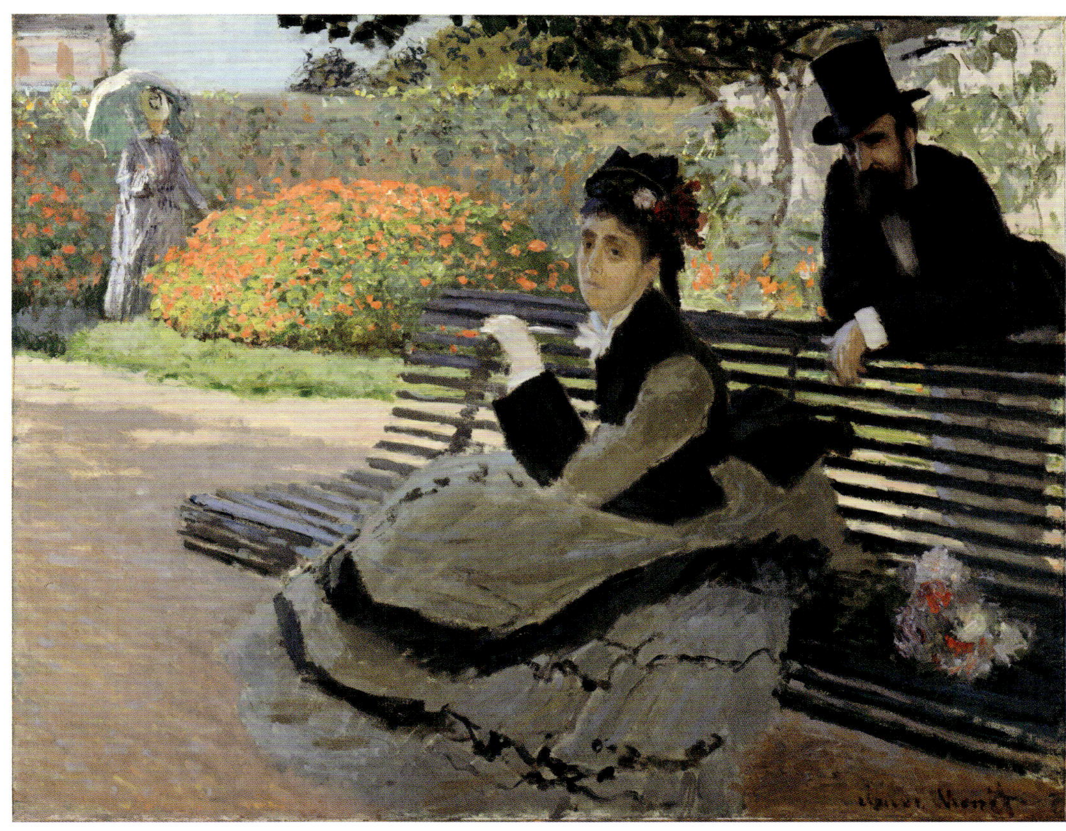

Claude Monet, *Camille Monet on a Garden Bench*, 1873, oil on canvas, 23 ⅞ × 31 ⅝ in. (60.6 × 80.3 cm). New York, The Metropolitan Museum of Art, The Walter H. and Leonore Annenberg Collection, Gift of Walter H. and Leonore Annenberg, 2002, Bequest of Walter H. Annenberg, 2002, 2002.62.1

handling, from Manet's remarkably loose brushwork, especially in the background, to the unblended colors and colored shadows visible throughout—Mantz called out the male figure's "blue hair," and other critics faulted Manet for the work's apparent lack of finish, likening it to "a rough draft."[49]

Although Manet received few favorable reviews in 1880, more progressive writers recognized the originality of Manet's modern-life subject. The critic Armand Silvestre wrote admiringly, "There is truly extraordinary vitality in this little scene of everyday life . . ." For Huysmans, Manet's canvas embodied "modernism": "Here is life, depicted without exaggeration, just as it is, in all its actuality, a daring work, unique from the point of view of modern painting in this prolific Salon." Yet, Huysmans maintained that the achievements of the Impressionists had surpassed Manet's early promise, "When all is said and done, Manet today is outdistanced by most of the painters who could once, and quite rightly, have considered him their leader."[50]

In the 1870s, Manet's art evolved in ongoing dialogue with Impressionism. Throughout the decade Manet's hoped-for success in the form of recognition at the state-sponsored Salon remained an elusive goal; he endured repeated rejections by the Salon jury, and he did not surpass the honorable mention awarded to his *Spanish Singer* at the start of his career at the Salon of 1861. In failing health, he was contemplating his artistic legacy by the end of the decade. In April 1879, he wrote to local government officials, proposing a series of paintings for the Municipal Council Chamber of the new City Hall; the works would represent, in his words, "the public and commercial life of our times," which he called "the Belly of Paris," borrowing the title of Zola's 1873 novel.[51] That June he sent a letter to the Under-Secretary of State, who had visited his studio the year before, requesting that the government consider purchasing one of his Salon paintings for the Musée du Luxembourg, which then housed works by living French artists.[52] Neither of his letters received a reply. By 1880, the same public that had hailed Manet as the leader of the avant-garde at the beginning of the decade saw him as having been eclipsed by his younger contemporaries.

1 Mary Dailey Desmarais, "Hunting for Light: *Luncheon on the Grass*," in George T. M. Shackelford, *Monet: The Early Years* [exhibition catalogue], Fort Worth, Kimbell Art Museum and Fine Arts Museums of San Francisco, 2016–17, 22.
2 Charles S. Moffett, "Manet and Impressionism," in Paris and New York 1983, 31.
3 On the significance of Argenteuil in the development of Impressionism, see Paul Hayes Tucker, *The Impressionists at Argenteuil* [exhibition catalogue], Washington, D.C., National Gallery of Art, 2000.
4 Degas's letter to James Tissot, dated "Friday 1874," cited in Moffett, Paris and New York 1983, 29.
5 Washington, D.C. 2000, 28.
6 Toledo and London 2012–13, 64.
7 *Great French Paintings from the Barnes Foundation: Impressionist, Post-Impressionist, and Early Modern* [exhibition catalogue], Washington, D.C., National Gallery of Art et al., 1993–95, 98 [n.b. there were 7 venues over 2½ years]
8 Robert Herbert, *Impressionism: Art, Leisure, and Parisian Society* (New Haven and London, Yale University Press, 1988), 235–36. Herbert identified Monet's work as *Sailboats on the Seine, Petit-Gennevilliers*, 1874 (Fine Arts Museums of San Francisco).
9 Willibald Sauerländer, *Manet Paints Monet: A Summer in Argenteuil* (Los Angeles, Getty Research Institute, 2014), 62–63.
10 Proust 1988, 46.
11 Sauerländer 2014, 62–63.
12 Herbert 1988, 236, no. 38.
13 Paris and New York 1983, 353.
14 Cited in Ibid., 353.
15 For a summary of Salon criticism, see Hamilton 1954, 187–94.
16 Cited in Paris and New York 1983, 355.
17 Mallarmé 1876, in Washington, D.C. and San Francisco 1986, 32.
18 On Manet's influence on and relationship to the new movement to which he was so closely linked in the 1870s, see Moffett, "Manet and Impressionism" in Paris and New York 1983, 29–35.
19 Mallarmé 1876, in Washington, D.C. and San Francisco 1986, 31.
20 On the portrait and their relationship, see Paris and New York 1983, 377–79.
21 On Manet's artistic dialogue with Degas, see Stephan Wolohojian and Ashley Dunn, *Manet/ Degas* [exhibition catalogue], New York, The Metropolitan Museum of Art and Paris, Musée d'Orsay, 2023.
22 Paris and New York 1983, 393.
23 Beth Archer Brombert, *Édouard Manet, Rebel in a Frock Coat* (Chicago, University of Chicago Press, 1997), 384.
24 Cited in Paris and New York 1983, 394.
25 Hamilton 1954, 201, no. 9; Tabarant 1947, 305–6.
26 Wilson-Bareau 1991, 180.
27 Letter to Émile Bergeret, early February 1880, reproduced in Chicago and Los Angeles 2019–20, 172.
28 See the analysis of the work in Leah Lehmbeck, "All the World's a Stage: Manet's Images of Model-Actresses," Chicago and Los Angeles 2019–20, 63–64.
29 Tabarant 1947, 305.
30 Cited in Paris and New York 1983, 394. On Degas's brothel monotypes in relation to Manet's painting, see 394–95.

31 Tabarant 1947, 314; along with *Nana* and *Plum Brandy*, the other work is *Skating*, 1877 (Harvard Art Museums, Cambridge, MA).

32 Chicago and Los Angeles 2019–20, 279–80.

33 Ketty Gottardo, *Goya to Impressionism: Masterpieces from the Oskar Reinhart Collection* [exhibition catalogue], London, Courtauld Gallery, 2025, 66.

34 Paris and New York 1983, 420.

35 Herbert 1988, 79.

36 See the discussion of the composition in Chicago and Los Angeles 2019–20, 281–82.

37 Samuel Rodary, "Édouard Manet: A Selection of Letters, 1878–83," in Chicago and Los Angeles 2019–20, 162.

38 Hamilton 1954, 229.

39 See the discussion of the work in Chicago and Los Angeles 2019–20, 275–76.

40 Paris and New York 1983, 436.

41 Tabarant 1947, 345.

42 On Manet and the Salon in this period, see Scott Allen, "Faux Frère: Manet and the Salon, 1879–82," in Chicago and Los Angeles 2019–20, 1–41, esp. 22–27.

43 Cited in Hamilton 1954, 212–13.

44 Ronald Pickvance, "Contemporary Popularity and Posthumous Neglect," in Washington, D.C. and San Francisco 1986, 261.

45 Paris and New York 1983, 356–57.

46 On *Chez le Père Lathuille* as a response to contemporary developments in plein air painting, see Allen in Chicago and Los Angeles 2019–20, 26–27.

47 Proust 1988, 55–56.

48 Wilson-Bareau 1991, 246; on the work's realization, see also Tabarant 1947, 352–53.

49 Hamilton 1954, 232, 234.

50 Ibid., 233, 237–38.

51 Wilson-Bareau 1991, 185.

52 Ibid., 186.

58

The Monet Family in their Garden at Argenteuil

1874
Oil on canvas, 24 × 39 ¼ in. (61 × 99.7 cm)
New York, The Metropolitan Museum of Art, Bequest of Joan Whitney Payson, 1975, 1976.201.14

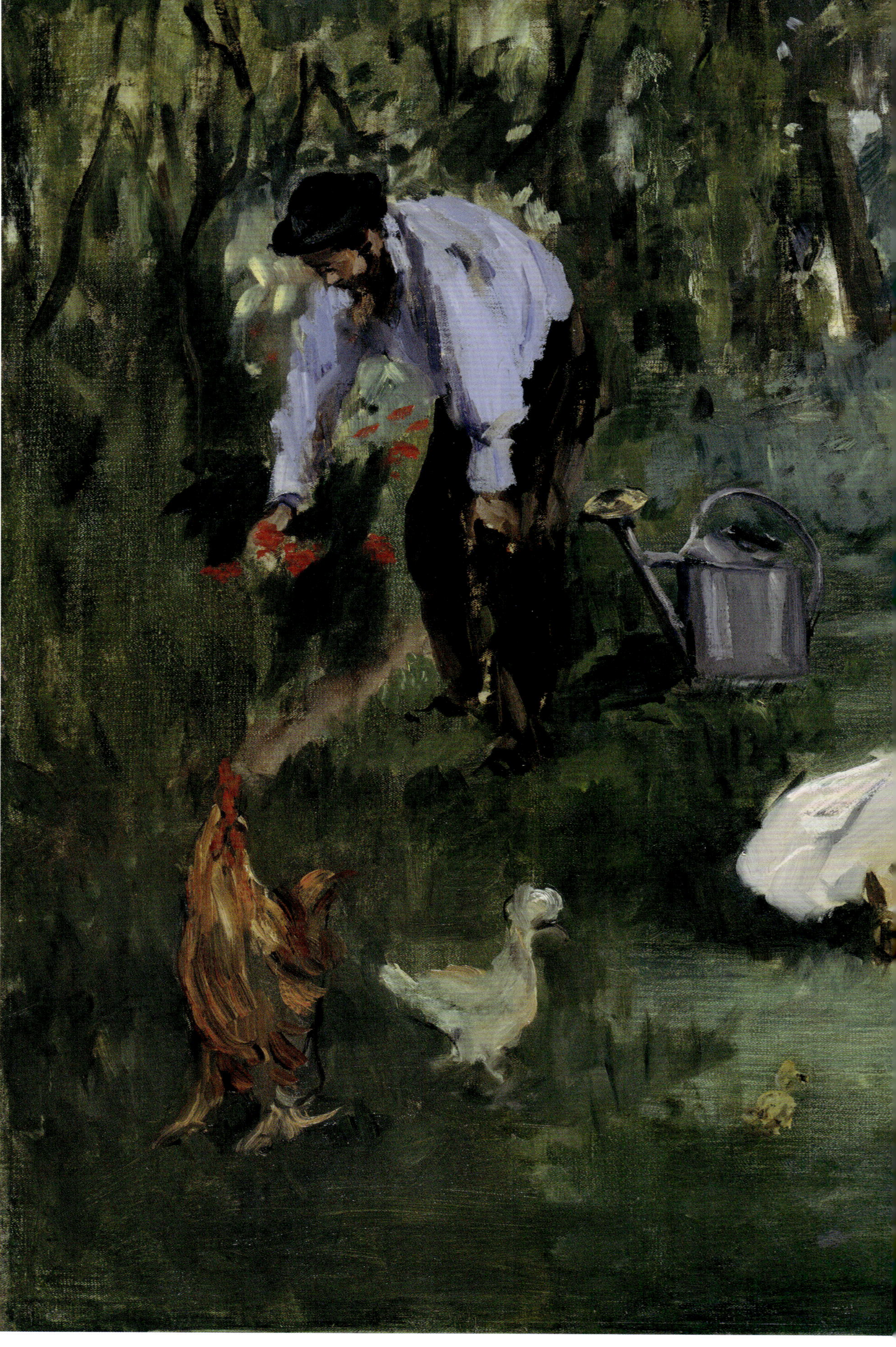

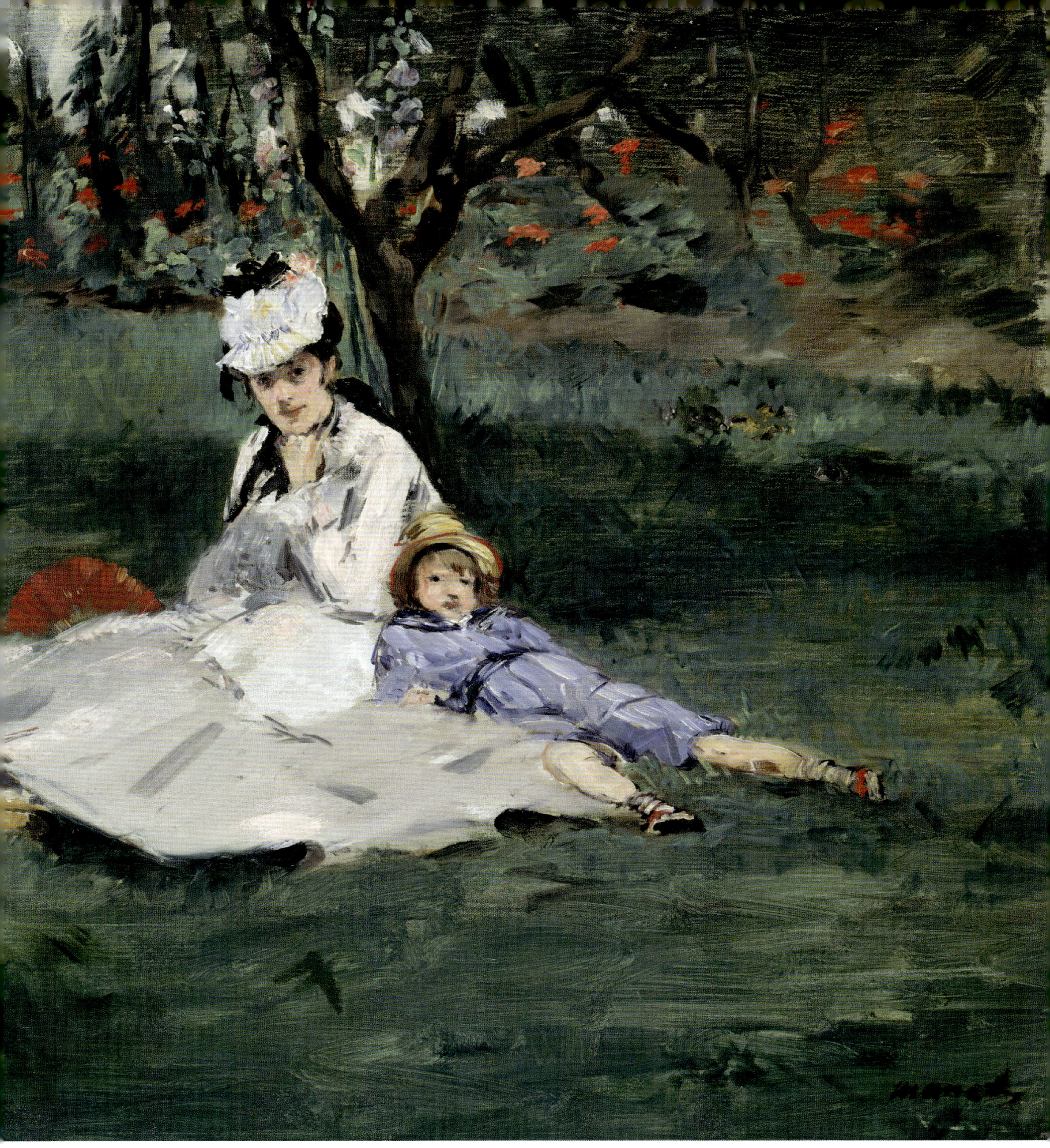
manet

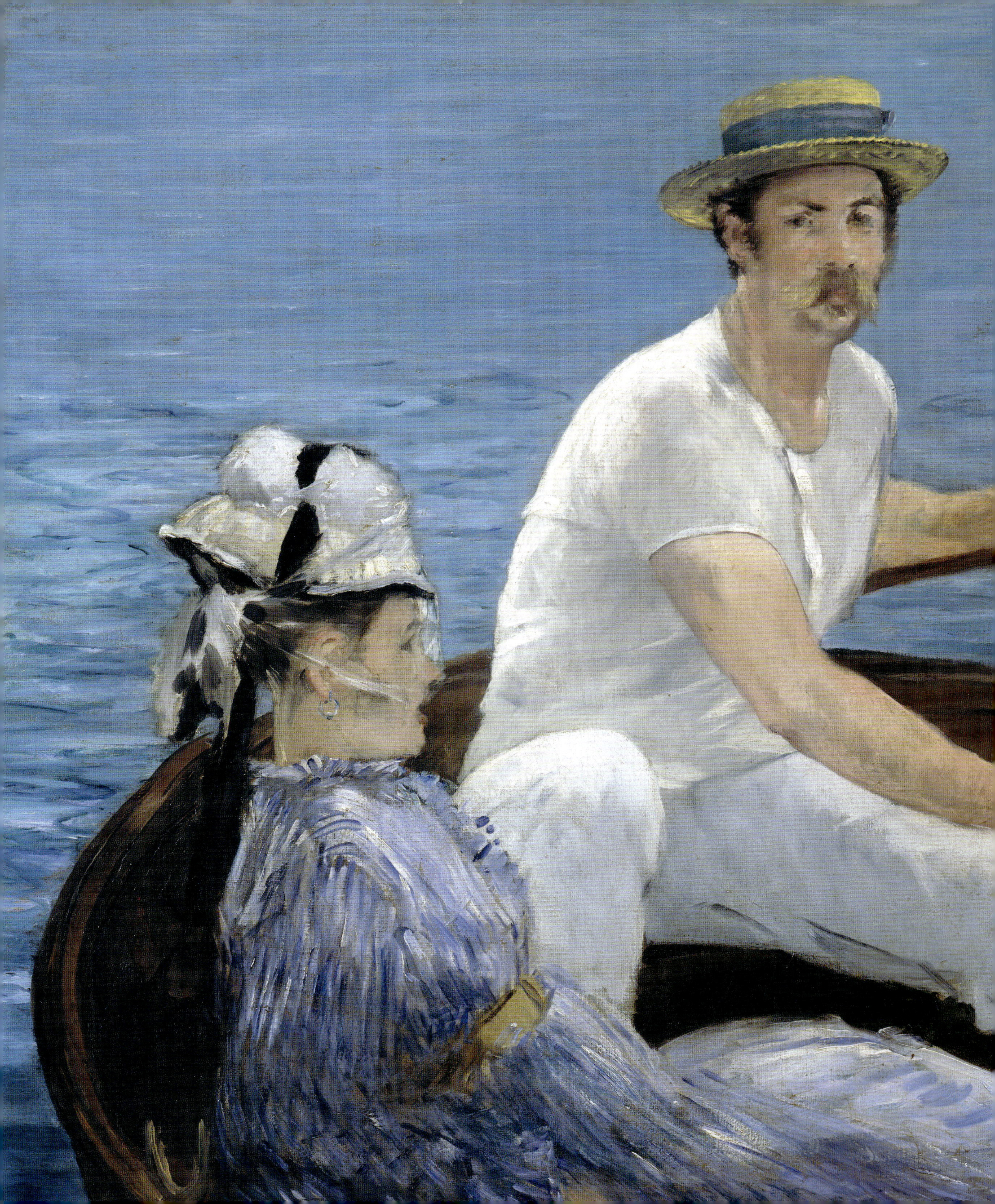

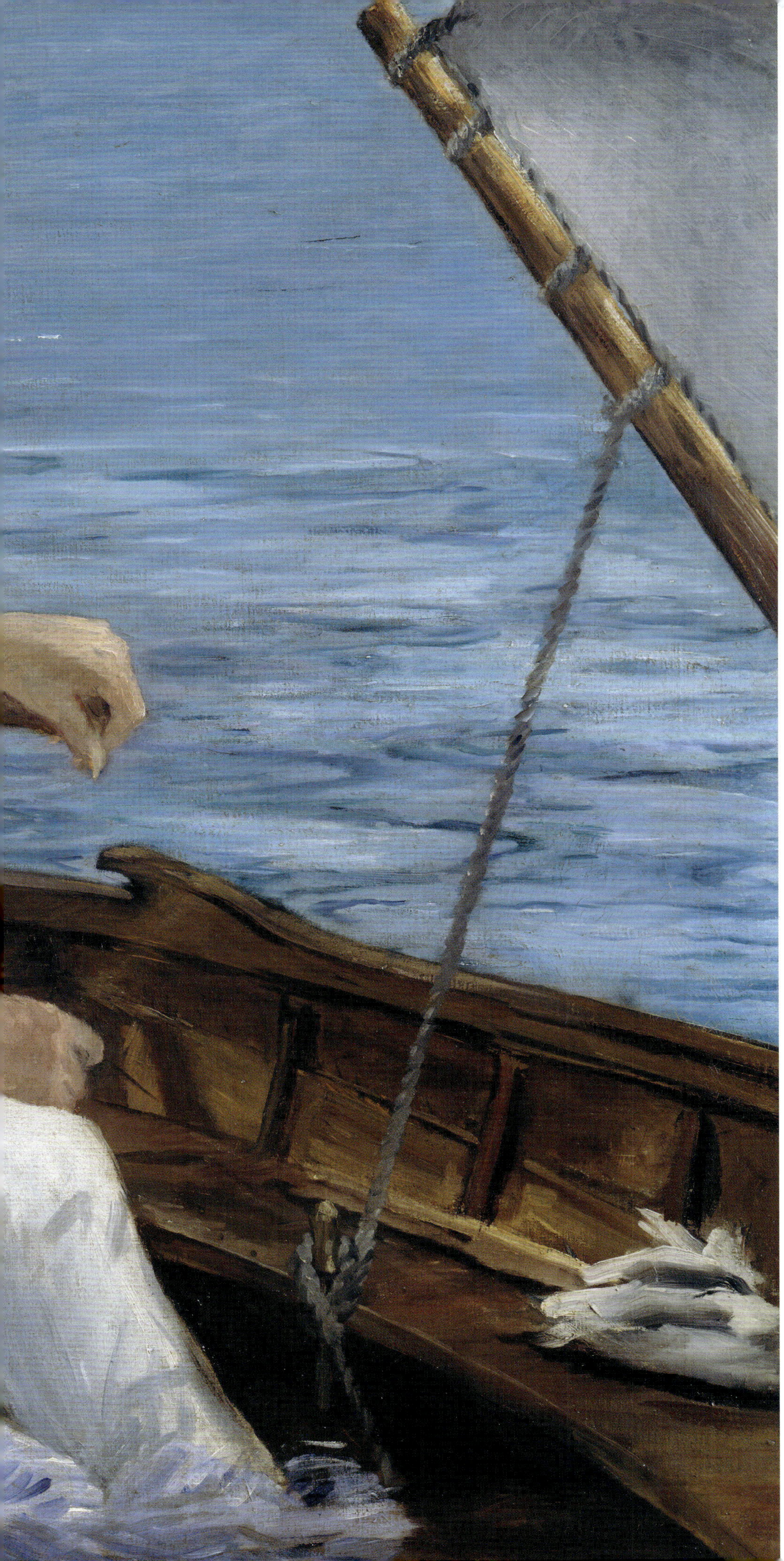

59

Boating

1874
Oil on canvas, 38 ¼ × 51 ¼ in. (97.2 × 130.2 cm)
New York, The Metropolitan Museum of Art, H. O. Havemeyer Collection, Bequest of Mrs. H. O. Havemeyer, 1929, 29.100.115

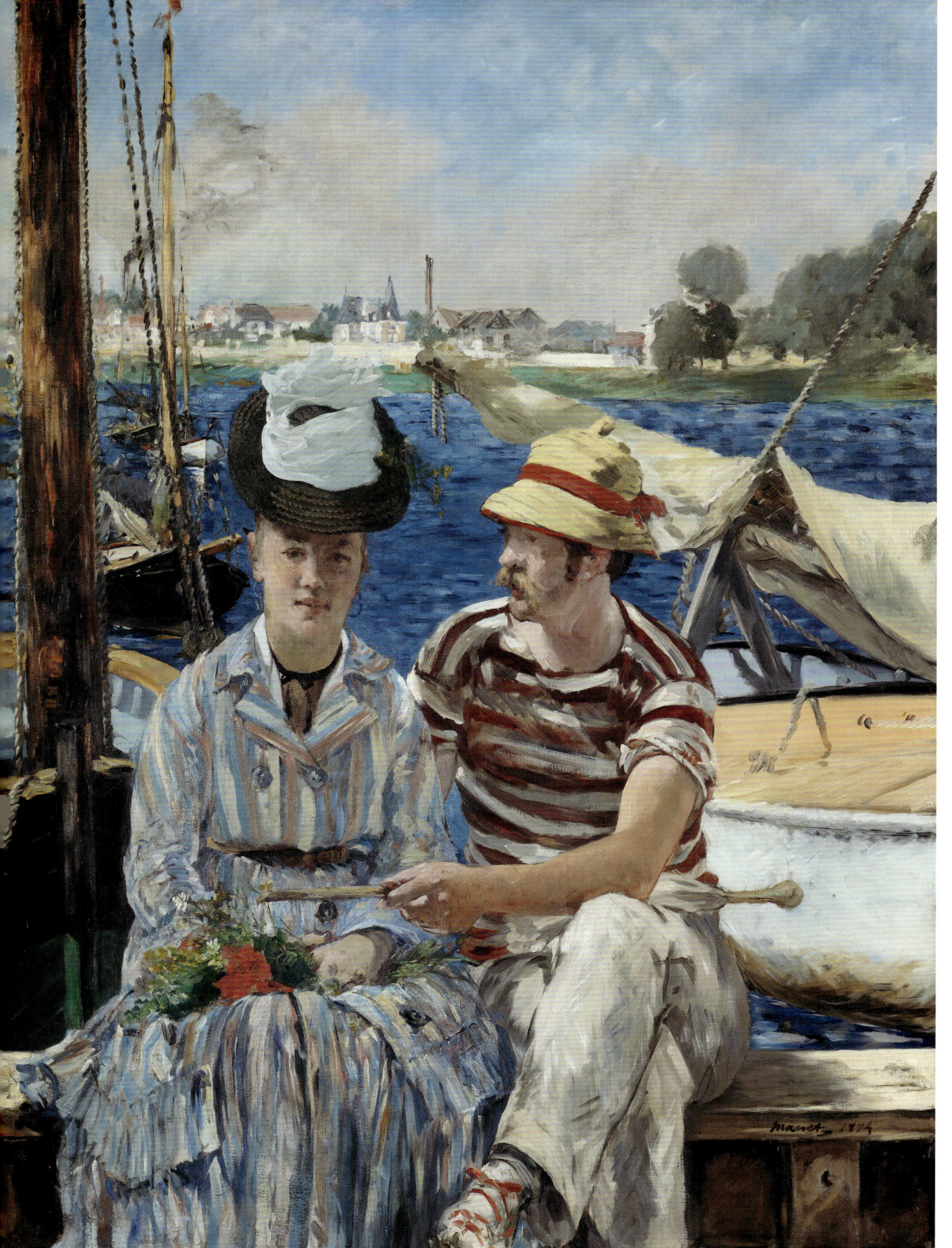
manet 1874

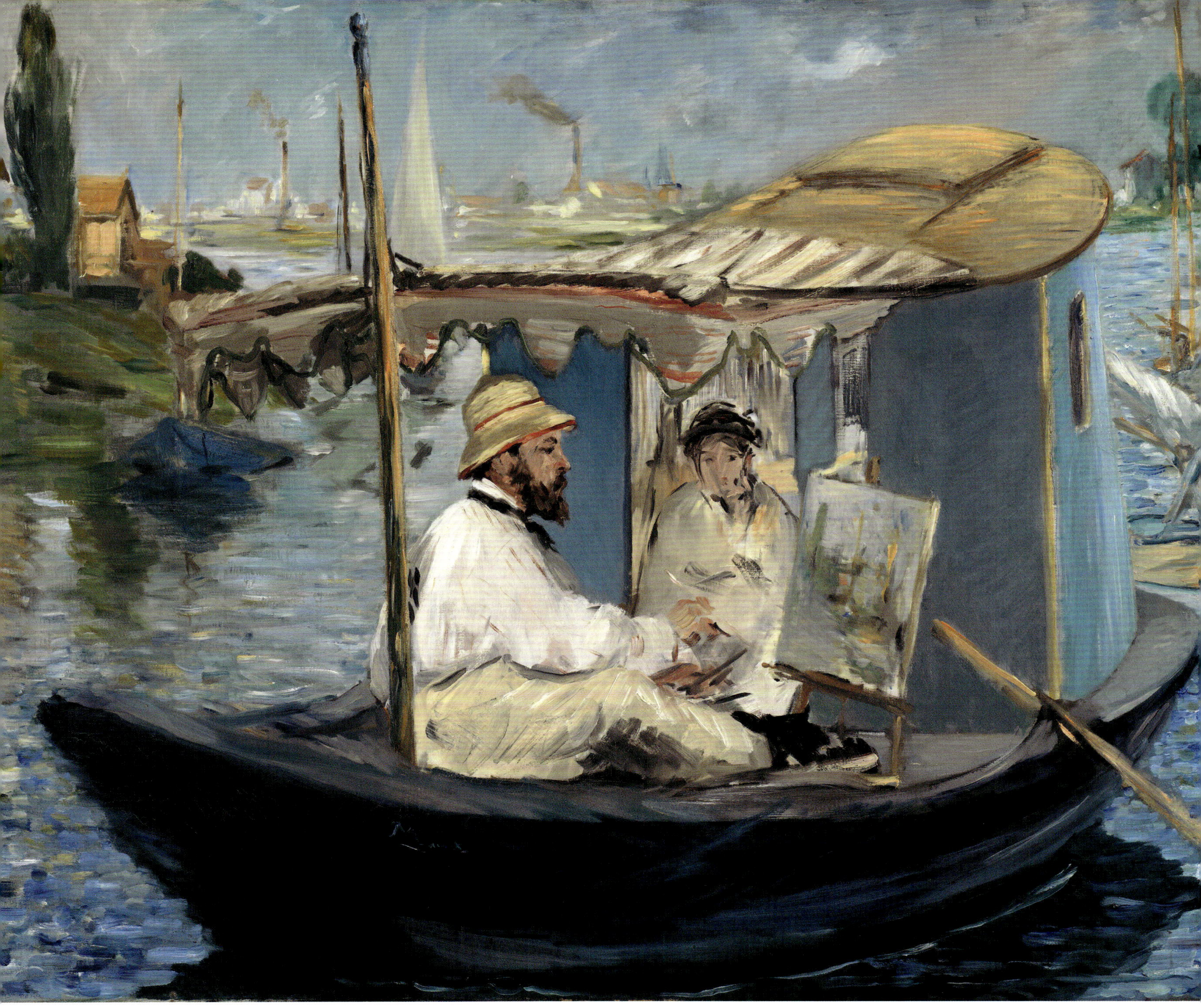

60

Argenteuil

1874
Oil on canvas, 58 ½ × 45 in.
(148.5 × 114.5 cm)
Tournai, Musée des Beaux-Arts de Tournai

61

Monet in his Studio Boat

1874
Oil on canvas, 32 ½ × 41 ⅓ in.
(82.7 × 105 cm)
Munich, Bayerische Staatsgemäldesammlungen – Neue Pinakothek München, 8759

62

Stéphane Mallarmé

1876
Oil on canvas, 10 ½ × 14 in.
(27.2 × 35.7 cm)
Paris, Musée d'Orsay, RF 2661

63

Nana

1877
Oil on canvas,
60 ⅔ × 59 ⅔ in.
(154 × 151.5 cm)
Hamburg, Hamburger
Kunsthalle, erworben 1924,
HK-2376

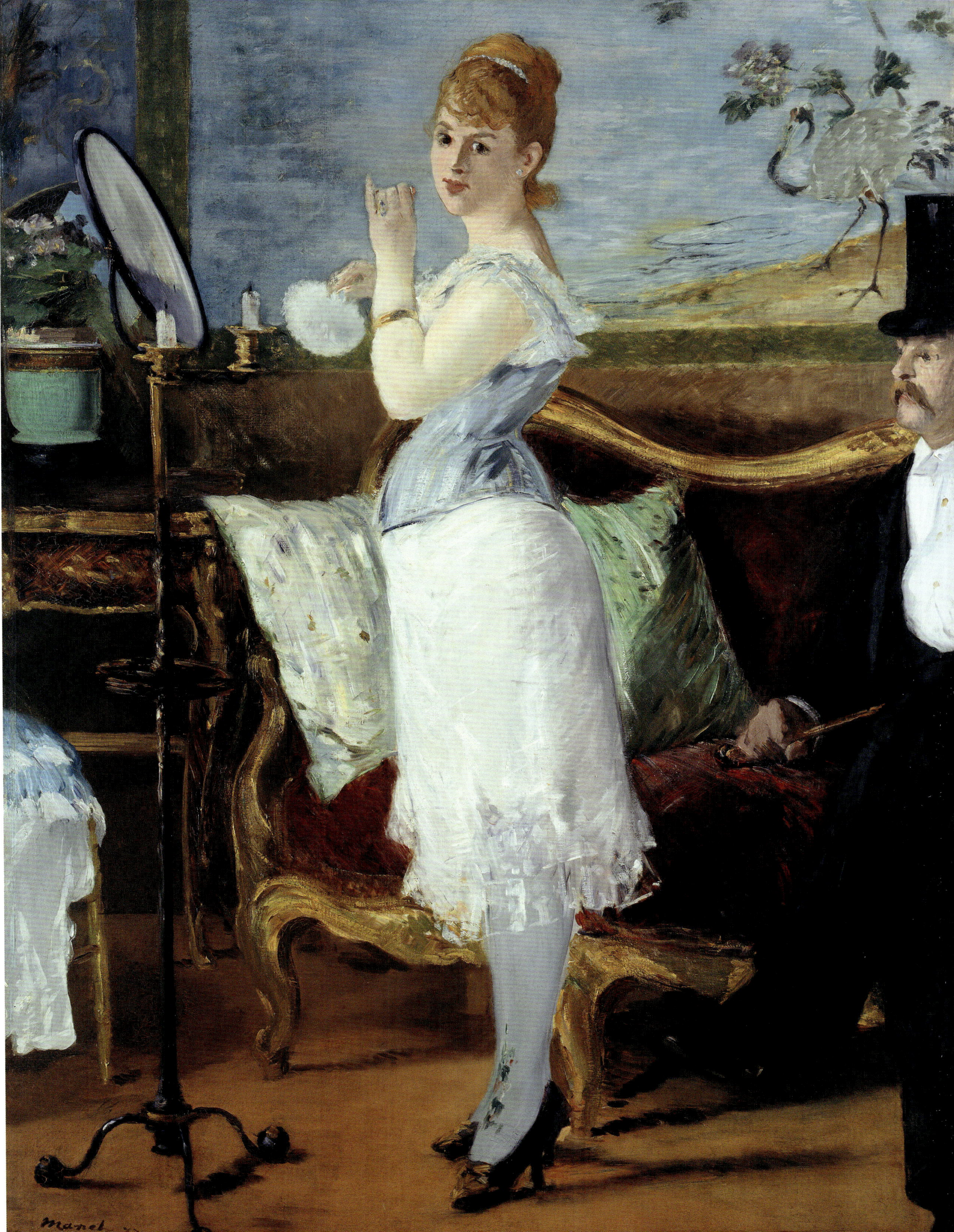

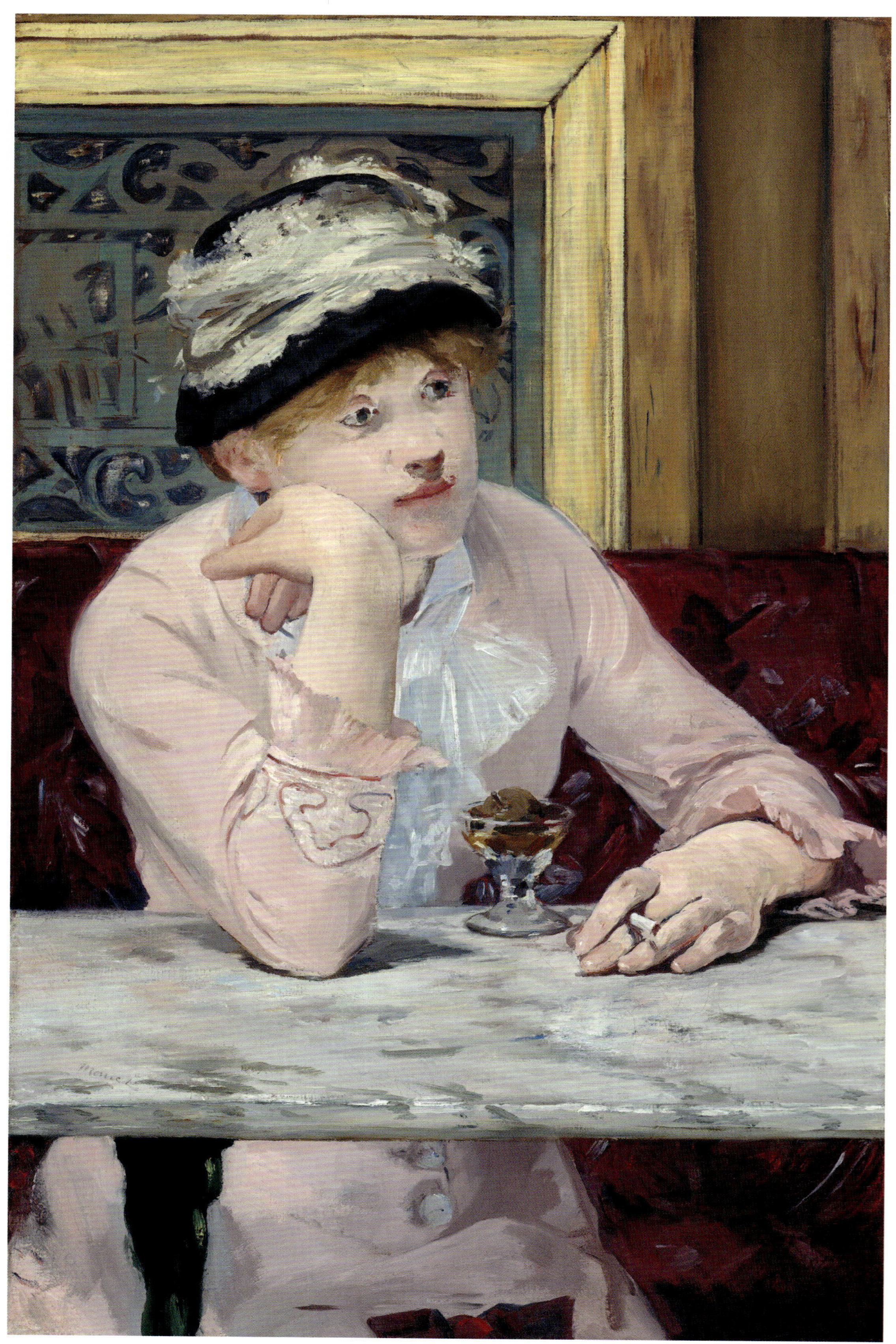

64

Plum Brandy

ca. 1877
Oil on canvas, 29 × 19 ¾ in.
(73.6 × 50.2 cm)
Washington, D.C., The National Gallery of Art, Collection of Mr. and Mrs. Paul Mellon

65

The Café Concert

1879–80
Oil on canvas, 18 ⅝ × 15 ⅜ in.
(47.3 × 39.1 cm)
Baltimore, The Walters Art Museum, Acquired by Henry Walters, 1909-10, 37.893

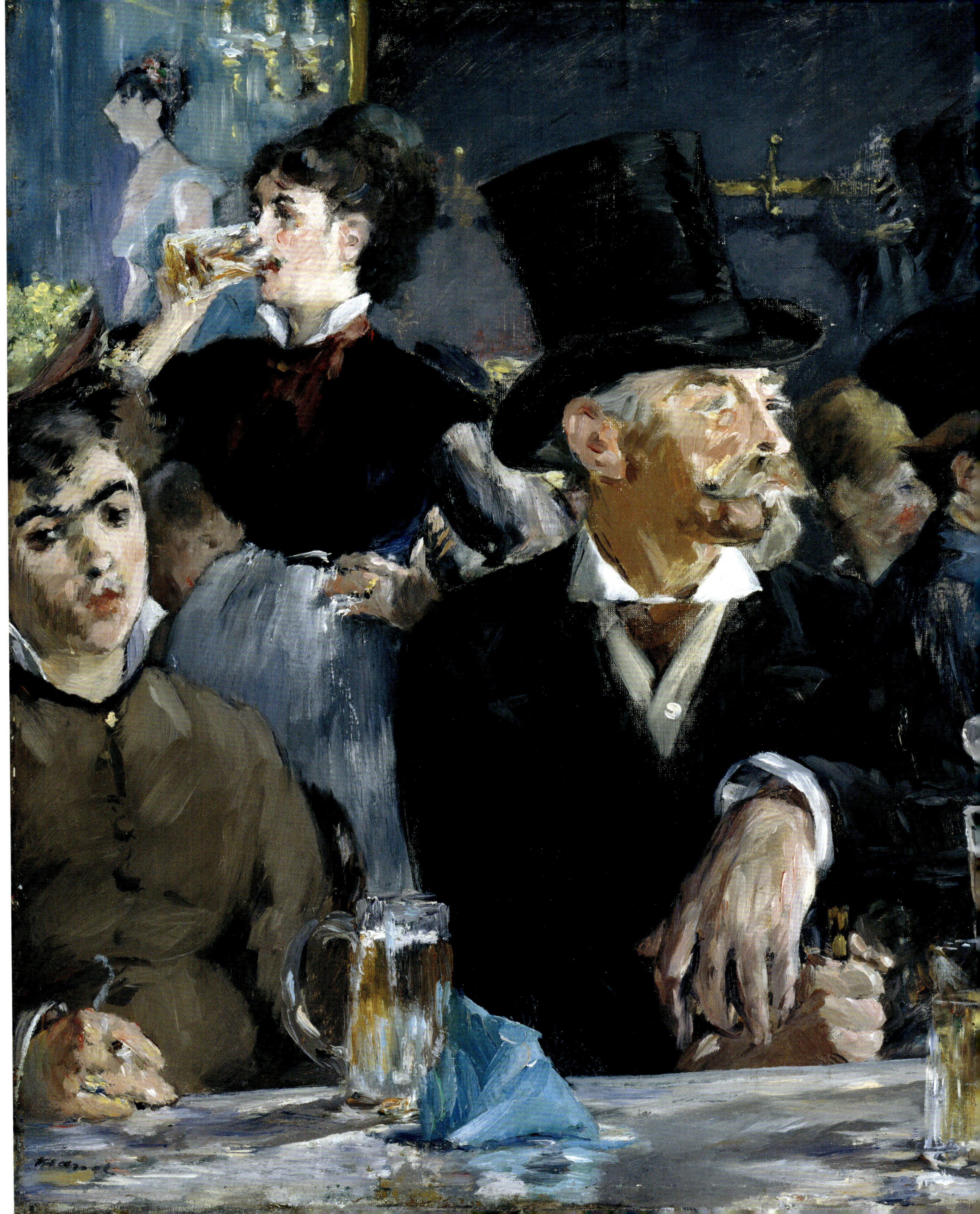

66

Au Café

1878
Oil on canvas, 30 ⅔ × 33 in.
(78 × 84 cm)
Winterthur, Sammlung Oskar Reinhart am Römerholz

67

Corner of a Café Concert

1878
Oil on canvas, 38 ¼ × 30 ½ in.
(97.1 × 77.5 cm)
London, The National Gallery, Bought, Courtauld Fund, 1924, NG3858

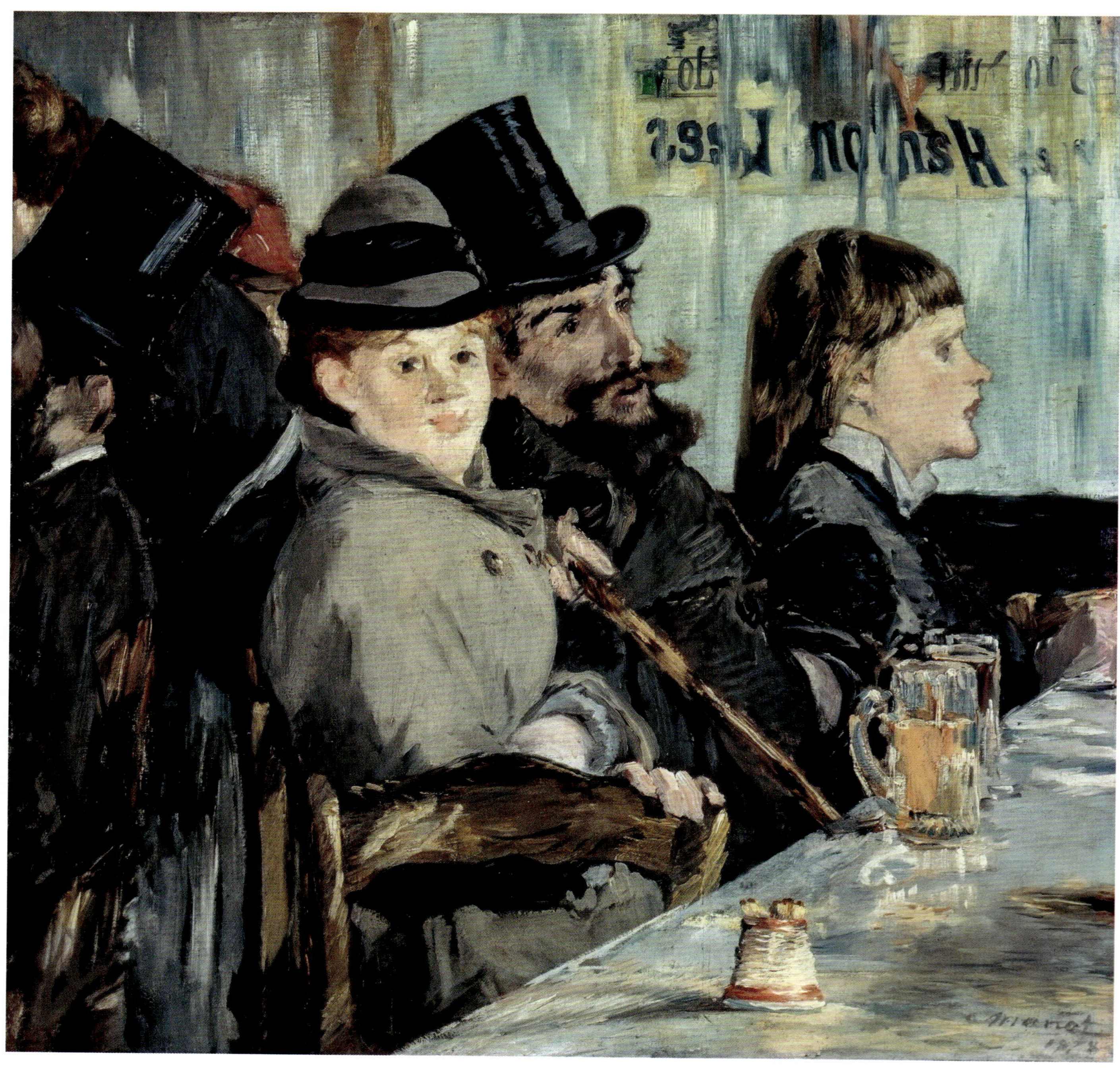

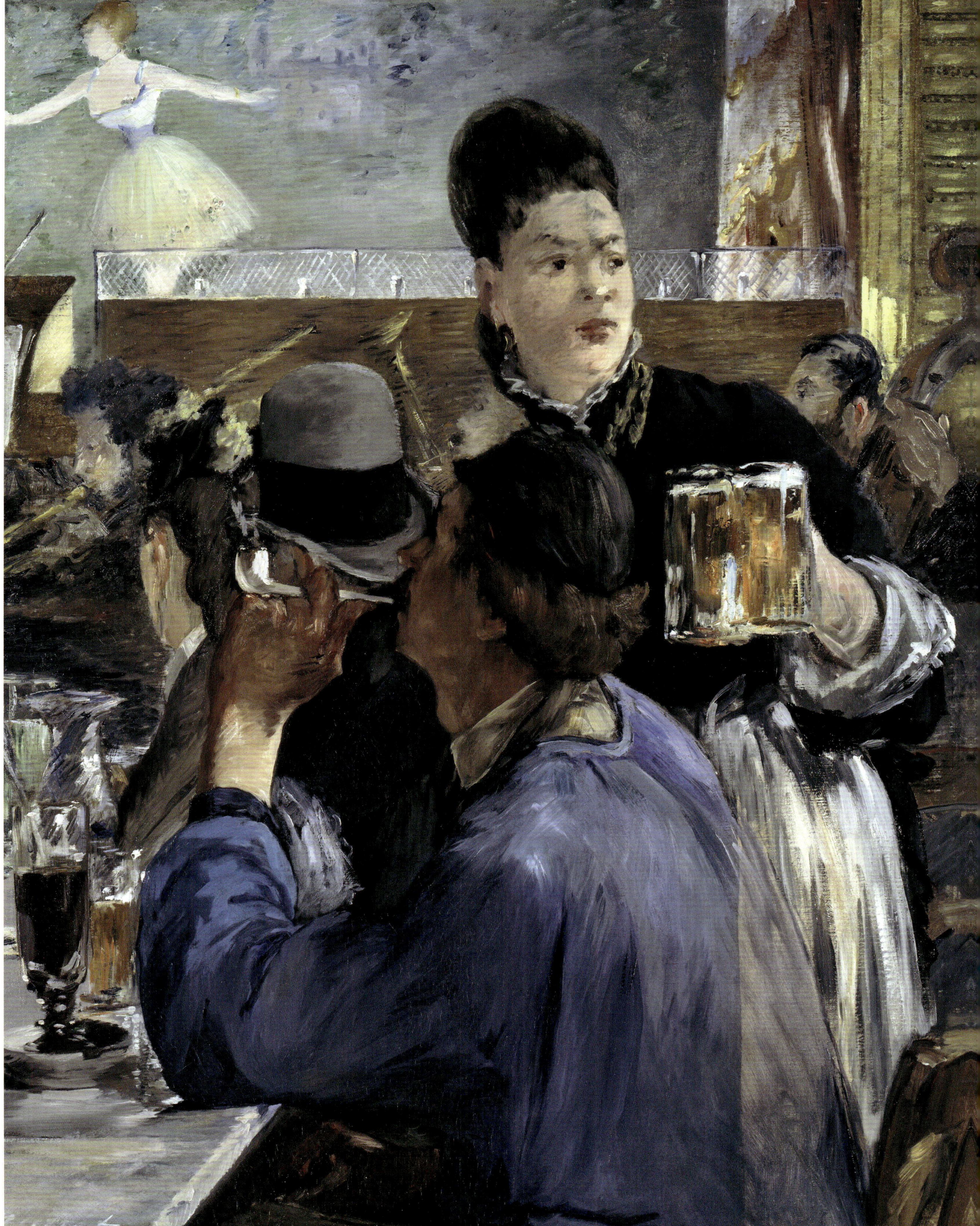

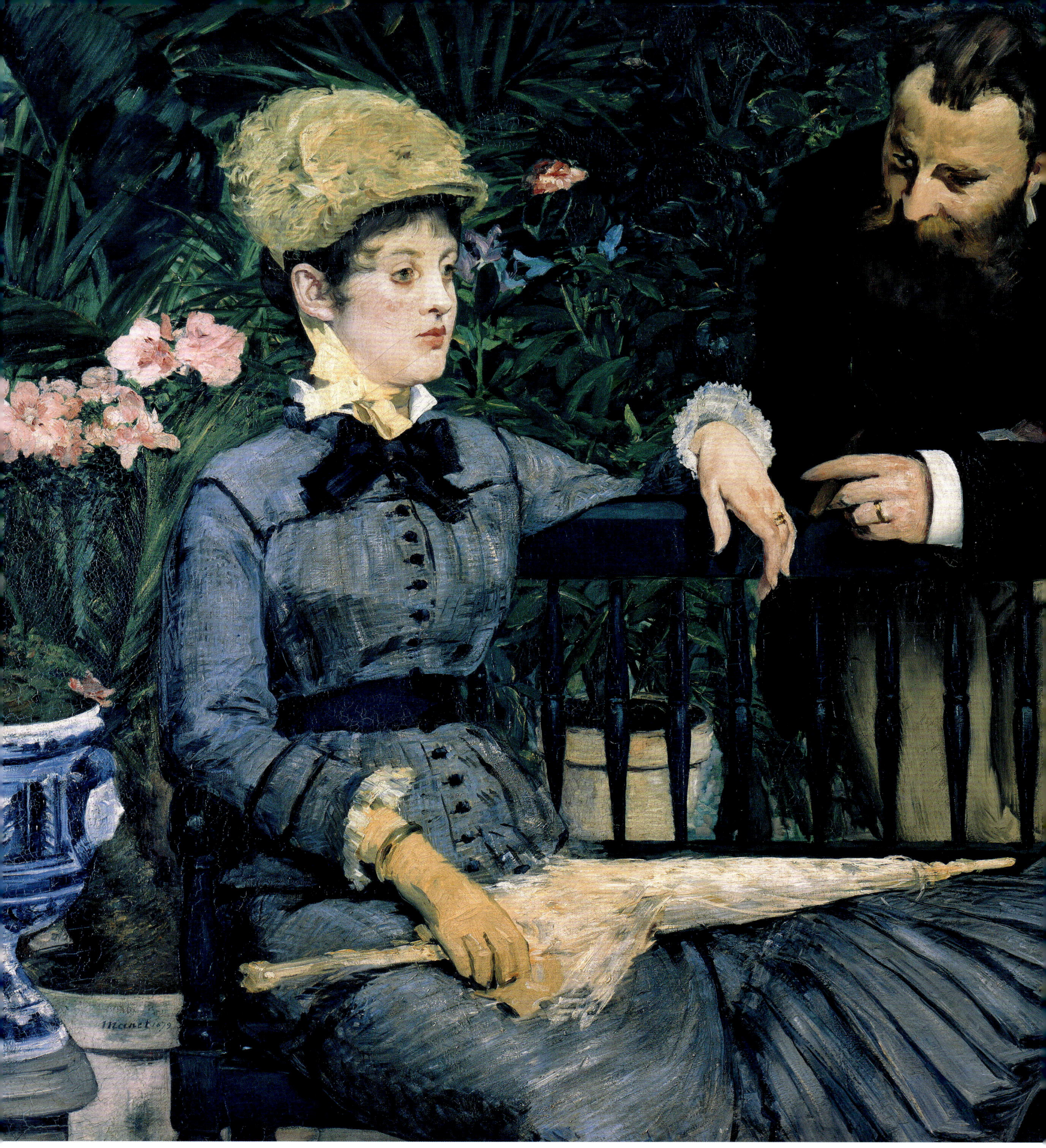
Manet 1879

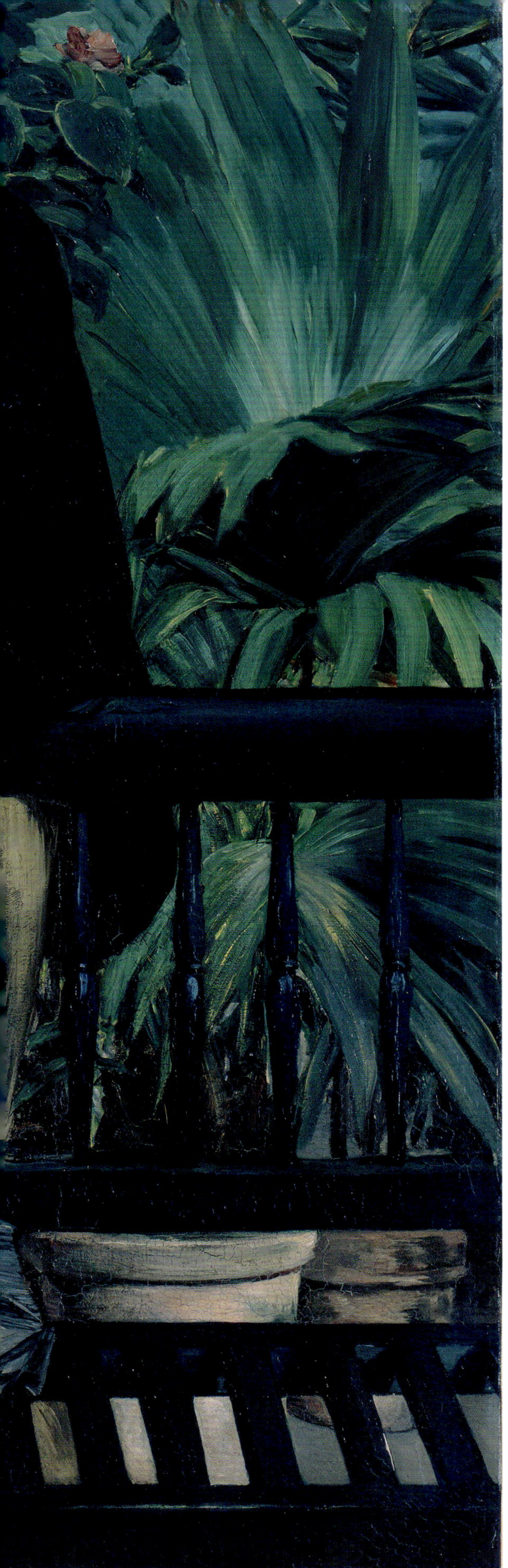

68

In the Conservatory

1878–79
Oil on canvas, 45 ¼ × 59 in.
(115 × 150 cm)
Berlin, Staatliche Museen zu
Berlin, Nationalgalerie, A I 550

69

Chez le Père Lathuille, en plein air

1879
Oil on canvas, 36 ¼ × 44 in.
(92 × 112 cm)
Tournai, Musée des
Beaux-Arts de Tournai

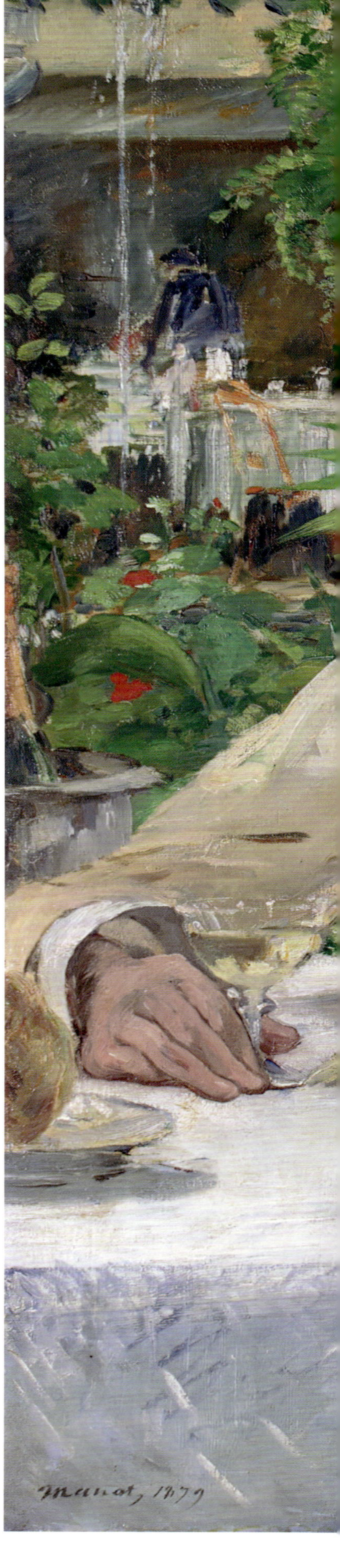

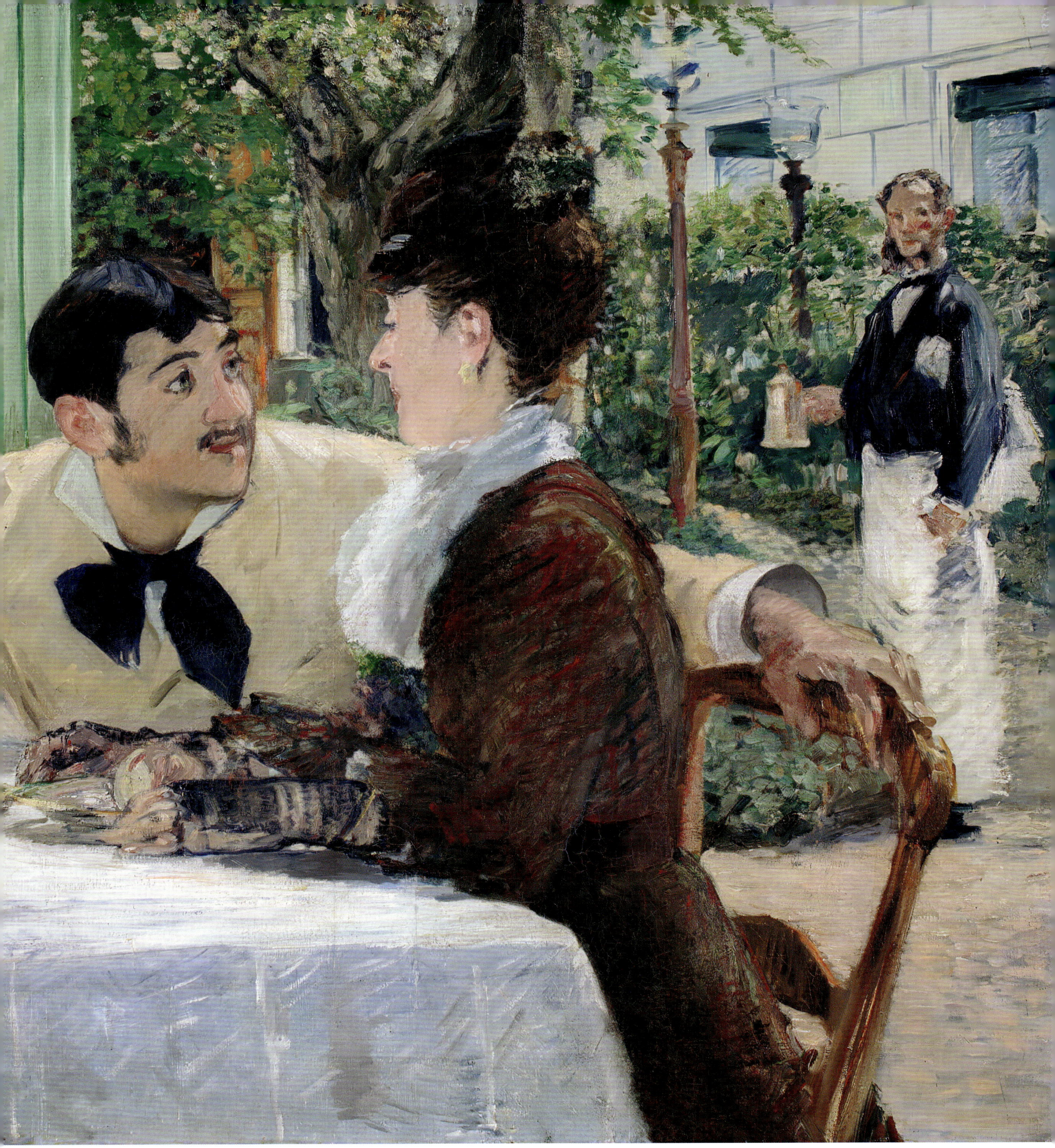

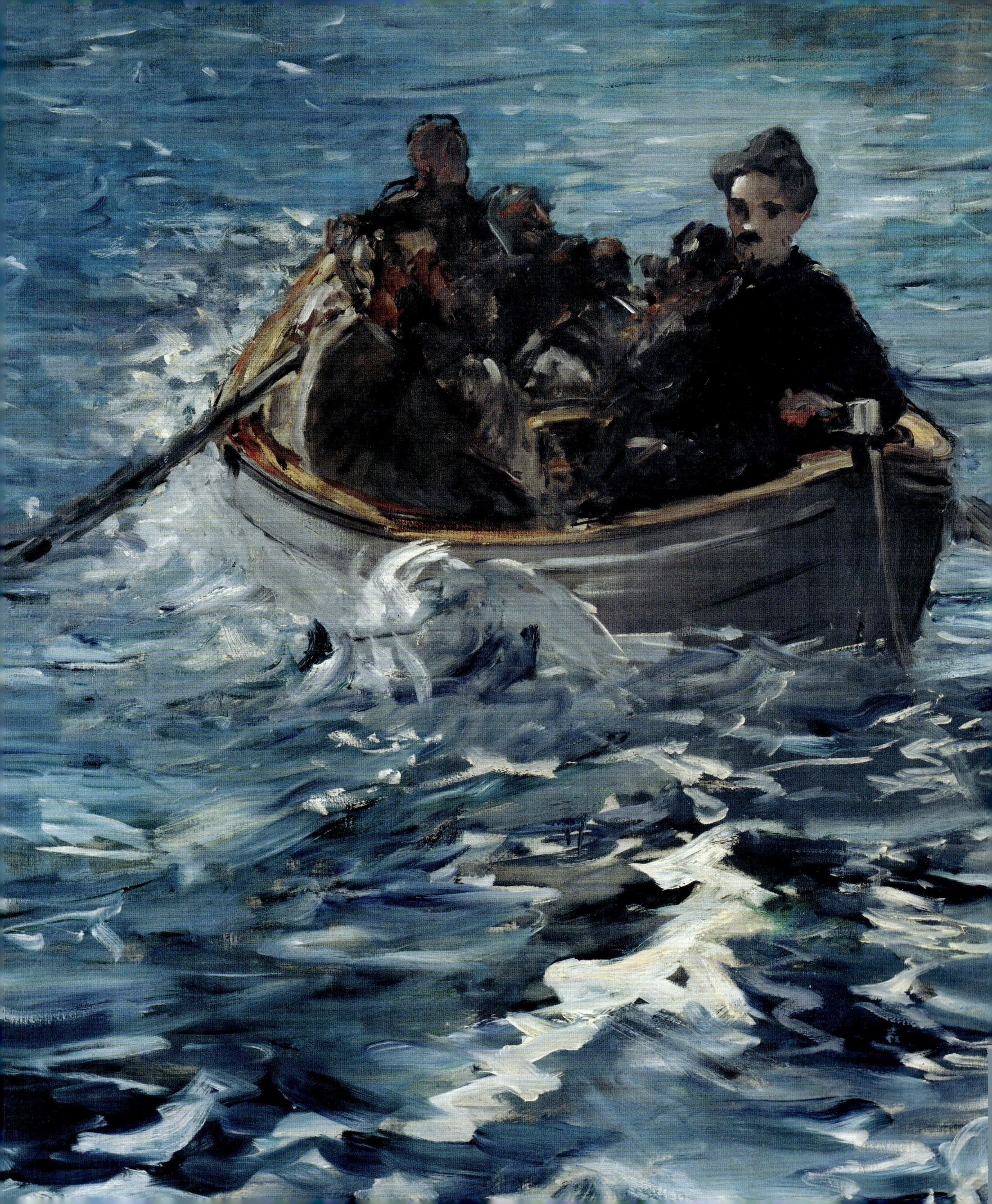

Brush with History

As a young student in Thomas Couture's atelier during the 1850s, Manet spoke dismissively of history painting, the genre prized by the Academy of Fine Arts and the Salon for its depiction of moralizing subjects from the Bible, mythology, and history: "Reconstructing historical figures—what a joke!" According to his friend Antonin Proust, "To his mind, 'history painter' was the nastiest insult you could throw at an artist."[1] At mid-century, history painting was widely believed to be in decline, and modern life was seen as lacking in terms of heroic and epic subjects worthy of history painting. In art, the elevated had been replaced by the everyday.[2] Yet Manet's art would manifest his ongoing engagement with contemporary history throughout his career, from a naval battle of the American Civil War to the execution of the Hapsburg Archduke Maximilian, Emperor of Mexico, and, in his own country, the Franco-Prussian War of 1870–71 and its aftermath. His paintings of contemporary events modernized history painting, just as his embrace of subjects from modern life redefined painting in the 1860s.[3]

Manet's engagement with important contemporary events represents a through line in his life. He was "very patriotic," according to Proust, a childhood friend, and a committed republican from a young age.[4] In the early days of the French Republic under President Louis-Napoleon Bonaparte (the future Napoleon III), a teenaged Manet, then a naval cadet, penned a letter to his father while at sea, writing in March 1849, "try and keep a decent republic against our return for I fear L[ouis] Napoleon is not a good republican . . ."[5] As an art student in Paris, he witnessed the aftermath of the 1851 coup d'état that led to the Second Empire under Napoleon III. During the 1871 Siege of Paris, Manet acted on his patriotism by volunteering to serve in the National Guard and chronicled the violence of the Paris Commune that followed. As an artist, he crossed paths with some of the leading political figures of his time, including Georges Clemenceau, the future prime minister of France, whose portrait he painted twice in the same year.

It was an episode from the American Civil War that inspired Manet's first contemporary history painting (fig. 70). On June 19, 1864, the *U.S.S. Kearsarge* was victorious over the Confederate

Detail of fig. 79

warship *Alabama* in a naval battle that took place just off the coast of France near Cherbourg. It was widely covered in newspaper accounts and illustrated journals in both France and England, and less than a month later Manet, who did not witness the event, exhibited a painting of the battle in the window of Alfred Cadart's print shop and studio in Paris. Departing from convention in marine painting, Manet depicted the battle along the distant horizon, whose sky is dominated by dark clouds of smoke emanating from the sinking Confederate ship, which largely obscures the victorious *U.S.S. Kearsarge* behind it. Manet instead lavished his brush on rendering the broad expanse of the sea itself, which dominates the composition.[6] Writing in *La Presse*, the critic Philippe Burty observed that Manet's canvas was "painted with an unusual power of realization, or, at the very least, of verisimilitude."[7] When Manet's battle scene was later shown at the Salon of 1872, the artist's unconventional composition was mocked in a caricature that depicted "Manet's faithful cat" watching the battle "from the bottom of the sea"—a reference to the black cat from *Olympia*, which had become the ubiquitous symbol of his artistic transgressions.

Manet's motivation in painting this historic naval event remains unknown. Perhaps he sought to capitalize on its topicality; it has also been suggested that the subject appealed as an expression of his anti-Bonapartist political sentiments, as Napoleon III was a known Confederate sympathizer. Whatever the reason, the American naval battle retained a hold on his imagination, as that July he visited the victorious *Kearsarge* anchored in Boulogne. Such was the public interest in this warship that boats ferried visitors to the *Kearsarge*; a member of the ship's crew recorded that "mostly Frenchmen" boarded the vessel on July 17.[8] In a letter to his friend, the artist Félix Bracquemond, Manet reported his visit to the ship that same day, adding, "I will bring back a study."[9] The "study" to which he refers is likely a preparatory watercolor (Musée des Beaux-Arts, Dijon), which served as the basis for another painting realized in his studio in Paris in late summer or fall (fig. 71). In the painting, as in his previous depiction of the battle itself, the *Kearsarge* hovers, off-center, on the distant horizon, here surrounded by sailing boats like those that transported Manet and his fellow tourists. In his 1867 defense of Manet, Zola ignored the historical significance of Manet's pair of canvases documenting the naval battle, instead considering them among a group of "marine subjects . . . in which the magnificent waves bear witness to the fact that the artist had sailed and loved the ocean."[10]

In summer 1867, the world's eyes were on Paris, the host city of the Exposition Universelle, which Napoleon III intended as a celebration of the Second Empire and its newly renovated capital city. Manet, whose work was not included in its Fine Arts section, had just opened his one-man show nearby on the Pont d'Alma. Meanwhile, across the Atlantic, Napoleon III's efforts at regime change in Mexico were failing. In 1864, he had installed the Habsburg Archduke Maximilian I as a puppet emperor of Mexico in a bid to expand France's imperial power; however, in the face of mounting opposition in Mexico and abroad, he withdrew French military support in February 1867, which led to Maximilian's capture by forces loyal to the elected president, Benito Juárez. Maximilian was executed at dawn on June 19, 1867, along with his two generals, Tomás Mejía and Miguel Miramón. When news of the emperor's assassination on a hillside overlooking the town of Querétaro reached France in early July, Manet was at work on a panoramic view of the site of the Exposition Universelle on the Champ-de-Mars, which he abandoned, never to finish (fig. 45).

By July, Manet embarked on the first of three large paintings representing the execution of Maximilian and his two generals (fig. 72). As has been widely acknowledged, its composition—victims on the left and firing squad on the right, with little space between them—reveals Manet's debt to Goya's *The Third of May, 1808*, painted in 1814. During his 1865 trip to Madrid, Manet had seen Goya's painting of an execution of Spanish civilians by French soldiers, an indictment of Napoleon I's invasion of Spain. Goya's work was also topical, as the first engraving of it was published in April 1867 in a monograph on Goya by Charles Yriarte, whom Manet knew.[11] There is an immediacy to Manet's painting, the most freely brushed of the three versions, which suggests the rapidity of his response to the event. The composition evolved as additional reports of the event as well as photographs reached Paris in the ensuing months.[12]

An account by journalist Théodore Duret details the prolonged evolution of Manet's series of paintings. According to Duret, Manet was first concerned with accuracy—"the circumstances and details of the drama." When he began painting, he worked from models, as was his practice—from members of an infantry platoon who posed in his studio for the firing squad and two friends who modeled for the generals (he later changed their heads). A photograph served as his source for Maximilian's likeness. Duret concludes, "When a first composition and even a second appeared not to match the detailed information he was finally able to obtain, he painted the work again, for the third time, in its final and definitive form."[13] Duret's account omits two additional works—a smaller oil sketch that served as a study for the third painting (Ny Carlsberg Glyptotek, Copenhagen) and a lithograph.[14]

Manet's two subsequent paintings of this subject retain the overall compositional structure of the first version. Manet began the second canvas in fall 1867 (fig. 73); it is marked by tighter handling and a greater formal clarity to the figures, now set in a barren landscape. For this version, Manet reportedly worked from models—soldiers who posed in his studio.[15] In this version, the uniforms worn by the members of the firing squad more closely resemble those of their French counterparts, reflecting Manet's assimilation of later newspaper accounts and photographs of the event; this change also serves to implicate the French government in the death of Maximilian and his generals—"France shooting Maximilian," as Zola later remarked.[16] Although the May issue of *L'Artiste* announced that Manet's "Death of Maximilian" would be exhibited at the Salon of 1868, it was not on

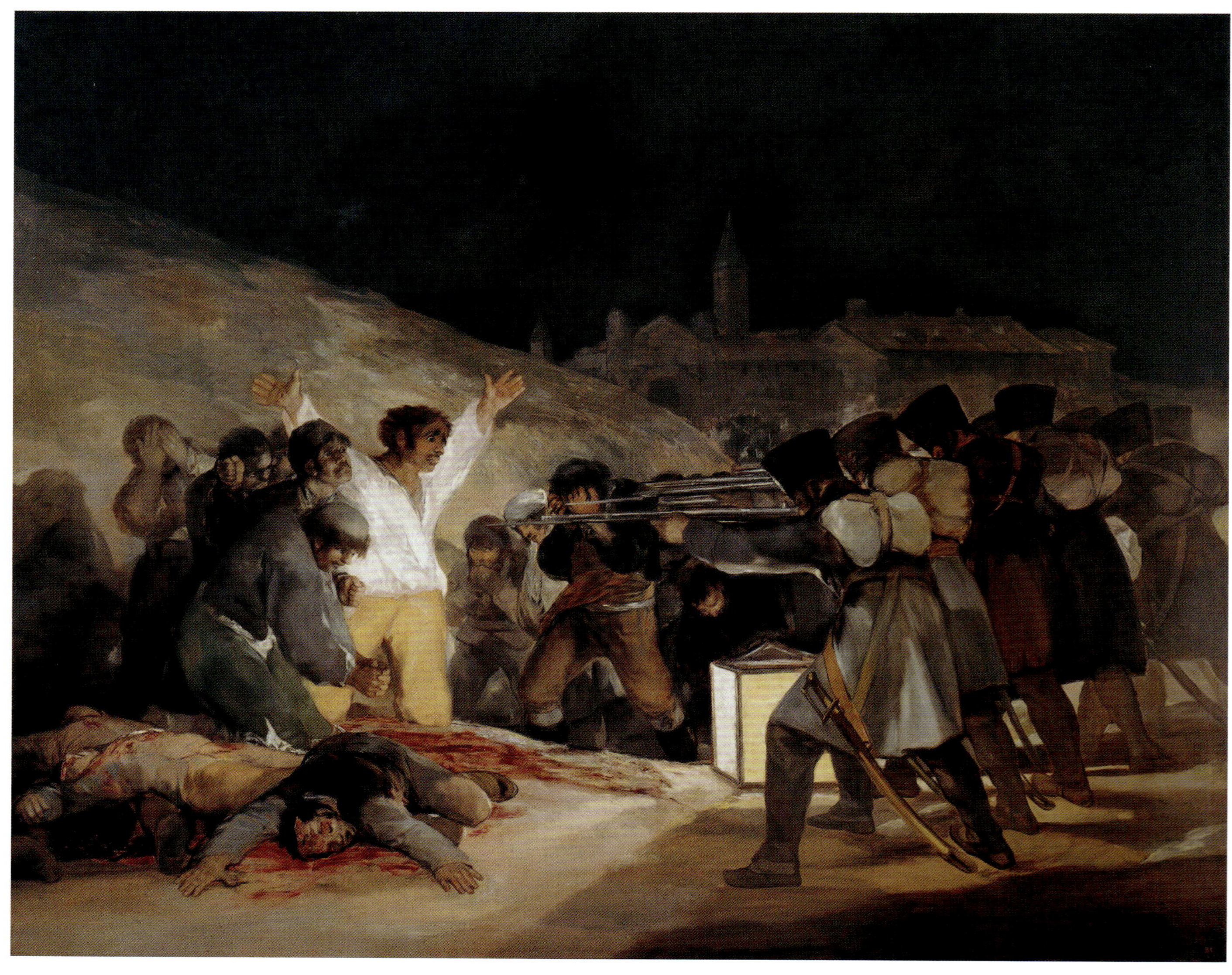

Francisco de Goya y Lucientes, *The Third of May, 1808*, 1814, oil on canvas, 105 ½ × 136 ⅔ in. (268 × 347 cm). Madrid, Museo Nacional del Prado, P749

view.[17] By 1883, the figures on the left had been cut out, likely due to damage to the canvas during storage; Suzanne Manet's son, Léon Leenhoff, subsequently cut what remained of the painting into four fragments, as it appears today. The third and final large canvas (fig. 74), painted in 1868–69, incorporates a wall behind the figures and, beyond that, a cluster of onlookers, whose rendering evokes the spectators in Goya's bullfighting prints, works that Manet knew.[18]

Manet's sustained engagement with this series from the summer of 1867 to early 1869 demonstrates its importance to him. That Manet's representation of the execution of Maximilian was seen as too politically charged is attested to by the fate of the lithograph he made of the subject in 1869. The government refused to allow it to be printed or published, which prompted Manet's comment to Zola, "it speaks well for the work, since there's no caption of any kind underneath it." The printer also threatened to destroy the lithographic stone. At Manet's request, Zola came to his defense in a damning critique of the imperial censors published in *La Tribune* on February 4, 1869.[19] Although the lithographic stone was returned to Manet, his lithograph was not published until 1884, one year after his death; Manet sent the final version of the painting to the United States for exhibition in 1879–80, and it then remained in his studio until his death.

By 1870, Manet had consolidated his place as the unofficial leader of the avant-garde, as commemorated that May at the Salon in Fantin-Latour's formal group portrait set in Manet's studio in the Batignolles (see p. 119). However, this gathering of like-minded artists and writers would soon be upended by contemporary events. On July 19, 1870, France declared war on Prussia. Frédéric Bazille, whose tall figure dominates the group, enlisted in the army and was killed in battle that November, while Monet, his figure is just visible behind Bazille, fled with his family to London in September. Renoir, standing to the right of Manet, served in the cavalry in the South of France. Following the crushing defeat of the French army at Sedan on September 1, under the command of Napoleon III, and the declaration of the Third Republic three days later, Manet sent his mother, Suzanne, and Léon to southwestern France for their safety while he and his brothers remained in Paris. Manet closed his studio the following week and preemptively stored his major works, including *Olympia* and *Luncheon on the Grass*, in the cellar of the home of his friend Duret.

For four months, Paris was surrounded by the Prussian army. In his near-daily letters to his wife during the Siege of Paris, as this period is known, Manet detailed the privations caused by the war, from isolation and illness to shortages of food and fuel. Soon after its onset, Manet wrote to his wife, "Everyone is a soldier now."[20] In November, along with Degas, he enlisted in the National Guard at the rank of lieutenant. In a letter of November 19, Manet told Suzanne: "there are now cat, dog, and rat butchers in Paris. We no longer eat anything but horsemeat, when we can get it." In the same letter Manet informed his wife, "I shall soon start to make some sketches from life."[21] In fact, Manet's work as an artist had effectively come to a halt as a result of the war and his attendant service in the National Guard. As a gunner in the artillery, he took part in a battle on December 1, which he recounted to his wife the following day—"What a bacchanale! The shells went off over our heads from all sides." Manet subsequently joined the General Staff: "The work in artillery was too demanding."[22]

In the aftermath of the Franco-Prussian War and the Commune, a period of civil unrest and violence that followed in spring 1871, Manet realized a group of three works on paper that evoke his lived experience. *Line in Front of the Butcher Shop*, an etching of 1870–71, recalls Manet's report to Suzanne in the early days of the Siege of Paris that "the butchers are open only three times a week, and that there are queues at their doors from four o'clock in the morning, and latecomers get nothing"[23] (fig. 75). Manet reduced the scene to its essentials: a cluster of faceless, cloaked women line up in front of a narrow door opening, guarded by a soldier, whose presence is signaled only by the tip of a bayonet that rises above the sea of umbrellas.

News of the violent insurrection in Paris, on March 18, 1871, that marked the beginning of the Paris Commune, elicited a rare political outburst from Manet, expressed in a letter to the artist Félix Bracquemond. Writing from Arcachon, where he had reunited with his family the month before (fig. 10), Manet exclaimed, "We're living in an unhappy country where people are only interested in overthrowing the government in order to join it." Reiterating his belief in a republican form of government, Manet lamented "the dreadful riots that have brought despair and disgust to the hearts of all true Frenchmen."[24]

Manet returned to Paris that May, and, according to Antonin Proust, he and Manet witnessed "the terrible repression of the troops entering Paris," a reference to the "Bloody Week" of May 21–28, 1871, in which twenty-five thousand people were killed in a violent conflict between government troops and Communards that led to the collapse of the Commune.[25] The experience inspired a lithograph, signed and dated 1871 but not published until 1874, titled *Civil War* (fig. 76). It depicts a National Guardsman lying dead near an improvised barricade while the feet of a civilian murdered by government troops are visible in the lower right corner; Manet reportedly encountered the aftermath of a battle near the Church of the Madeleine, which he then sketched from life.[26] It has also been suggested that the figure of the fallen soldier is based on Manet's earlier *Dead Toreador*,[27] while the composition itself recalls the foreshortened central figure and use of cropping in Honoré Daumier's *Rue Transnonain, le 15 Avril 1834*, a charged political caricature that exposed the violent repression by the government of Louis-Philippe during the July Monarchy (1830–48).[28]

The Barricade depicts the execution of Communards by government soldiers in the streets of Paris (fig. 77). Manet himself witnessed the execution of three Communards at a military camp near Versailles on November 28, 1871.[29] However, neither the episode nor the date of the work can be identified with certainty. What is clear is Manet's deliberate reference to the *Execution of Maximilian* in a scene that documents the violence of the Paris Commune. On the reverse of the drawing, a traci ng of Maximilian and his generals and one of the soldiers from the earlier work appears in reverse, based on his then-unpublished lithograph; the artist then used its indented contours to outline the central figures in *The Barricade*.[30] A drawing of soldiers on the street, sketched from life, likely served as the source for its background.[31] Manet's large drawing, transformed into a vertical format with the addition of a second sheet of paper pasted above the figures, might have served as a study for a painting intended for the Salon that was never realized. As scholar Juliet Wilson-Bareau observed of *The Barricade*: "Here Manet created a grand new historical subject from his own imagery."[32]

In 1878, Paris once again hosted the Exposition Universelle, and the French government declared June 30 a national holiday called the *Fête de la Paix*. Intended as a celebration of the Exposition and France's return to peace and prosperity following the Franco-Prussian War and

Honoré Daumier (drawing) and Delaunois (printer), *Rue Transnonain, le 15 Avril*, lithograph in *Association Mensuelle* (July 1834), 11 ¼ × 17 ⅜ in. (28.6 × 44.1 cm) (image). New York, The Metropolitan Museum of Art, Rogers Fund, 1920, 20.23

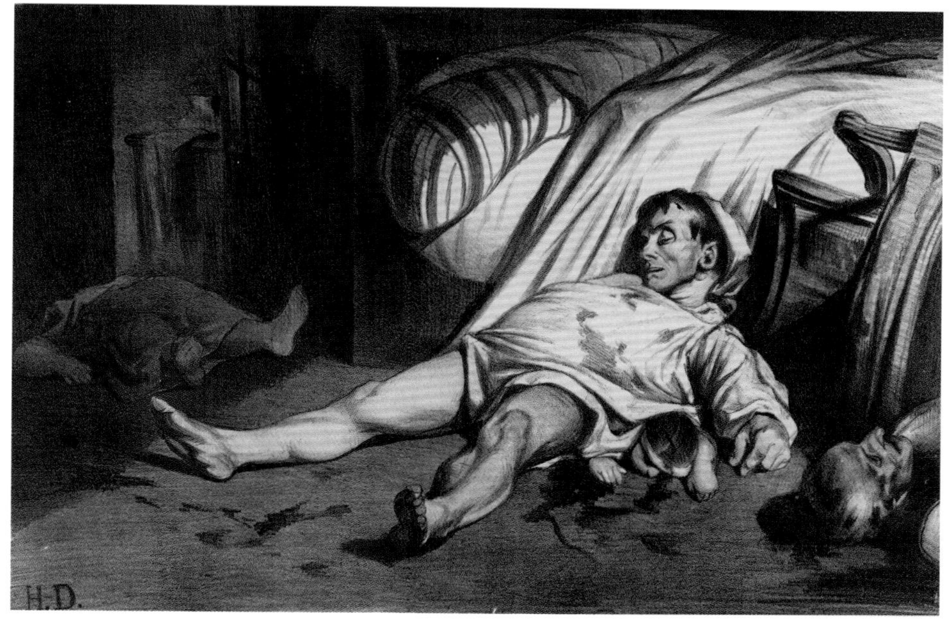

its aftermath, the holiday was politically divisive, seen by critics of the government as an attempt to distract from the realities of political discord and economic hardship. Manet's 1878 canvas of the rue Mosnier bedecked with flags in celebration of the Fête de la Paix, as seen from the window of his studio on the rue de Saint-Pétersbourg, embodies these divisions (fig. 78). Its profusion of flags, reinforced by the tricolor palette Manet deployed, evokes a patriotic sentiment that is countered by the presence of an amputee wearing a worker's blue smock, walking on crutches in the foreground. His figure conjures both the socially marginalized and the victims of the recent violence in contrast to the top-hatted *flâneur* on the opposite sidewalk. Manet's scene, from a group of three painted views of the rue Mosnier realized in 1878, conjures the ambivalence this holiday engendered in the nascent Third Republic.[33]

In addition to representing contemporary history as it unfolded, Manet also portrayed some of the leading political figures of the Third Republic (1870–1940), the democratic, parliamentary government that succeeded the Second Empire. Manet admired Léon Gambetta, the lawyer and republican politician who helped to found the Third Republic. Gambetta also attended the twice-weekly soirées at the Manet family apartment, along with other politicians, writers, and artists. In 1871, Manet sketched him during sessions of the National Assembly in Versailles, but his hoped-for "portrait of Gambetta at the podium" was never realized, according to Antonin Proust, who recalled several visits by the deputy to the artist's studio. Those sittings did not provide enough time for Manet to paint his portrait, which he regretted.[34] Manet confided to Proust, "That's always been my principal concern, to make sure of getting regular sittings. Whenever I start something, I'm always afraid the model will let me down . . . They come, they pose, then away they go, telling themselves that he can finish it off on his own. Well, no, one can't finish anything on one's own, particularly since one only finishes on the day one starts, and that means starting often and having plenty of days available."[35]

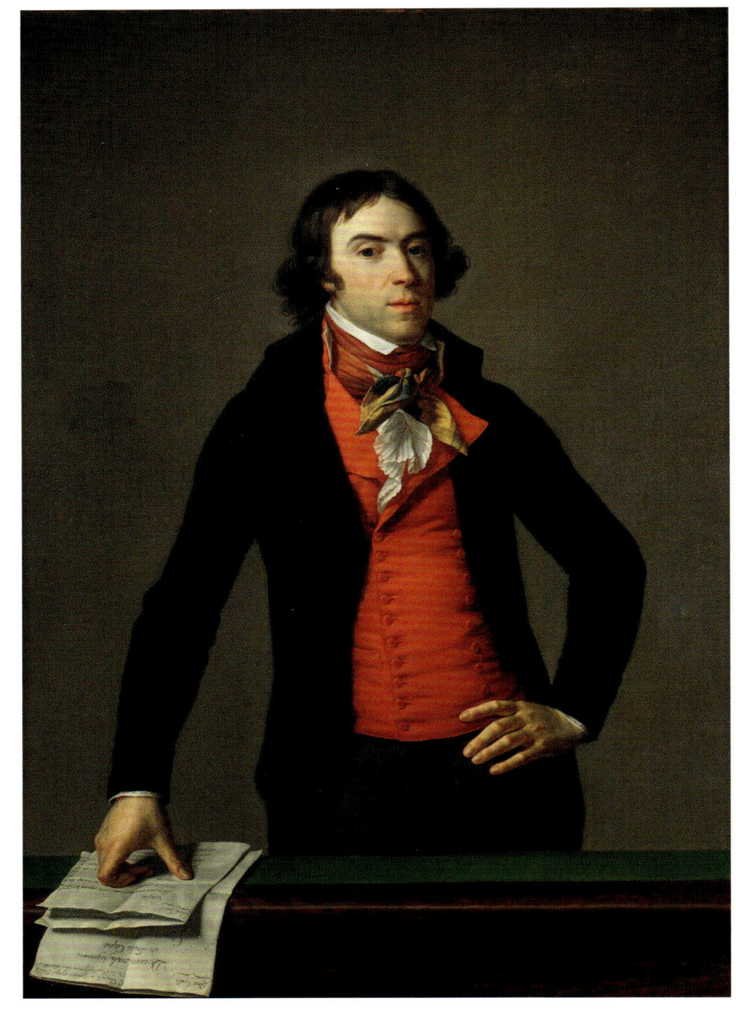

Jean-Louis Laneuville, *Portrait of Bertrand Barère de Vieuzac*, ca. 1793–94, oil on cavas, 51 × 38 in. (129.5 × 96.8 cm). Bremen, Kunsthalle Bremen - Der Kunstverein in Bremen

In the winter of 1879–80, Manet undertook two similar portraits of Georges Clemenceau, the future prime minister of France, "at the podium," as he had envisioned portraying Gambetta (fig. 80). At the time, Clemenceau, a journalist, served as a deputy on the Paris municipal council and would launch *La Justice*, a radical republican journal, in January 1880. In both portraits, which remain unfinished, the deputy stands before a neutral background, arms authoritatively crossed, as if poised to deliver a speech at the tribune of the Chamber of Deputies in the Luxembourg Palace.[36] The format recalls portraits of deputies from the first French Republic (1792–1804), thereby underscoring Clemenceau's republicanism, as art historian Mary Anne Stevens has suggested.[37] The sitter's pose and attire are the same in both portraits, suggesting that Manet was aided by a photograph. Although Clemenceau would complain that he sat "forty times" for Manet, he also enjoyed his conversations with the artist during his sittings: "I had such good times talking with Manet! He was so witty!"[38]

While the unfinished portraits of Clemenceau reflect Manet's dialogue with the tradition of political portraiture, his portrayal of the radical journalist and former Communard Henri Rochefort innovatively fuses portraiture and history painting (fig. 79). In the aftermath of the Paris Commune, Rochefort had been deported to a penal colony on the island of New Caledonia, from which he escaped in 1874. On July 14, 1880, the National Assembly granted amnesty to former Communards, and he returned to France on the same day. Manet had read Rochefort's fictionalized account of his escape, *L'Évadé*, which became a bestseller following its publication in June 1880, and he sought to commemorate Rochefort's dramatic escape in the form of a contemporary history painting. Rochefort agreed to Manet's proposal, as reported by the artist Marcellin Desboutin, who acted as intermediary: "The idea of an *Alabama* sea carried the day!!" By December 1880, Manet was at work on "a sensational painting for the Salon—Rochefort escaping in a rowboat on the open sea," according to Monet.[39]

Indeed, Manet's canvas recalls his *Battle of the U.S.S. Kearsarge and the C.S.S. Alabama* in its vertical format and scale (its dimensions are almost the same) and the wide expanse of sea that dominates the composition. The whaleboat carrying the six fugitives occupies the center of the canvas; Manet had a whaleboat delivered to the courtyard of his studio to use as a model and painted it "dark gray" to conform with Rochefort's account. However, Manet's work departs from historical fact in its setting in the open sea in lieu of a harbor and in its depiction of Rochefort heroically manning the boat's tiller during his escape. Manet also painted another, smaller version of this subject; in it, the boat and its occupants are set further back, closer to the horizon, and the figures are less clearly rendered (*The Escape of Rochefort*, ca. 1881, Musée d'Orsay, Paris).

The larger version of the escape of Rochefort remains in an unfinished state, and neither work was shown at the Salon. Instead, at Manet's request, Rochefort posed for a more conventional, half-length portrait, arms crossed, no longer the heroic escapee who had first captured Manet's imagination (Hamburger Kunsthalle). It was this portrait that Manet chose to exhibit at the Salon of 1881. Manet's reason for abandoning his "sensational painting" of Rochefort's escape seven years earlier is unknown.[40]

In the fall of 1878, Manet wrote to his friend Duret, "today Proust asked me to do his portrait for the next Salon."[41] Manet's portrait, dedicated "a mon ami Antonin Proust" was completed in 1880 and shown in the Salon the same year (fig. 81). Manet's childhood friend was then a deputy in the National Assembly. However, Manet's portrait eschews the conventions of political portraiture; set against a neutral background, Proust is more flâneur than statesman. It has been suggested that Manet was inspired by his own 1867 portrait by Fantin-Latour (see p. 13) in his portrayal of Proust: both men sport frock coats and top hats (that of Proust was reportedly "begun anew twenty times" by Manet) and carry walking sticks.[42] After the opening of the Salon in 1880, where the portrait was "badly hung . . . and received even worse than it's hung," as Manet wrote to Proust, the artist told his friend, "Your portrait is the sincerest work there can be."[43]

During Proust's brief tenure as Minister of Fine Arts in Leon Gambetta's short-lived government from November 1881 to January 1882, Manet was named *chevalier*, or knight, of the *Légion d'honneur*, conferring the official recognition that he had so long desired. By this date Manet's health was declining, and his world was increasingly circumscribed. His paintings of modern life and contemporary history would give way to more intimate and personal imagery—portraits of friends and small-scale still-life paintings.

1 Proust 1988, 21.
2 On this subject, see John House, "Manet's Maximilian: History Painting, Censorship, and Ambiguity" in Juliet Wilson-Bareau, *Manet: The Execution of Maximilian, Painting, Politics, and Censorship* [exhibition catalogue], London, National Gallery, 1992, 87–111.
3 On Manet's history paintings, see Anne Coffin Hanson, *Manet and the Modern Tradition* (New Haven, Yale University Press, 1977), 103–27.
4 Proust 1988, 36.
5 Wilson-Bareau 1991, 25.
6 See Juliet Wilson-Bareau and David Degener, "*Manet and th e Sea*," in Juliet Wilson-Bareau et al., *Manet and the Sea* [exhibition catalogue], Chicago, Art Institute of Chicago, Philadelphia, Philadelphia Museum of Art, and Amsterdam, Van Gogh Museum, 2003–4, 57–61.
7 Hamilton 1954, 64.
8 Juliet Wilson-Bareau and David C. Degener, *Manet and the American Civil War: The Battle of the USS Kearsarge and the CSS Alabama* [exhibition catalogue], New York, The Metropolitan Museum of Art, 2003, 41, 53–55.
9 Jean-Paul Bouillon, *Manet to Braquemond, Newly Discovered Letters to an Artist and Friend* (Paris, Fondation Custodia/Collection Frits Lugt, 2020), 106.
10 Zola 1867 in Los Angeles 2013, 86.
11 London 1992, 47.
12 Paris and New York 1983, 273.
13 John Elderfield, *Manet and the Execution of Maximilian* [exhibition catalogue], New York, The Museum of Modern Art, 2006, 62.
14 New York 2006, 108.
15 London 1992, 55.
16 Ibid., 69.
17 Ibid., 58.
18 Paris and New York 1983, 277–78.
19 For all documents related to this controversy, see Appendix II, ed. by Juliet Wilson-Bareau in Paris and New York 1983, 531–34.
20 Letter of September 24, 1870, in Curtiss 1983, 381.
21 Ibid., 384.
22 Letters of December 2, and December 7, 1870, Ibid., 385.
23 Letter of September 30, 1870, Ibid., 381.
24 Letter of March 21 to Bracquemond in Wilson-Bareau 1991, 160–61.
25 Proust 1988, 37.
26 James H. Rubin, "Manet's Heroic Corpses and the Politics of Their Time," in Therese Dolan (ed.), *Perspectives on Manet* (Ashgate, 2012), 130.
27 Hanson 1977, 119.
28 For the comparison with Daumier, see Paris and New York 1983, 328.
29 London 1992, 73.
30 Paris and New York 1983, 323–24.
31 Hanson 1977, 119.
32 Paris and New York 1983, 328.
33 See the discussion of this work in Paris and Washington, D.C. 1998, 131–43, and Herbert 1988, 30–32.
34 Proust 1988, 37–38.
35 Wilson-Bareau 1991, 184; Proust 1988, 53.
36 See also *Portrait of Georges Clemenceau*, 1879–80, Fort Worth, Kimbell Art Museum.
37 Toledo and London 2012–13, 194.
38 Paris and New York 1983, 443.
39 Ibid., 467–68.
40 See Juliet Wilson-Bareau and David Degener, "Manet and the Sea" in Chicago-Philadelphia-Amsterdam 2003–4, 86–89.
41 Wilson-Bareau 1991, 182.
42 Paris and New York 1983, 449–50.
43 Cited in Lawrence W. Nichols, "Manet and Hals: Two Geniuses, One Vision," in Toledo and London 2012–13, 71.

70

The Battle of the "U.S.S. Kearsage" and the "C.S.S. Alabama"

1864
Oil on canvas, 54 ¼ × 50 ¾ in. (137.8 × 128.9 cm)
Philadelphia, Philadelphia Musuem of Art, John G. Johnson Collection, 1917, cat. 1027

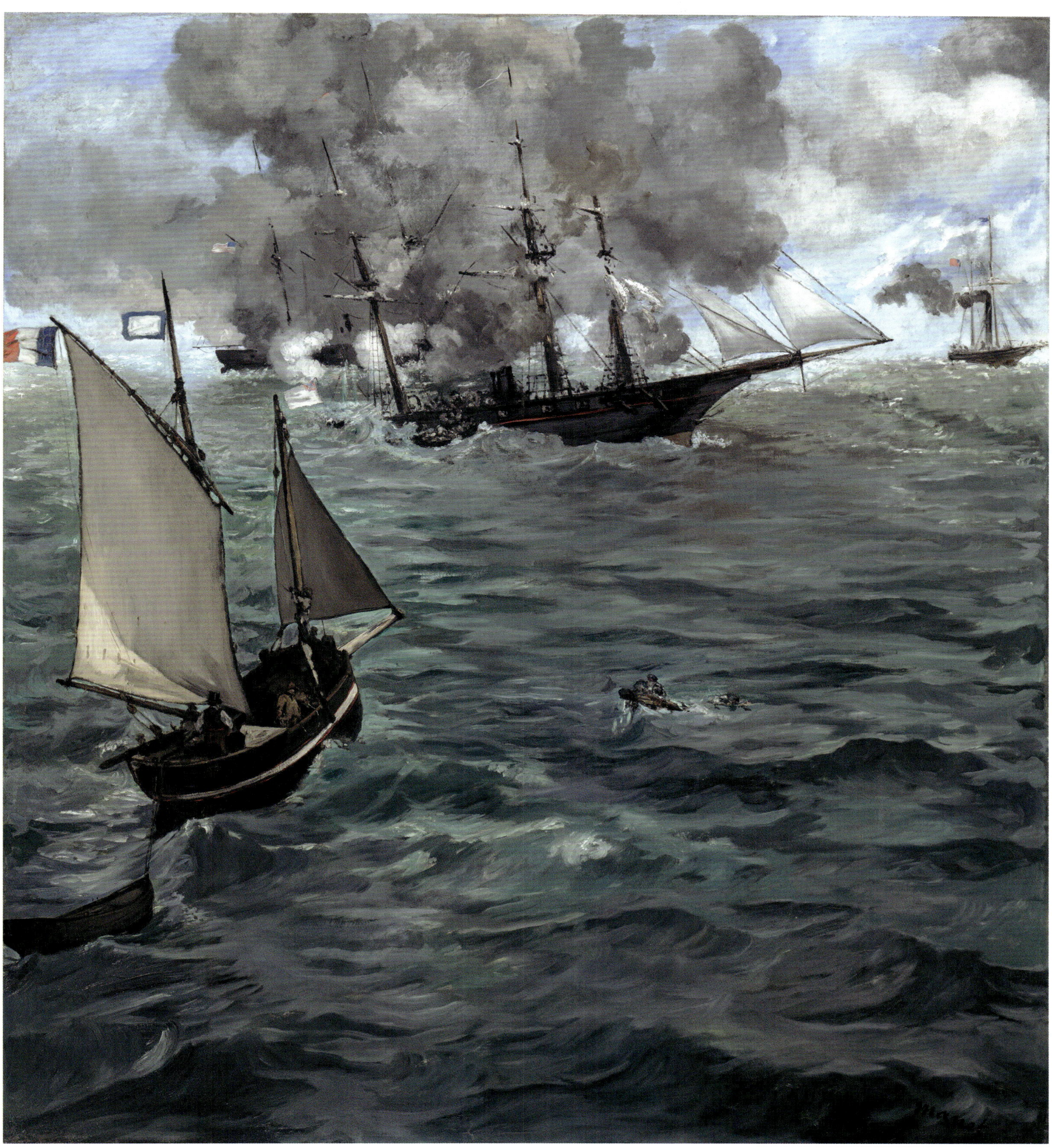

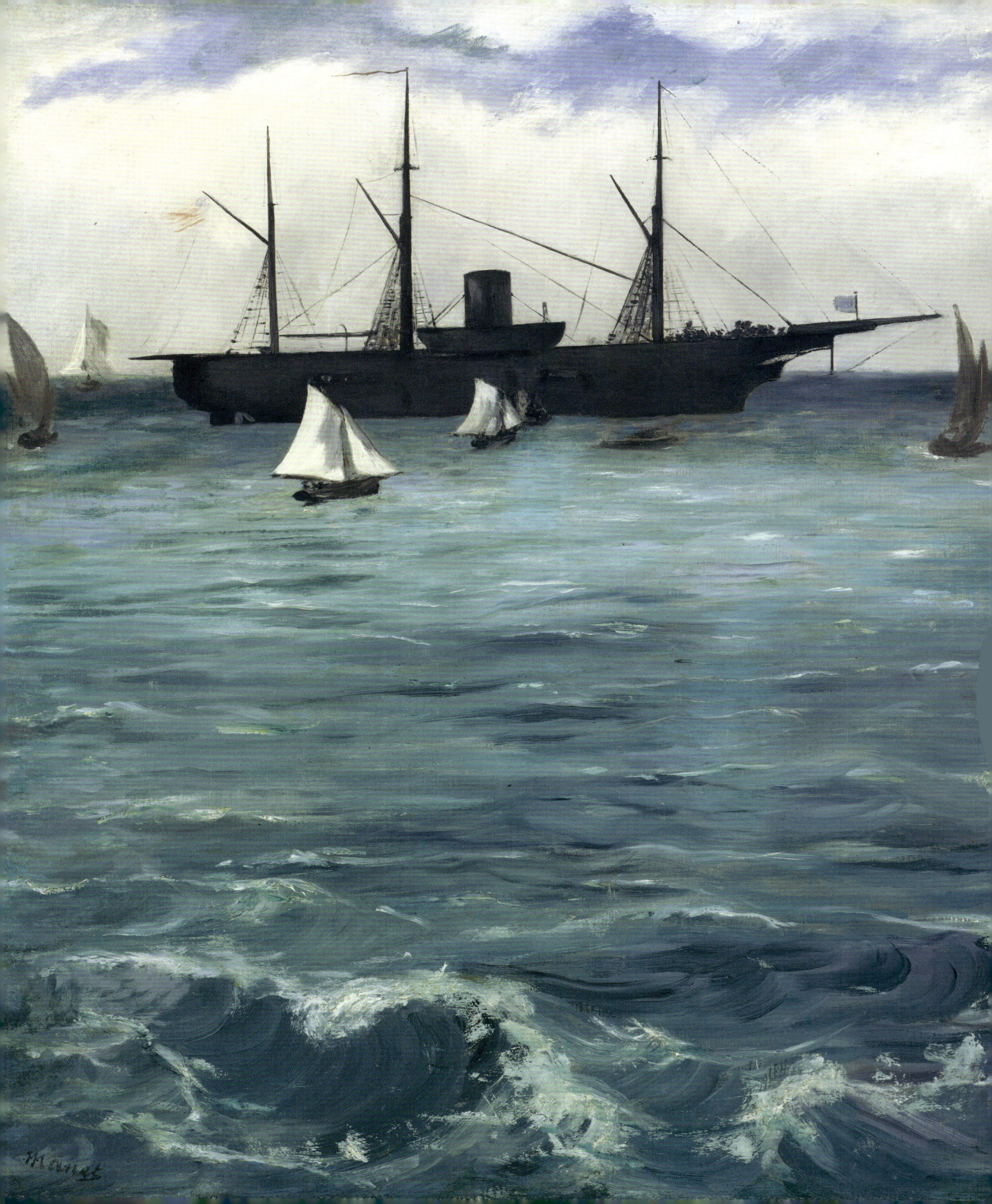
Manet

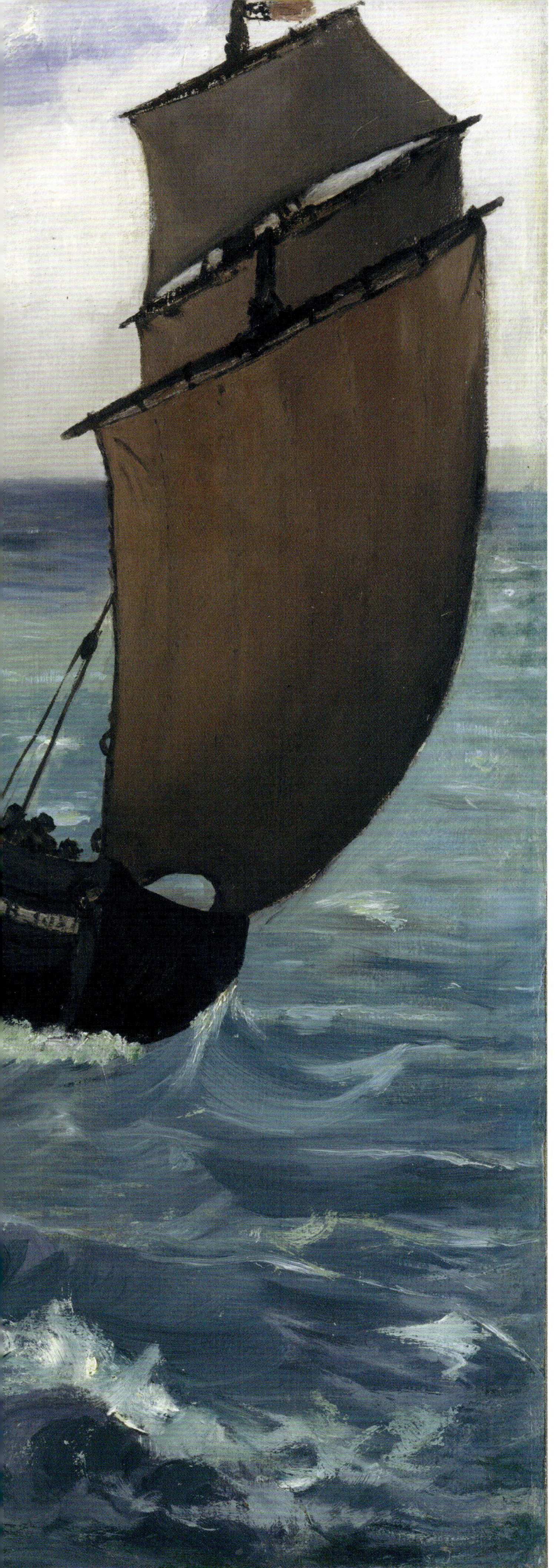

71

The "Kearsarge" at Boulogne

1864
Oil on canvas, 32 ⅛ × 39 ⅜ in. (81.6 × 100 cm)
New York, The Metropolitan Musuem of Art, Gift of Peter H. B. Frelinghuysen, and Purchase, Mr. and Mrs. Richard J. Bernhard Gift, by exchange, Gifts of Mr. and Mrs. Richard Rodgers and Joanne Toor Cummings, by exchange, and Drue Heinz Trust, The Dillon Fund, The Vincent Astor Foundation, Mr. and Mrs. Henry R. Kravis, The Charles Engelhard Foundation, and Florence and Herbert Irving Gifts, 1999, 1999.442

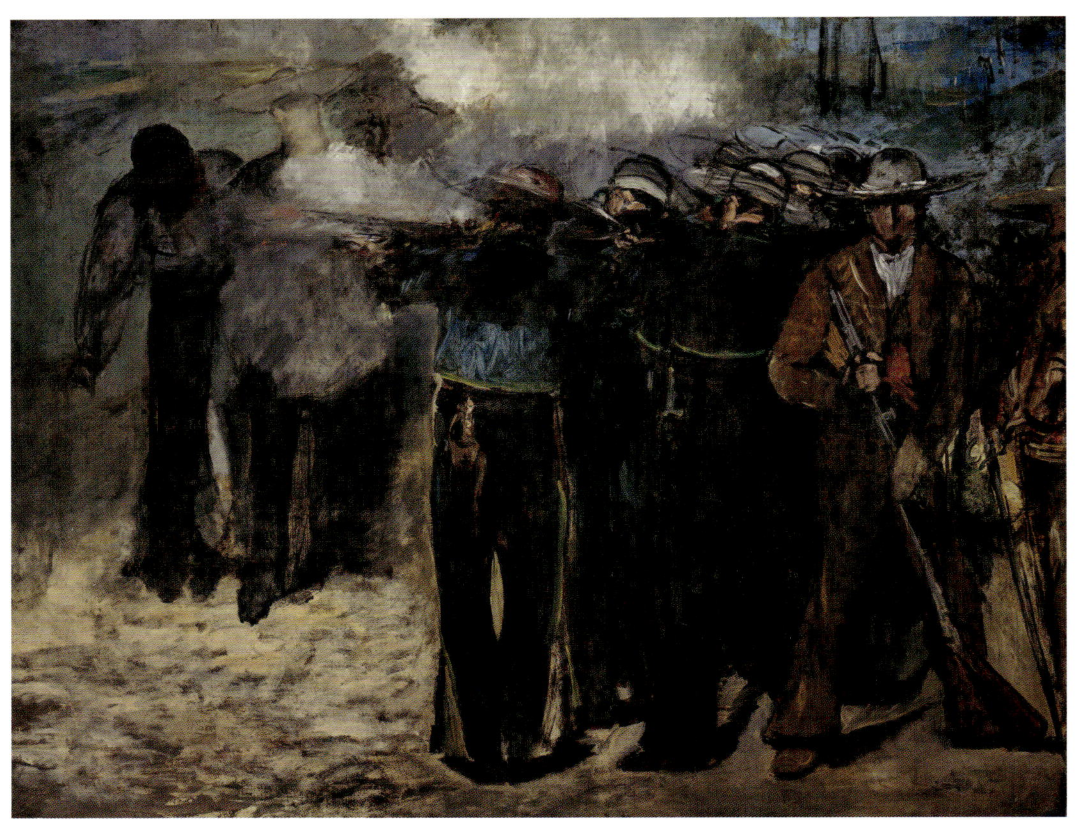

72

The Execution of Maximilian

1867
Oil on canvas, 77 ⅛ × 102 ¼ in. (195.9 × 259.7 cm)
Boston, The Museum of Fine Arts, Gift of Mr. and Mrs. Frank Gair Macomber, 30.444

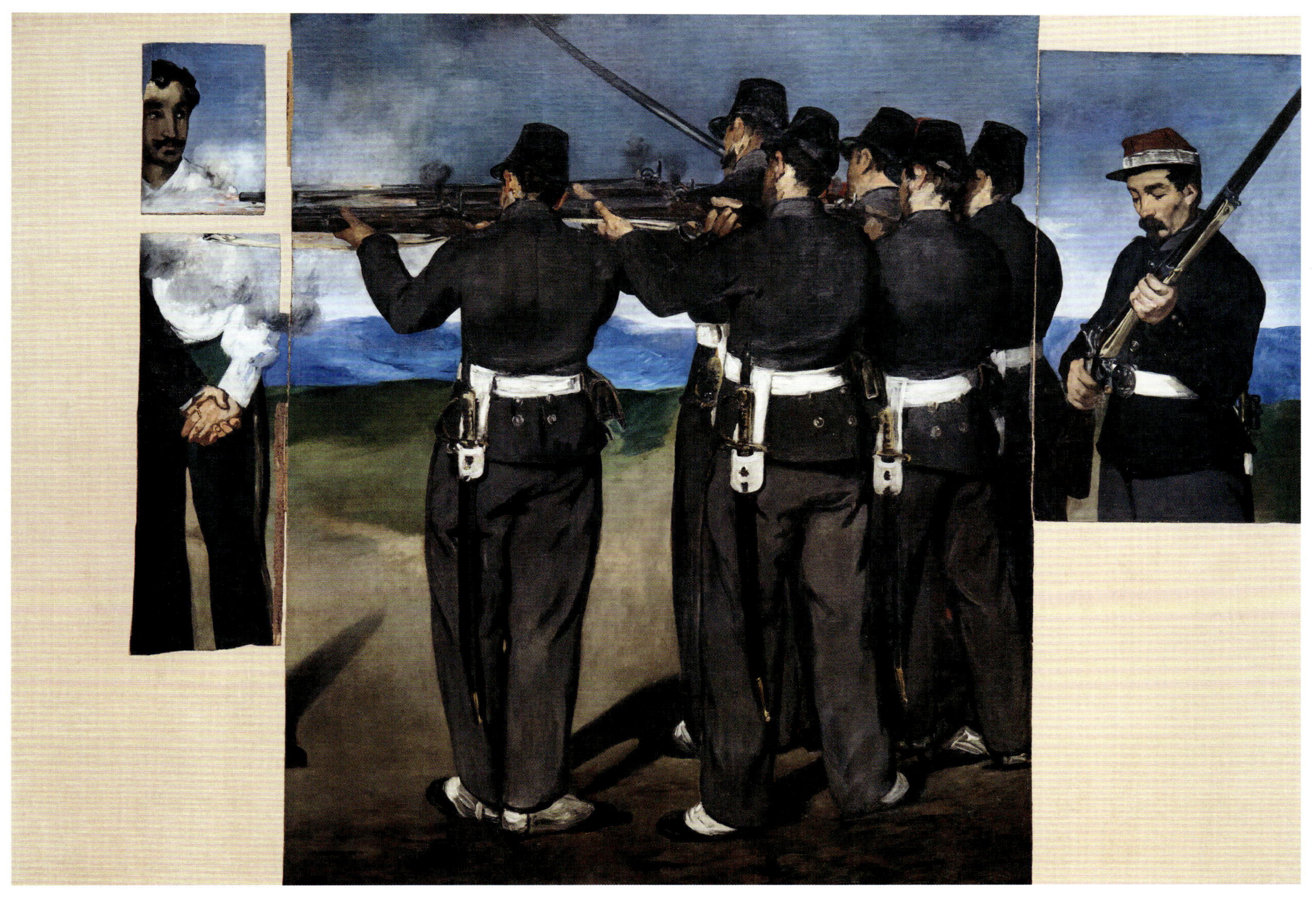

73

The Execution of Maximilian

1868–69
Oil on canvas, 76 × 112 in.
(193 × 284 cm)
London, The National
Gallery, NG3294

74

The Execution of Maximilian

1867
Oil on canvas, 99 ¼ × 120 in.
(252 × 305 cm)
Mannheim, Kunsthalle
Mannheim

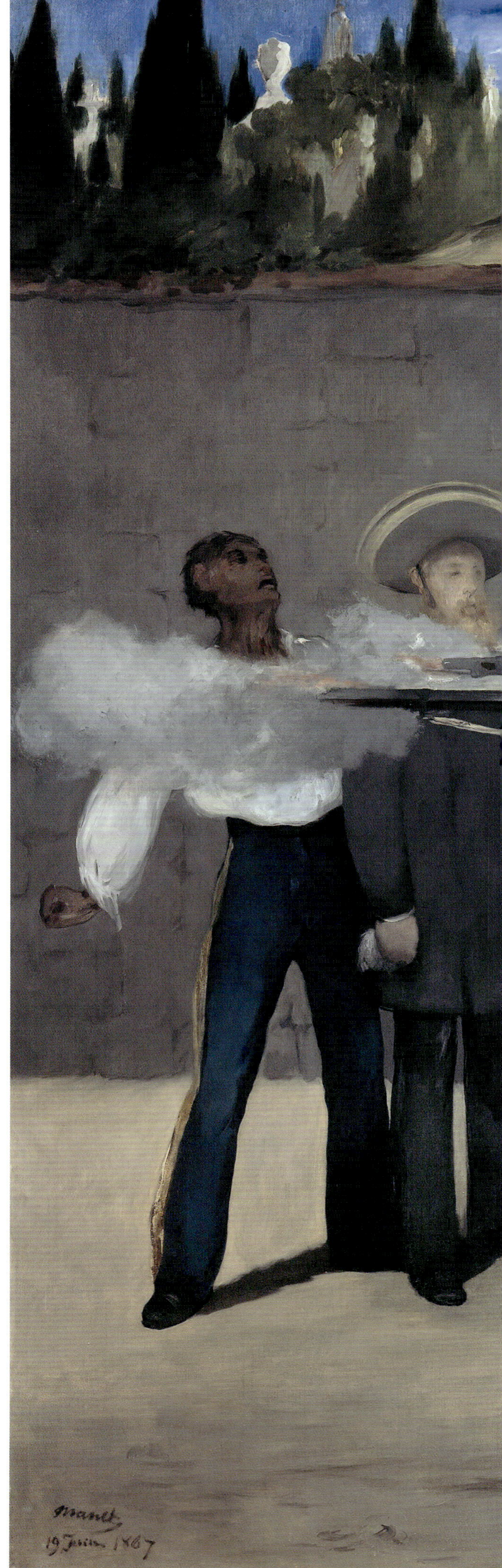

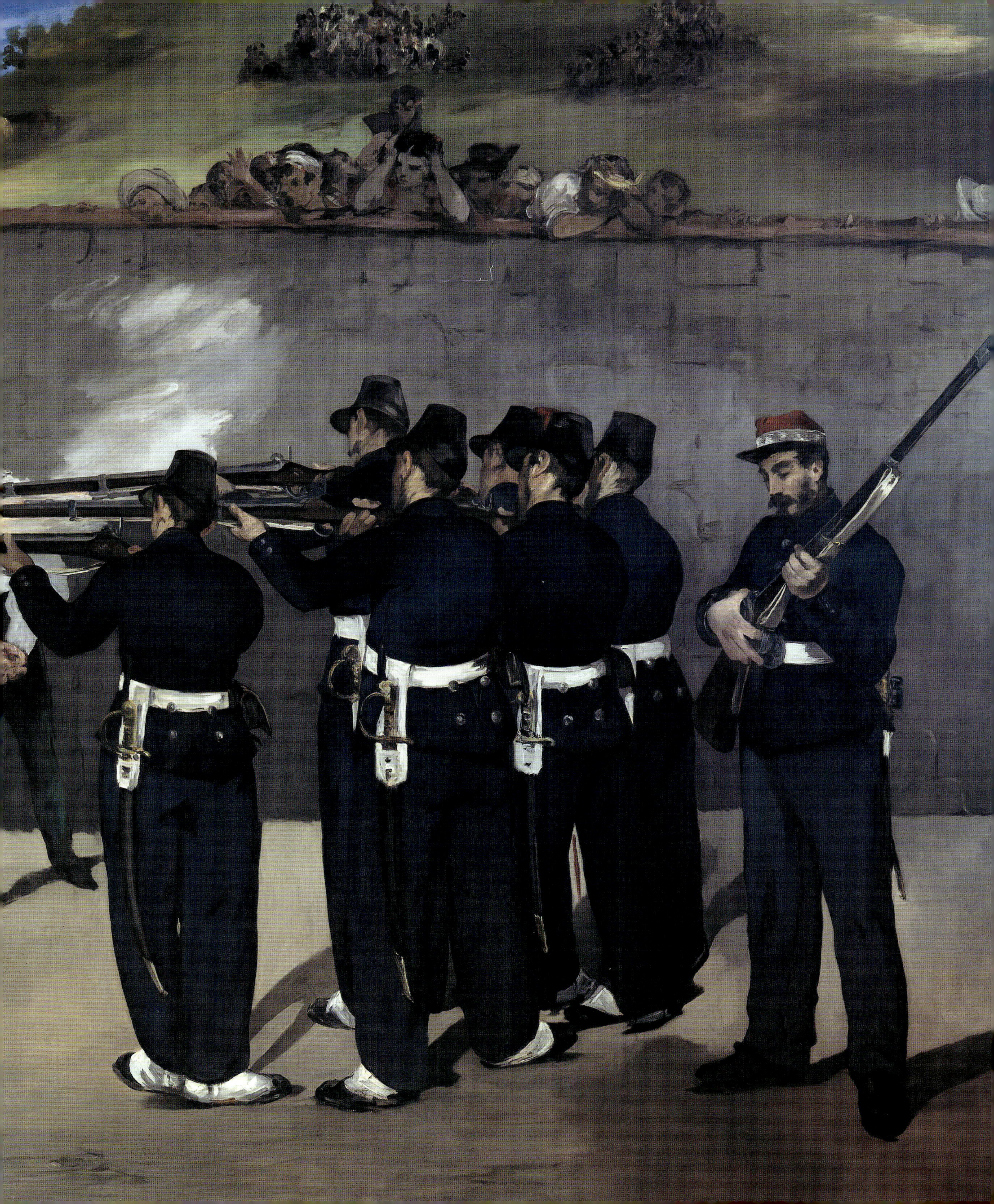

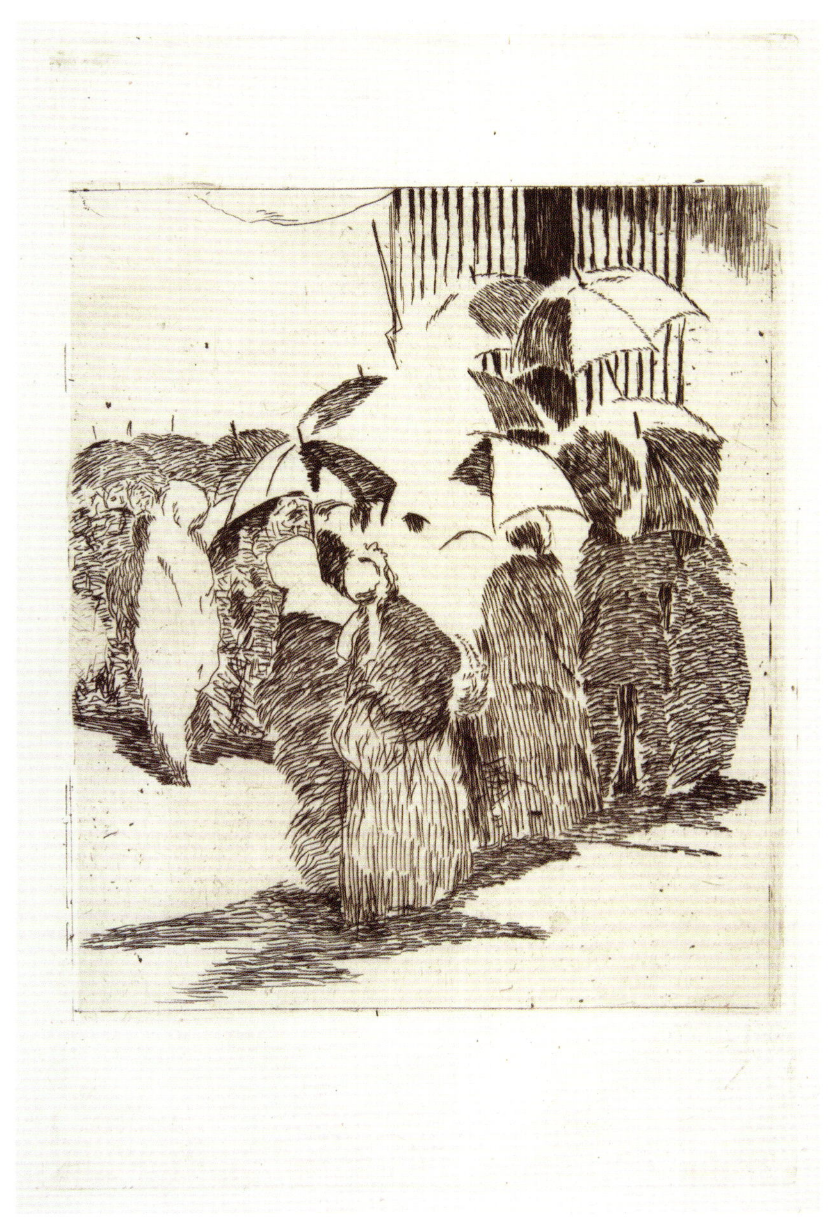

75

Line in Front of the Butcher Shop

1870–71
Etching in warm black on laid paper, 9 5⁄16 × 6 ¼ in. (23.6 × 15.8 cm) (plate)
New York, The Metropolitan Museum of Art, Rogers Fund, 1921, 21.76.28

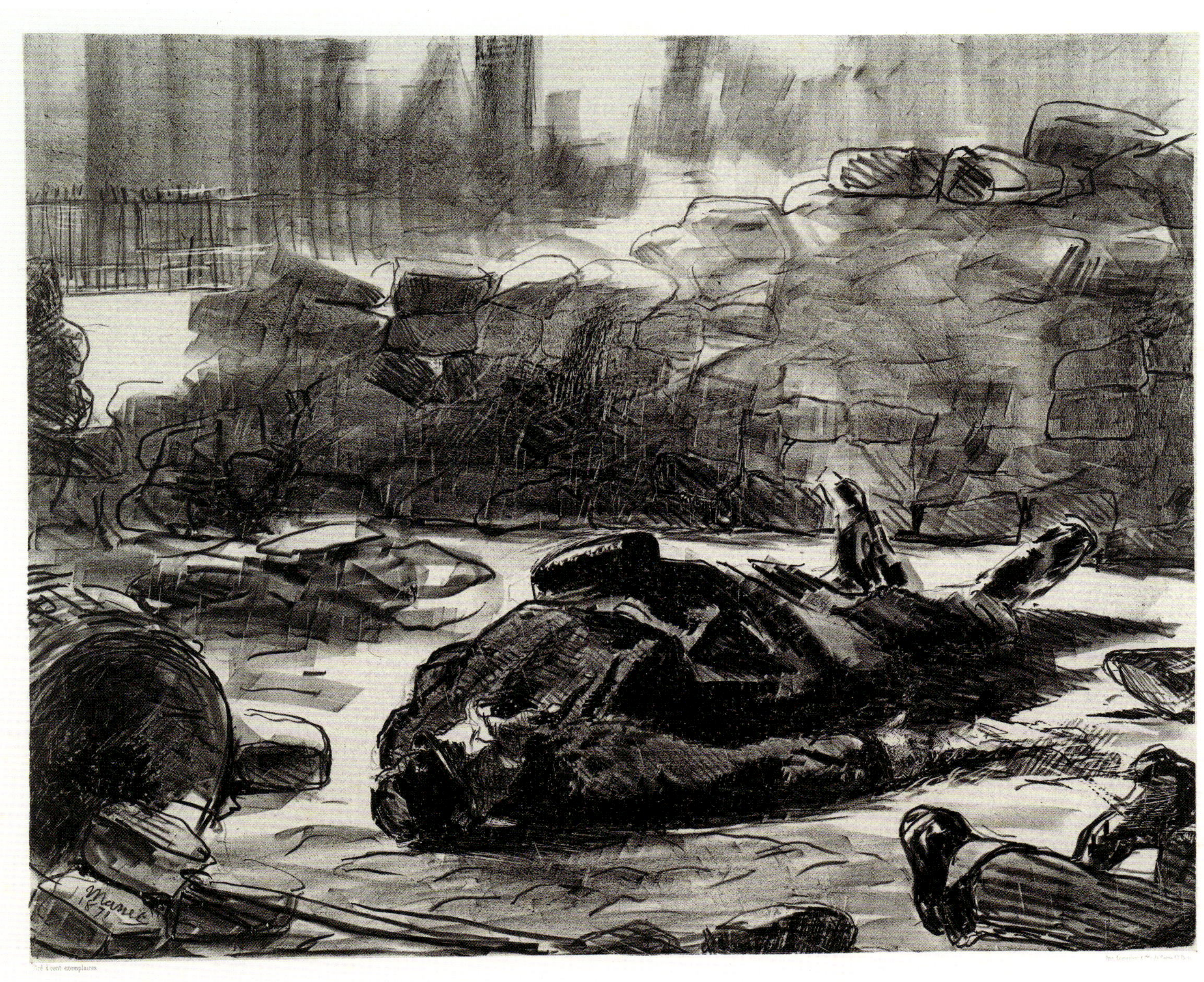

76

Civil War

1871–73
Lithograph on paper,
15 ⅝ × 20 in. (39.7 × 50.8 cm) (image)
New York, The Metropolitan
Museum of Art, Rogers Fund,
1922, 22.60.18

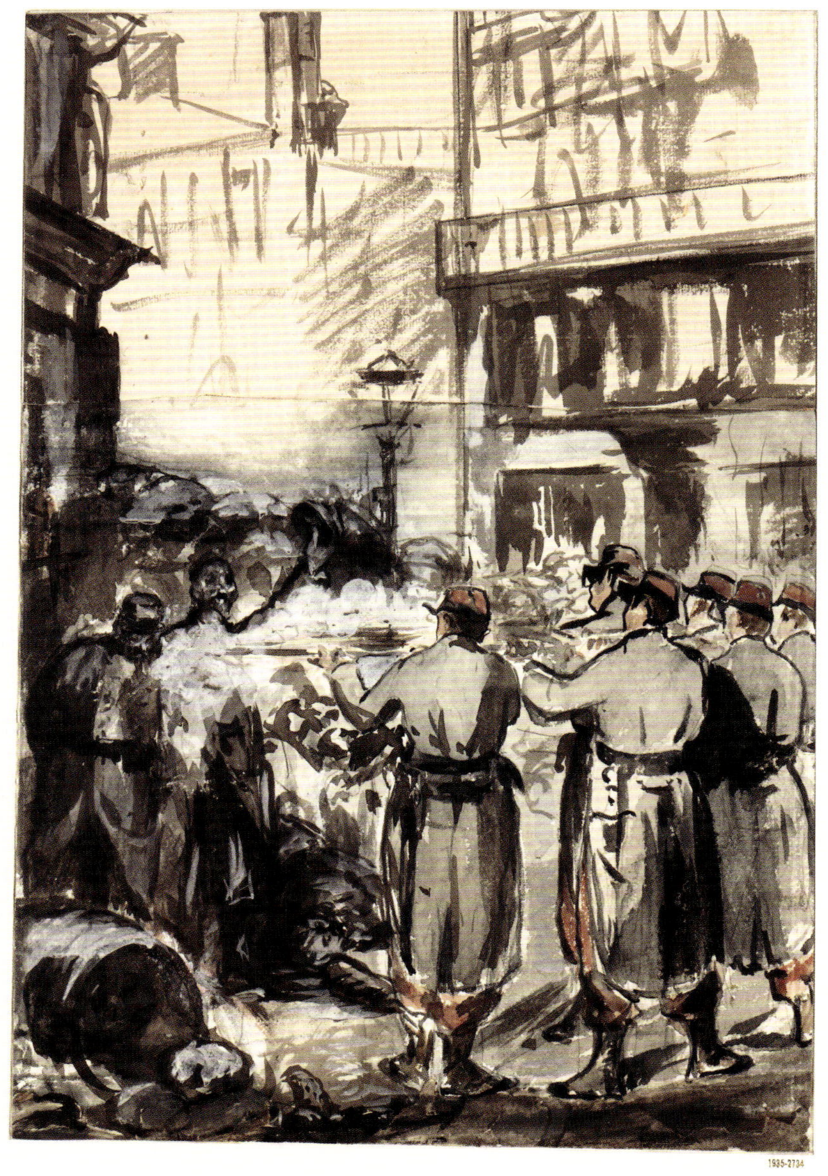

77

The Barricade

ca. 1871
Brush and ink wash,
watercolor and gouache
over graphite on paper,
18 3/16 × 12 13/16 in. (46.2 × 32.5 cm)
Budapest, Szépművészeti
Múzeum / Museum of Fine Arts
(1935-2734)

78

The Rue Mosnier with Flags

1878
Oil on canvas, 25 ¾ × 31 ½ in.
(65.4 × 80 cm)
Los Angeles, Getty Museum,
89.PA.71.

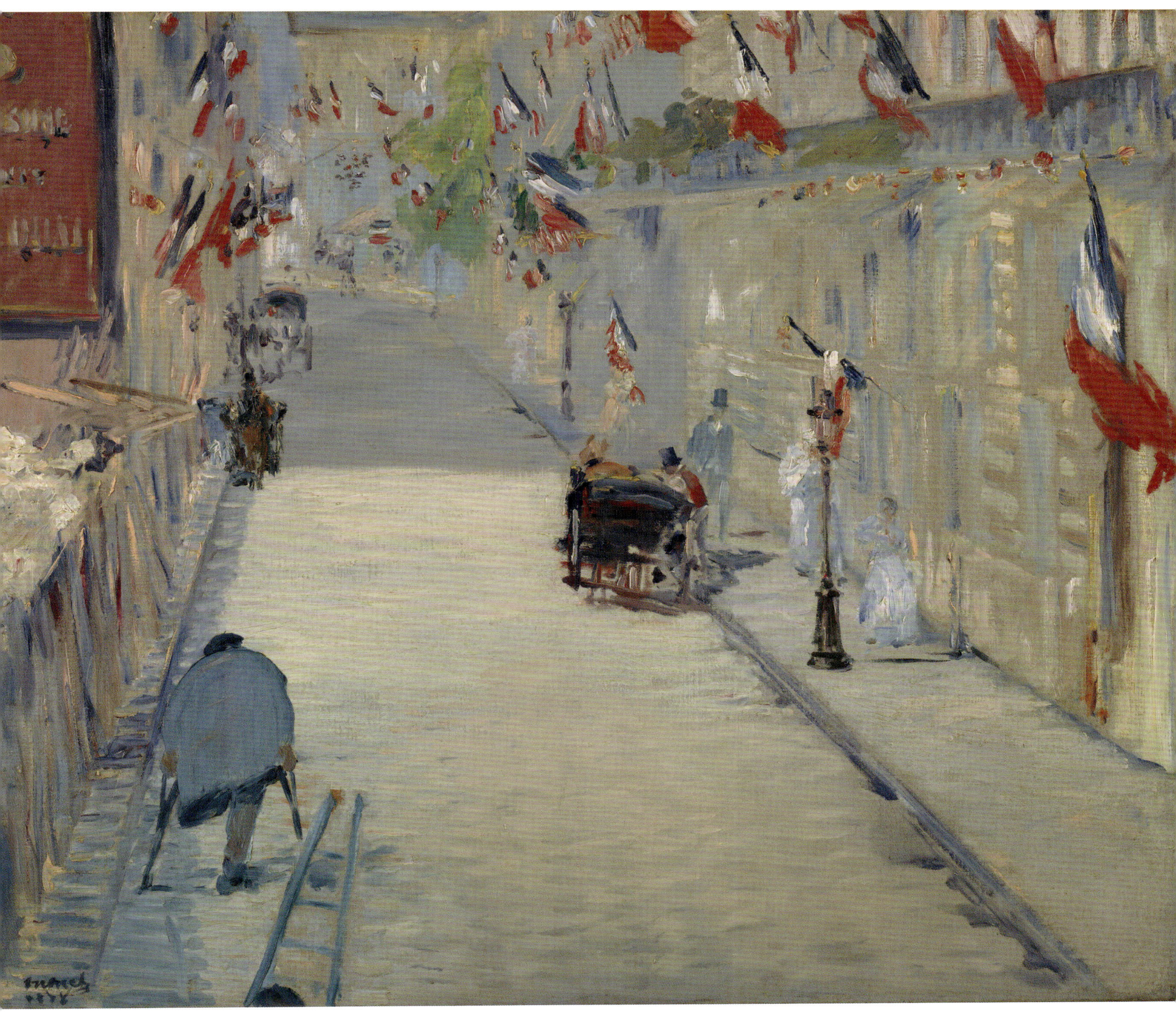

79

Rochefort's Escape

1880–81
Oil on canvas, 56 ¼ × 45 in.
(143 × 114 cm)
Zurich, Vereinigung Zürcher
Kunstfreunde, purchased
with the bequest
of Dr. Adolf Jöhr, 1955

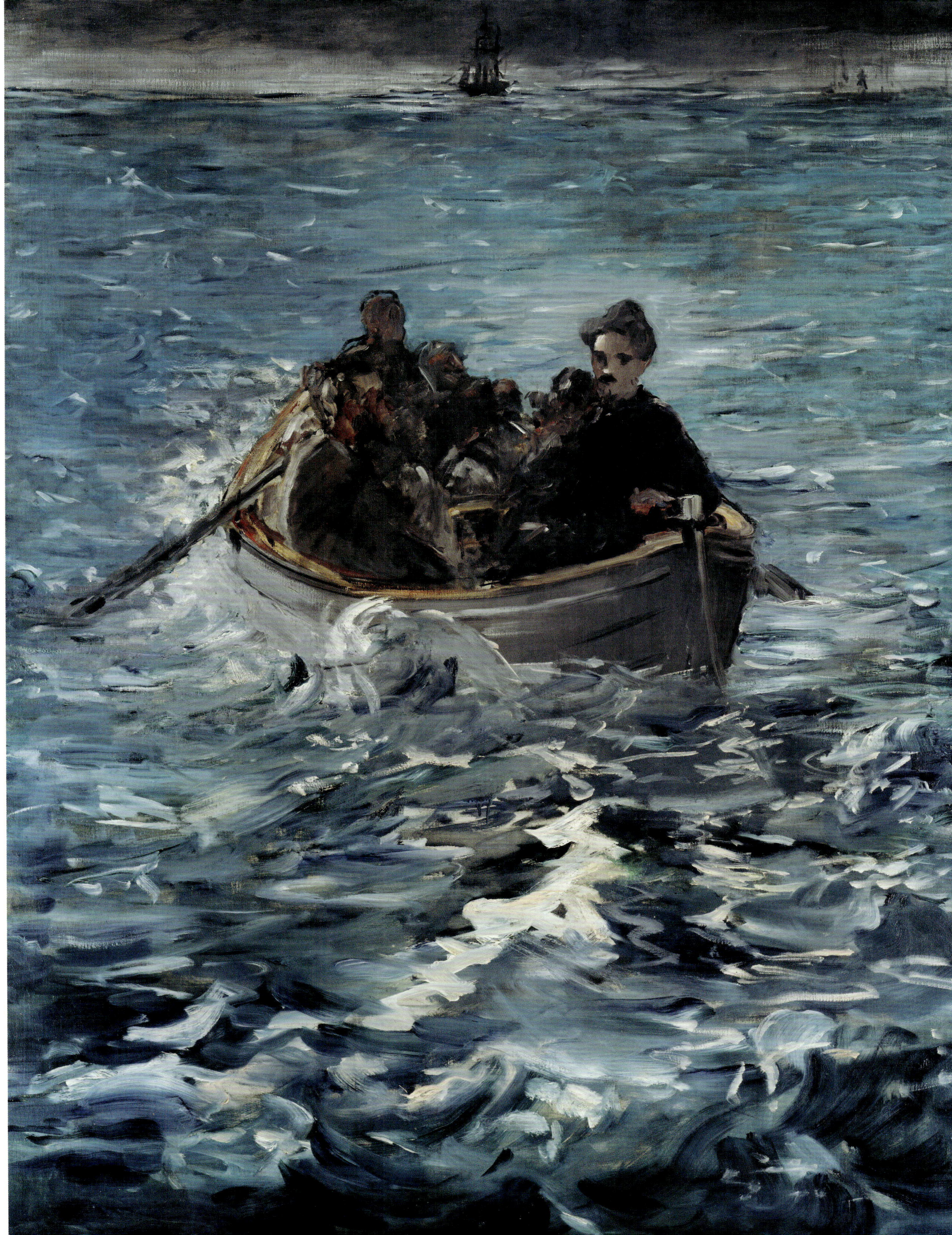

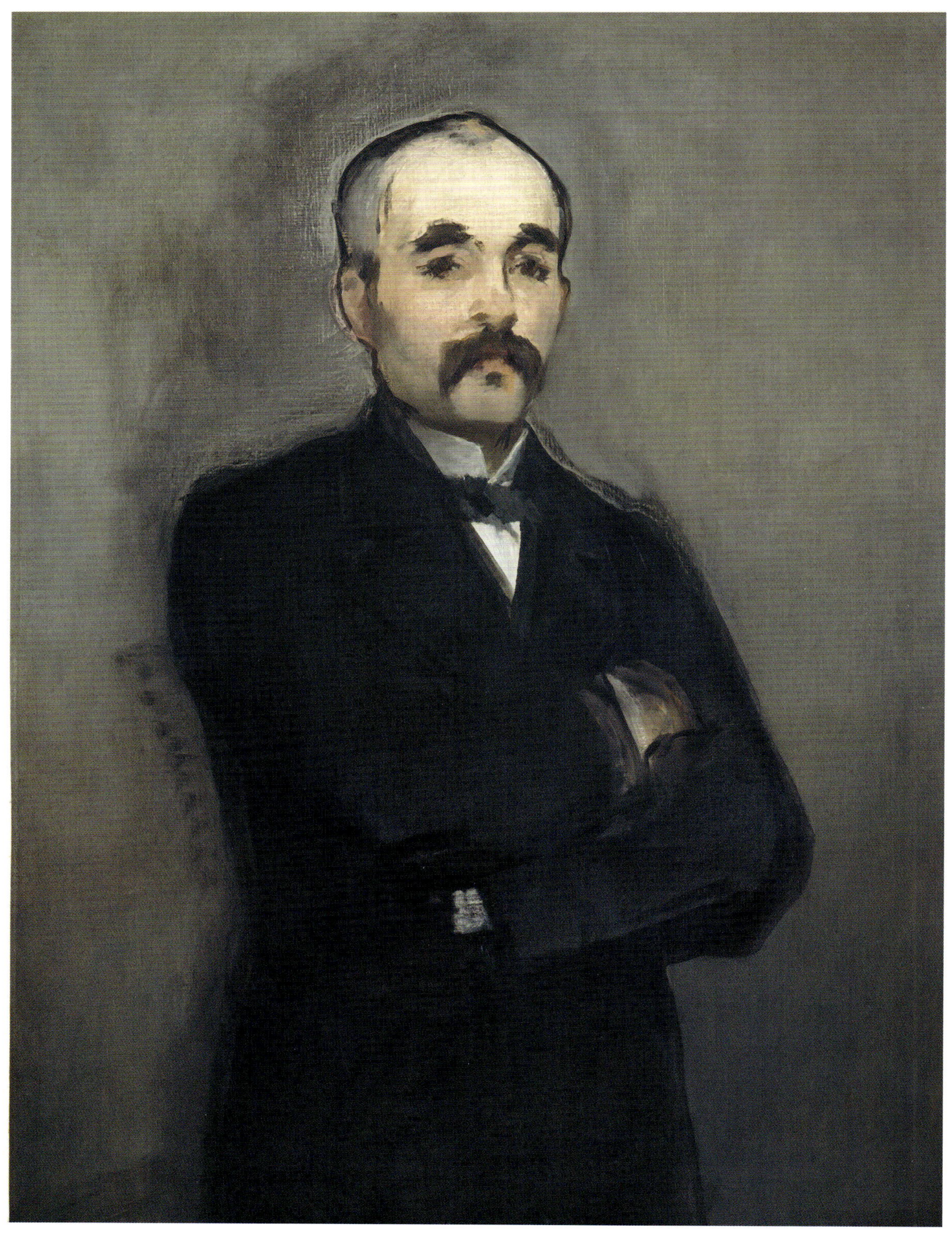

80

Georges Clemenceau

1879–80
Oil on canvas, 37 × 29 in.
(94 × 73,8 cm)
Paris, Musee d'Orsay,
RF 2641

81

Antonin Proust

1880
Oil on canvas, 51 × 37 ¾ in.
(129.5 × 95.9 cm)
Toledo, Toledo Museum
of Art, Gift of Edward
Drummond Libbey, 1925.108

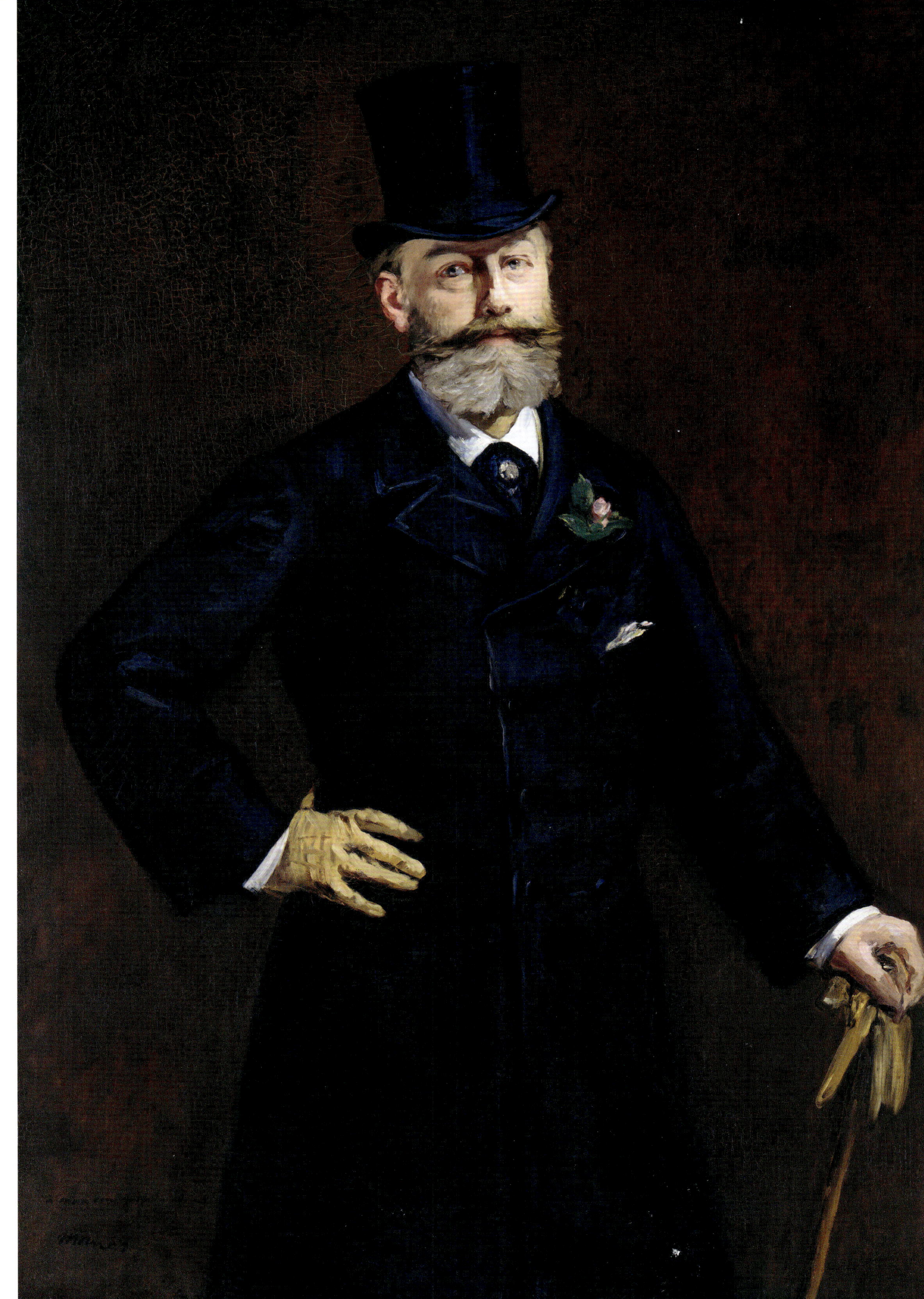

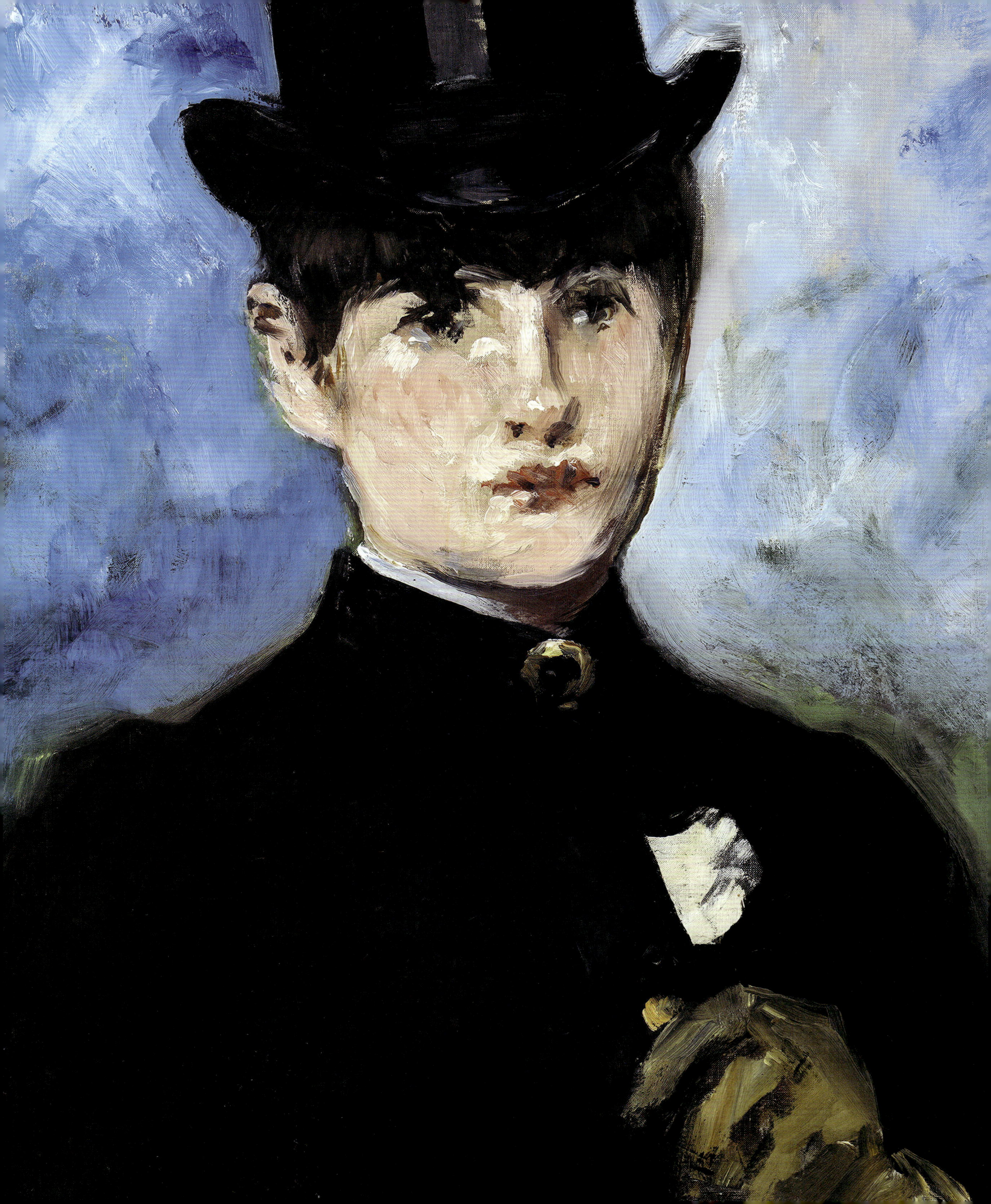

Legacy

In 1881, Manet attained the official recognition he had long been seeking. The de facto leader of the avant-garde for nearly two decades, he received a second-class medal at the Salon for his portrait of Eugène Pertuiset as a lion hunter (Museu de Arte de São Paulo Assis Chateaubriand), exempting his submissions from future review by the Salon jury. By the end of the year, he was also named *chevalier* of the *Légion d'honneur*, thanks to the efforts of his friend Antonin Proust, then France's Minister of Fine Arts. By this date he was also suffering from the effects of advanced syphilis, which forced him to seek treatment outside of Paris. Although his world would narrow even further, he continued to push the boundaries of his art, engaging in a dialogue with his earlier work while also experimenting with new media and subjects. His last years, far from marked by stagnancy or decline, represent both artistic growth and efforts to ensure his legacy.[1]

In late May 1880, Manet left Paris with his family for the spa town of Bellevue, in Meudon, where he underwent water therapy as prescribed by his doctor. During his nearly six-month stay, his ability to work was limited. Ever the consummate Parisian, he chafed at the boredom of his enforced isolation, complaining to his old friend Zacharie Astruc, "the countryside only has charms for those who are not obliged to stay there."[2] Seeking subjects to paint, he invited Marguerite Besnier de la Pontonnerie to model for him at Bellevue in July; "Mademoiselle Marguerite," as he called her, was the younger sister of Madame Jules Guillemet, who had posed with her husband for *In the Conservatory* (fig. 68). He instructed her, "Bring your needlework and the light-colored summer dress you told me about, and if you have a pretty garden hat don't leave it behind."[3] Later that summer he reported to an artist friend, "I've begun painting the young sister [Marguerite] but don't know if I'll have time to finish."[4] Manet realized his vision in *A Corner of the Garden at Bellevue*, one of three paintings depicting his model reading in the garden of his rented villa.[5] Its vibrant palette and loose brushwork reflect Manet's ongoing engagement with Impressionist plein air painting. It has been suggested that his garden scenes from this summer might have served as faux plein-air backgrounds for later figure paintings realized in his Paris studio.[6]

Detail of fig. 89

Manet's isolation in Bellevue inspired a body of letters sent to friends and potential models that he variously embellished with watercolor illustrations, whose subjects ranged from fruit and flowers from his garden to a watering can and Suzanne Manet's cat, Zizi. Manet occasionally added a portrait of the missive's intended recipient, painted from memory or with the aid of a photograph. These letters were mostly addressed to women, among them Isabelle Lemonnier, the sister-in-law of the publisher Georges Charpentier, Méry Laurent, a demimondaine and salon hostess, and Madame Jules Guillemet. Often flirtatious in tone, they recall his earlier still life of a bunch of violets and a fan, a painted billet-doux dedicated to Berthe Morisot (fig. 50).[7] One of his series of letters to Isabelle Lemonnier wittily fuses image, text, and recipient (fig. 83). In it, a single plum and its cast shadow float above a poem in four lines that plays on the rhyme of the sitter's surname with "mirabelle," the type of plum that Manet depicted.[8]

The illustrated letters naturally accord with Manet's renewed interest in still-life painting in 1880. However, instead of the large-scale, complex arrangements reminiscent of seventeenth-century Dutch prototypes that he favored in his first group of still lifes from the 1860s, Manet narrowed his focus to fruits and vegetables, shown individually or clustered together on a marble tabletop. A bunch of asparagus bound in twine, painted in 1880, embodies these small-scale works, which are at once intimate and monumental in their pared-down simplicity (fig. 85). Manet lavished his brush in rendering the different textures of the tender stalks and distinctive rose-purple tips of the asparagus, grown nearby in Argenteuil. The work was acquired that same year by Manet's patron Charles Ephrussi, who paid more than the asking price, prompting the artist's painted rejoinder in the form of a single asparagus spear that hovers just over the edge of the marble tabletop (fig. 84). Its placement mirrors that of the knives in Manet's earlier still lifes, a compositional device borrowed from Chardin (figs. 42 and 43). Manet sent the painting of the lone asparagus to Ephrussi, accompanied by a note: "There was one missing from your bunch."[9]

In addition to revisiting still life as a subject, Manet had begun experimenting with a new medium: pastel. Popularized in the eighteenth century, pastel was enjoying a resurgence among the Impressionists in the 1870s, including Berthe Morisot, Edgar Degas, and Manet's former student Eva Gonzalès. In Manet's one-man show in the galleries of *La Vie Moderne* in April 1880, he exhibited pastels for the first time; fifteen pastels figured among the twenty-five works on view. He reserved the medium for portraits and figure paintings, and between 1879 and 1883 he realized some ninety works in pastel, mostly of women. A laudatory review of Manet's 1880 exhibition declared him "the painter of elegant women."[10] According to his first biographer, Edmond Bazire, "models . . . were multiplied, and for everyone that sat, there are three, four, six likenesses."[11] In the context of the chronic pain that afflicted Manet in the final years of his life, pastel was also less demanding than painting, as Duret observed, "Pastel was for him a comparatively easy exercise, a diversion, and gained him the company of the engaging women who came to pose for him."[12]

One of the "engaging women" was Méry Laurent, whom Manet met when she visited his studio in 1876. It was she who encouraged Manet to paint "this series of pastel portraits," most of which were painted in his studio on rue d'Amsterdam, according to Manet's friend Proust.[13] She became the artist's close friend and favorite model in his final years. An 1882 portrait of Laurent reveals Manet's facility with pastel (fig. 86). In keeping with the informality of the pose, the handling is loose and seemingly rapid, underscored by the slight blurring of the sitter's facial features.[14] The artist's touch evokes a range of textures, from the white-dotted netting covering her toque to the fur boa around her neck and the glint of a highlight applied to the tip of her nose. Manet's attention to the details of the sitter's fashionable attire is typical of his portraits of women from this period. Works such as the portrait of Méry Laurent reflect Manet's abiding interest in portraying the women of the Third Republic, as recorded by Proust. In a comment that might reflect his anti-Bonapartist sentiments, he said, "I didn't do the women of the Second Empire, but I did those who came afterward."[15]

Manet's interest in painting the women of the Third Republic further manifested itself in a planned series of allegorical portraits of the four seasons, of which only two works were realized, *Jeanne (Spring)* (fig. 87) and *Autumn (Méry Laurent)* (1881 or 1882, Musée des Beaux-Arts, Nancy). *Jeanne* features a teenage model as the personification of spring, who later made her name as the actress known as Mademoiselle Demarsy. Silhouetted against a background of rhododendrons, she wears a hat trimmed with roses and daisies and a floral-patterned dress, as styled by Manet.[16] While the format of the work recalls fifteenth-century profile portraits of women, the subject is an unmistakably modern type that had interested Manet since the 1860s (fig. 53). The sitter's fashionable ensemble and bearing as well as her pert, upturned nose, which Manet accented with a reddish-brown contour line, identify her as a *Parisienne*, which his contemporaries were quick to recognize. Manet exhibited the work at the Salon of 1882 where, exceptionally, it was widely acclaimed. One reviewer enthused, "This nice little face, pink beneath the rice powder, this turned-up nose . . . this whole image of the smart *parisienne* walking in a garden under a transparent parasol—it's simply exquisite."[17] Another critic proclaimed the work "an absolute masterpiece, the Mona Lisa of the master, or even better, a true *Parisienne* from the tip of her charming upturned nose to the end of the parasol that she holds with so much chic."[18]

At the Salon of 1882, Manet exhibited *Jeanne* with another modern subject that marked his return to the world of Parisian leisure and entertainment that he had explored in his café scenes from the later 1870s. *A Bar at the Folies-Bergère* (fig. 88) recreates the promenade encircling the theatre inside the popular entertainment venue. Contemporary Naturalist literature emphasized its seamier side; in his 1885 novel, *Bel-Ami*, Guy de Maupassant described a scene that conjures Manet's painting: "the circular promenade where . . . a group of women awaited arrivals at one or another of the three bars behind which, heavily made-up and wilting, three vendors of refreshments and of love held court."[19] A woman who worked as a barmaid at the Foliès-Bergère, identified as Suzon, served as Manet's model; the artist Gaston La Touche, Manet's friend and neighbor, posed as her top-hatted customer, seen only as a reflected image in a mirror. Working from sketches made on site, Manet staged the scene in his studio, using the same marble table that appears in his first café subject, *Plum Brandy* (fig. 64).

Manet captured the spectacle of modern life on display at the Folies-Bergère, from the well-stocked bar, its bottles of Champagne, liquor, and Bass ale rendered with portrait-like specificity, to the mirrored reflection of the audience seated in the balcony, which includes loosely sketched portraits of Jeanne Demarsy and Méry Laurent, and the disembodied legs of a trapeze artist floating above the scene. Manet's barmaid was seen as the embodiment of the place—"truly modern, truly 'Folies-Bergère.'"[20] However, the obvious divergence of Suzon's figure from its reflected image flummoxed Salon audiences in 1882; its artifice "bewilders the throng of visitors, who exchange puzzled remarks concerning the mirage of this canvas,"[21] as one reviewer wrote. A Salon caricature went so far as to add the "missing" figure of the male customer, its caption explaining, "We believe we must correct this omission."[22] In a preliminary oil sketch (private collection), the reflected image is more convincingly real, while technical analysis of the final canvas reveals that the disjuncture between image and reflection was deliberate, as evidenced by changes that Manet made as he worked.[23] In January 1882, the artist Georges Jeanniot witnessed Manet in his studio at work on the canvas, painting Suzon posed behind the marble table; in a remark that encapsulates the modernity of Manet's approach to painting, Jeanniot observed, "Manet, though painting from life, was in no way copying nature."[24] More than a century later, Manet's impossible reflection continues to provoke a range of interpretive responses.[25]

By this date, his mobility increasingly impaired, Manet was forced to paint sitting down, and visitors to his studio reported the visible toll it took on him. He rarely ventured beyond his apartment and studio, and the latter had become a substitute for the cafés that he once frequented in the company of his friends and fellow artists, prompting his wife to call it "an annex of the Café de Bade," then nearby on the boulevard des Italiens.[26]

A Bar at the Folies-Bergère has long been viewed as Manet's swan song as a painter of modern life in the tradition of Baudelaire. However, in the months before his death Manet was working on a painting of a modern type, a woman in riding costume (*en amazone*), which he intended to exhibit at the Salon of 1883.[27] Three unfinished canvases, all depicting the same model,[28] reveal his effort to capture his fashionable subject, a recurrent motif in contemporary literature and paintings as well as popular illustrations (fig. 89). These late works mark Manet's return to this subject: a woman on horseback occupies the center of Manet's view of the 1867 Exposition Universelle (fig. 45), and Manet also painted an equestrian portrait of Mademoiselle Marie Lefébure (*The Amazon*, ca. 1875, Museu de São Paulo Assis Chateaubriand).[29] Manet's renewed interest in this type might have been stimulated by Gustave Courbet's 1856 portrait of a woman in a riding habit (The Metropolitan Museum of Art, New York), then in the collection of Manet's friend Duret.[30] Manet's admiration of Courbet's paintings dates to the 1850s, when the Realist painter scandalized Salon audiences with his large-scale scenes of modern life in his native Ornans. Silhouetted against an unfinished landscape background, Manet's model wears a riding costume borrowed from a fellow artist.[31] The work's format and scale attest to Manet's ambition despite his failing health, and its subject manifests his ongoing engagement with painting the women of his time.

A final series of still-life subjects, begun in 1882, occupied the artist in the last year of his life. His fondness for flowers was well known, as Proust recalled: "The sight of a flower was enough to restore all his gaiety."[32] Gifts of flowers brought to him during his illness became the subject of intimate still-life paintings that Manet offered as tokens of friendship (fig. 90). A recipient of one of Manet's painted bouquets in late 1882 expressed her gratitude: "I love flowers . . . In sending me some that will never wilt, you have given me the greatest pleasure."[33]

All but two of the twenty known late still-life paintings depict a variety of flowers arranged in one of seven glass vases and displayed on the same marble tabletop that appears in *A Bar at the Folies-Bergère*; the arrangements are set against neutral backgrounds recalling those of Manet's early figure paintings. Despite their limited range, the works are neither repetitious nor formulaic. They reveal Manet's bravura brushwork in capturing the different textures of flowers and leaves, the play of reflected light on clear glass, and the clarity or turbidity of the water. In a biography of Manet, published the year after his death, Edmond Bazire recounted the circumstances in which Manet realized his final floral still-life paintings in his studio: "It was to paint [these flowers] that Manet took up his brush for the last time . . . Having finished, he returned to his room and never left it again."[34] One of the works cited by Bazire, *Vase of White Lilacs and Roses*, was shown at Manet's posthumous retrospective in 1884, where it was dated February 28, 1883—two months before Manet died (fig. 91). Accounts such as Bazire's contributed to the mythical aura that surrounds Manet's late flower paintings, which have become inextricably linked with the artist's untimely death.

In April 1883, Manet's left leg was amputated because of gangrene, and he died ten days later, the day before the Salon opened, at the age of fifty-one. Monet, Zola, and his childhood friend Proust were among the pallbearers at his funeral. Degas, stricken by the loss, allegedly remarked, "He was greater than we thought."[35] After Manet's death, Degas focused on adding

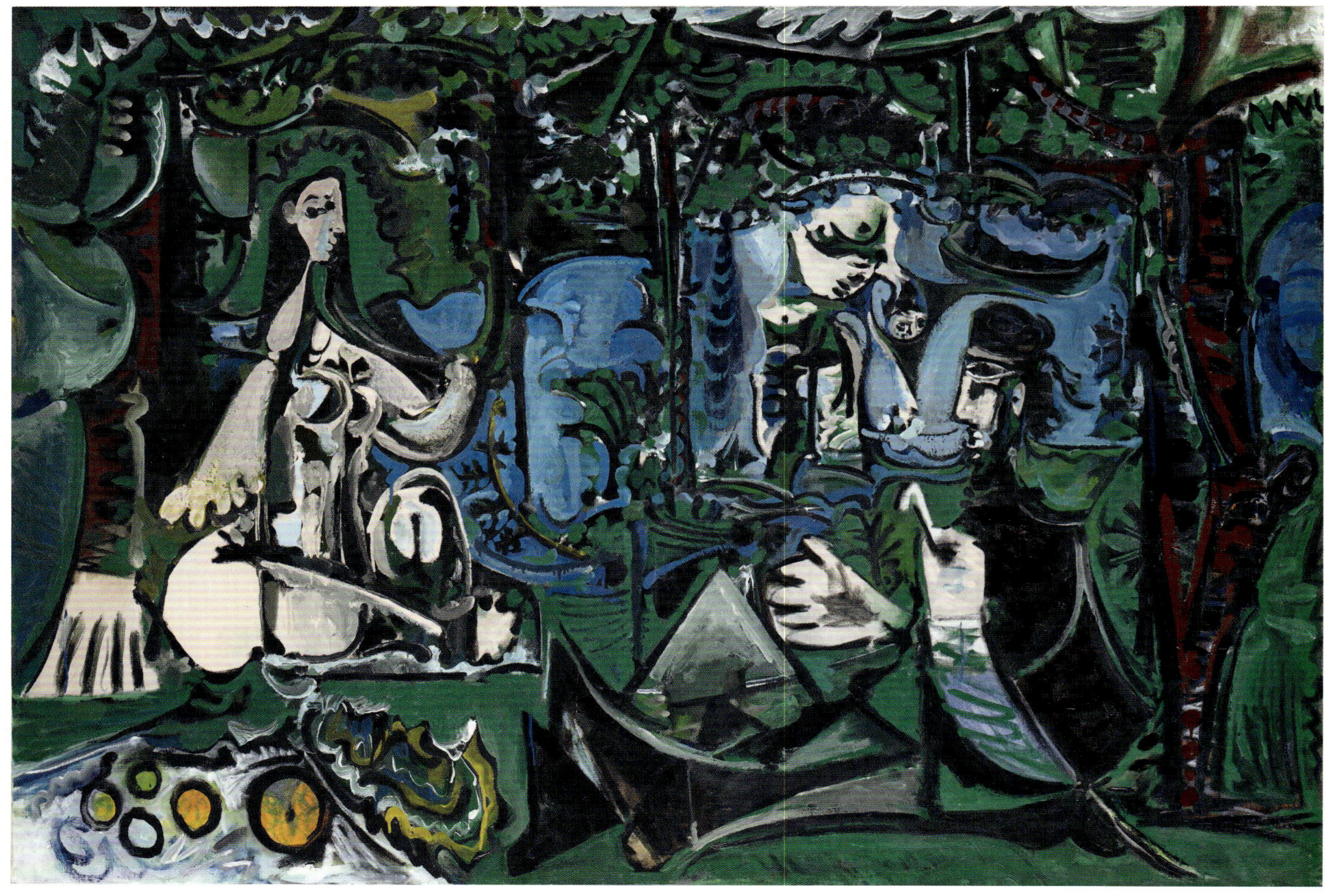

Pablo Picasso, *Luncheon on the Grass after Manet*, 1960, oil on canvas, 51 × 76 ¾ in. (130 × 195 cm). Paris, Musée Picasso, MP215

his friend's works to his private art collection.[36] Among the eighty works by Manet in his collection were Manet's portrait of *Berthe Morisot in Mourning* (fig. 51), a late, unfinished portrait of Suzanne Manet (fig. 3), as well as an 1874 pastel, *Madame Manet on a Blue Sofa* (Musée d'Orsay, Paris). Around 1894, when he learned that the second version of *The Execution of Maximilian* (fig. 73), damaged during Manet's lifetime, had been cut into four fragments after Manet's death, he embarked on a mission "to try to put the painting back as it was," according to the artist's niece Julie Manet[37]. Its fragments reunited on a new canvas support, Manet's history painting became the centerpiece of Degas's private gallery.

Degas was not alone in his efforts to preserve Manet's artistic legacy. In 1889, Monet launched a public subscription to raise money to purchase *Olympia* from Manet's widow and donate the work to the state. Degas was among the contributors. In February 1890, Monet justified the campaign for *Olympia* in a letter in *Le Figaro* that argued that the work belonged in the national collection: "It therefore seems to us impossible that such a work should not have its place in our national collections, that the master is not represented where his disciples already reside" and concluded that the work belonged in the Louvre as "simply an act of justice." In November 1890, despite objections in the conservative press, *Olympia* entered the collection of the state-run Musée du Luxembourg, which then housed works by living French artists; it reportedly hung there in total isolation. More than once, Manet had asked his friend Proust, "please, promise me one thing, never to let me enter a museum piecemeal, at least without making a protest," adding, "I would be incomplete and I want to remain complete."[38] Manet's canvas was finally transferred to the Louvre in 1907 as ordered by Georges Clemenceau, France's new prime minister (fig. 80).

The belated—and reluctant—admission of *Olympia* into the Louvre, which conferred upon it the status of an Old Master, did not diminish its influence on Manet's contemporaries and beyond. Paul Cézanne declared about Olympia: "Our Renaissance dates from it."[39] One of his two painted responses to Manet's work, *A Modern Olympia*, was shown at the First Impressionist Exhibition (Musée d'Orsay, Paris); in keeping with the overt eroticism of his imagery, Cézanne included Manet's unseen client, playing upon the implicit voyeurism of Manet's original. In 1891, Paul Gauguin painted a copy of *Olympia* not long after it was installed in the Musée du Luxembourg; Degas acquired Gauguin's copy for his own collection four years later. When Gauguin left for Tahiti in 1891, he brought with him a photograph of Manet's painting, which resonates in his *Manaò tupapaú (Spirit of the Dead Watching)*, painted the following year (Buffalo AKG Art Museum). Its adolescent model, Teha'amana, was referred to by Gauguin's contemporaries as a "brown Olympia" and the "Olympia of Tahiti." Their response attests to the cultural relevance of Manet's modern nude nearly a decade after his death.

Mickalene Thomas, *Le Déjeuner sur l'herbe: Les trois femmes noires*, 2010, rhinestones, acrylic, and enamel on wood panel, 120 × 288 in. (304.8 × 731.5 cm). New York, The Rachel and Jean-Pierre Lehmann Collection

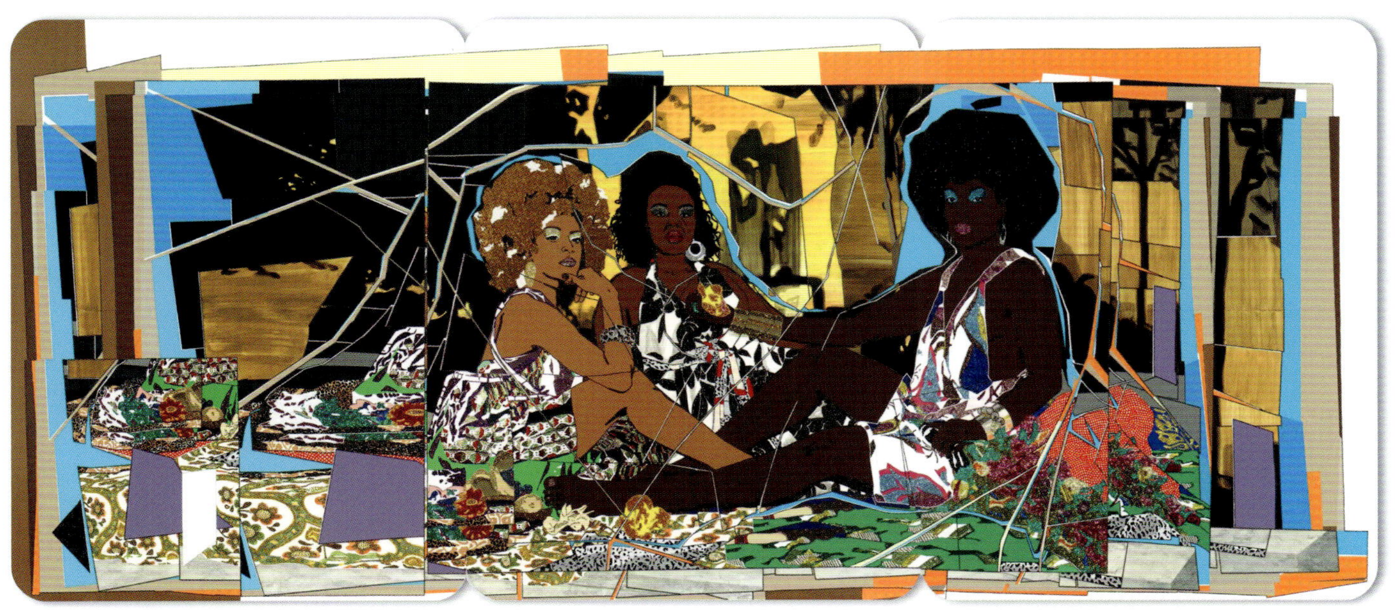

The radical nature of Manet's art has not lost its resonance in the nearly one hundred fifty years since his death. In 1932, Henri Matisse observed that Manet was "the first painter to have translated his sensations immediately."[40] Around the same time, Pablo Picasso wrote on the back of an envelope, "When I see Manet's *Luncheon on the Grass* I tell myself there is pain ahead." He later embarked on an extensive series of twenty-seven paintings and 150 works on paper based on Manet's iconic work. With the rise of modernism in the twentieth century, Manet's eschewal of conventional modeling and his assertion of the flatness of the pictorial surface were seen as harbingers of the modernist aesthetic. In 1960, the American critic Clement Greenberg, an early champion of Abstract Expressionism, called Manet's paintings "the first Modernist ones by virtue of the frankness with which they declared the surfaces on which they were painted."[41]

In the postmodern era, *Luncheon on the Grass* has been variously reimagined by other artists as pixelated Pop Art (Alain Jacquet, *Le Déjeuner sur l'herbe*, 1964), as a family picnic set in a nudist camp in Pennsylvania (Diane Arbus, *A family one evening in a nudist camp, Pa., 1965*), and as a photo-collaged trio of Black women, fully clothed amid a sensual profusion of color and pattern, by Mickalene Thomas.[42] In its exploration of gender, race, and sexuality, Thomas's work represents twenty-first-century modernity just as Manet's art embodies that of the nineteenth century.

The renewed interest in figurative painting since the 1980s has also led to new artistic

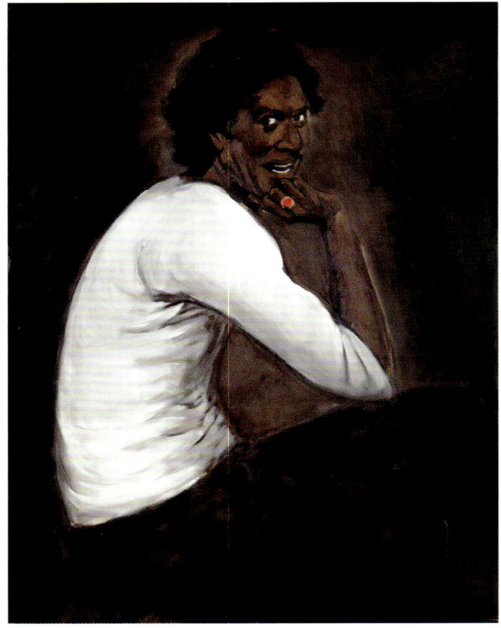

Lynette Yiadom-Boakye, *King for an Hour*, 2011, oil on canvas, 90 ½ × 78 ¾ in. (230 × 200 cm). Miami, Pérez Art Museum

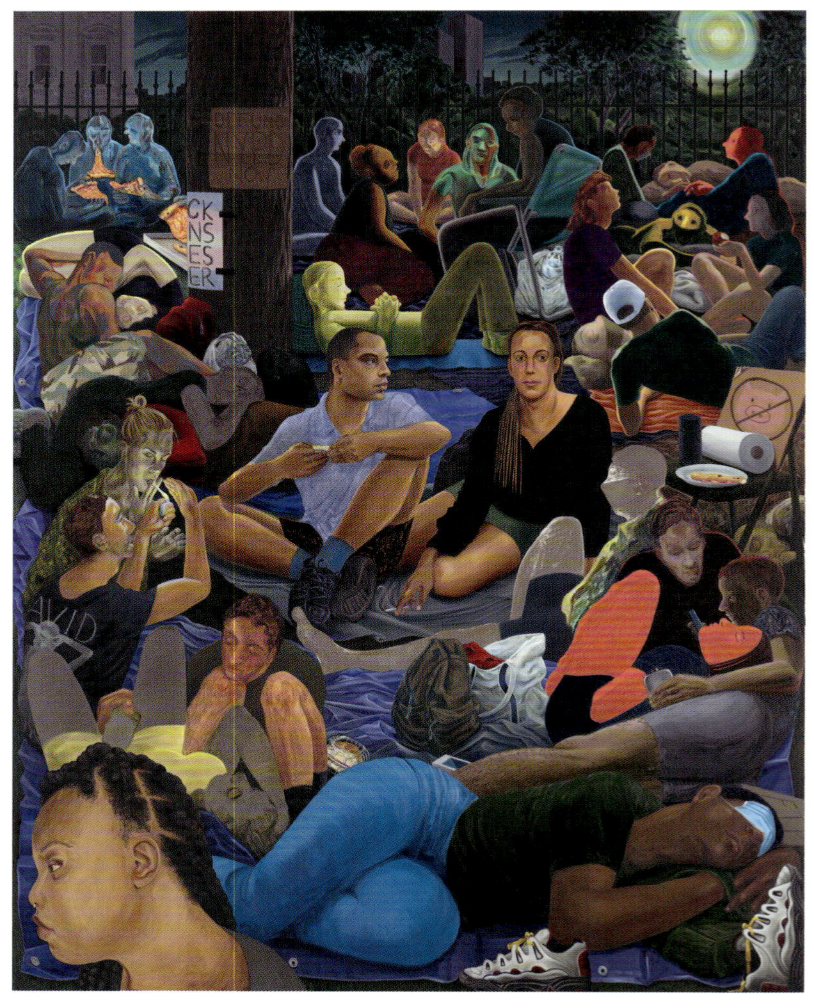

Nicole Eisenman, *The Abolitionists in the Park*, 2020–2022, oil on canvas, 10 ft. 8 ¼ in. × 8 ft. 9 ⅛ in. (325.8 × 267 cm). New York, The Metropolitan Museum of Art, Purchase, Green Family Art Foundation Gift, courtesy of Adam Green Art Advisory, 2022, 2022.259

dialogues with Manet's imagery. The contemporary British artist Lynette Yiadom-Boakye paints imagined Black figures in works marked by their narrative ambiguity, which subvert conventions of Western art. Her imagery is allusive, often embedded with subtle references to works by earlier European artists. The pose of the provocative nude figure modeled by Victorine Meurent in *Luncheon on the Grass* variously recurs in her paintings of a Black man clad in a long-sleeved white sweatshirt and black pants, who, like Victorine, looks outward.[43]

Like Yiadom-Boakye, Brooklyn-based artist Nicole Eisenman simultaneously engages with and subverts the canon of Western art. *The Abolitionists in the Park* of 2020–2021 is a contemporary history painting realized in the aftermath of Occupy City Hall, a monthlong encampment in the summer of 2020 at the height of the Covid-19 pandemic, which took place in the park of City Hall in downtown Manhattan.[44] Eisenman's response to this event recalls the immediacy of Manet's painted reaction to news of the execution of Emperor Maximilian in 1867. Eisenman was among those at City Hall who protested the murder of George Floyd, a Black man killed by a white police officer in Minneapolis, on May 25, 2020, which launched the global Black Lives Matter protest movement. Eisenman appears twice on the margins of the scene: on the left, as the green-faced figure behind the woman with the cigarette, and at the apex of the trio of figures opposite. Among the other portraits in the composition are the two seated figures in the center, friends of the artist whose poses subtly echo those of the central figure group in Manet's *Luncheon on the Grass*. Eisenman also borrowed the direct gaze of Victorine, using it to anchor the crowded composition. Manet's imagery and approach infuse the scene, whose innovative fusion of history painting, contemporary genre scenes, and portraiture represents a twenty-first-century response to the poet Baudelaire's call for artists to paint the "heroism of modern life."

How fitting that Manet, an artist who revered and learned from the art of the past, has inspired other artists since the 1860s, when his radical technique and subject matter galvanized the avant-garde. His legacy extends beyond his own body of work, housed in museums and collections around the world. It continues to resonate in the work of contemporary artists like Thomas, Yiadom-Boakye, and Eisenman, who similarly engage with artistic tradition and, in so doing, write a new chapter in the evolving history of art.

1 On this subject see Chicago and Los Angeles 2019–20.
2 Wilson-Bareau 1991, 250.
3 Ibid., 252.
4 Ibid., letter to Henri Guérard [August–September 1880], 255.
5 On this work see the entry by Samuel Rodary in Lukas Gloor and Sylvie Wuhrmann (eds.), *La Collection Emil Bührle* (Paris, Éditions Gallimard, 2019), 52.
6 Gloria Groom, "Foregrounding Manet's Backgrounds," in Chicago and Los Angeles 2019–20, 79–80.
7 Paris and Baltimore 2000, 46.
8 Carol Armstrong, "Manet's Little Nothings," in Chicago and Los Angeles 2019–20, 121.
9 Tabarant 1947, 388.
10 Chicago and Los Angeles 2019–20, 4–5.
11 Paris and New York 1983, 366.
12 Cited in Manet 1983, 429.
13 Proust 1988, 44.
14 On this work see Sarah Lees in *Nineteenth-century European Paintings at the Clark Art Institute* 2012, cat. no. 206, 477–79.
15 Proust 1988, 51.
16 Ibid., 58.
17 Chicago and Los Angeles 2019–20, 2, 35, 157.
18 Ibid., 311.
19 Paris and New York 1983, 478.
20 Clark 1984, 239.
21 Joris-Karl Huysmans, *Oeuvres completes*, vol. 7 (Geneva, Slatkine Reprints, 1972), 295.
22 Paris and New York 1983, 481.
23 Munich and London 2004, 66.
24 Paris and New York 1983, 482.
25 See Clark 1984, 205–58; Armstrong 2002, 269–301; Bradford Collins (ed.), *Twelve Views of Manet's Bar* (Princeton, Princeton University Press, 1986).
26 Scott Allan, "Faux Frère: Manet and the Salon, 1879–82," in Chicago and Los Angeles 2019–20, 36.
27 See Juliet Wilson-Bareau, "Manet's 'Amazon': A Final Salon Painting," *The Burlington Magazine* 154, 1309 (April 2012): 256–59.
28 On the identity of Manet's model, see Chicago and Los Angeles 2019–20, 314.
29 On the latter work, see Toledo and London 2012–13, 193.
30 Wilson-Bareau 2012, 257.
31 Ibid., 258.
32 Chicago and Los Angeles 2019–20, 320.
33 Paris and Baltimore 2000, 168; see also Tabarant 1947, 461.
34 Cited in Lees (ed.) 2012, 481.
35 J-E Blanche, *Essaies et Portraits*, Paris, 1912, 160.
36 On this subject see *The Private Collection of Edgar Degas* [exhibition catalogue], Ann Dumas et al., New York, The Metropolitan Museum of Art, 1997.
37 Stephan Wolohojian, "Degas, after Manet," in Paris and New York 2023, 64.
38 Proust 1988, 62–64.
39 https://salmagundi.skidmore.edu/articles/504-the-intrepid-manet-degas-dialogue-at-the-musee-d-orsay.
40 Cited in Robert Gordon and Andrew Forge, *The Last Flowers of Manet* (New York, Harry N. Abrams, Inc., 1986), 9.
41 Cited in John House, "Face to Face with Le déjeuner and Un bar aux Folies-Bergère," in London and Munich 2004–5, 56.
42 On artists' interpretations of *Luncheon on the Grass*, see Jeffrey Deitch et al., *Luncheons on the Grass: Reimagining Manet's Le Déjeuner sur l'herbe* (New York, Rizzoli Electa, 2024).
43 Andrea Schlieker, "Quiet Fires: the paintings of Lynette Yiadom-Boakye," in Isabella Maidment and Andrea Schlieker (eds.), *Lynette Yiadom-Boakye: Fly in League with the Night* [exhibition catalogue], London, Tate Britain, Bilbao, Museo Guggenheim, and San Francisco, San Francisco Museum of Modern Art, 18–19.
44 Monika Bayer-Wermuth and Mark Godfrey (eds.), *Nicole Eisenman: What Happened* [exhibition catalogue], Munich, Museum Brandhorst, London, Whitechapel Gallery, and Chicago, Museum of Contemporary Art, 2023–24, 26–27, 237, 244.

82

Corner of the Garden at Bellevue

1880
Oil on canvas, 36 × 27 ½ in. (91 × 70 cm)
Zurich, Emil Bührle Collection

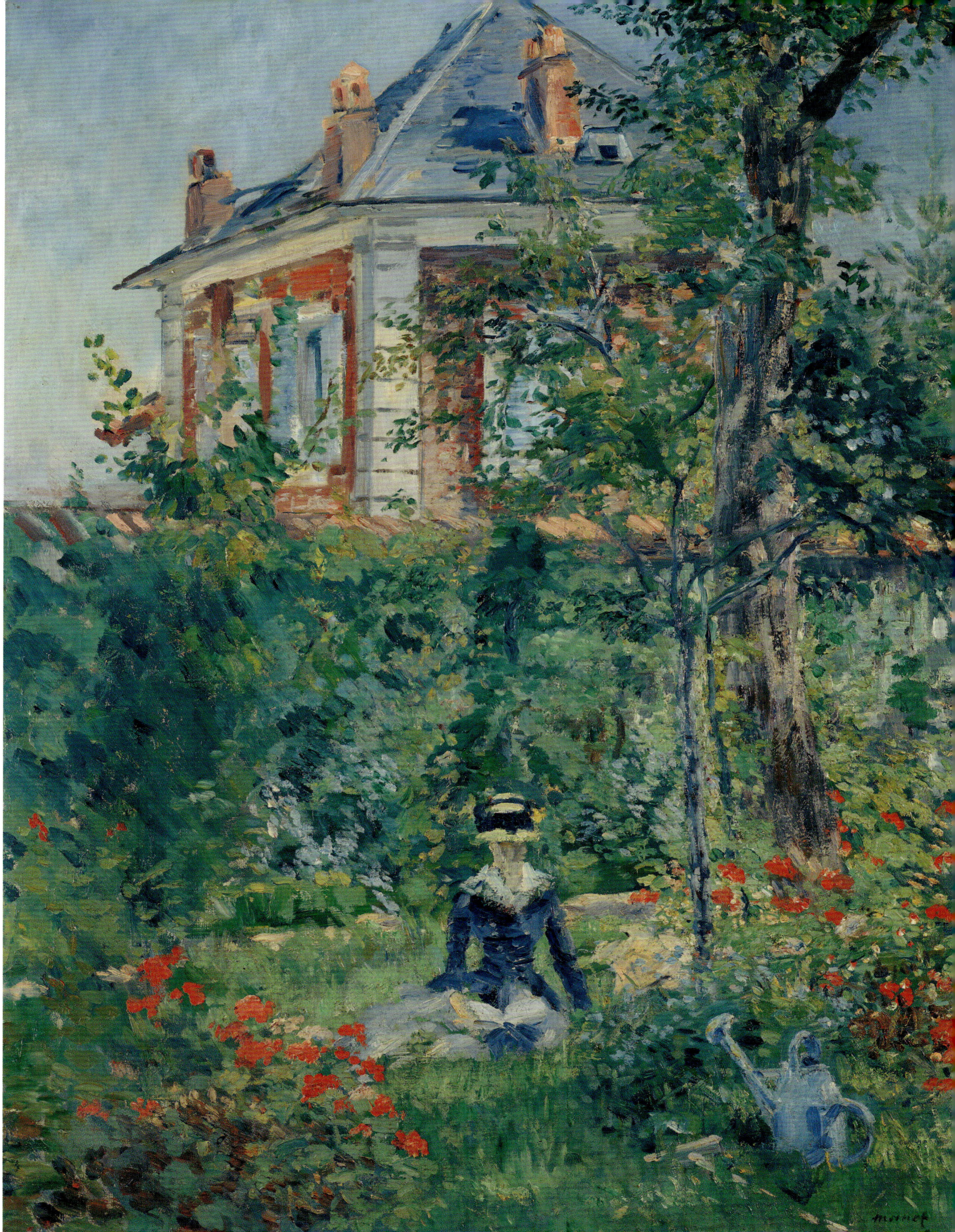

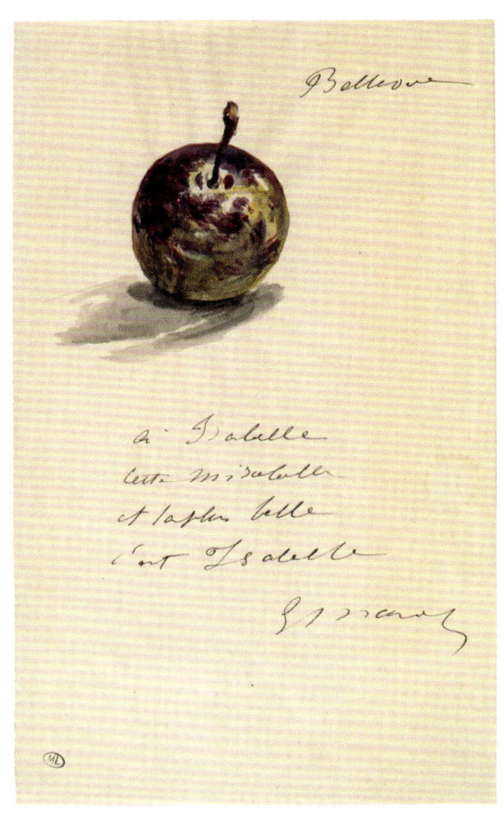

Bellevue

à Isabelle
cette mirabelle
et la plus belle
c'est Isabelle

E Manet

83

Letter to Isabelle Lemonnier with a Plum

Unknown date
Watercolor and ink on paper,
8 ¼ × 6 in. (21 × 14.8 cm)
Paris, Musée d'Orsay,
RF 11180

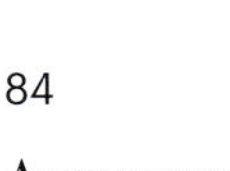

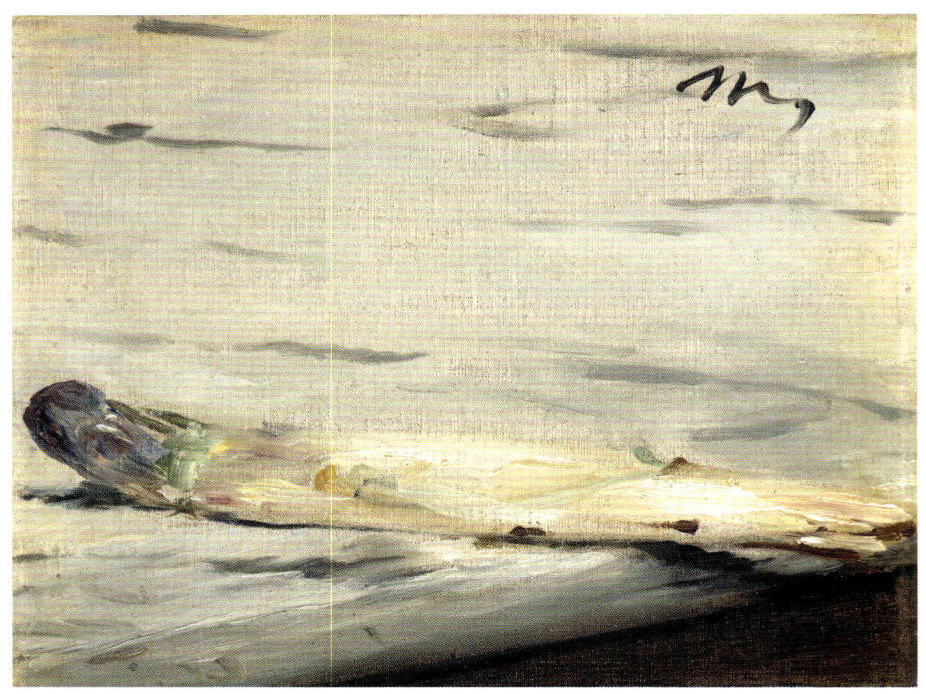

84

Asparagus

1880
Oil on canvas, 6 ⅔ × 8 ⅔ in.
(16.9 × 21.9 cm)
Paris, Musée d'Orsay,
RF 1959 18

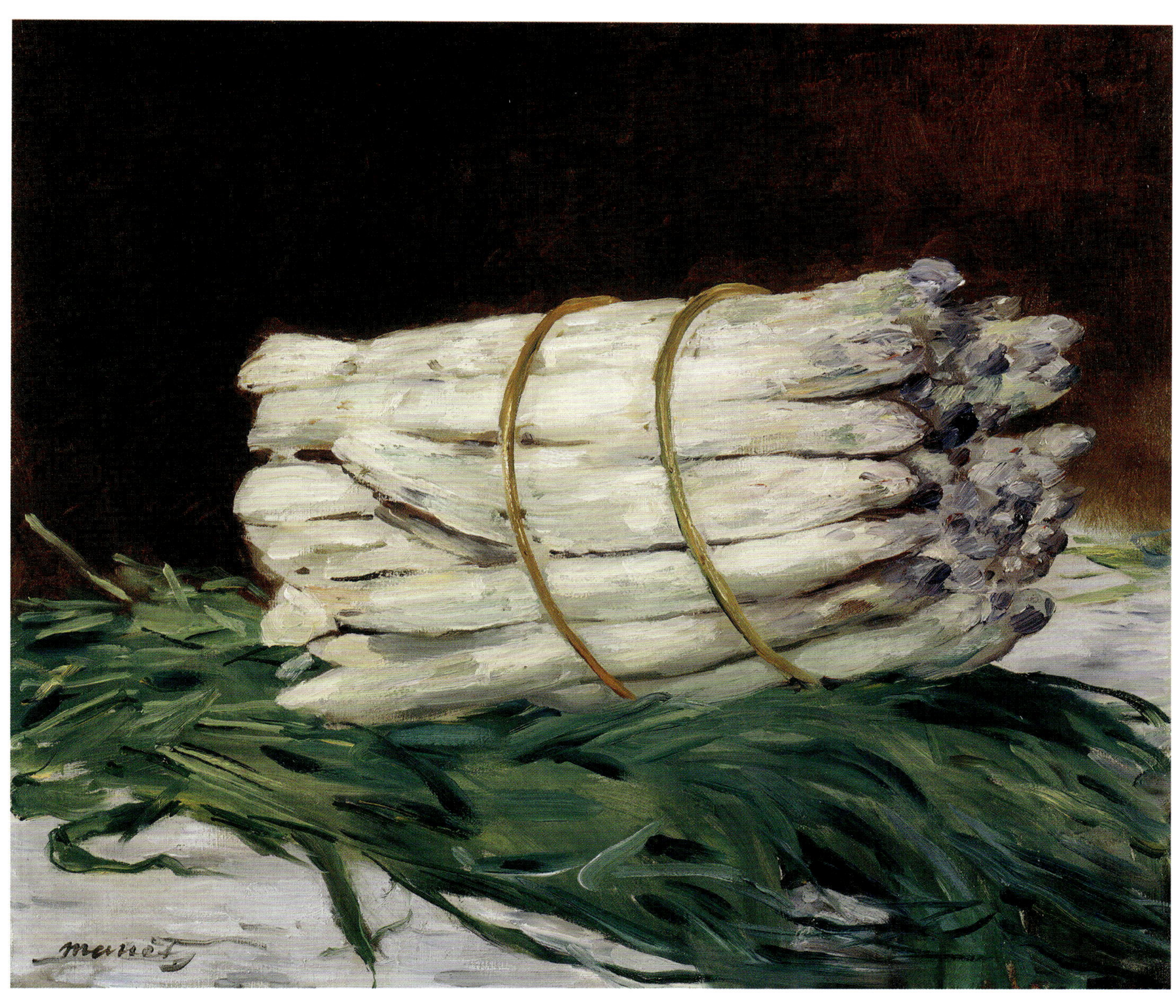

85

Bunch of Asparagus

1880
Oil on canvas, 18 × 21 ⅔ in.
(46 × 55 cm)
Cologne, Wallraf-Richartz
Museum, Dep. 0318

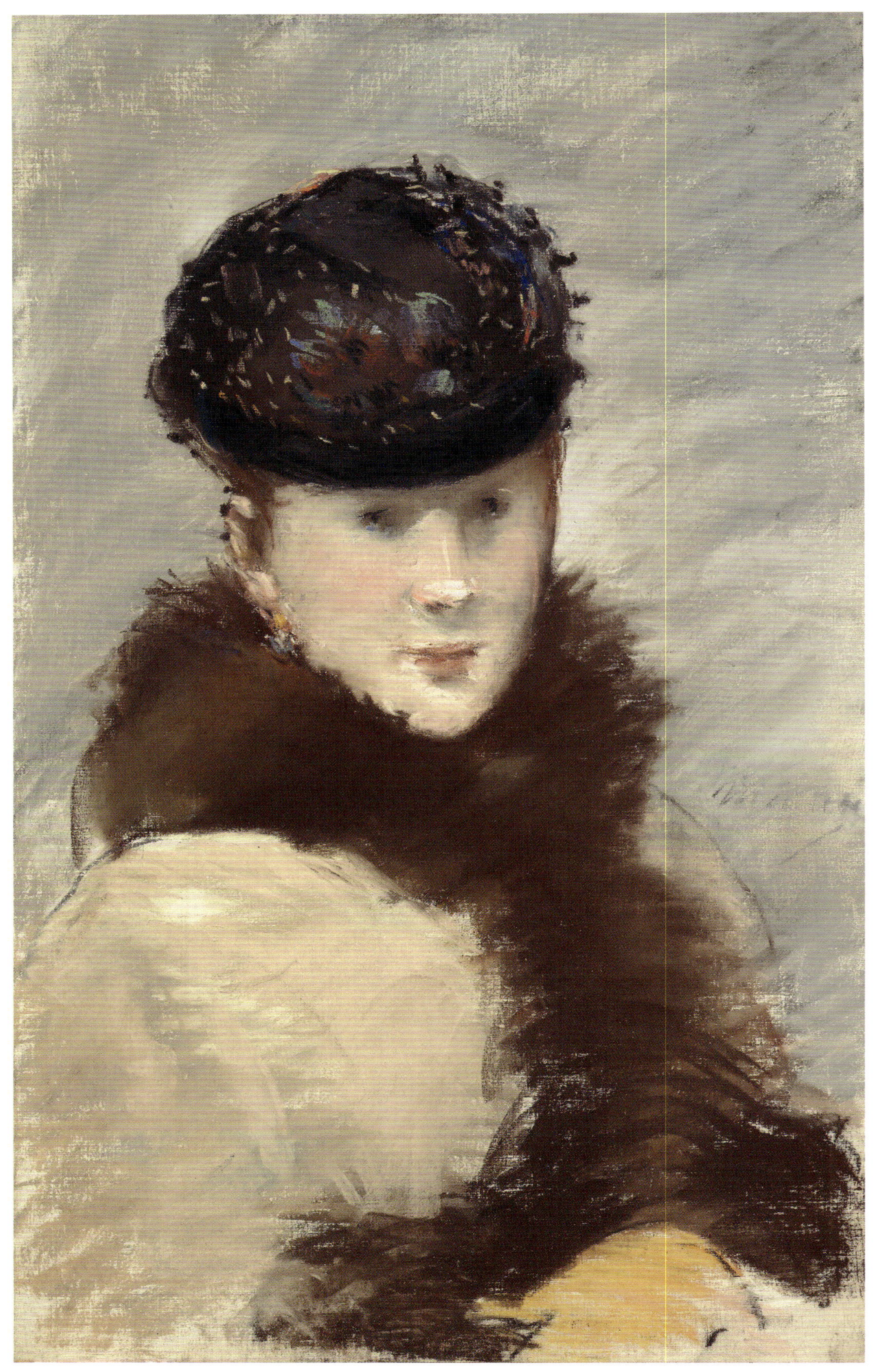

86

Méry Laurent Wearing a Small Toque

1882
Oil on canvas, 21 ¾ × 13 ⅝ in.
(55.3 × 34.6 cm)
Williamstown, The Clark Institute, 1955.565

87

Jeanne (Spring)

1881
Oil on canvas, 29 ⅛ × 20 ¼ in.
(74 × 51.5 cm)
Los Angeles, Getty Museum, 2014.62

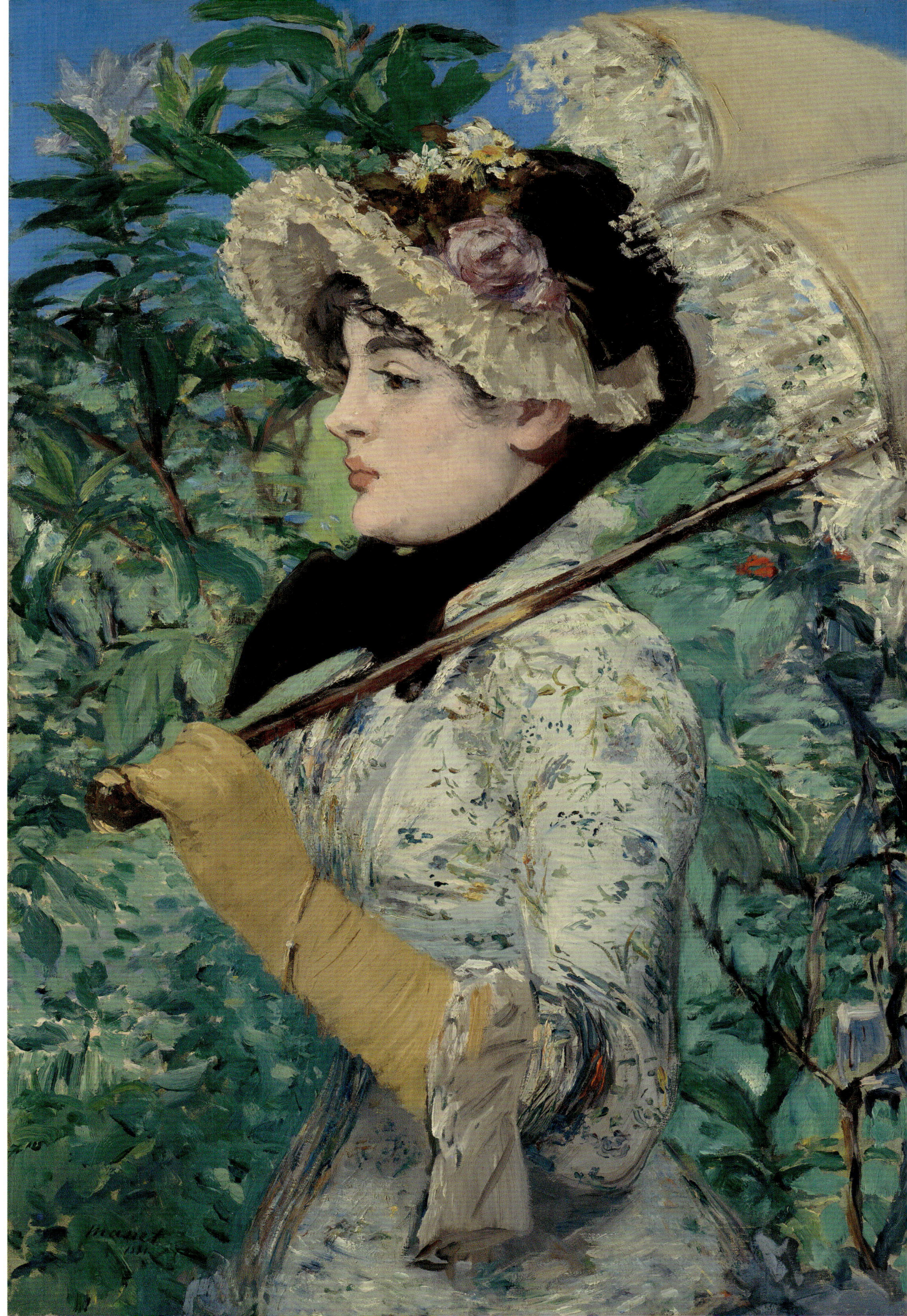

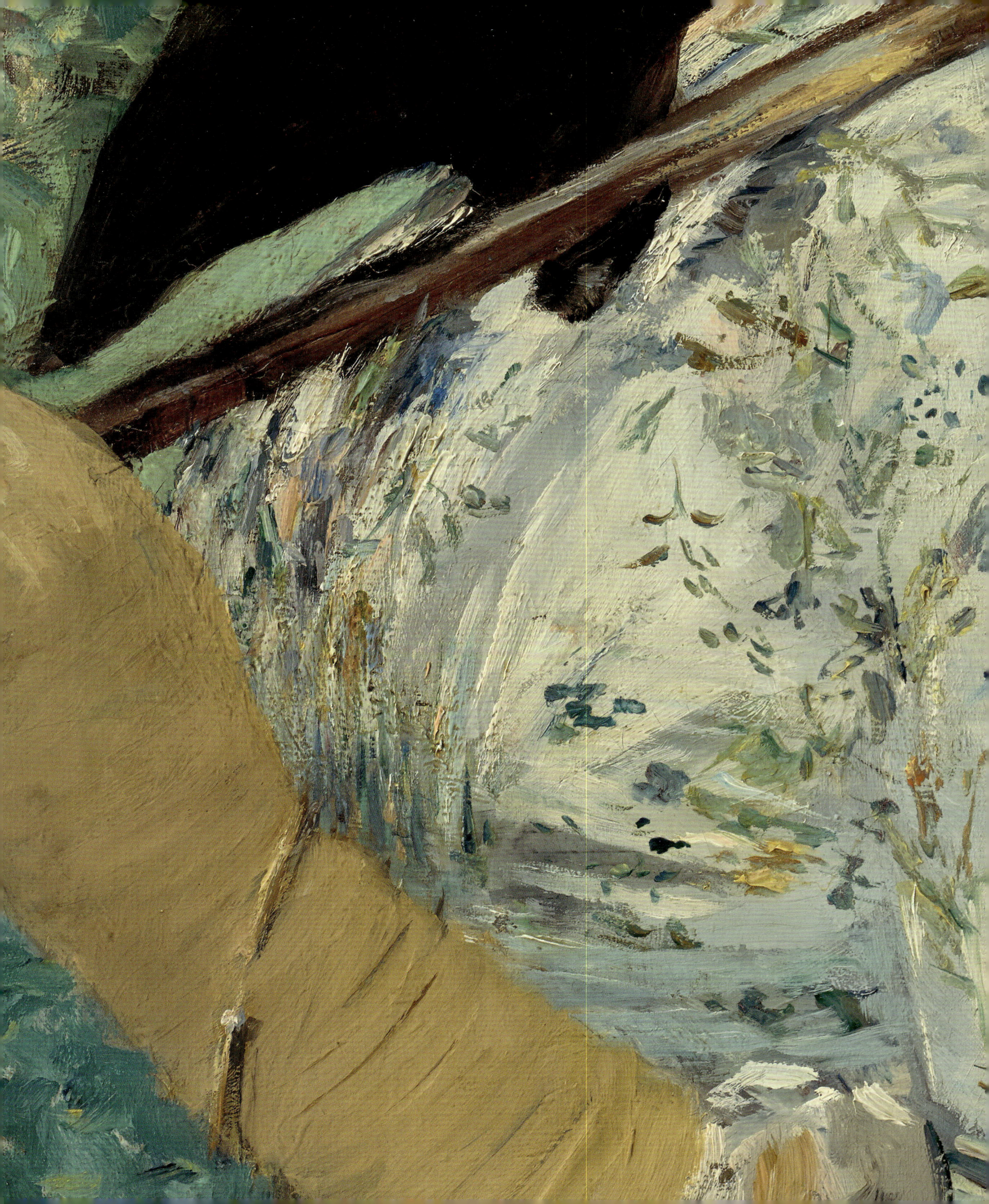

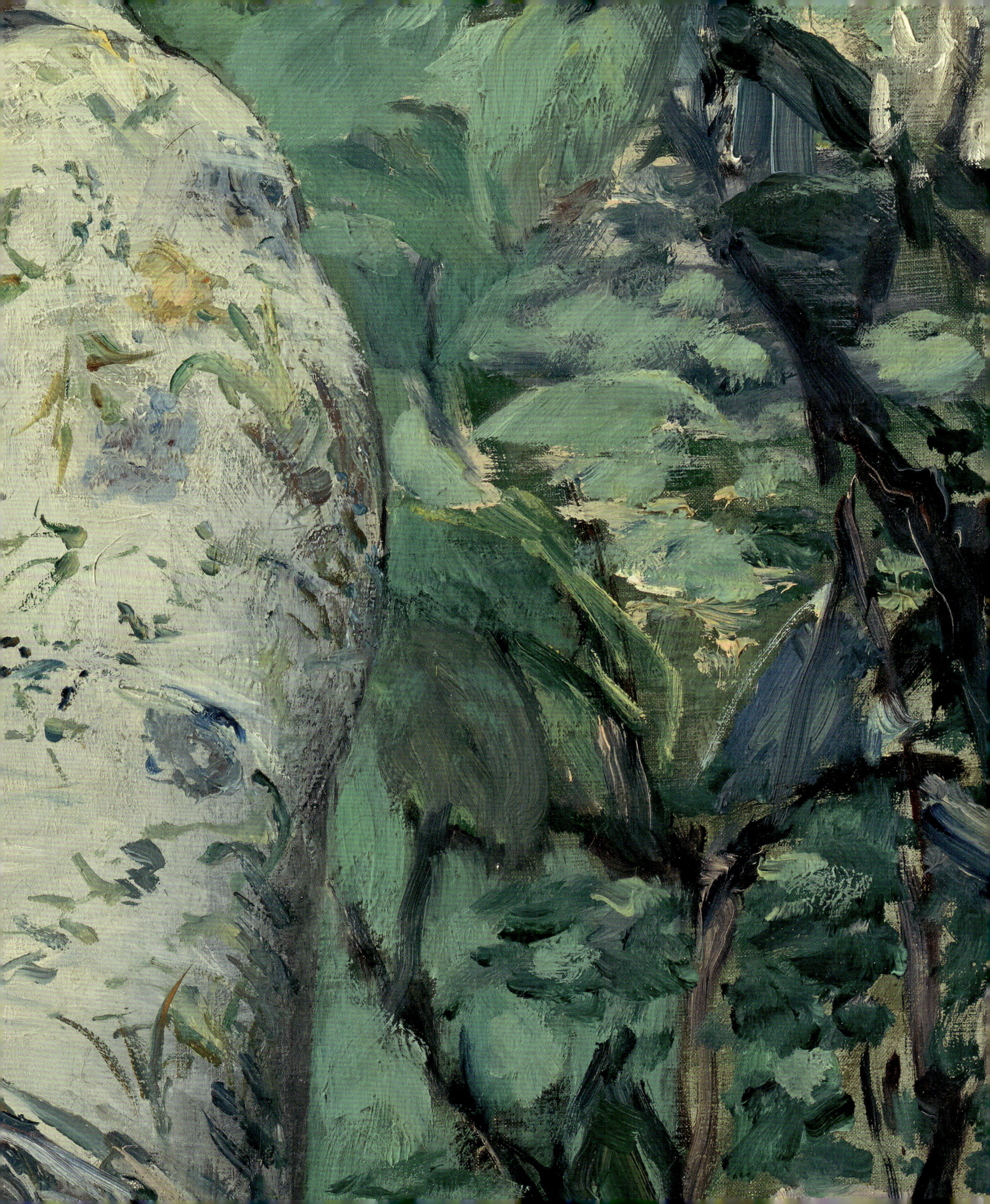

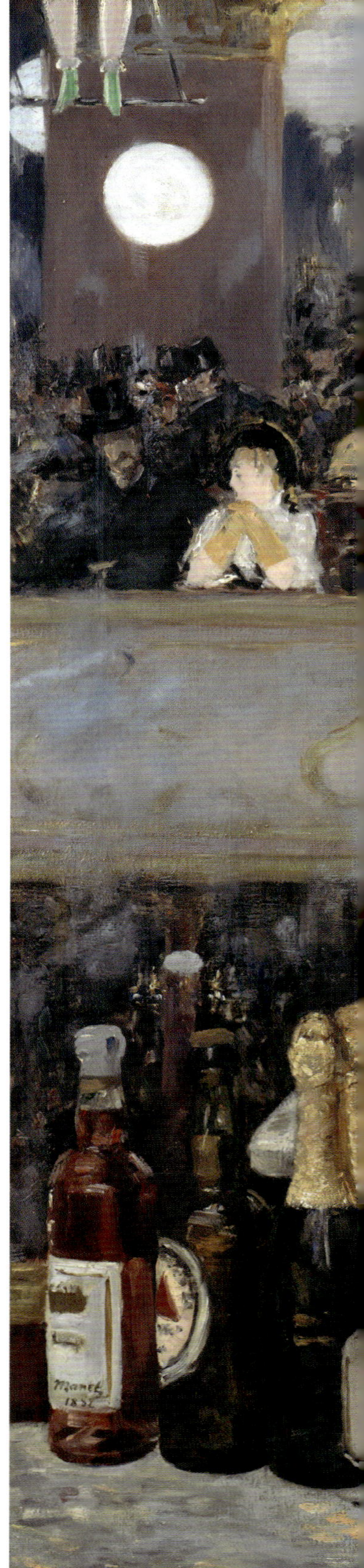

88

A Bar at
the Folies-Bergère

1882
Oil on canvas, 37 ¾ × 54 in.
(96 × 137.3 cm)
London, The Courtauld

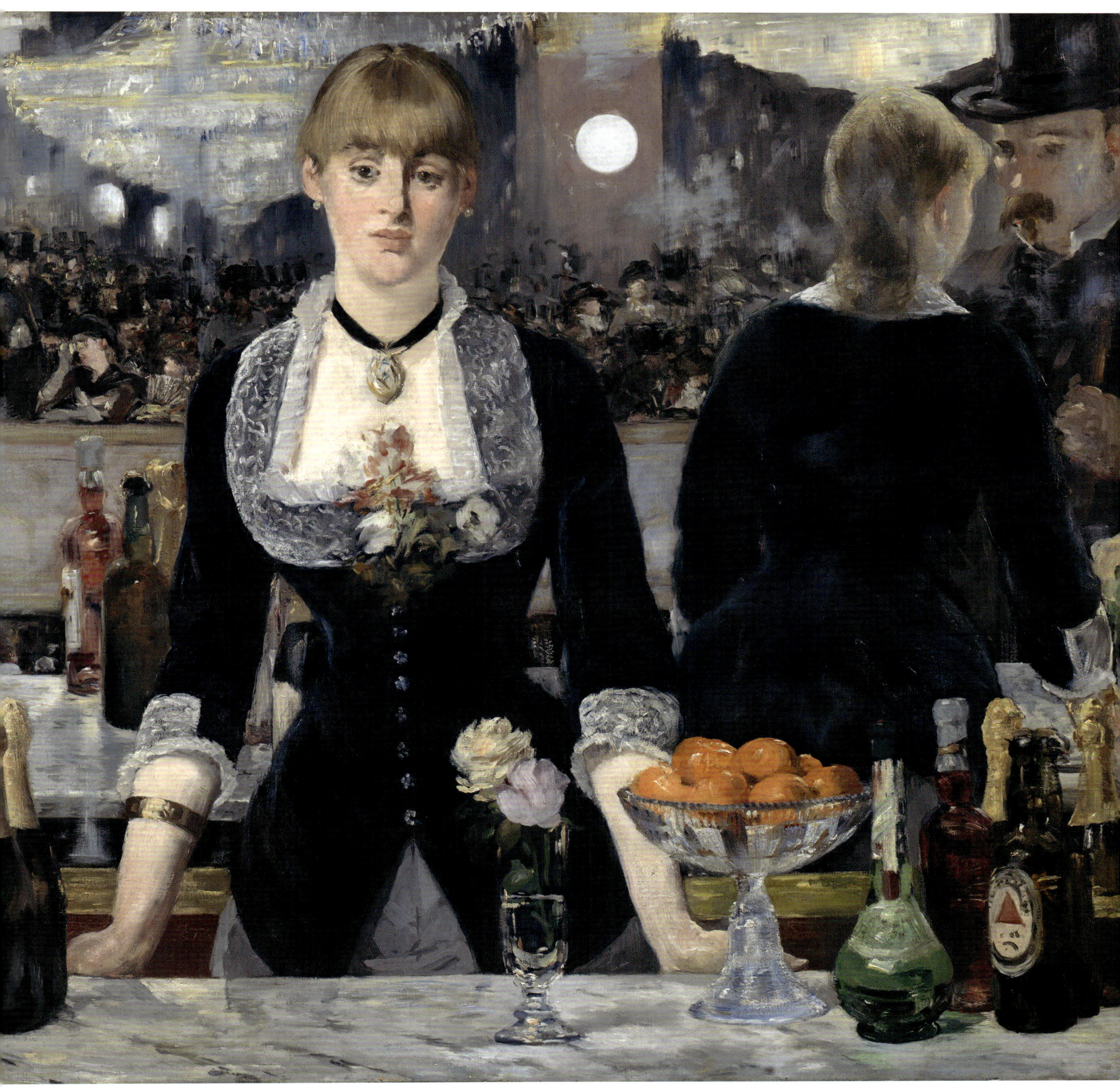

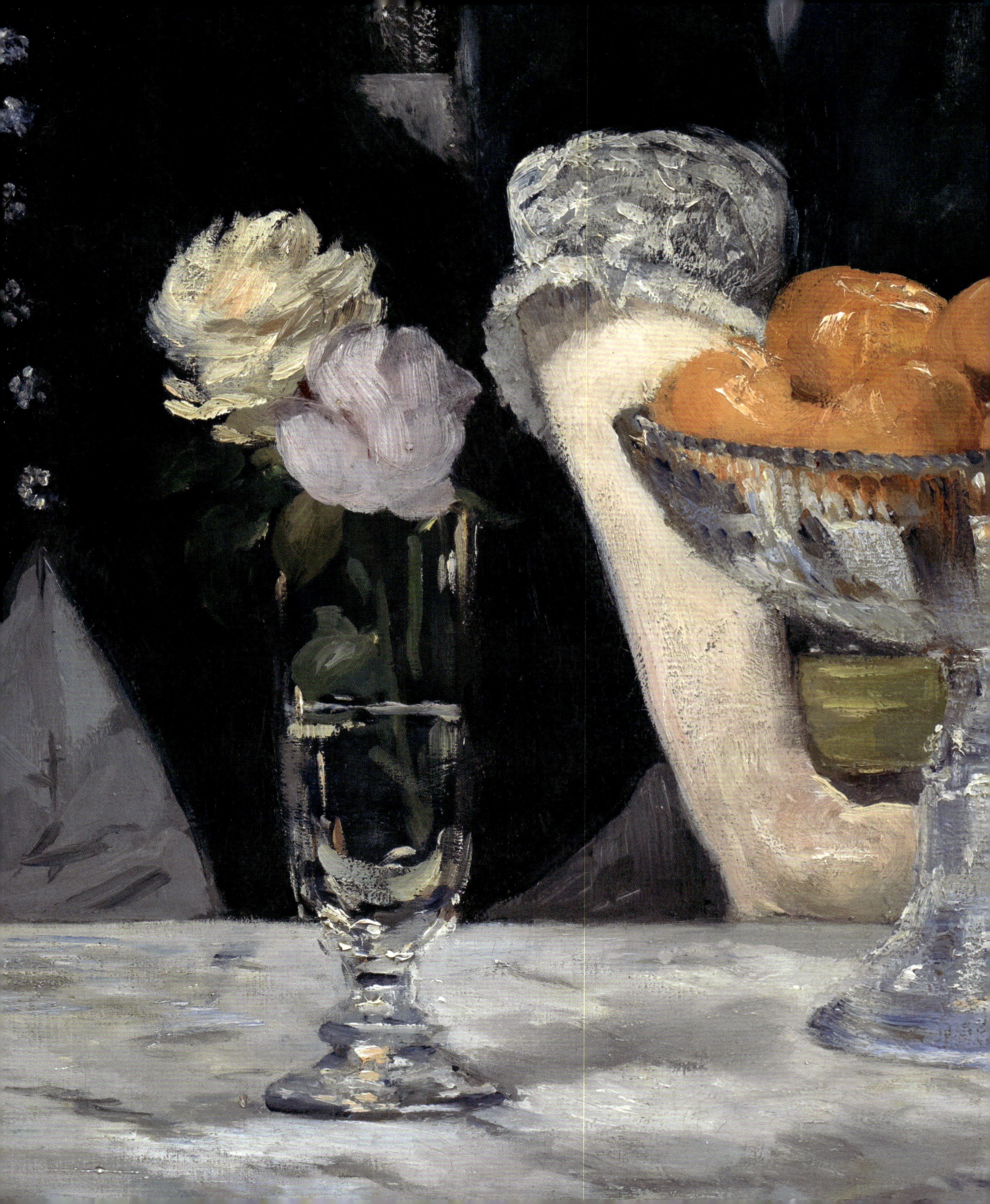

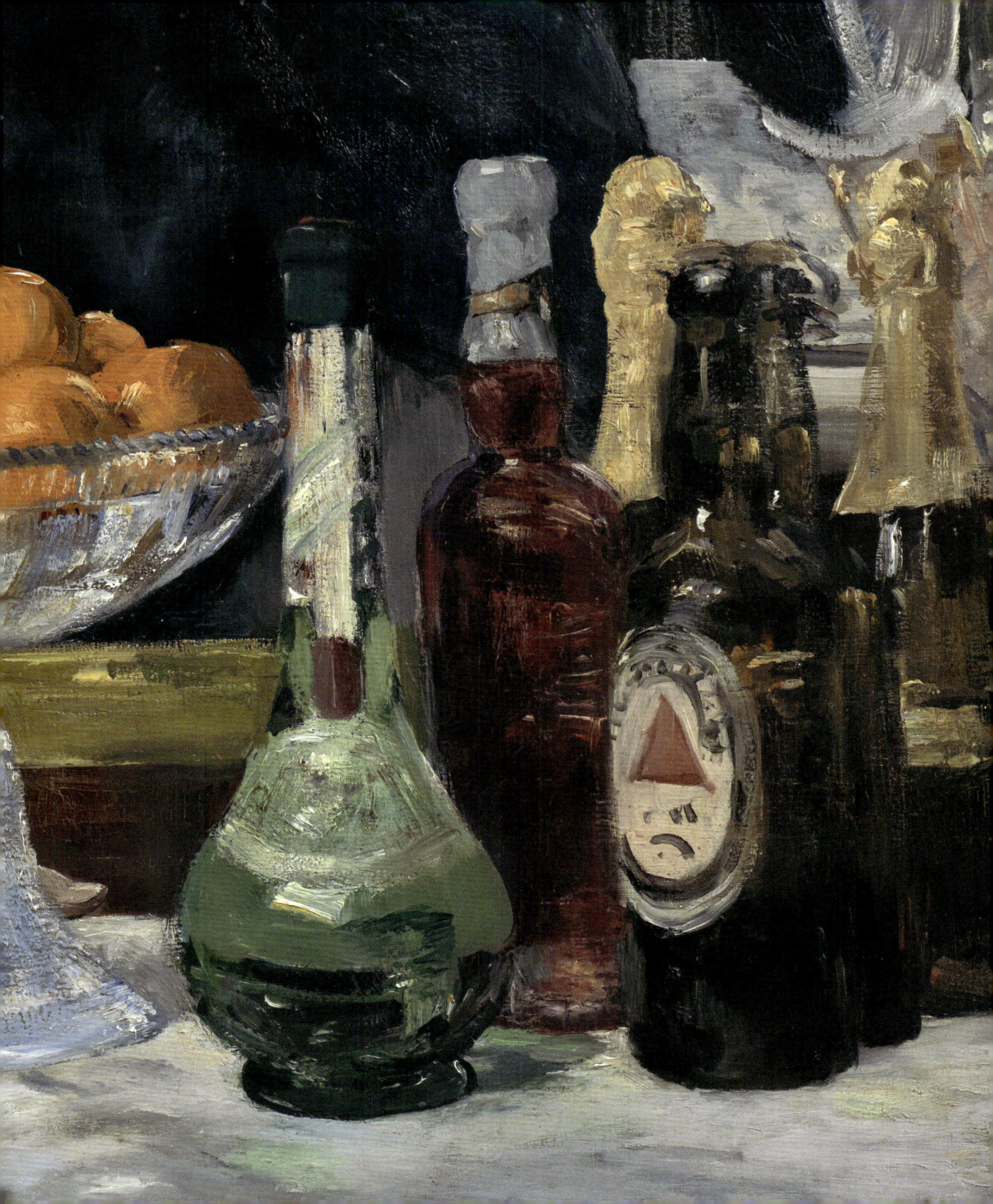

89

Horsewoman, Full-Face (L'Amazone)

ca. 1882
Oil on canvas, 28 ¾ × 20 ½ in.
(73 × 52 cm)
Madrid, Museo Nacional
Thyssen-Bornemisza, 659
(1980.5)

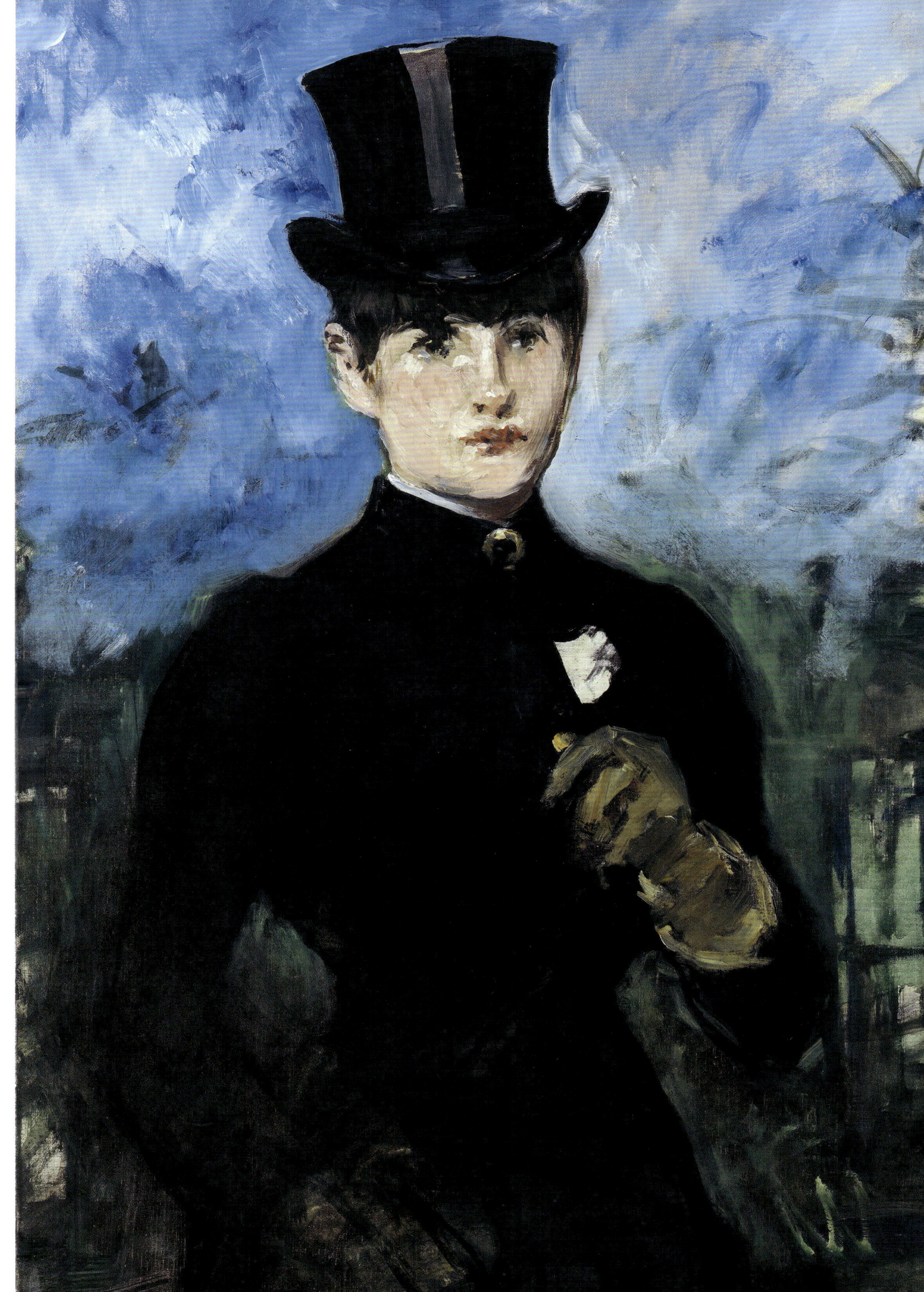

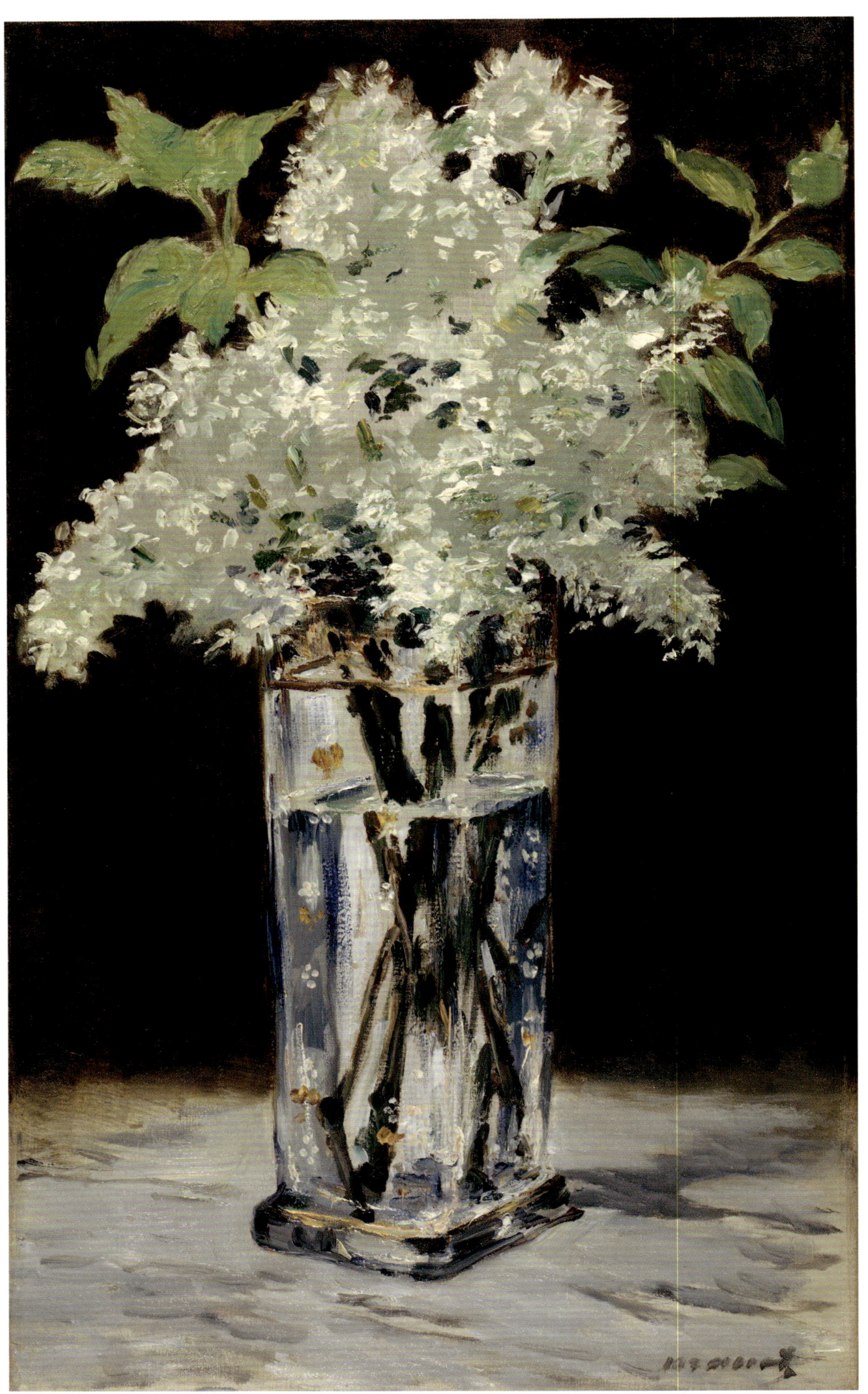

90

White Lilacs in a Crystal Vase

ca. 1882
Oil on canvas, 22 ⅛ × 13 ¾ in. (56.2 × 34.93 cm)
Kansas City, Nelson Atkins Museum of Art, Gift of Henry W. and Marion H. Bloch, 2015.13.12

91

Vase of White Lilacs and Roses

1883
Oil on canvas, 22 × 18 ⅛ in. (55.88 × 46.04 cm)
Dallas, Dallas Museum of Art, The Wendy and Emery Reves Collection, 1985.R.34

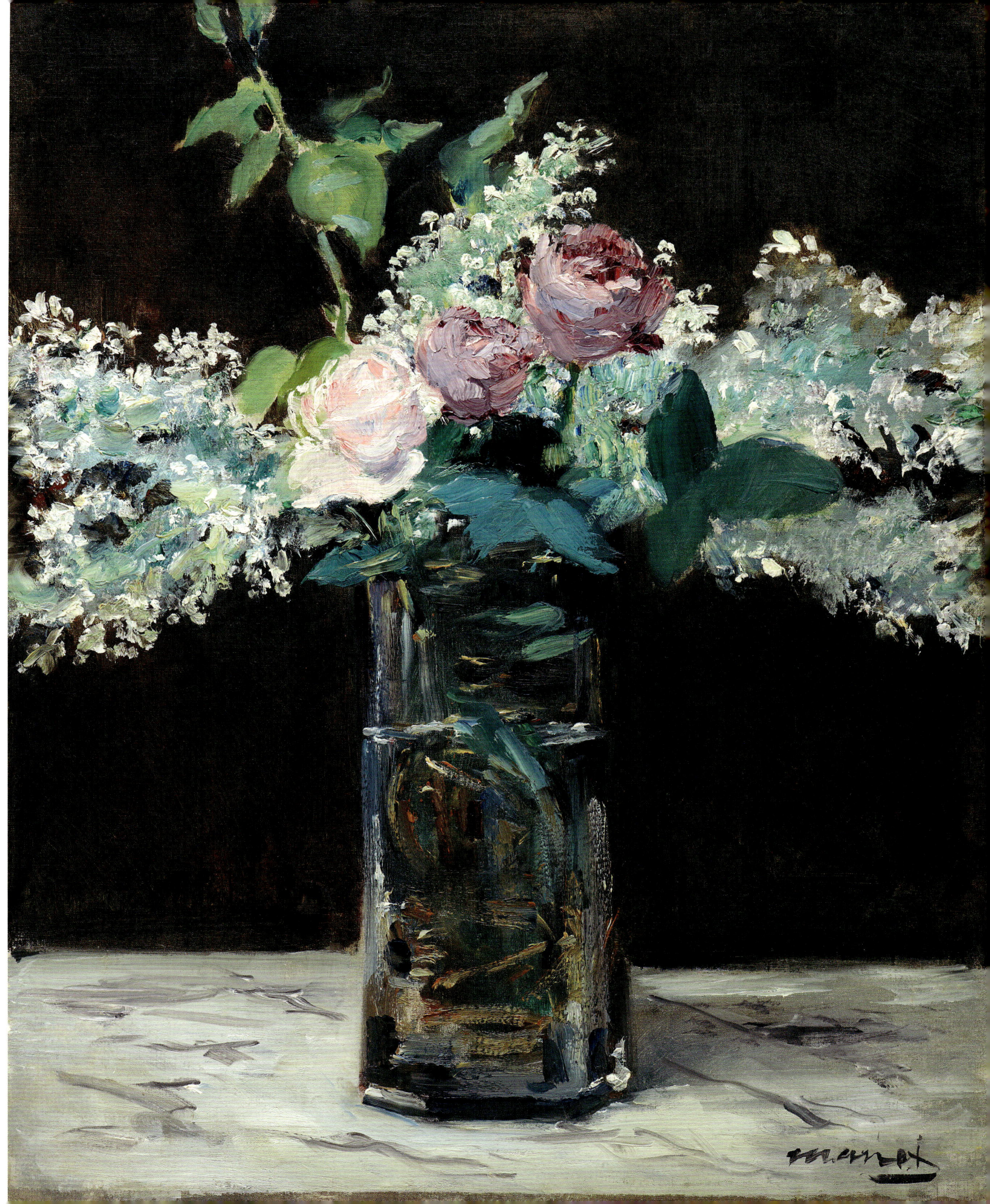
manet

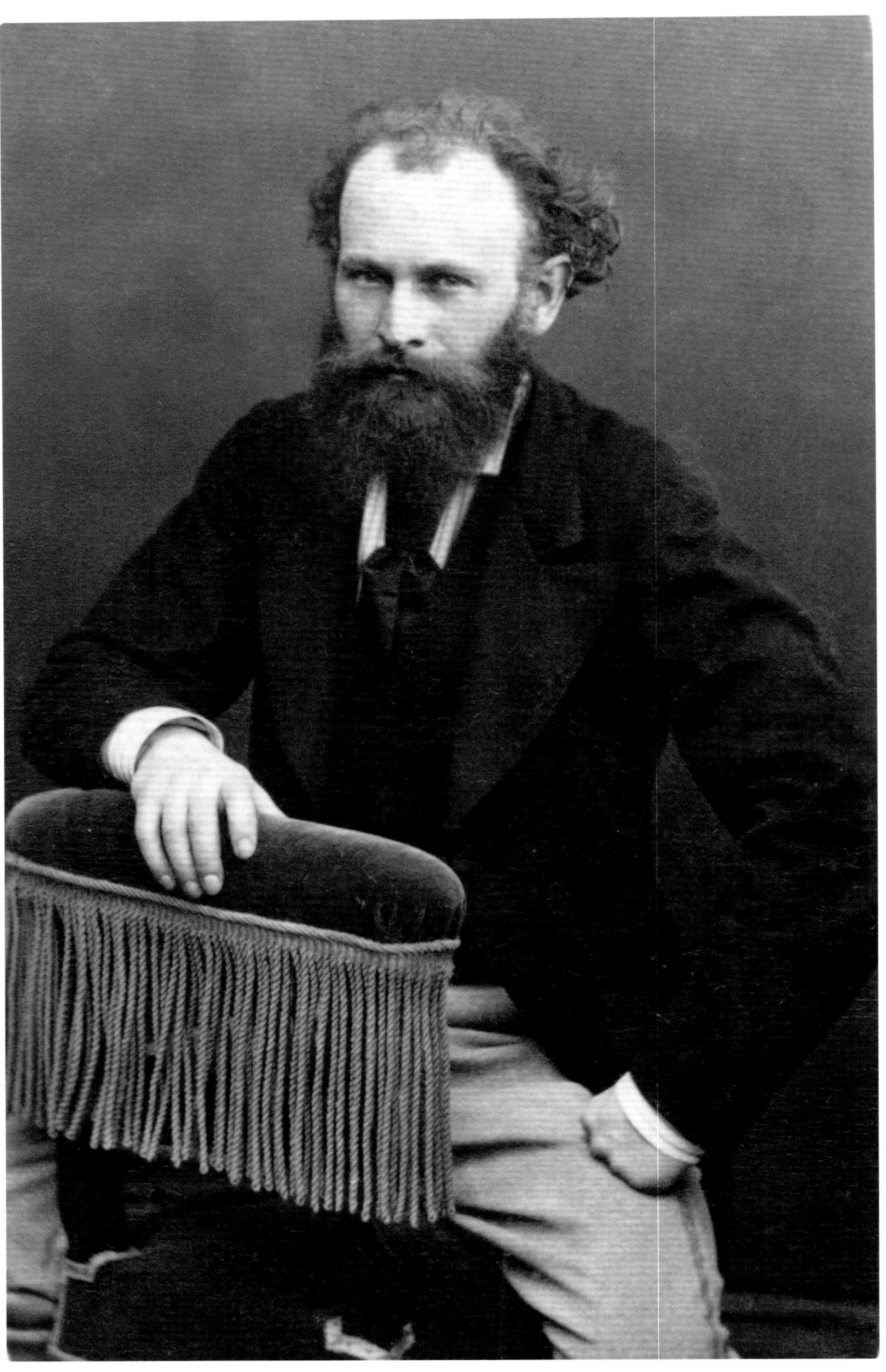

Timeline

Édouard Manet sitting on a chair, ca. 1865. Photograph by Félix Nadar. Paris, Bibliothèque nationale de France

1832

January 23: Birth of Édouard Manet, the eldest son of Auguste Manet, a division chief at the Ministry of Justice, and his wife Eugénie-Désirée Fournier in Paris. His brothers Eugène and Gustave are born in 1833 and 1835 respectively.

1844

October: Manet enters secondary school at the Collège Rollin, where he is a mediocre student; his classmate Antonin Proust becomes a lifelong friend.

1848

December: Having failed the entrance exam for the Naval Academy, Manet departs France for Rio de Janeiro as a cadet onboard the *Le Havre et Guadeloupe*, a training vessel. He returns to France on June 13, 1849, and persuades his parents to allow him to pursue a career as an artist.

1850

January 29: Manet registers as a copyist in the Louvre.

September: He enters the studio of the successful Salon artist Thomas Couture along with his friend Proust. Manet's interest in painting modern-life subjects, at odds with Couture's emphasis on history painting, leads to frequent clashes between the two. Manet remains there for six years.

1851

December 2: Manet and Proust experience the rioting in the streets of Paris in response to the coup d'état of Louis-Napoléon Bonaparte. Two days later, on a visit to the cemetery in Montmartre, where the bodies of those killed in the riots were brought, Manet sketches one of the corpses.

1852

January 29: Suzanne Leenhoff, piano teacher to Manet's younger brothers, gives birth to a son, Léon Édouard Koëlla, known as Léon Leenhoff, whose paternity remains unknown. Publicly, Léon is known as Suzanne's younger brother and Manet's godson.

1856

Manet makes his second trip to Italy, where he copies Titian's *Venus of Urbino* at the Uffizi Gallery in Florence. Seven years later, he would paint a modern nude in response: *Olympia* (fig. 36).

1859

The Salon jury rejects Manet's submission, *The Absinthe Drinker* (fig. 13); Couture also dismissed the work, which led to Manet's break with his teacher. The figure of the absinthe drinker reappears in *The Old Musician* of 1862 (fig. 18).

July 1: Manet registers again as a copyist at the Louvre. Among the works that he likely copies is a painting then attributed to Velázquez,

Gathering of Gentleman, which inspires his own *The Little Cavaliers* of around 1860 (fig. 15).

1861

May: Manet debuts at the Salon with two paintings: *Portrait of Monsieur and Madame Auguste Manet* (fig. 4) and *The Spanish Singer* (fig. 14); the latter is awarded an honorable mention. His success attracts a contingent of young artists and writers to his studio on rue Guyot, among them the painter Henri Fantin-Latour and the poet Charles Baudelaire.

1862

Manet meets the professional model and dancer, Victorine Meurent, who appears in five major paintings dating from 1862 to 1873, including *Luncheon on the Grass* (fig. 31) and *Olympia* (fig. 36).

September 25: Manet's father dies of syphilis. His death brings Manet financial independence.

1863

March 1: Manet's first solo exhibition opens at the Galerie Martinet in Paris; the fourteen paintings on view attest to his interest in Spanish subjects, notably *Lola de Valence* (fig. 17), *Reclining Young Woman in Spanish Costume* (fig. 24), and *The Spanish Ballet* (fig. 16).

May 15: Manet exhibits his work at the landmark *Salon des refusés*, which features some eight hundred works rejected by the Salon jury; it is held at the same venue as the official Salon, separated by only a turnstile. Flanked by *Mademoiselle V . . . in the Costume of an Espada* (fig. 32) and *Young Man in the Costume of a Majo* (fig. 33), *Luncheon on the Grass* (fig. 31) scandalizes the public.

October 28: Manet marries Suzanne Leenhoff in her native Netherlands; around this time, Manet portrays the couple along with Suzanne's son, Léon, in a work known as *Fishing* (fig. 7), which probably commemorates their union.

Charles Baudelaire, whom Manet met in 1858, publishes "The Painter of Modern Life" in *Le Figaro*. His essay becomes a rallying cry for the rising generation of avant-garde artists.

1864

May: Manet exhibits *Incident at a Bullfight* (see fig. 20) and *The Dead Christ with Angels* (fig. 34) at the Salon; reviews are overwhelmingly hostile.

June 19: A naval battle of the American Civil War takes place off the coast of Cherbourg, France; less than a month later, Manet's painting of the battle between the *U.S.S. Kearsarge* and the *C.S.S. Alabama*, which he did not witness, is on view in the window of a print shop in Paris (fig. 90).

1865

Manet is photographed by Félix Nadar, the pioneering French portrait photographer (see pp. 10 and 232).

May: Manet exhibits *Jesus Mocked by the Soldiers* (fig. 35) and *Olympia* (fig. 36) at the Salon. Both works are ravaged by the critics, whose vitriol upsets him.

September: Manet travels by train from Paris to Spain, where he visits Burgos, Valladolid, Toledo, and Madrid. In the Spanish capital, he meets the writer and collector Théodore Duret; the two visit the Prado together, where Manet is struck by the portrait of Pablo de Valladolid by Velázquez (see p. 41). During his week in the Spanish capital, he attends his first bullfight, which inspires future paintings of this subject.

1866

The Salon jury rejects both *The Fifer* (fig. 37) and *The Tragic Actor* (fig. 21). Manet displays the rejected works in a private exhibition in his studio. In his review of the Salon, published on May 7 in *L'Evenément*, Zola calls *The Fifer* his favorite work. Manet, who has yet to sell a painting, sends the critic a note of thanks for his support.

In the fall, Manet and his family move in with his mother at 49, rue de Saint-Pétersbourg.

1867

January 1: Zola publishes a study of Manet and his art in *L'Artiste. Revue du XIXe Siècle*, in which he declares that Manet's work will one day hang in the Louvre.

April 1–October 31: Paris serves as the venue for the Exposition Universelle, intended to showcase the newly modernized city, transformed by the urban renewal projects led by Baron Georges-Eugène Haussmann, prefect of the Seine. Manet and other avant-garde artists are excluded from its display of Fine Arts.

May: In response, Manet stages an independent exhibition of his work in a purpose-built pavilion on the avenue d'Alma, adjacent to the grounds of the Exposition Universelle. *Olympia* (fig. 36), *Luncheon on the Grass* (fig. 31), and *The Tragic Actor* (fig. 21) figure among the fifty paintings on view. In the preface to the exhibition catalogue, Manet writes, "it is a vital matter . . . for an artist to be able to exhibit his work." A financial failure, his exhibition is virtually ignored by both the press and the public.

June 19: Maximilian I, emperor of Mexico, and his two generals are killed by a firing squad in Querétaro; news of the assassination reaches France in early July. Manet produces three paintings of the execution (figs. 72–74) as well as an oil sketch and lithograph. In 1869, Manet is told that the Salon would refuse his painting of the subject (fig. 74), and his lithograph is banned by government censors.

August 31: Baudelaire dies from syphilis. Manet attends his funeral on September 2; his unfinished painting, *The Funeral* (fig. 44), is thought to represent Baudelaire's funeral procession.

1868

May: Manet's portrait of Émile Zola (fig, 39) and *Young Lady in 1866* (fig. 38) are exhibited at the Salon. The latter represents Manet's response to Gustave Courbet's *Woman with a Parrot* (see p. 84), shown at the Salon in 1866.

July: At the Louvre, Fantin-Latour introduces Manet to the sisters Berthe and Edma Morisot, both of whom are artists. From September into the spring of the following year, Berthe poses for Manet's *The Balcony* (fig. 25), the first of ten canvases in which she features from 1868 to 1874.

1869

Manet invites Claude Monet to join the Monday evening gatherings of avant-garde artists and writers at the Café Guerbois in the Batignolles neighborhood. Monet recalls meeting Henri Fantin-Latour, Paul Cézanne, and Edgar Degas there, while he in turn introduces Frédéric Bazille and Auguste Renoir to the group.

May: Manet exhibits *The Balcony* (fig. 25) and *Luncheon in the Studio* (fig. 43) at the Salon.

1870

May: At the Salon, Manet exhibits *Music Lesson* (Museum of Fine Arts, Boston) and a portrait of the artist Eva Gonzalès (fig. 47), his only formal pupil. Fantin-Latour's *Studio in the Batignolles*, a group portrait that shows Manet at work on a portrait and surrounded by avant-garde artists and writers, is also on view (see p. 119).

July 19: France declares war against Prussia; on September 4, the end of the Second Republic is declared, and the Third Republic is inaugurated. Less than a week later, Manet sends his mother, Suzanne, and Léon to southwestern France for their safety. He closes his studio on rue Guyot on September 16.

September 19: Prussian troops surround Paris. During the Siege of Paris, Manet writes almost daily letters to Suzanne, many of which are sent from Paris via balloon.

November 7: Both Manet and Degas, who also stayed in Paris, voluntarily enlist in the National Guard.

1871

January 24–27: Paris capitulates, and on February 12, Manet leaves to join his family in southwestern France.

March 18–May 28: In opposition to the French government, the radical Paris Commune governs Paris and controls parts of the city. Manet and his family spend March in the seaside town of Arcachon, southwest of Bordeaux (fig. 10).

May 21–28: Government troops enter Paris to suppress the Commune. During what is known as the Bloody Week, some twenty-five thousand people are killed. Manet returns to Paris and witnesses the aftermath of its violence as captured in *Civil War*, a lithograph not published until 1874 (fig. 76).

1872

January: The dealer Paul Durand-Ruel, one of the first to champion the Impressionists, buys twenty-four paintings from Manet, including *The Spanish Singer* (fig. 14), *The Dead Christ with Angels* (fig. 34), *The Fifer* (fig. 37), and *Repose* (fig. 48).

May: Manet visits Haarlem and Amsterdam in The Netherlands, where he sees the work of the seventeenth-century Dutch painter Frans Hals, whose art was recently rediscovered.

1873

May: Manet exhibits *Repose* (fig. 48) and *Le Bon Bock* (Philadelphia Museum of Art) at the Salon. While the image of a beer drinker evocative of seventeenth-century Dutch genre subjects represents the first critical success of Manet's career, the compositional daring of *Repose*, modeled by Berthe Morisot, is skewered by the critics.

1874

April 15: The group of artists later known as the Impressionists hold their first exhibition in the former studio of the photographer Nadar on the boulevard des Capucines in Paris. Manet declines their invitation to participate, preferring to exhibit his work at the Salon, as he would continue to do for the rest of his career.

April: The Salon jury rejects two of Manet's four submitted works: *The Swallows* (Zurich, Foundation E.G. Bührle Collection) and *Masked Ball at the Opera* (fig. 56). In response, Manet's new friend, Stéphane Mallarmé, publishes a defense of the artist in *La Renaissance Littéraire et Artistique* the following month.

May: Manet exhibits *The Railway* (fig. 57) along with a watercolor at the Salon. *The Railway* is the last work for which Victorine Meurent serves as his model.

July–August: Manet summers at his family's property in Gennevilliers, across the Seine from Argenteuil, where Monet and his family are living. Manet spends time painting en plein air with Monet; they are joined on at least one occasion by Renoir (figs. 58, 59).

December 22: Berthe Morisot marries Manet's younger brother, Eugène; following her marriage, she never again poses for Manet.

1875

May: Manet exhibits *Argenteuil* (fig. 60) at the Salon. Its plein air subject and handling of paint lead critics to proclaim Manet the leader of the Impressionists.

1876

April 15–May 1: Manet mounts a public exhibition of his work in his studio, sending printed invitations to friends and acquaintances "to see his paintings rejected by the jury of 1876." His exhibition opens two weeks before the official Salon. Among the visitors to his studio is a former actress, Méry Laurent, who becomes a close friend and favorite model (fig. 86).

September 30: Stéphane Mallarmé's ardent defense of Manet, "The Impressionists and Édouard Manet," is published in an English journal.

1877

Manet begins a series of paintings and pastels of café subjects (fig. 64), an interest that he shares with Degas. Both men are regulars at the Café de la Nouvelle Athènes, which is also frequented by the Impressionists.

May: Following the rejection of *Nana* (fig. 63) by the Salon jury, Manet displays the painting in a shop window on the boulevard des Capucines on the opening day of the Salon. Crowds flock to see Manet's provocative image of a courtesan.

1879

April 1: Manet moves into his final studio on 77, rue d'Amsterdam, a light-filled space where he receives visitors and displays his major works, including *Olympia*, *The Balcony*, and *The Execution of Maximilian*.

April 8: Manet submits a proposal for a series of paintings of "the public and commercial life of our times" as decoration for the Municipal Council of the new City Hall in Paris, but it goes unanswered.

May: Manet exhibits *Boating* (fig. 59) and *In the Conservatory* (fig. 68) at the Salon.

June 6: Manet proposes to the under-secretary of state for fine arts that the French state purchase one of his Salon paintings for the Musée de Luxembourg, which then housed works by living French artists. He does not receive a reply.

Summer: Manet experiences symptoms of advanced syphilis, which would eventually kill him, and undergoes hydrotherapy treatment in the spa town of Bellevue. For the next three summers, he would seek rest and treatment in the suburbs of Paris.

December–January 1880: *The Execution of Maximilian* (fig. 74) is shown in New York and Boston through the efforts of the opera singer Emilie Ambre, whom Manet had recently met. None of Manet's paintings of this politically sensitive subject are publicly exhibited in France during the artist's lifetime.

1880

Manet focuses increasingly on the painting of intimately scaled still-life paintings of fruit and flowers, which are popular among collectors.

April 8–30: Manet shows a group of twenty-five recent works, including his first pastels and a selection of café subjects at the gallery of the journal *La Vie Moderne*. The exhibition is a commercial success.

May: Manet exhibits a portrait of his lifelong friend Antonin Proust and *Chez le Père Lathuille* at the Salon (figs. 69, 81).

June 1–early November: During a period of medical treatment and enforced rest in suburban Bellevue, Manet composes letters illustrated with watercolors that he sends to his friends, including Isabelle Lemonnier (fig. 83).

1881

May: At the Salon, Manet is awarded a second-class medal for *Portrait of Monsieur Pertuiset, the Lion Hunter* (Museu de Arte de São Paulo Assis Chateaubriand). This award will allow him to exhibit his work without review by the Salon jury.

December: Manet is named a chevalier of the Legion of Honor, France's highest civilian honor, following the recent appointment of Antonin Proust as Minister of Fine Arts.

1882

Visitors to Manet's studio note that he now paints sitting down and takes frequent breaks, a sign of his declining health. Manet begins his final series of still-life subjects.

May: Manet exhibits *Jeanne (Spring)* (fig. 87) and *A Bar at the Folies-Bergère* (fig. 88) at the Salon, his last. *Jeanne*, an image of a Parisienne modeled by aspiring actress Jeanne Demarsy, elicits widespread praise from reviewers.

September 30: Manet draws up his will, naming Suzanne his sole heir and Léon residual legatee.

1883

February 28: Manet paints his final still life, *Vase of White Lilacs and Roses* (fig. 91), exhibited with this date at the artist's posthumous retrospective in 1884.

April 30: Manet dies at home ten days after his gangrenous left leg was amputated. Among the pallbearers at his funeral were Duret, Fantin-Latour, Monet, Proust, and Zola.

1884

Edmond Bazire publishes a biography of Manet.

January: A memorial exhibition of 179 works by Manet is held at the École des Beaux-Arts in Paris; Zola pens the preface to the accompanying catalogue.

1890

The Impressionist painter Claude Monet, who met Manet in 1866, leads a public subscription campaign to buy *Olympia* from the artist's widow and donate it to the French state, generating a controversy in the press. The painter Edgar Degas is among the contributors, while Proust refuses his support.

1897

February to May: Antonin Proust's memoir of Manet appears in a series of articles in the journal *La Revue Blanche*; it would be republished posthumously in 1913 as *Édouard Manet, Souvenirs*.

First published in the United States of America
in 2026 by
Rizzoli Electa, a Division of
Rizzoli International Publications, Inc.
49 West 27th Street
New York, NY 10001
rizzoliusa.com

Edited by
Rizzoli Electa

Produced by
Ediciones El Viso
Gonzalo Saavedra
María Boluda
Cristina Gil Ramón
Raquel Ochoa
Teresa Santiago

Design
Subiela Bernat

Typesetting
Ana Martín de la Casa

Prepress
Emilio Breton

Printing and Binding
Printer Trento S.r.l., Trento

For Rizzoli Electa
Publisher: Charles Miers
Associate Publisher: Margaret Rennolds Chace
Editor: Klaus Kirschbaum
Assistant Editor: Emily Ligniti

ISBN: 978-0-8478-7621-1
Library of Congress Control Number: 2025947592

Printed In Italy
2026 2027 2028 2029 / 10 9 8 7 6 5 4 3 2 1

The authorized representative in the EU for product safety and compliance is Mondadori Libri S.p.A., via Gian Battista Vico 42, Milan, Italy, 20123
mondadori.it

Visit us online
Instagram.com/RizzoliBooks
Facebook.com/RizzoliNewYork
Youtube.com/user/RizzoliNY

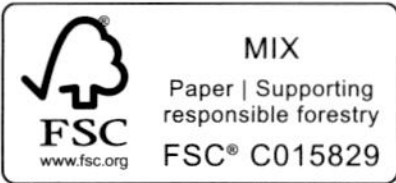

Photo Credits

© Bridgeman Images: fig. 50

© Nicole Eisenman. New York, © The Metropolitan Museum of Art / Art Resource/ Florence, Photo Scala: p. 214 (bottom)

© Sucession Pablo Picasso, VEGAP, Madrid, 2025. París, © Grand Palais RMN (Musée National Picasso-Paris) / Mathieu Rabeau: p. 212

© Mickalene Thomas, VEGAP, Madrid, 2025: p. 213

© Lynette Yiadom-Boakye. Courtesy of the artist, Jack Shainman Gallery, New York and Corvi-Mora, London: p. 215 (top)

Album: pp. 18, 41, 44, 47, 156, 184, 206; fig. 89

Album / adoc-photos: p. 10

Album / Alamy: figs. 16, 19, 47, 81

Album / akg-images / André Held: fig. 51

Album / Artelan: fig. 73

Album / Bridgeman Images: p. 81

Album / Fine Art Images: p. 118; fig. 66

Album / Joseph Martin: p. 79

Album / Supertsock: p. 123; figs. 3, 67

Baltimore, The Walters Art Museum: p. 5, fig. 65

Berlin, bpk, Bildagentur fuer Kunst, Kultur und Geschichte / Florence, Photo Scala: figs. 43, 61, 63, 68, 74

Boston © 2025, Museum of Fine Arts: p. 90; figs. 29, 30, 72

Boston © Isabella Stewart Gardner Museum / Bridgeman Images: fig. 8

Bremen, Kunsthalle Bremen - The Kunstverein: p. 188

Buenos Aires, Documentation and Registrer Area of Museo Nacional de Bellas Artes: fig. 5

Budapest, The Museum of Fine Arts / Florence, Photo Scala: fig. 77

CC 0: pp. 84, 187; figs. 42, 75, 76

Chicago, The Art Institute of Chicago / New York, Art Resource / Florence, Photo Scala: pp. 13, 98-99; figs. 23, 35, 46

Cologne, photo: Historisches Archiv mit Rheinischem Bildarchiv, Wallraf-Richartz: fig. 85

Copenhaguen, Ny Carlsberg Glyptotek: fig. 13

Dallas, Dallas Museum of Art, The Wendy and Emery Reves Collection: p. 4; fig. 91

Florence © Gabinetto fotografico delle Galerie degli Uffizi: p. 80

Florence, Photo Scala: p. 180, fig. 79

Kansas City, courtesy of the Nelson-Atkins Digital Production & Preservation: fig. 55, 90

Kitakyushu, Municipal Museum of Art: p. 21,

Lisbon, Calouste Gulbenkian Museum. Photo: Catarina Gomes Ferreira: p. 71, fig. 27

London, Christie's Images / Florence, Photo Scala: p. 6, fig. 1

London, The Courtauld. Samuel Courtauld Trust © The Courtauld / Bridgeman Images: cover, pp. 226-227; fig. 88

Los Angeles, The J. Paul Getty Museum: pp. 222-223; figs. 78, 87

New Haven, Connecticut, courtesy of Yale University Art Gallery: fig. 24

New York © The Metropolitan Museum of Art / Art Resource / Florence, Photo Scala: pp. 8-9, 104, 128-129, 159; figs. 6, 7, 14, 28, 32, 33, 34, 38, 44, 58, 59, 71

Norfolk, Chrysler Museum of Art. Photo: Ed Pollard: fig. 15

Oslo, photo: Nasjonalmuseet / Børre Høstland: fig. 45

Paris © GrandPalaisRmn (Musée d'Orsay) / Michèle Bellot: fig. 83

Paris © GrandPalaisRmn (Musée d'Orsay) / Adrien Didierjean: backcover, p. 74; figs. 39, 80

Paris © GrandPalaisRmn (Musée d'Orsay) / Tony Querrec: fig. 9

Paris © GrandPalaisRmn (Musée d'Orsay) / Hervé Lewandowski: pp. 34, 36, 108; figs. 11, 12, 25, 40, 41, 49, 52, 62, 84

Paris © GrandPalaisRmn (Musée d'Orsay) / Mathieu Rabeau / Benoît Touchard: fig. 31

Paris © GrandPalaisRmn (Musée d'Orsay) / Patrice Schmidt: p. 3, figs. 4, 17, 36

Paris © GrandPalaisRmn (Musée d'Orsay) / Benoît Touchard: p. 119

Paris © GrandPalaisRmn (Musée d'Orsay) / Michel Urtado: p. 2, fig. 37

Paris © GrandPalaisRmn (Musée du Louvre) / Agence Bulloz: fig. 26

Paris, BnF – Bibliothèque nationale de France: p. 223

Paris, Frits Lugt Collection, Fondation Custodia: p. 76

Philadelphia, courtesy of the Philadelphia Museum of Art: fig. 70

Providence, Rhode Island, courtesy of RISD Museum: p. 134; fig. 48

Shelburne, Vermont © Shelburne Museum / Gift of the Electra Havemeyer Webb Fund, Inc. / Bridgeman Images: fig. 54

Stockholm, photo: Erik Cornelius / Nationalmuseum: fig. 53

Tokyo, Artizon Museum, Ishibashi Foundation: fig. 2

Tournai, Musée des Beaux-Arts: figs. 60, 69

Washington, D.C., courtesy of the National Gallery of Art: pp. 38, 114, 146-147, 150, 153; figs. 18, 20, 21, 56, 57, 64

Williamstown, Massachusetts, courtesy of Clark Art Institute. clarkart.edu: p. 16; figs. 10, 22, 86

Zurich, courtesy of the Fondation E.G. Buhrle Collection: fig. 82

Jacket front: *A Bar at the Folies-Bergère*, 1882 (detail of fig. 88)
Jacket back: *Émile Zola*, 1868 (detail of fig. 39)
Page 2: *The Fifer*, 1866 (detail of fig. 37)
Page 3: *Olympia*, 1863 (detail of fig. 36)
Page 4: *Vase of White Lilacs and Roses*, 1883 (detail of fig. 91)
Page 5: *The Café Concert*, 1879–80 (detail of fig. 65)
Page 6: *Self-portrait with a Palette*, 1878–79 (detail of fig. 1)
Page 8: *Boating*, 1874 (detail of fig. 59)

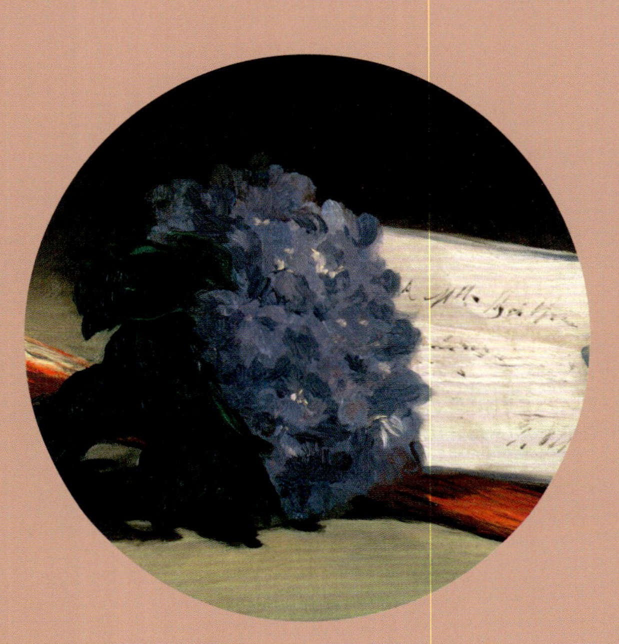